The Ancient World :

An Historical Perspective

HENRY C. BOREN
University of North Carolina

Prentice-Hall, Inc., *Englewood Cliffs, New Jersey*

The Ancient World:

An Historical Perspective

Library of Congress Cataloging in Publication Data

BOREN, HENRY CHARLES (date)
 The ancient world.

 Includes bibliographies and index.
 1. Civilization, Ancient. 2. Bronze age. I. Title.
CB311.B65   930   75-37897
ISBN 0-13-036442-8

The Ancient World: An Historical Perspective
Henry C. Boren

Printed in the United States of America.

10   9   8   7   6   5   4

Prentice-Hall International, Inc., *London*
Prentice-Hall of Australia Pty. Limited, *Sydney*
Prentice-Hall of Canada, Ltd., *Toronto*
Prentice-Hall of India Private Limited, *New Delhi*
Prentice-Hall of Japan, Inc., *Tokyo*
Prentice-Hall of Southeast Asia Pte. Ltd., *Singapore*

To My Wife, Martha

Contents

Greece: The Hellenic and Hellenistic Periods
115

Introduction

A. History: its nature

In one sense history is all that ever happened to mankind. In another, the term applies to the survivals of the human past, in whatever form: documents mostly, but also buildings, tools, and the like. History is in another sense a discipline which includes both the techniques for recovering and evaluating materials (again, primarily, written documents) and also the process of writing it in logical and readable form for the use of others. Finally, the word history sometimes means the finished product of the historian.

Because history (in the sense of discipline and finished product) can never be altogether scientific, and because the world changes, so that what is important in one age seems less so in another, history must constantly be rewritten. This necessity is interestingly illustrated in the case of three great historians of antiquity, of succeeding generations. When Eduard Meyer wrote the obituary of the great historian of ancient Rome, Theodor Mommsen, he said, "Many have regretted that the man whom they looked upon with deep reverence identified himself so completely with a view which to them seemed to belong to the past and no longer to provide an adequate standard for judging the present and its great tasks." When Meyer's own obituary was written years later, by Victor Ehrenberg, the same words were quoted as being equally applicable to him.[1]

History also has to be rewritten, of course, because of the recovery of new materials out of the past. In a sense, because of this, ancient history

[1] See Ehrenberg, *Aspects of the Ancient World* (New York, 1946), p. 231.

xiii

is not ancient at all, but most modern. Advances have been most spectacular in the Near East, for there huge quantities of written documents have come to light, best known of which are the Dead Sea Scrolls.

B. History: its role

"Know Thyself," the ancient Greeks wisely said. The dictum is as important for groups as for individuals. Here, of course, is the chief role of History. It does not predict the future nor does it give easy solutions for present problems. As each generation of historians tries to illuminate the past in terms of the pressing concerns of the present, history is made continuously relevant, helpful to present understanding and to wise planning for the future.

Professional historians for the most part disavow any intention of producing work which can adequately serve either as a standard of judgment for the present or as a guide for the future. But they do think that those who are aware of the past are better equipped to face present and future decisions.

C. History: its concerns

History lies in change, in process, consequently in chronology. Historians usually investigate dynamic societies, not static ones. They seek development—which may or may not be progress. Also, they emphasize those dynamics of the past which point to the present, which inspire our own traditions, culture, outlook, direction. Western civilization is still the most dynamic element in the modern world; its history therefore speaks to every educated man. The tap roots of our civilization are firmly grounded in the ancient world. Thus the study of the present should begin with antiquity.

Historians ordinarily concentrate on human institutions more than on individuals. Single persons are considered as they influence the group. This is inevitable, for the actions and policies of the group expressed through its leaders—heads of state, for example—impinge upon the lives and well-being of every person.

An important concern of history reflected in this volume involves the antithetical struggle between group security and individual freedom. This human struggle is presented more completely than is the parallel struggle to control the physical environment.

Some historians emphasize social and intellectual material. They investigate religion, science, philosophy, medicine, or psychology. All these are intimately relevant to man's development, and in some periods they are supremely important. Such material is most meaningful when studied in the chronological context provided by traditional history.

This volume traces the development of human institutions from the prehistoric family to the sprawling Roman Empire. In the first section, the Ancient Near East, the emphasis is often placed on early, pioneering archaeology rather than upon recent refinements. This is deliberate. The history of the recovery of the past is important in itself, and quite interesting, as well. Moreover, the greatest strides, the most significant discoveries, often were the earlier ones. More recent developments have not, of course, been neglected where they suggest important revision of accepted views. Somewhat greater space is devoted to religion than in most textbooks.

The Greeks provide us the best examples of states which permitted the greatest individual freedom; however, they were often unstable and warlike: the city-state of Athens illustrates this best. The state which achieved the greatest degree of security for its members was the Roman Empire. Better than any preceding state, Rome developed the institutions of government and law to establish justice for her huge population; yet she also tended to stifle dynamic individuals and to relegate huge populations in provinces to a secondary role in public affairs, at best.

This volume is a scant summary, the merest introduction. There are gaps; usually these reflect a lack of available evidence; sometimes the material has been pared in conformity with the author's purpose, to produce a book which is long enough to contain sufficient structure to serve as an orderly core for either a semester's or a year's study, and yet is brief enough to permit assignment of significant amounts of collateral reading. Specialists in the Ancient Near East will doubtless think that this section, "covering" a period of thousands of years, has been slighted. Others who have used textbooks which emphasize only Greece and Rome will find that section comparatively overabundant. Brief summaries of early civilization in the Indus valley and in China are included but these areas are ignored in the later sections. The reason is that there is a greater common theme in the rise of civilization than in the subsequent development of it. Even with limitations of space it seemed useful to include these geographically extraneous but intellectually—historically—homogenous small sections.

The balance of the finished work represents, of course, the author's best judgment, based on a quarter of a century's teaching experience, during which much has changed. In any case, the size and organization of this volume will allow teachers to vary the balance through omissions of sections or whole chapters and through assignment of additional readings, either from collections of source documents or from the list of hardcover and paperbacks suggested in the bibliographies appended to each chapter.

CHART 1 Prehistory

PERIOD	AREA	PEOPLE	CULTURE
Lower Paleolithic c. 5,000,000 to c. 125,000 years ago	East Africa: Kenya, Tanzania Java, China	Australopithecus Homo erectus	Pebble tools Rough, chipped tools Family unit
Middle Paleolithic c. 125,000 to c. 35,000 years ago	Europe, North Africa, Near East	Neanderthaloids (homo sapiens?)	Mousterian: flaked tools; shafted tools Ceremonial burials Use of fire
Upper Paleolithic c. 35,000 to c. 9,000 B.C.	Europe	Cro-Magnon (and other) homo sapiens	Magdalenian (and other): Cave art forms; sophisticated stone tools, bone tools (harpoons, etc.); bow and arrow, spear thrower Extended family unit
Mesolithic (transitional) c. 9,000 B.C. to c. 7,000 B.C.	Near East: Mount Carmel and many other sites		More sophisticated food gathering; beginnings, domestication of animals; invention of sickles; extensive use of microliths
Neolithic c. 7,000 B.C. to c. 4,000 B.C.	Near East		Production of food; domestication of animals; agriculture; ground and polished stone tools; pottery; weaving Village life; tribal organization
Chalcolithic c. 4,000 B.C. to c. 3,000 B.C.	Near East		Use of copper, primarily for ornaments; beginnings of writing; wheel used for pottery and carts Larger villages; division of labor (craftsmen)

Prehistory
and the
Ancient Near East

I

Metaphors have been freely invented by historians to describe the primacy of the ancient Near East in the rise and development of human culture. The Nile and Mesopotamian regions have been called the "cradle" of civilization, the "fountain" of inventive genius, the "birthplace" of the world's greatest religions. There can be found the "roots" of Western Civilization. All these figures of speech describe the "central role played" by the peoples of this area in the late phases of prehistory and in the Bronze and Iron Ages. Any study of the classical world of Greece and Rome—indeed any study of modern civilization, whether it emphasizes the Western tradition or a broader world view—should start with the ancient Near East.

The treatment of the periods of both prehistory and history must to some extent be regional rather than strictly chronological. The student, therefore, should use the charts here and in Chapter 2 to note the chronological relationships between the various areas and to develop a proper sense of perspective. To some degree the charts also indicate the necessary chronological overlap between the parts of the book.

This section—Part I—of this book sketches human development over a tremendously long period. Prehistory, the subject of Chapter 1, involves countless aeons of time. As for the ages since, it should be noted, for the sake of perspective, that fully half of it—half of all of human history—is dealt with in this part. These few pages, then, encompass more long years of historical time than all the rest of history from the 4th century B.C. down to the last quarter of our own, the 20th century A.D.

Before History

1

History is written primarily from documents. The Age of History, therefore, must necessarily be defined as that period which follows the invention of writing and the production of documents, only some of which endure. That date—with respect to the ancient Near East and Western civilization—is about 3,000 B.C. The emphasis on this date is to some degree a convention, for no documents exist for the history of most peoples even long after that date. Important civilizations must often be studied chiefly from the unwritten materials dug up by archaeologists. The date is convenient, however, for other reasons: the invention of bronze and the dawn of the age of metals occurred at about this time, and the agricultural towns of Mesopotamia began developing what may properly be called the first real civilization. But some attention must first be directed to the long, long ages before this comparatively brief period we call "history."

A. Phases of Human Development in Prehistory

No character out of prehistory can come alive except through the imagination. We can know little of the aspirations, hopes, and dreams of early man. Even so, archaeologists have provided us with an astonishing amount of information on prehistoric ways of life. They have sifted through ancient garbage heaps and the ashes of centuries of campfires. Caves and graves have been made to yield those durable objects that endlessly endure, usually bones and tools fashioned of bone and stone. Careful study of all these objects makes it possible to detail the physical conditions of prehistoric life and something of the social conditions as well. The written accounts of these conditions tend to be either technical, almost devoid of the human warmth and color that can enliven the pages of "history," or semifictional, going far beyond what may be inferred from the facts. The historian cannot, however, permit himself to indulge in fancy.

Classification by Stone Age Tools

It was natural for the early students of prehistory, a century or so ago, to arrange their findings through classification of surviving tools. They invented descriptive terminology: the Paleolithic or Early Stone Age, the Mesolithic or Middle Stone Age, and the Neolithic or New Stone Age. Paleolithic tools were made from frangible stone, mostly flint. Many Neolithic tools were fashioned by a new process, grinding and polishing. Dense stones such as granite could then be used to produce better axes and adzes, new types of tools needed for a settled life. These ages cannot be assigned specific time periods, for they describe levels of accomplishment. Thus Columbus found a neolithic technology when he arrived in the New World, and indeed some cultures today are still neolithic—and a few, paleolithic, as that of the Tasaday in the Philippines.

In some ways the old terms, paleolithic and neolithic, are now seen to be inadequate because the usage of tools is not sufficiently descriptive of the cultural development of these times. New terms have been invented that are more indicative of the actual conditions of life in the various phases of progress toward civilization. Some speak of the "Age of Savagery," of the "Age of Barbarism," and of the "Age of Civilization" in place of the Paleolithic, Neolithic, and Bronze ages. Others prefer to substitute for "paleolithic" and "neolithic" the phrases "food-gathering" and "food-producing." The older terms, however, have become so entrenched in the language of both the specialist and the general public that it seems best to continue to use them—understanding them, however, not as literal terms but as relative terms within a broad context.

Classification by Human Remains

There were men before there were tools. Another approach to learning about man before history, therefore, is to study his bones. Some anthropologists and biologists or paleontologists are primarily concerned with the physical development of man as a biological creature. The historian, even in a survey, must give some space to their findings.

A century ago Darwin's theories of the descent of man produced furious opposition from religious leaders. Today his general ideas, with modifications, are a part of routine education and are no longer considered a threat to religion. Still, there is nothing in the factual basis of evolution that rules out the possibility that it is a matter of divine creation. Nor does the historian's preoccupation with human causation —motives and actions of individuals—rule out the possibility of divine intervention in history.

Human remains before history may be classified in terms of cultures. A culture in this sense means the total way of life of a particular group of people as shown by the things they made and the ways in which they made them, the ways in which they gathered or produced their food, buried their dead, and so on. A culture is usually named after the site where it is first identified. When a culture becomes complex and involves proto-urban centers, writing, and specialized craftsmen, historians call it a civilization.

New scientific techniques have aided greatly in establishing dates in the prehistoric as well as historic period. The geologist dates the rocks of the earth's surface by determining what percentage of the uranium in some of them has turned to lead. Bones and other organic objects can also be dated by various methods because they too involve the gradual decay of one element as it is transformed into another. Most useful in this analysis is the Carbon 14 method, despite recent discoveries that demonstrate previously unsuspected variables. Every organic or living thing absorbs this radioactive isotope, which begins to deteriorate at a regular rate on the death of the organism. A careful measurement by a skilled technician of an uncontaminated sample of, say, bone, leather, or charcoal can yield a fairly reliable date within a relatively narrow range. A potassium-argon technique has been used to date several lava deposits in East Africa in which some of the most significant and oldest fossil remains of hominids—manlike creatures— have been found. Since the half-life of Carbon 14 is only a bit over 5,700 years, it can be applied to the historic period. A new technique, involving measurement of "thermoluminescence," permits the dating, within limits, of ceramic objects. Thermoluminescence is an atomic "glow" that takes place when the object is heated, as displaced atomic particles move back into a regular pattern. Obviously, this process is useless for any period before the invention of pottery. However, within the period of history—at least in connection with major civilizations—the ordinary, comparative methods used by historians are usually more precise and accurate for determining dates.

B. Paleolithic Man

Early Human Remains

Read Know

Bones of men or manlike creatures such as those discovered in Java in 1890 and again in 1937-1940 (Java man, *Pithecanthropus erectus*) and in the 1920s, 1930s, and again since the 1960s near Peking (Peking man, *Sinanthropus erectus*) and dated to about 500,000 years ago were once thought to represent the earliest "men" (*Homo erectus*). But subsequent discoveries, especially by the late L. S. B. Leakey and his wife Mary at Olduvai Gorge in Tanzania and more recently by their son Richard and others in Kenya, have forced revisions of older views. Homo erectus may date back to one million years. And creatures approaching the biological features of modern man are now thought to have lived millions of years ago.

The Leakeys found remains of a type of *Australopithecus* (southern ape-man; they called it *Zinjanthropus*) among lava deposits that date back nearly two million years. This hominid may have used pebble tools. Richard Leakey in 1972 found a skull of a relatively advanced type in Kenya, along with hundreds of stone tools, which he dates to nearly three million years ago. And a Harvard expedition to Kenya in 1971 reported bone fragments of a hominid dated to five and a half million years ago. It is now apparent that several different types of hominids lived contemporaneously in that East African region, some of which have simply disappeared in a biological dead end.

As so often occurs, greater knowledge has brought with it greater problems. No consensus of opinion among scholars as to the meaning of all these findings can be reported at this time. Remains of many other types of early men have been unearthed all over the world. Even an anthropology textbook could do no more than outline the major finds and the work done in connection with them. Our sketch is intended merely to provide some perspective.

A rather widespread type of early man who lived chiefly in Europe and adjacent areas during the Middle Paleolithic Age (from about 125,000 to 35,000 years ago) is called Neanderthal, after the valley in Germany where his remains were first identified. His bones have been discovered not only in Europe but also in the entire Mediterranean area and as far east as Iran. Neanderthaloid types ranged still farther. The disappearance of Neanderthal man at the beginning of the Upper Paleolithic Age, about 35,000 years ago, is something of a mystery. In Asia it appears that he may have interbred with other types, but in Europe it seems more likely that he was annihilated by more advanced types of men, such as the Cro-Magnon, who flourished in the Upper Paleolithic. The Cro-Magnon, named after a rock shelter in France

6

where his skeletal remains were first discovered, or some earlier relative, was perhaps the first true *Homo sapiens.* Neanderthal men were short and heavy. Their skulls had a capacity at least as large as ours, but their brains were less developed in certain critical areas. Their heavy brow-ridges and sloping foreheads are well known. Cro-Magnon men had high foreheads and were much taller.

Life in the Paleolithic Age

Paleolithic man was a predator and a scavenger; he survived, doggedly, by his wits and skill in the use of simple weapons and tools. A food-gatherer, he was extraordinarily dependent upon his environment for the nature and quality of what he ate—and how he dressed. If the herds he hunted migrated, he had to move with them; if crustaceans and fish were scarce at his seaside habitation, he changed his location and perhaps his eating habits as well.

The search for security in paleolithic times was primarily the struggle for food and for protection from the elements. These early men fought with beasts and with each other, but the savagery of the age has probably been overemphasized. To survive, paleolithic men had to give full attention to hunting and fishing, to the manufacture of simple weapons, to the preparation of skins for clothing. The social unit was the family or the extended family, not the large community. No environment would support a dense population of food-gatherers. Many a modern city has more inhabitants than the entire globe supported in the Paleolithic Age.

Much, if not most, of our information about men in the Paleolithic Age has come from caves, primarily because other habitation sites have disappeared. Evidence has survived, in other words, in the protected place. It should be assumed that paleolithic men learned to construct rude shelters and then huts, perhaps partially buried in the ground for warmth, in the manner common in later ages. They learned to use fire, a most important achievement, probably, of the Lower Paleolithic Age, though the means of kindling it may not have been invented until the Upper Paleolithic.

Paleolithic Tools

In the Lower Paleolithic Age tools were quite simple. A very early type was the crude hand ax, formed from a pebble that had only to be chipped on one side to make a useful implement. Scrapers and borers, needed to prepare skins for human use, also came rather early. For thousands of years, however, only a few new tools and new methods of manufacture were developed. Then came hafted tools, a brilliant accomplishment, and the invention of the spear, which greatly eased the task of the hunter. Meanwhile, skilled toolmakers devised new ways of flaking and chipping stone and some of them became real artists. Delicately chipped knives, axes, and spearheads became things of beauty to be treasured.

In the Upper Paleolithic Age (from about 35,000 to 9,000 B.C. in Europe) men invented important new tools and weapons. The spear-thrower had greater range and penetrative ability, though probably at the expense of accuracy. The bow and arrow was perhaps the first tool with the capacity to store up energy for sudden release, and greatly increased the productivity of the hunter. A similar device was soon used for making fire and for boring or drilling holes, the bowstring looped around a straight stick. Fishermen now fashioned bone harpoons and, eventually, fishhooks. Bone needles were invented, and bone whistles, which were probably used to control hunting parties.

Paleolithic Cultures: Mousterian, Magdalenian

A typical culture of the Middle Paleolithic Age was the Mousterian, first found at Le Moustier in France, and associated with the Neanderthal man. Mousterian tools were typical of the period, but of distinctive design. Neanderthals, who like other men were cannibals, knew the technique of pressure flaking and produced fine spear points. In some caves, bear skulls have been found carefully arranged and covered with slabs of stone, which implies some sort of animal cult. These men also buried tools and food with their dead. Their very primitive belief in life after death was no doubt originally simple ignorance of the physical nature of death: the individual might revive and need his possessions. But the burial of small children with ceremony—one was found within a ring of horns—indicates a more complex belief. The family already seems to have been a strong social unit in the Mousterian culture.

The best-known culture of the Upper Paleolithic Age is the Magdalenian, associated with Cro-Magnon man. The major new tools of the period have already been mentioned. The Magdalenians made particular use of reindeer bone, which was plentiful for these hunting groups. Their society was somewhat more complex than that of the previous ages, most likely because the newer weapons, including the harpoon, spear-thrower, and bow and arrow, made possible a somewhat denser population. The clan organization typical in later ages probably developed in this culture, and society may have been matriarchal, with descent reckoned through the female line.

The most startling and impressive development of Cro-Magnon and other upper paleolithic types in southwestern Europe was in art, samples of which were discovered only in the last century. When a Spanish nobleman, Don Marcelino de Sautuola, accidentally discovered realistic, perfectly preserved paintings of long extinct animals in a cave on his property at Altamira, he was ridiculed even by scholars. But later discoveries by archaeological expeditions excavating caves blocked for centuries by debris proved the astonishing truth: the Cro-Magnon man could paint. His technique was developed over thousands of years, through crude beginnings to fine realism and a sort of impressionism. Various techniques and methods were used, including finger painting, "crayons," and the blowing of powdered pigments onto a fat-covered surface. Preliminary sketches were sometimes made. Engraved and half-relief figures have also been found in the cave rock.

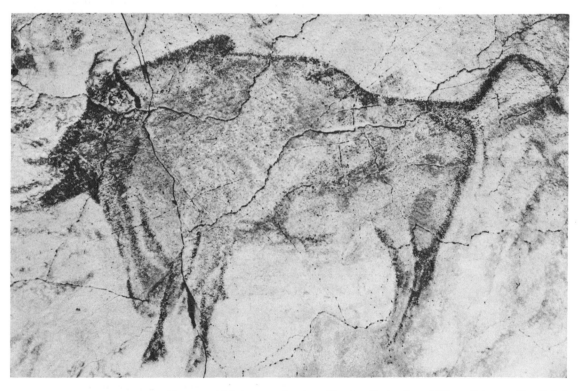

Bison, prehistoric cave drawing, Altamira, Spain. *(Les Editions Braun et Cie, Paris)*

9

Much of the painting was hidden, with some difficulty, in remote recesses of caves. It appears, therefore, that its purpose was magical: to assist hunters in finding game. Pregnant animals occasionally appear, and one fertility scene portrays human beings. These paintings were probably intended to assure plentiful game and to make women fertile. Nonetheless, some of the work was surely done for pleasure alone—art for art's sake.

Small statuettes from this period, often of pregnant women or of phallic symbols, were also found in the late 19th century. Again, the intention was probably magical—or perhaps it should be called "religious." For here we may have the earliest evidence for worship of a great mother goddess, so familiar in later human history.

Magdalenian culture disappeared with the end of the last Ice Age, about 10,000 years ago. It is difficult to account for the decline and disappearance of this rather highly developed culture. One is tempted to speculate that a much greater use of shelters outside of caves—houses of poles covered with skins are known to have existed in the Upper Paleolithic Age—may simply have caused what is really just a gap in our evidence. But this hypothesis cannot be a complete explanation.

Paleolithic Man in the Western Hemisphere

Homo sapiens made his entry into America during the Upper Paleolithic Age, crossing over the land bridge that then existed at what is now the Bering Strait. Certain animals—mammoths, elephants, bison—went along at the same time, during one of the thaws of the last Ice Age (called the Wisconsin in America) it has usually been thought. Eskimos seem to have taken the same route at a somewhat later time.

Spear points have been found among the bones of mammoths and elephants at several sites in the southwest and Great Plains regions of the United States, graphic evidence that these early men were efficient big-game hunters. Charcoal from one occupation site in southern California has been dated back as much as 100,000 years and other occupation sites have been attributed to even earlier times. It is now believed by some scholars, therefore, that the human crossing of the Bering Strait bridge dates back to the third, or the second Ice Age (Illinoisian or Kansan).

The fine spear points, the Sandia, Clovis, and Folsom among others, usually considered to be 10,000 to 12,000 years old, indicate a culture comparable with that of contemporary western Europe, though they have some distinctive features. Clovis and Folsom points, for ex-

Examples of early stone tools. Core tools on the left, flake tools on the right. *(American Museum of Natural History)*

ample, are fluted for better hafting and more effective penetration. At a site in Utah dated to the end of the Paleolithic or the beginning of the Mesolithic Age, there is evidence of the art of basket-weaving—earlier than anywhere else known. The question of the development of agriculture in the Western Hemisphere is much-argued. It probably evolved independently of the Old World cultures—and much later.

The Mesolithic Age

The Mesolithic Age, about 9,000 to 7,000 B.C.—in the Near East, which was advanced—was one of transition from food-gathering to food-producing. Men still hunted, but they were learning to domesticate wild animals. Perhaps wild dogs aided hunters in the hope of sharing the spoils and in the process became tame; or perhaps men just began rearing the orphaned young. Hunters who jealously protected a herd or flock may have claimed ownership of the animals and gradually asserted their control. Other men were learning the mysteries of the germination and growth of grains, noting which were useful. Some genius invented the sickle, made of small chips of sharp-edged flint (microliths, typical of the age) set in a split stick or bone. Quite likely these first steps toward agriculture were taken by women, whose husbands, the great hunters, might not of late have been doing so well. When

11

these new techniques became better understood and developed they would produce a revolution in human affairs.

C. A Quickening Pace: The Neolithic "Revolution"

Food Production:
Agriculture, Domestication of Animals

Agriculture first began, it now appears, somewhere in the grassy uplands of the Near East, though its inception may have been on the soil of an oasis like that at Jericho, with its marvelous spring. There is some evidence for agricultural beginnings in southwest Asia about as early; future investigation may show parallel and independent development at two or more sites far removed from each other. Simple types of barley, wheat, and other grasses were the earliest crops, and their first cultivation was by hoe. At first, it may be, the flint ax was made to do; then someone came up with the idea of changing the haft and turning the implement into a hoe. The ground-stone technique, which developed about the same time, made better hoes possible as well as axes and such new tools as the adze. The plow, invented before many centuries, was at first of wood.

Several varieties of animals now were domesticated in the region. Flocks and herds became the measure of life and wealth for many. Men still hunted and fished, but dependence upon the environment was being replaced by a measure of ability to control it. No longer mere parasites of sorts, families cooperated to produce food and create other forms of wealth.

To maintain flocks and herds does not demand an altogether settled existence; neolithic shepherds, in fact, were forced to move from one area to another as the seasons changed or as forage was consumed. Such shepherds were not rootless nomads, however; they moved about within certain areas and built wells and cisterns, which they jealously guarded. They usually lived in tents, suited to their roving existence, and thus could migrate with relative ease when necessary.

Social and Economic Consequences of Agriculture

Neolithic farmers found that they had to stay in one place for at least a season, preferably longer, and that they needed homes near their fields. They also found that they had to protect their crops from animals and thieves, and that they had to keep noxious weeds from choking the grain. Storage space for the crops, and some facilities to care for a few domestic animals, also had to be provided.

Food production—especially the new agriculture—made possible a denser population. Farmers in the same region came together for mutual protection and social benefit to form villages. By day they went to work their fields; by night they retired to their homes. Soon, walls protected their houses and stores. Certain persons kept guard over flocks and herds in common pastures. With the villages housing several families, social structures based on family and tribe were extended. New groups required new rules—for example, new forms of government. There seems to have been a natural tendency to entrust regulatory matters to a council formed of the heads of families, with one of their number chosen as chief; a larger council was made up of all able-bodied men.

A changing world creates its own problems. As agriculture advanced, it made a better life possible, but it also made greater demands upon men in the political and social spheres. The most profitable land, it was learned, was in the river valleys; in the flood plains of the Near East, only minimal crops could be raised without irrigation. But to irrigate the rich alluvial soil was no simple task. It was not enough for one man to dip water out of the river for his own tiny crop. In short, irrigation systems were essential and, by trial and error were eventually devised. Canals were built and maintained, and for consistent supplies of water reservoirs were constructed. Natural lagoons formed at high water were probably dammed to create the first reservoirs. An irrigation system, in turn, demanded large-scale cooperation. Villages at these irrigation complexes grew into towns and ultimately, in the Bronze Age, into cities.

Technological advances largely determined the physical conditions of human existence in the Neolithic Age. Denser populations required greater cooperative action. But what sort of action was by no means predetermined. Men were forced to find new ways of living together with some degree of security. How they managed varied according to purely human decisions. The development of villages and towns was also accompanied by advanced techniques in construction. In Mesopotamia, for example, sun-dried bricks were invented, which made for better housing, better public buildings—temples, chiefly—and town walls.

Invention of Pottery

The early neolithic men learned to make pottery from clay. Metals were unknown, so the development of pottery was vastly important for storage and cookery. Another achievement was the making of thread from animal and vegetable fibers and the weaving of thread into cloth. Weaving and pottery manufacture were both the result of long processes of experimentation that are beyond our knowledge to appreciate.

The invention of pottery has proved to be the greatest possible boon to the archaeologist. A pot was easily broken, of course, and scarcely ever mended, but the discarded sherds are virtually indestructible. Careful study of developmental sequences in the techniques and styles employed in the manufacture of pottery has made it possible for archaeologists to date sites and strata quite accurately, within relatively narrow limits, by potsherds alone. By a new technique involving what is called thermoluminescence, potsherds can be separately dated within somewhat broader limits, usually. Different methods in manufacture, different sizes and types, changing decorative patterns, incised or painted, and the composition of the clay itself, all have their story to tell. Occasionally, to the delight of the excavators, sherds are found inscribed with the name of a maker or client, or with correspondence, written in ink. These ostraka (the Greek word for potsherds is used in this restricted sense by archaeologists) have preserved written documents that would have decayed centuries ago had they been written on paper. Such ostraka have produced valuable information in recent years in Palestinian archaeology.

Division of Labor: The Craftsman

The developing crafts, tool-making, pottery-making, weaving, and a host of others, soon produced craftsmen—specialists in one or another of these manufactures. The Paleolithic Age may have seen craftsmen who worked full-time making flint tools, but artisans as a class came only with the late Neolithic Age. These craftsmen fashioned finer tools than most individuals could, and in turn, through barter, they obtained more food and other necessary things than they themselves could have grown or made.

Toward the end of the Neolithic Age came other great achievements. This period, in the Near East about 4,000 to 3,000 B.C., is sometimes called the Chalcolithic (copper-stone) Age because copper came into use, first as decorative beads and later, when it was learned that hammering hardened and compacted the metal, for somewhat satisfactory tools. The wheel appeared; used initially in pottery-making, perhaps, it was soon adapted to crude transport. And sailing vessels now plied the rivers, aiding the development of extensive trade. In Mesopotamia, where the soil was rich, raw materials—even stone—had to be brought in from a distance.

Most important, at the end of the age, systems of writing slowly evolved from pictures and pictographs. Written documents made possible more extensive business activity and efficiency; they also allowed the accumulation of knowledge in reliable and systematic form. Scholars in the last several decades have learned, however, that oral transmission of information may have been both more extensive and more reliable than was once believed.

Civilization: Social and Political Change

Civilization may be described as a complex, literate, urban-centered culture. When a town became something more than the focal point of an agricultural operation, it became a city, a political and social center, with a population more diversified than that of an agricultural village. Some of the population of these Bronze Age cities were craftsmen, some were administrators, some were priests. In some cities there were full-time warriors; in others there were also merchants and traders. The surplus food produced by the cities' adjacent irrigated land allowed their upper classes to enjoy leisure time; they could engage in cultural pursuits or patronize artists and writers.

Bronze Age cities required new social structures. The old relationships based on kinship that had endured the Paleolithic Age, and with modifications through the Neolithic Age as well, gave way to new structures based on occupation and position. Kinship was still a factor, but its importance receded. Artisans such as potters, builders, and weavers formed guilds of sorts. Administrators, priests, and warriors also joined forces to support common goals; together, they tended to form an upper class or nobility. Below them were freemen, whether artisans, farmers, or traders, and, still lower, serfs and slaves. The primitive egalitarianism that had seemed so characteristic of earlier ages was gone.

In a primitive world, the natural variation in individual abilities may mean the difference between the great hunter and the poor one, the warrior-leader and the second-rate follower. But when technology extends the power and potential of certain men who can use it, the inevitable result is that individual differences will be accentuated. If the whole group does not somehow prevent it, the relative distance between the rich and the poor, the strong and the weak, will become greater. In the modern world, of course, this tendency is even more pronounced, though modern governments do intervene massively to rectify the balance.

The various groups within the growing new cities of the Bronze Age, and the competition between cities, created conditions that demanded new political institutions. The new class structure and the new political structure developed simultaneously. The most crucial single factor to cause political change was probably warfare, for it was necessary to protect both the irrigation system and the increasing wealth within the city's walls. There were also, to be sure, wars of expansion, which no political leader of the ancient world ever thought it necessary to justify. Successful warfare in all ages necessitates the efficient organization of both manpower and resources and an unambiguous command structure as well. The wars between emergent Bronze Age cities certainly helped to produce the characteristic political unit that then evolved: the city-state.

The City-State

The city-state embraced an area no larger than an average county in one of the United States. The city was the center—political, economic, and religious. The leader of the city-state was often the leader of the army. Whatever his title, he was a sort of warrior-king, and sometimes the chief priest as well. And whatever his actions, he and his people recognized that the outcome of their struggle to protect themselves from neighbors or outlanders was in the hands of the gods. The priest, who could propitiate the gods and interpret their will, thus ranked as a very important person. Not surprisingly, the priests, who administered the property of the gods, were often wealthy.

The emphasis in religion long before the Bronze Age had shifted from paleolithic magic and the worship of a great mother to a neolithic worship of a great sky-father god and earth-mother goddess, to correspond with the rise of agriculture. Numberless local deities also entered the pantheon, but gods playing the role of great mother remained important, as religion tends to combine new and old. In the Bronze Age the focus of worship was upon a patron deity of the city. Pseudo-scientific observation of the heavens also meant that celestial deities were stressed, sometimes in abstract, conceptual terms. In Babylon, for example, Shamash, the sun god, came to be also the god of law or justice; in Egypt a similar role was attributed to Horus and a daughter of Re, both also associated with the sun.

Riverine Civilizations

Civilizations arose in the great river valleys for reasons, as we have seen, that were economic. All civilizations must have an economic basis. It has also always been true that only when agriculture produces a surplus, so that not all men have to work at food production, can some men be free to work at tasks that enrich human existence. In the modern world, mineral wealth and industrial production are vital—though an agricultural surplus is still absolutely basic to progress in other spheres. In the Bronze Age, metals began to form a new source of wealth, but

Aerial photograph taken from a Gemini space capsule shows the area from eastern Egypt to the Persian Gulf (upper right). *(National Aeronautics and Space Administration)*

throughout the ancient period, even in the Iron Age, good land was fundamental.

The earliest civilization arose in the great river valley formed by the Tigris and Euphrates, in an area called Mesopotamia—"between the rivers." Almost as early was the civilization of the great Nile valley. Not much later came those civilizations developed in the Indus River valley to the east, in the valleys of the Yellow and Yangtze Rivers in China, as well as others bordering Mesopotamia on the east and south. The early development on Crete seems to have depended partly upon wealth produced overseas and brought to the island.

In the next chapters we shall consider these civilizations, giving particular attention to those that are distinctly in the Western tradition.

18

Books for Further Reading

BURKITT, MILES, *The Old Stone Age,* New York, 1963.

CHILDE, V. G., *What Happened in History,* Baltimore, 1954.

DEETZ, JAMES, *Invitation to Archaeology,* New York, 1967.

FRANKFORT, H., *Before Philosophy,* Baltimore, 1951.

FRANKFORT, H., *Birth of Civilization in the Near East,* New York, 1956.

GABEL, C., *Man Before History,* Englewood Cliffs, N.J., 1964.

HAWKES, J., and WOOLLEY, L., *Prehistory and the Beginnings of Civilization,* New York, 1963.

LEAKEY, L. S. B., *Adam's Ancestors: the Evolution of Man and His Culture,* New York, 1960.

MELLAART, J., *Catal Huyuk,* New York, 1967.

MELLAART, J. *Earliest Civilizations of the Near East,* New York, 1965.

VLAKOS, O., *New World Beginnings,* New York, 1970.

Ancient Mesopotamia
in the Bronze Age

2

Whole millennia of Mesopotamian history are now known that were never dreamed of little more than a century ago. To a Judeo-Christian world predisposed to great interest in the area because of its Biblical associations, some of the discoveries of archaeologists have at times taken on an aura of romance. In December 1872 George Smith of the British Museum reported to the British Society of Biblical Archaeology that among the museum's clay tablets excavated decades before at Nineveh, he had found a Chaldean account of the Flood. At the expense of a London newspaper and with considerable fanfare, Smith made an expedition to Nineveh on the Tigris in modern Iraq to seek a missing fragment from one of the tablets. Astonishingly, he quickly found it. The tablet was part of the Gilgamesh epic, discussed later in this chapter.

Earlier excavators had offered notice that extraordinary discoveries in the Mesopotamian region could be made. Austen Henry Layard, a British diplomat-scholar, had found the remarkable library of Assurbanipal; the publication in 1852 of his fascinating account of the Nineveh excavation had been widely read. Other extensive if superficial excavations had also yielded significant materials. Another British scholar-soldier-diplomat of the period was Henry (later Sir Henry) Rawlinson. Using the trilingual inscription of King Darius the Great of Persia that had been carved on a rocky bluff near Behistun on the fringe of northern Mesopotamia, Rawlinson did much to decipher cuneiform writing; he published his work in 1847—and the study of "Assyriology" was well under way. More, and more careful, excavations of the great "tells"— flat-topped eminences that contain, in layer upon layer, the remains of

CHART 2 Period of Early History, 3,000–500 B.C.

	MESOPOTAMIA	EGYPT	OTHER AREAS
Early Bronze Age c. 3000 B.C. to c. 2100 B.C.	Protoliterate, predynastic age. Growth of cities. Early Dynastic Age. Gilgamesh king of Uruk. Sargon's empire.	Archaic Period. Thinite Period (unification); First and Second Dynasties. Old Kingdom, pyramids; Third and Fourth Dynasties.	Rise of civilization in Aegean, Indus areas, probably in China. Syrian cities important.
Middle Bronze Age c. 2100 B.C. to c. 1600 B.C.	Third Dynasty of Ur; Ur-Nammu, first known law code. Kingdoms of Babylon (Hammurabi), Mari, Assyria. Kassites.	First Intermediate Period; Seventh through Eleventh Dynasties. Middle Kingdom; Twelfth Dynasty. Second Intermediate Period; Thirteenth through Seventeenth Dynasties. Hyksos. Expulsion of Hyksos.	Height of Knossos, other Aegean centers. Shang Dynasty, China. Mycenaean Age. Decline of Knossos, other Cretan sites. Hittite Old Kingdom.
Late Bronze Age c. 1600 B.C. to c. 1200 B.C.	Assyria strong.	Empire; Eighteenth through Twentieth Dynasties. Hatshepsut. Thutmoses III. Akhnaton. Ramses II.	Destruction of Indus civilization. Kingdom of Mitanni. Hittite Empire. Suppiluliumas. Israelite entry into Palestine.
Iron Age 1200 B.C. 1000 B.C.		Ramses III repels invasion of the Sea peoples. End of Egyptian Empire. Twenty-first Dynasty. Twenty-second Dynasty.	Sea peoples destroy Hittite Empire, cities of Syria, Byblos, and so forth. Period of Judges in Israel, then Kingdom. Phoenician cities flourish. Kings Saul, David, Solomon, then Divided Monarchy: Israel, Judah. Ahab King of Israel; Jezebel.
900 B.C.	Assyrian Empire expands under Shalmaneser III.		
800 B.C.	Tiglath-pileser III. Shalmaneser V. Sargon II. Sennacherib. Assurbanipal.	Twenty-third Dynasty. Twenty-fourth Dynasty. Twenty-fifth Dynasty. Twenty-sixth Dynasty. Necho II	Phoenicians colonize Carthage, other sites. Fall of Kingdom of Israel to Assyria; Judah subjected. Phoenicians sent by Egyptian king Necho around Africa. Rise of Empire of Medes and Persians. Destruction of Jerusalem; Babylonian captivity.
700 B.C.			
600 B.C.	Fall of Assyria; Neo-Babylonian or Chaldean Empire. Nebuchadnezzar, Nabonidus.	**PERSIAN EMPIRE**	
500 B.C.	Fall of Babylon to Persia under Cyrus. Darius III, the Great. Xerxes I.	Twenty-seventh Dynasty, Persian, established by Cambyses.	Asia Minor conquered by Cyrus. First Jewish exiles permitted to return. Thrace taken by Persia; Scythians repel Persians. Greeks defeat Persians at Marathon. Greeks defeat Persians at Salamis, Plataea. Athenians lead Greeks, establish empire. Peloponnesian War; victory of Sparta, allies. March of the 10,000 against Persia. Persia involved in Greek wars.
400 B.C.	Artaxerxes I, Darius II. Artaxerxes II. Artaxerxes III. Darius III, defeated by Alexander.	Egyptians encouraged by Athens to revolt against Persia.	
330 B.C.	Alexander the Great destroys the Persian Empire.		

ancient cities—have produced information about a far earlier civilization than that of the Assyrians so well known from the Bible.

One of the oldest agricultural villages known is Jericho, just above the Dead Sea in Palestine. It was excavated by the British archaeologist Kathleen Kenyon, who dug down through seventy feet of debris representing nearly 7,000 years of human habitation. Carbon 14 dates confirm that a settlement existed at Jericho by about 8,000 B.C. After another thousand years there was a town at the site encompassing several acres and surrounded by a stone wall several feet thick, with a large tower. Houses in this neolithic town were made of sun-dried brick, with compacted clay floors and domed roofs not unlike those still seen in the Middle East. There was evidence of agriculture; pottery came along considerably later. The term "pre-pottery neolithic" was coined by Kenyon to fit the evidence turned up at Jericho. Agriculture at Jericho was possible only with irrigation from the large spring that gives life to the spot. Thus, a certain complexity of social and political organization as well as of technology may be inferred. Though the people produced food, they still hunted, as the bones found testify. Animals were domesticated also, but which ones and at what point it is difficult to say. Evidence of religious practices was unearthed including cult statues, some apparently of a mother goddess, with small shrines. And perhaps the people worshiped ancestors: skulls of the dead were sometimes plastered and fitted with artificial eyes to make them into something like portrait busts.

Another neolithic site about as early as Jericho but more recently excavated is that of Zawi Chemi-Shanidar in northern Iraq; it is located along the Great Zab River, a tributary of the Tigris. Somewhat less old but quite important for its contribution to our understanding of the age is Catal Hüyük, on the southern Anatolian plateau in modern Turkey. This site was well developed, considerably larger than Jericho, and with a record of continuous habitation throughout the early neolithic period, for more than a millennium after 6,700 B.C. Here, too, both agriculture and hunting were simultaneously important. Archaeologists have identified a dozen or more products of cultivation, including three types of wheat, fruits, and nuts. More than fifty types of tools were used. Excellent pottery was produced by 5,900 B.C., and the inhabitants wove several kinds of fibers into cloth. As for art (and religion) at this exceptional site, not only statuettes but also wall paintings were discovered. The reasons for Catal Hüyük's "decline and fall" are still subject to speculation.

Other early neolithic towns have been turned up by the spade in widely separated places: elsewhere in Anatolia, in northern Iraq, in Iran (recently at the foot of the Zagros Mountains) and in as far removed an area as Southeast Asia, where scholars naturally have found it difficult to work in recent years.

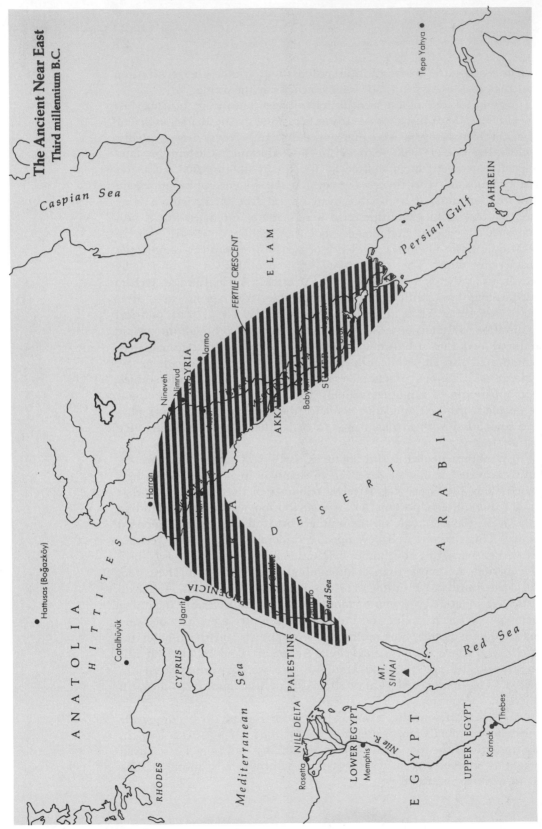

The Ancient Near East
Third millennium B.C.

Caspian Sea

Tepe Yahya

BAHREIN

Persian Gulf

FERTILE CRESCENT

ELAM

Jarmo

Nimrud

SYRIA

Nineveh

AKKAD

Babylon

Uruk

Harran

DESERT

ARABIA

PHOENICIA

Dead Sea

Hattusas (Boğazköy)

ANATOLIA

HITTITES

Çatalhüyük

CYPRUS

Ugarit

RHODES

Mediterranean Sea

PALESTINE

MT. SINAI

Red Sea

NILE DELTA

Rosetta

LOWER EGYPT

Memphis

Nile R.

EGYPT

UPPER EGYPT

Karnak

Thebes

Adapted from Brinton, Christopher, and Wolff, Civilization in the West, third edition, volume one.

A. City-states of the Tigris-Euphrates Basin

An amazing amount of early history was made in the Asian Near East within the bounds of a region called "the Fertile Crescent." This semicircular band of land stretches from Palestine and Syria on the west up, over, and down through Mesopotamia on the east. (Syria should not be confused with Assyria, located farther to the east on the upper Tigris River.) It is bounded by the Mediterranean Sea on the west, by the mountains of eastern Anatolia and Armenia on the north, and by the Zagros Mountains on the east. Within the crescent's two horns and to the south lies the Arabian Desert. There are many easy avenues of access into the Fertile Crescent, and throughout history immigrants and invaders on occasion have swarmed into the region. Although Jericho is one of the earliest known neolithic villages, the earliest true civilization developed in the eastern horn of the crescent—above the Persian Gulf in lower Mesopotamia.

Mesopotamia: Climate, Geography

Mesopotamia is the rather large area between and along the two great rivers of the Near East, the Euphrates and the Tigris. Both arise in the Armenian mountains to the north, and at one point near their sources they are rather close together. The Tigris flows mostly south; the Euphrates swings west and then south. In far antiquity they debouched separately into the Persian Gulf, but today they join together a few miles north of the gulf.

Lower Mesopotamia is conventionally subdivided into two parts: Sumer and Akkad. Sumer, the lower section, was unsuitable for permanent settlement until a few centuries before 4000 B.C. because it was once a marsh. A long-held view that the waters of the Persian Gulf once extended far north of the present coastline has been challenged by geologists using new data. Perhaps the Euphrates formed a lagoon near the city of Ur which connected with the gulf. The rivers have built up the land during their characteristic annual flooding, but the basin has subsided as the soil accumulated. The soil is thus alluvial and quite deep.

The climate of Mesopotamia is hot and humid, and because the winter rains are not substantial, only the most primitive agriculture is possible without irrigation. The Tigris and Euphrates often overflow in spring, from rains and melting snows to the north. These floods are irregular and can be terrifyingly destructive, as is known from both modern and ancient experience. They also gave rise to the story of the Flood in the book of Genesis and in earlier Semitic and Sumerian accounts as well. Successful irrigation on any scale has always required careful organization.

The land was rich, though under intensive irrigation it tended to become gradually less productive through salinization. The staple crop, barley, however, tolerated salt somewhat better than wheat. Beer was made early, both from dates and from barley. And though minerals and fuel were scarce, the palm tree was marvelously useful—fruit, trunk, and leaves. Even the outer layers of bark furnished fiber for rope.

The Sumerians

Who were the Sumerians? There is as yet no exact answer to that question. Certain of their practices, especially the building of *ziggurats*—the pyramidal platforms imitative of mountains upon which they built temples—suggest they came from mountainous country to the east. Some of their traditions, however, suggest that they lived near the sea long before the historic period. Perhaps they were indigenous to lower Mesopotamia. Probably the people who created the first civilization were already a racially mixed group. In any event, the term "Sumerian" is more a linguistic than a racial one.

The Early Dynastic Age

A Sumerian tradition has it that their oldest town was Eridu. By the middle of the 3rd millennium B.C., several other cities stood out, including Ur, Uruk, Lagash, and Umma. In Akkad to the north, the cities of Nippur and Kish were prominent. These cities were ruled over by successive dynasties of kings or priest-kings. Hence the Early Bronze Age, down to about 2400 B.C., is called the Early Dynastic Age. Writers of a later period preserved the remembrance of these various dynasties in lists of kings, which, in the lengths of reigns indicated, are in many instances totally unbelievable. The kings are divided into two groups, those who reigned before the Flood and those who reigned after. One list contains eight antediluvian kings who ruled a total of 241,200 years! The list remarks that "kingship was sent down from heaven," a comment repeated after the Flood. The statement gives us some understanding of the idea of the divine origin of the kingship which Sumerians apparently held, at least at the time when the lists were compiled.

Some of the lists of later kings assign more believable reigns. When the British archaeologist Sir Leonard Woolley was excavating at al-Ubaid near Ur, he found a temple dedication inscription that proved the existence of the first king of the first dynasty of Ur, Mes Anni Padda, who ruled in approximately 2500 B.C. On the same site, deeper down, Woolley uncovered evidence of a great flood—the one he thought was so

The ziggurat at Ur, much restored.
(Courtesy of T. Edward Franklin.)

firmly implanted in the memory of all the peoples of the region. It has not been possible, however, to identify a single flood as *the* Flood, and to place all the postdiluvial dynasties immediately after it. All attempts to collate evidence relating either to the Flood or to the king lists are inconclusive.

Tomb Excavations at Ur

The riches of the kings of the Early Dynastic Age were also demonstrated in the excavations of Woolley in a cemetery near Ur. These royal tombs contained rich helmets, vessels, harps, and pots along with the remains of human beings who had been slain and buried with the kings (and queens) to serve them beyond the grave. The tombs contained as many as seventy to eighty skeletons. Mrs. Woolley's sculptured bust of one queen, Shub-Ad (Pu-Abi), adorned in wig and hair jewelry has made this wife of King Akalamdug a familiar face in textbooks. The king and queen were buried at different times. With them were dancing girls, musicians, personal attendants, a sledge-chariot drawn by a yoke of asses, and two ox-drawn carts. One harp of magnificent workmanship was decorated with a bull's head in gold and lapis lazuli. A kind of "standard" with ivory carved panels set in bitumen is important for what it shows

25

of the life and achievements of the king. These objects are among the
most prized possessions of the British Museum.

Cities of the Early Dynastic Period

Almost all construction in these cities was of sun-dried bricks. At first
the cities were not walled but as they grew rich they required protection.
The most notable feature of each was the temple to the patron god,
which was erected atop a ziggurat large enough to raise it well above
the walls. These ziggurats were usually built up in layers, growing with
the town. Some, as that at Ur where the best-preserved one is to be
found, were irrigated on the top levels. To the approaching traveler, its
greenery must have seemed to float in the sky, especially in the dry
season when the plain, the walls, and the buildings, all of clay, were a
scorched dun color.

The ziggurat was not only the religious center of town, it was
the social, political, and economic focal point as well. In some Sumerian
cities the ruler was the *en* or *ensi* (Semitic *ishakku*), probably originally
a priest; later the term means approximately governor, a man subordinate
to the *lugal,* or king, who may initially have been a military leader. Much
of the city's property, both real and movable, belonged in theory to the
patron god. In each of these cities a sort of council of city notables and
an assembly made up of the army—presumably all male, able-bodied
full citizens—tended to develop.

So far as possible the Sumerians made do with the materials at
hand. They used clay for sun-dried and baked bricks (though fuel was
expensive); they even used clay, baked until vitrified, for such objects
as sickles; these broke easily, no doubt, but they must have been fairly
satisfactory. Stone, both for building and for making flint tools had to
be imported. Copper was available at no great distance. Tin, however—
which makes up about 10 per cent of bronze, the other element being
copper—had to be brought in from a distance, perhaps from Elam, in
modern Iran.

B. The First Empires

Conflict and Consolidation

In human terms it seems inevitable that the new city-states, once just
small villages with their irrigation complexes, should have become embroiled in wars. We hear of boundary disputes and struggles over water
rights along canals. King Agga of Kish may have been one of the earliest
monarchs whose imperialistic expansion brought other rulers under his

sway, possibly including the renowned Gilgamesh of Uruk (Biblical Erech), who will be mentioned later. A "stele of vultures," now in the Louvre, celebrated a victory of Lagash over Umma. Ur probably controlled a rather large area at one point. At last, however, Lugalzaggisi, king of Umma, conquered Lagash and Ur and came to dominate all Sumer, with Uruk as his new capital.

Sargon of Agade: A Semitic Empire

Lugalzaggisi's empire soon fell in turn to a storied king, Sargon (Sharrumkin) of Agade in Akkad, about 2340 B.C. Sargon reputedly reigned for fifty-six years. Our sources have it that his empire extended through all of Mesopotamia and westward over the Fertile Crescent to the Mediterranean, possibly on to Cyprus and up into Anatolia. To some degree the existence of such a sizable empire has been confirmed by archaeology. One of its most significant consequences was that it disseminated Sumero-Semitic culture throughout the entire region.

Third in succession after Sargon was his grandson, Naram-Sin. This vigorous king pushed into the lands bordering the Persian Gulf as far south as Oman. He was a prosperous monarch. Literary and archaeological evidence indicates he was paid an extensive tribute and that his trade extended as far east as distant India. Naram-Sin called himself "King of the Four World Regions," and for centuries every monarch in Mesopotamia with imperialistic ambitions would assume that grandiloquent title. Mysterious, unlucky events ultimately weakened the empire in the latter days of Naram-Sin, and soon after his death it fell to pieces. Most likely, the Akkadian kings had simply overreached themselves.

Depredations of the semibarbarous Guti from regions to the east had blunted the power of the Agade dynasty. These Gutians finally overwhelmed the Akkadian portion of the empire and gained control over parts of Sumer as well. The confusion of the period is despairingly echoed on the king list: "Who was king? Who was not king?" Some of the Sumerian cities held back the tide, however—principally Lagash, whose king, Gudea, is well known through the several statuettes of him that have been found. Gudea undertook only defensive wars and gave his attention to building temples and canals.

Ur III: A Sumerian Empire

The famed Third Dynasty of Ur (or simply Ur III), founded by Ur-Nammu about 2111 B.C., finally stabilized the whole area of lower Mesopotamia. In the brilliant and prosperous period that followed, a late flowering of Sumerian culture occurred. The ziggurat at Ur, the capital, was built to magnificent proportions and temples were constructed or restored in several other cities. The canals so important to the irrigation complexes were renewed, and an extensive trade developed. The literature which, along with Ur-Nammu's law code, will be discussed later, centered about legendary earlier figures such as Gilgamesh and was probably compiled chiefly in this age.

The empire of Ur III fell shortly before 2000 B.C., partly because of Elamite revolts in the east and partly because of attacks by a new incursion of Semites called Amorites, who moved into Mesopotamia from their homeland in Syria or Arabia. These Amorites had been immigrating for some decades. The successor states to Ur included Isin in Akkad, Larsa in Sumer, Mari on the middle Euphrates 300 miles upstream, and Assyria on the upper Tigris. The final end of Ur under Elamite attack shocked its people. A poignant poem, *Lamentation over the Destruction of Ur,* suggests that the fall was by divine decree; Ur's patron deity could not thwart the decree of Enlil, leader of the gods.

Hammurabi the Amorite: A Second Semitic Empire

Ur III was the last predominantly Sumerian empire. As new waves of Semites swept into Mesopotamia, its population became increasingly Semitic. It was the Amorite dynasty established at Babylon in Akkad that next achieved dominion over the whole region—the feat of the sixth king of the dynasty, the famous Hammurabi (c. 1792–1750 B.C., or 1728–1686 by a late chronology).

Hammurabi is best known for his code of laws, discovered in 1901 in ancient Elam. Excavations at Mari, chiefly in the 1930s, have turned up clay tablet archives of great benefit in understanding the diplomatic history of the time. We learn how the wily Hammurabi played off one enemy against the other to conquer his opponents one by one. He took Larsa in about his thirtieth year and Mari a few years later. Hammurabi administered his dominions vigorously, giving attention to the welfare of his subjects as the introduction to his law code testifies. But his successors were less competent. Southern Mesopotamia broke away from the empire, and a raid of the Hittites from Asia Minor about 1595 B.C. caused devastation all the way to Babylon itself. Soon after, a semibarbarous people from the mountainous country to the northeast—the Kassites—overran Akkad and established themselves as rulers of what remained. Indo-European names appear among the gods of the Kassites, though they seem not to have been an Indo-European people.

Other invaders of the upper Euphrates and of the lands north of Assyria were the Hurrians (Biblical Horites), who later, led by Indo-European elements, founded a kingdom called Mitanni, which extended

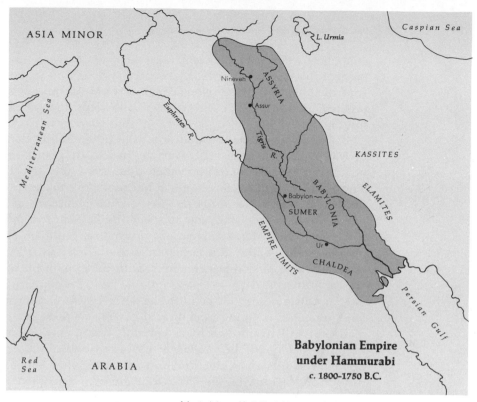

Adapted from Modell, A History of the Western World, volume one.

from the Euphrates to parts of what is now Armenia. Very recent archaeological evidence shows that some Indo-European-speaking peoples had been in the area south of the Caspian Sea a thousand years before this. The weakness of all the great powers—from the Hittites in Anatolia to the Assyrians and Babylonians—permitted the Kassites and Hurrians to establish themselves firmly and begin to absorb the culture of their captives. The success of these invaders—and later of the Hittites as well—was in part assured by their intensive use of horse-drawn chariots.

C. Cultural Development of Early Mesopotamia: Writing System

Evolution of Writing Systems

One marked distinction between animal and human intelligence (though it may be a distinction only of degree) relates to man's ability to symbolize, an ability most clearly demonstrated in connection with language. Most animals have some means of audible communication, but no great complexity is possible without the ability to conceive and understand symbolically. Such development came first, of course, with spoken language, which always precedes any written system. This sequence must be kept in mind, for the development of writing has always involved the problem of conveying by visual symbols words that already exist in spoken form.

Writing systems seem always to have developed along a pattern in which pictures came first. Then followed pictographs in which the picture symbolized something other than what was actually pictured. Thus, a foot meant not merely a foot but to walk or to go. In an ideogram the symbol stands for an abstraction. In the Sumerian system, for example, the sign for a star came to symbolize heaven; it could also represent a god. Moreover, combinations of symbols could be utilized for a new meaning. Again illustrating from the Sumerian, the symbol for bowl—meaning food—when combined with the symbol for mouth meant "to eat."

Obviously, at this point in the development of a language, a very large number of quite complicated characters existed that for the most part still retained their pictographic qualities. Further steps were required to simplify the symbols or characters and to reduce their number. For the Sumerians, simplification meant the slow elimination of the pictographic nature of the characters. Students had then to recognize characters, not pictures. The solution to the need to pare down the vast numbers of characters lay in phonetics. Characters could be made to represent phonetically—that is, by sound rather than by visual representation—all the aural nuances of spoken language. Thus the Sumerians used the symbol for water (the original pictograph looked somewhat like a stream) to mean "in" because the word for "water" and the word for "in" sounded alike. This phonetic principle made possible the representation of words for which no pictograph or ideograph could easily be invented, and when widely applied—it could even be applied to new languages with a totally new vocabulary—led to a gradually simplified system using basic sets of symbols. During the transition period there would still be thousands of symbols, some used phonetically and some not—doubtless a difficult time for students of the art of writing!

The protracted changes in the symbols for simpler and faster writing, and the cutback in their number, can be traced, often in detail, in the Sumerian system. A totally phonetic system at length emerged with a limited number of symbols, each standing for a syllable (syllabary). Finally, after more centuries of development, the idea of individual symbols for each separate sound led to a true alphabet. Improvement often came in the application of the writing system to a new language, when old traditions no longer exercised a restraining influence. Real alphabets developed somewhat later than the Sumerian period under consideration here.

The Sumerians probably produced the first writing system. A separate one, little known and undeciphered, was developed only a little later in Elam, and those created in the Nile and Indus River valleys—the last currently being deciphered—were almost as early. We call the Sumerian system "cuneiform," from Latin words meaning wedge-shaped, because the symbols were impressed on damp clay tablets with a square-cut, triangular-shaped reed. To the untrained eye, the result looks like chicken tracks. Numerous tablets designed for teaching the writing system in schools have been found. Valuable to modern scholars as well, some are much like dictionaries; others are lists of synonyms involving different languages.

The fact that the Sumerians chose to write on clay—as did, for many centuries, most peoples who lived in and about the Fertile Crescent—has been supremely fortunate for modern scholars. Once baked, these clay tablets are almost as indestructible as potsherds. Even if only sun-dried, they can with care be excavated intact from the damp Mesopotamian soil and redried or baked, if it seems desirable. Tens of thousands of these tablets have been discovered, preserving for today's scholars invaluable information that otherwise would have been irretrievably lost.

The cuneiform writing system endured for an astonishingly long period. It was used almost exclusively throughout the Fertile Crescent and surrounding area at least until the middle of the 2nd millennium B.C., and in diminishing degree until about the beginning of the Christian era. The most used language, however, was not Sumerian but Akkadian and its later variations.

D. Early Mesopotamian Literature

Many of the greatest works of ancient Mesopotamian literature have Sumerian antecedents, but the popular and enduring forms are Semitic. Gilgamesh, the mythical-legendary king of Uruk, was a sort of semi-divine hero of the Sumerians, but the tablets that preserved the finished poem, and which were dug up at Nippur and Nineveh, give the story in Akkadian, with Semitic overtones.

An Early Great Epic Poem: Gilgamesh

The story of Gilgamesh is one of the world's first great epics. Gilgamesh is portrayed as a swashbuckling monarch somewhat resented by the citizens of his city, Uruk, who begged the gods for relief. They sent him a competitor, a primitive, hairy savage, Enkidu. But Gilgamesh employed a prostitute who civilized him a bit—a "modern" theme that is clearly as old as literature. Gilgamesh and Enkidu then became great companions and performed heroic tasks, among them the slaying of the terrible monster of the cedar forest, Huwawa. The love goddess Ishtar (Sumerian Inanna) herself fell in love with Gilgamesh, but to little avail. In rejecting her, Gilgamesh pointed out how most of her former lovers had come to grief. In reprisal Ishtar persuaded Anu, the great sky god and her father, to send a terrible "bull of heaven" to kill Gilgamesh and Enkidu. The two, however, succeeded in killing the bull. But then a council of gods decreed that one of them must die. Enlil, god of the air, caused the decision to go against Enkidu, who fell sick and expired. Gilgamesh, now brought up short and faced with the finality of man's common lot, set out to seek immortality, one of humanity's great quests.

Gilgamesh learned of a man who had found immortality, one Utnapishtim (Sumerian Ziusudra), and went to find him. A friendly and philosophical (and semidivine) bar girl tried to persuade him to accept man's fate, and to eat, drink, and be merry. But Gilgamesh continued his search and at length found Utnapishtim—the Babylonian Noah who had survived the Flood. (It was this account that George Smith found on a tablet in the British Museum and presented to the world.) Utnapishtim's story is told in language strikingly similar to that of the book of Genesis, though without the moral background or the polytheistic form. Warned by a god of the coming deluge, Utnapishtim built a huge square vessel as instructed and loaded it with people and all living things. Then,

> *With the first glow of dawn,*
> *A black cloud rose up from the horizon.*
> *Inside it Adad thunders, . . .*
> *Who turned to blackness all that had been light.*
> *The wide land was shattered like a pot! . . . .*
> *No one can see his fellow,*
> *Nor can the people be recognized from heaven.*
> *The gods were frightened by the deluge,*
> *And, shrinking back, they ascended to the heaven of Anu . . .*
> *The gods, all humbled, sit and weep, ...*
> *Six days and six nights*
> *Blows the flood wind, as the south-storm sweeps the land.*
> *When the seventh day arrived, ...*
> *The sea grew quiet, the tempest was still, the flood ceased.*
> *I looked at the weather: stillness had set in,*
> *And all of mankind had returned to clay.*
> *The landscape was as level as a flat roof.*[1]

[1] From J. B. Pritchard, ed., *The Ancient Near East: An Anthology of Texts and Pictures* (Princeton, 1958), p. 68.

The "ark" landed on a mountain called Nisir. Utnapishtim sent out, at intervals, a dove, a swallow, and a raven. When the raven did not return, he left the vessel and poured out a libation to the gods. The gods, feeling rather sorry about what they had done, gave Utnapishtim immortal life by way of compensation. The secret of rejuvenation he now gave to Gilgamesh: he was to dive to the bottom of the river and find a specific plant. This he did, but before he could eat it, a snake stole it away. As for Gilgamesh, he went the way of all the world, but humans later deified him.

Other Babylonian Literary Works

Fragments of many other pieces of Mesopotamian literature are known to us. Most of them belong to the period of Assyrian greatness, but derive from early history of Mesopotamia. One famous myth tells how the great Marduk, patron god of Babylon, created the world from the body of the great dragon-goddess Tiamat, slicing her in half to form the heavens and the earth. Another tale with Sumerian origins offers an etiological explanation of the seasons. Inanna (Semitic Ishtar) made a journey to the nether world, perhaps seeking Dumuzi (Tammuz), her dead lover, and was held there, lifeless and hanging on a nail! But because Inanna—the goddess of love—was a fertility deity, the earth dried up and yielded no fruit. The wise god Enki eventually persuaded the rulers of the underworld to give up Inanna; she was sprinkled with the water of life and, of course, the world again became fruitful. Various forms of this myth persisted to Greco-Roman times. Other well-known Greek myths, as for example those preserved in Hesiod's *Theogony,* likely have their origins in Mesopotamian literature.

E. Early Mesopotamian Law and Society

The Earliest Law Codes

The black diorite stele which contains the Hammurabic code almost intact, one of the prizes of the Louvre Museum, was discovered in 1901 on the site of ancient Susa. Earlier codes are now known. The Sumerian code of a king of Isin, Lipit-Ishtar, dates nearly 150 years earlier than the Hammurabic code. And one king, Bilalama, a Semite, promulgated a code (Laws of Eshnunna) some seventy years before that. Earlier still is the code of Ur-Nammu, founder of the Third Dynasty of Ur. Fragmentary as these last codes are, they all nonetheless show clearly a direct line of development that came down to—and continued past—Ham-

34

The Stele of Hammurabi. Hammurabi stands before the sun god, the "Lord of Justice and Lawgiver." *(Cliché des Musées Nationaux)*

murabi. Through a 1,500-year period, the codes grew more strict and severe.

A certain king of Lagash named Urukagina issued a series of laws around 2400 B.C. that already shows a degree of comprehensiveness and organization, though it can hardly be termed a "code." These laws illustrate the way in which collections of the edicts of a king formed a sort of transitional stage that led to the more ordered and more extensive compilations that came later and that may properly be termed "codes." Urukagina wished to protect his people from the depredations of official bureaucrats and priests, and from the domineering upper classes. He reduced taxes and fees, which were exorbitant even for burial of the dead. A wealthy man could no longer force a poorer and less powerful man to sell his property if he did not wish to do so. Unfortunately, neither Urukagina nor Lagash seems to have been very strong, for the city was soon conquered.

The social, political, and economic implications of these codes are notable, though a word of warning as to the nature and degree of their significance is in order. Written laws do not necessarily indicate the real situation. Was Urukagina, for example, able to control his own bureaucracy and his rapacious nobles? Modern experience with similar situations would tend to suggest a skeptical answer. His laws may reflect only one monarch's good intentions. What is law, really? One pragmatic reply is that it is what the magistrates and courts actually enforce. As historical evidence, then, laws and law codes must be evaluated with great care. Incidental information in them about social classes or areas of social and economic activity is more dependable than is the information about exaction of penalties.

The Law Codes and the Social Classes

Three social classes are mentioned in the Hammurabic code. The upper class was a rather broad group (at least in law) and to call them nobles is somewhat misleading. They were full citizens and included officials, priests, and warriors. The second class, that of freemen ("middle class" would also be misleading), included craftsmen, professional people, merchants and traders, and some farmers. At the bottom were serfs and slaves, some of whom had certain rights: they could own property, for instance.

To commit an offense against one of the upper class called for a more severe penalty than to commit the same offense against one of the lower classes. On the other hand, for certain offenses the upper-class felon was punished more severely because he was expected to behave as one of the elite. The principle of revenge—an eye for an eye, a tooth for a tooth (*jus talionis*)—was applied, but not for all situations. In particular, when the offense was against the lower classes, a money payment could be made. When fines were permitted as alternatives to physical punishment the rich were obviously in a favored position. Of course, money compensation could mean more than vengeance to an aggrieved poor man.

The very complexity and sophistication of the sections of the Hammurabic Code dealing with such matters as marriage and the family, property, inheritance, and slander and other crimes show long development and wide experience in all sorts of situations. For example, if one of the upper class was captured in war, what of his spouse? If she was well fixed financially, she was expected to stay at home and take care of family matters for her absent husband. If, however, she could not maintain herself, she could remarry. If the first husband came home, the decision was his whether she should come back to him. If she had children by both husbands, each father took his own. Women could engage in business; they seem often to have run beer halls, frequently of questionable character.

Other sections of the code fixed prices for commodities of all sorts, as well as for physicians and builders. The code also set penalties for malpractice as it did for shoddy construction. Inheritance and dowry were closely controlled; a man could not capriciously disinherit his son, for example. Commerce and exchange were carefully regulated as well. Records had to be kept if recourse to the law was to be taken. In general, strict justice was the ideal, with no room for mercy.

F. Early Mesopotamian Religion

Religion is extremely important in history—as it still is today—and it deserves much more space than it is usually given in a work of this kind. At its historical best, religion is a unifying, integrating force, providing the basic value structure that holds the society together. At its historical worst, it is, as Marxists have charged, a ruler's instrument for oppression of the masses. In the nations of the West today, the role of religion seems of little consequence, though this may be an illusion. Even when religion plays a passive rather than a dynamic role in societal affairs it is still a salient factor in history, for religious beliefs and the religious organizations reflect the nature of a society almost as well as does its government, if with different emphases.

Mesopotamian Gods

The early Mesopotamian religion contained leftovers from the earlier peasant culture—the Inanna-Dumuzi (Akkadian Ishtar-Tammuz) story has already been mentioned, for example—and some elements from more primitive times. It adapted to civilization and city-state organization primarily through its emphasis on both a single patron deity for each city and local religious festivals as well as through its development of bodies of priests and priestesses with high social and sometimes political standing.

In the Mesopotamian pantheon, there was a hierarchy of gods. The big three of the Babylonian gods were Anu, the sky god; Enlil, the god of air or wind; and Enki (Akkadian Ea), the god of earth with its subsoil water. Other important deities were associated with the heavenly bodies: Inanna (Ishtar), goddess of love and fertility, was identified with the planet Venus; Utu (Shamash), god of justice, with the sun; Nanna (Sin), with the moon. Also of great importance were Adad the storm god and the Semitic Marduk, the storm god of Babylon. Enlil, patron deity of Nippur, by 2500 B.C. was considered the general ruler of the rest of the gods.

Religion at all times represents an effort to come to grips with problems for which every thinking man must find answers. The origins and destiny of humanity and all that exists, the causes of good and evil, the genesis of the physical phenomena that affect human life—these and similar questions lie at the root of all religion. In later history, philosophy and science, sometimes artificially separated from religion, would provide answers to some of these questions. But in this early age, answers were sought in the realm not only of religion but of magic—the mechanical means by which people, events, and sometimes the gods may be manipulated by one who has power. Mostly, however, explanations to the questions that troubled the Mesopotamians involved the nature of the gods themselves and their relationships with men. Even in those ancient times, however, thinking persons had already developed relatively high concepts. Enlil, for example, came to be viewed not only as perhaps the most powerful god, he was also considered a creator of an orderly cosmos and a benefactor who gave to mortals such gifts as the plow and the pickax. His decrees fixed the destinies of humans and sometimes gods.

Religion in Life and Afterlife

Some of the early dynastic kings, as we have noted from their tombs, evidently hoped for a pleasant life after death, and took along with them servants, dancers, and harpists. In general, however, there was no great emphasis on an afterlife. The emphasis was rather on life on earth. Of greatest importance in religion was the necessity to placate the gods, to learn what life had in store, and to find an explanation for the apparent illogic of a world in which the good sometimes suffer and the evil prosper. To placate the gods was largely a matter of supporting the temples and priests and offering sacrifices as they demanded. The contradictions of an otherwise orderly universe were partially explained by positing the existence of demons, often conceived as composite monsters; one, for example, had the features of a lion, a snake, and an eagle. The spirits of the dead were sometimes thought to be malevolent also. Even so, in spite of all precautions, the ancient Mesopotamian was still aware that he might be victimized by these evil influences.

Practitioners of the "Religious" Arts

A host of religionists and conjurers helped to exorcise the demons, to rid the body of its ills (a connection with medicine is obvious), and, above all, to foretell the future. "Omen texts" have been discovered in large numbers. The Mesopotamian practitioners forecast the future through astrology, the pseudoscience of the stars, through the inspection of livers or of all the entrails of sacrificed animals, through the observation of smoke from burning incense and the spreading of oil dropped in water, or through the interpretation of dreams. Clearly, religion entered intimately into every facet of human life. One recent definition of religion describes it as what an individual feels toward his deity in times of solitude. It is a definition, however, that is deficient even for the present; for the majority of peoples in antiquity, it almost completely misses the mark.

G. Other Mesopotamian Achievements

Art and Architecture

Art in ancient Mesopotamia was highly developed. At one time the most valued treasures might be pottery or cylinder seals; at another, jewelry or statuary. Sculpture became important in the middle 3rd millennium: the "standard of Ur," for example, illustrates well the skill in bas-relief in the Early Dynastic period. Gudea, ruler of Lagash, left several statues, and Naram-Sin and Hammurabi were portrayed on famous reliefs.

Much of the architecture might seem unattractively monotonous today. But many of the greater structures, mostly temples, with typically low rectangular lines and crenellated wall surfaces that catch the interesting interplay of light and shadow, seem quite modern. The "white temple" of early Uruk is an example. With its imported limestone facing, horizontal and vertical lines, and interior columns made of clay decorated with ceramic cones set in geometric patterns, this temple illustrates well the abilities of early Sumerian architects and artists. The use of baked and ceramic bricks partly offset the lack of stone in the area, though fuel for baking was limited. The Mesopotamians even knew how to form the true arch and dome, as Woolley found in the graves near Ur. They did not apply these architectural feats, however, to structures of any size.

Numbers: Weights and Measures

Any agricultural society must work out a system of weights and measures. In the early barter economy, barley was a common medium of exchange, with the value of an ox as a standard unit. With the development of cities, silver became the medium of exchange—though traded by weight. True coinage was an invention of a much later period. The system that evolved was based on a talent of about sixty-seven pounds; one sixtieth of a talent was a mina, and one sixtieth of the mina was a shekel. This system was widely used throughout the ancient world; the Greeks used it, with variations, as did the Romans.

The numbers system was based upon a combination of sixes and tens. Sixty was thus a much used number; our inheritance from the system in measuring time and degrees in angles is plain. For practical arithmetic, the system was easier to use than our decimal system. As an example, the number 360 (the number of degrees in a circle) can be divided by 10, 9, 8, 6, 5, 4, 3, and 2. Our typical number 100 can be divided only by 10, 5, 4, and 2. Sixty was considered a kind of complete number (it was the basis for expressing fractions) and it was assigned to the god Anu. Enlil, who originally was second in importance, was assigned the number 50, and so on down the ranks. A fairly well-developed system of geometry was necessary in an agricultural society—particularly in the river valleys with their irrigation complexes and flood problems. Some indications of the development of what we would call algebra and some logarithmic tables have also been found.

These scanty paragraphs can do no more than hint at the astonishing accomplishments of the people who inhabited that great cradle of civilization, Mesopotamia.

Books for Further Reading

BOTTÉRO, J., E. CASSIN, J. VERCOUTTER, eds., *The Near East: The Early Civilizations,* New York, 1967.

CHIERA, E., *They Wrote on Clay,* Chicago, 1938.

CONTENAU, G., *Everyday Life in Babylon and Assyria,* New York, 1966.

KRAMER, S. N., *From the Tablets of Sumer,* Indian Hills, Colo., 1956.

KRAMER, S. N., *The Sumerians,* Chicago, 1963.

LLOYD, S., *Foundations in the Dust,* Baltimore, 1955.

MALLOWAN, M., *Early Mesopotamia and Iran,* New York, 1965.

MOSCATI, S., *Ancient Semitic Civilizations,* London, 1957.

MOSCATI, S., *Face of the Ancient Orient,* Chicago, 1960.

OPPENIIEIM, A. L., *Ancient Mesopotamia,* Chicago, 1964.

PRITCHARD, J. B., *Ancient Near Eastern Texts,* Princeton, 1954.

PRITCHARD, J. B., *The Ancient Near East: Supplementary Texts,* Princeton, 1969.

ROUX, G., *Ancient Iraq,* London, 1966.

SAGGS, H., *The Greatness That Was Babylon,* New York, 1962.

WOOLLEY, C. L., *Excavations at Ur,* New York, 1965.

3

Ancient Egypt

Ancient Egypt has never faded from human memory. The great cities of ancient Mesopotamia moldered into tells marking sites whose very names were forgotten, but the monuments of ancient Egypt, built of enduring stone, have given mute testimony for century after century of the magnificence of its antique civilization. Lively literary accounts, moreover, especially by Herodotus, the Greek historian of the 5th century B.C., kept alive additional information about early Egypt. Herodotus wrote not only of the well-known Giza pyramids, he also described other works that later disappeared, such as the labyrinthine buildings and hydraulic works in the Fayum region. He estimated that these works exceeded in cubic volume all the masonry of all types built by the Greeks up to his own time. Remains of this "labyrinth" have been discovered in recent years.

In spite of the eminent visibility of the Egyptian monuments, the country was not well known to the West during the Middle Ages and early modern period. It was a military expedition that revived interest in the area: Napoleon's invasion of Egypt in 1798. Perhaps consciously imitating Alexander the Great—for Napoleon knew Plutarch well—he took along with him on the expedition some 150 *savants*. These scholars traveled from Lower to Upper Egypt and copied monuments that exceeded in size and grandeur anything they had expected. The results were published in the popular multivolume *Description de l'Egypte*. Ultimately more important, in digging a trench the French soldiers in 1799 found the famous Rosetta stone. Because the British were the ultimate victors in the Egyptian campaign, the Rosetta stone is in the British Museum. Copies were made, however, and widely circulated.

From the inscription on the Rosetta stone, Jean Champollion was able by 1822 to announce the decipherment of hieroglyphics. By mid-century Egypt, like Mesopotamia, was being ransacked for portable antiquities for Western museums. A Frenchman, Auguste Mariette, was able to persuade the Khedive of Egypt to start a museum with Mariette himself as director, and to control somewhat the sale and export of antiquities. He and his successor, Gaston Maspero, partially curtailed clandestine digging and saved some of the finest objects for display in the Cairo museum. A truly scientific survey and excavation, however, came only when an Englishman, Flinders Petrie, began a careful measurement of the pyramids at Giza in 1881. Petrie also pioneered in the analysis of potsherds in sequence-dating (see p. 14).

Probably the most publicized archaeological find ever made was Howard Carter's discovery of the almost intact tomb of Pharaoh Tutankhamon in 1922. The incredible variety and richness of the finds of that tomb still dazzle visitors to the Cairo museum. Yet Tutankhamon was one of the least important of the pharaohs.

A. The Land and the People

Only in the 6th millennium B.C. was Egypt thickly settled. Most of the populace was typically Mediterranean, though there were frequent admixtures of Nubian and Ethiopian immigrants from the south all during antiquity, especially in periods of governmental weakness. What first brought men to the Nile valley was the desiccation that followed the last Ice Age and that gradually reduced a great mass of land to desert or semi-aridity. The African Sahara, as large as the United States, was only a part of a vast arid belt that stretched from the Atlantic Ocean to the Arabic peninsula and from there through Iraq and Iran to modern Pakistan, where the monsoon rains finally contained the dryness.

The Nile

From far antiquity men remarked that Egypt was the gift of the Nile, one of the world's notable rivers. The inhabitants recognized their dependence upon the river, and gave it reverence. The Nile flows out of Lakes Victoria and Albert in East Africa, nearly 4,000 winding miles from the Mediterranean. For about the last half of their ninety-day journey to the sea, the Nile waters course through an almost rainless desert. The annual miracle of the Nile's astonishingly high and predictable flood cannot be explained by anything observable downstream. The floods result from rains in the watersheds of the White Nile and two major tributaries, the Blue Nile and the Atbara. Before construction of

Golden throne of Tutankhamen; the Pharaoh and his wife. *(Photograph by Harry Burton, The Metropolitan Museum of Art)*

modern dams, the flood reached an average depth of about forty-five feet at Elephantine on the southern border of Egypt, some 600 miles from the sea. The water normally begins to rise in July, reaches a peak in September, slacks a bit and then reaches a still higher level in October. Thereafter the river ebbs to a low from about April through June.

Water for a parched land was not the only gift of the Nile. The silt it deposited each year also renewed the soil. Egypt's farmers, therefore, could not exhaust the land, nor was it subject to salinization, as in

42

Mesopotamia. One ancient name for Egypt was the Black Land. Photographs made by some of the first U.S. astronauts dramatically show the contrast between that long, narrow strip of dark and productive soil and the flanking desert sands, scorched and sterile. No agriculture above primitive levels was possible in ancient Egypt without irrigation, and there, as in Mesopotamia, impelling necessity demanded human cooperation to water the land. Because irrigation was easier in Egypt, because there was less trade, and because the habitable portion of the country was a serpentine, narrow strip hundreds of miles long, Egypt remained more rural, less urban than Mesopotamia.

The Nile furnished food, too—fish and fowl. It was, in addition, an easy transportation route. Men could drift down the river, of course, and since the wind blows upriver to the south most of the year, they could easily sail back upstream. The delta region is called Lower Egypt, and the land to its south is Upper Egypt. Sometimes the term "Middle Egypt" is employed to designate the area around Memphis near modern Cairo and the Fayum west of the river, a basin below sea level where a lake would form when the river overflowed. Temperatures are high but the air is less humid in Egypt than in Mesopotamia, and the climate is healthful. The land provided stone of fine quality and variety; gold could be mined in the eastern desert and copper in the Sinai across the Red Sea. Timber and most other metals were imported.

Topographical Isolation

Egypt was protected from outsiders by her topography. To the east lay desert, low mountains, and the Red Sea. To the north was the Mediterranean. To the west sprawled the great and inhospitable Sahara. To the south along the Nile, cataracts (rapids rather than falls) and the narrowness of the river's gorge made defense easy. Access to the country along the coasts to the west and to the northeast could easily be cut off. For centuries Egypt controlled her own destinies without serious external threat.

The regularity with which the Nile bestowed its blessings and the protection of topography gave to Egypt's people a sense of security, of optimism and confidence. With this went also a feeling of changelessness, of almost no sense of history. One year was much like every other; from generation to generation all was the same. Egypt's very security, however, meant that less pressure was exerted to make improvements. As an example, Egypt used only copper and almost no bronze down to about 2000 B.C., and as we shall see, the arrival of the Iron Age meant decline. Still, Egypt's accomplishments in the 3rd and 2nd millennia B.C. were tremendous. Culturally, it was part African, part Asian.

B. Earliest Egypt

From the predynastic (and prehistoric) age, which ends about 3000 B.C., through the era of Egyptian greatness, Egypt can be divided into historical segments. These segments are known as the Archaic, or Thinite Period; the Old Kingdom; the Middle Kingdom; and the New Kingdom or Empire. Sandwiched between the last three are two intermediate stages.

The Dynastic King Lists

Egyptian history is discussed in terms of dynasties, that is, in accordance with the way in which the ancients grouped their kings. Several lists of the kings have been preserved: two were inscribed in stone on temple walls, one has survived on a famous papyrus roll, and fragments of the 3rd century B.C. historian Manetho give us further information. The papyrus (Turin papyrus) adds the names of gods who ruled before men. Some of the lists—Manetho is most important here—supply lengths of reigns as well. It would seem, then, that modern historians could compile a chronologically accurate history from the earliest period. But there are always complications. The names vary. Moreover, each king had several names, and those listed are not always the names used on monuments or tombs. Further, the earliest of the lists mentioned above was compiled about 1,500 years after the founding of the First Dynasty—which naturally left ample room for error. Manetho seems to have used an older list for the first two dynasties, one that we have but only in fragments. The largest piece of this early inscription is called the Palermo stone, because it is located in a museum at Palermo. Predictably, modern scholars also disagree on the date for the founding of the First Dynasty. Most would place it within a 400-year period, from about 3200 B.C. to about 2800 B.C. The chronology becomes more exactly determinable in later periods, and after the founding of the Middle Kingdom it is probably accurate to within a margin of error of ten or fifteen years.

Early Mesopotamian Influences

Egypt was unified far earlier than Mesopotamia. Political unification, however, is not the all-important criterion of civilization, and in some very significant ways Mesopotamia seems to have been more advanced. Writing, for example, developed earlier in Mesopotamia. In concept, Egyptian hieroglyphics are much like Mesopotamian cuneiform, and it is usually thought that the Egyptians got the idea from the Sumerians. In other ways also, Egyptians seem to have learned from Asians. Both in materials and in form, major architectural monuments of the Archaic Period bear a close resemblance to Mesopotamian models. Cylinder seals were imported into Egypt, and stylized artistic motifs appear in Egypt that are characteristic of Mesopotamia. Evidence of this sort seems sufficient to establish a chronological priority for Mesopotamia. However, it does not establish any argument for qualitative priority in achievement. In some ways Egyptian achievements are more impressive. Early sculpture in Egypt, for instance, is much superior to that of contemporary Mesopotamia. And Egypt's influence endured. When a new cycle of ancient civilization began with the ancient Greeks, the Egyptian influence was immediate and profound.

C. Unification: the Thinite Period (c. 3000–2700 B.C.)

In the prehistoric age, Egypt's progress toward unification followed the usual pattern of development from smaller to larger states until finally, along with a sudden flowering of civilization, two kingdoms were formed corresponding to the geography of the country, Lower Egypt and Upper Egypt. This sudden advance may have been the result of an invasion from Mesopotamia or Syria. By about 3000 B.C., the two kingdoms were combined into one.

Just who was the first pharaoh of all Egypt is difficult to determine. Manetho's list and two others say Menes. Archaeological evidence indicates it was a man with the Horus name Aha. A mace head found near Memphis shows a man wearing the crown of Upper Egypt and calls him Scorpion (at least his name is written with that sign); he seems also to be celebrating a victory over Lower Egypt. A famous palette shows on one side a ruler called Narmer wearing the crown of Upper Egypt conquering his enemies of Lower (or Northern) Egypt; the other side shows him wearing the crown of Lower Egypt. It is possible though not probable that all these names refer to one and the same pharaoh. Possibly Scorpion began the unification, which was completed by Narmer-Menes, the first king of the First Dynasty. Aha, possibly the same as Teti on the king lists, may be the second monarch of the First Dynasty.

Other matters relating to the Thinite Period are equally difficult. The capital was apparently at This. However, a tradition preserved in Egyptian literature has it that Memphis was built by Menes and became the first capital. Archaeology does not solve this contradiction. Memphis certainly became important quite early. And monarchs of the First Dynasty built two tombs: one near This, the other at Memphis. (It was not unusual later for kings to have two tombs, one a cenotaph.) Perhaps the future will bring new evidence regarding the "Union of the Two Lands." What is certain, nonetheless, is that the unification of Egypt was crucial for its people: central authority was urgently needed, for any disruption usually meant famine shortly thereafter. The irrigation system, above all, required order.

D. The Old Kingdom (c. 2700–2300 B.C.)

The God-King

The Third through the Sixth dynasties, about 2700 to about 2300 B.C., constitute the Old Kingdom. Its capital was at Memphis, and its kings, as in the Archaic Period, were god-kings. In Mesopotamia, as we have seen, even those rulers who were not priest-kings thought their kingship was divinely ordained. But in Egypt the king was god; at the same time he was also the son of a god who at death took his place between Re, the sun god, and Horus, a falcon-deity also identified with the sun, sometimes with the son of Re. The implications of this god-king doctrine for the theory of government can be easily deduced. All authority and power went back to the pharaoh, a title meaning literally "great house." In practice, however, the pharaoh was not so absolute because an old nobility, whose members retained high status and position, helped to set limits on the pharaoh's power. Chief officials included a vizier, a chief architect, and a chief judge—all "seal-bearers" and all supposed to look out for the interests of the "Lord of the Two Lands." About forty provinces or Nomes were each under a governor whose hellenized title is Nomarch.

The very position of the pharaohs was so lofty that they left little evidence giving any inkling of personal feelings or views. We can know little of the essential character of the great kings who constructed the massive works that have endured for so many centuries.

The Pyramid Age

In many ways the Old Kingdom was the most brilliant age of ancient Egypt. The first king of the Third Dynasty, Zoser or Djoser, left a most impressive monument in the first of the great pyramids, the Step Pyramid at Sakkara. The pyramid began as a mastaba tomb of traditional type, but was enlarged in stages into a huge structure enclosed within a walled area containing subsidiary monuments. The architect, Imhotep, was renowned also for his wisdom. Sometime after his death he was accorded divine honors, and centuries later he was still worshiped at numerous shrines. Reconstructions of the Step Pyramid with its thirty-foot white wall, regularly recessed, make it clear enough to the appreciative modern eye why Egyptians revered Imhotep.

The true pyramid with the typical pattern—causeway to the Nile with a valley temple, a mortuary temple near the pyramid itself, and a boat pit, all within an enclosure—came with the Fourth Dynasty, about 2600 B.C. The first king of that dynasty, Sneferu, actually built three pyramids, the largest called the Bent Pyramid, located at Dashur. It was about 620 feet square at the base, and 336 feet high. It is "bent" because the angle changes about halfway up; perhaps the original height was reduced because the great weight of rock was threatening to collapse the tomb chamber. All the great pyramids were flanked by smaller tombs for relatives and high nobles.

The Great Pyramid

The pyramids at Giza are, of course, the largest and best known. The Great Pyramid there was built by Khufu, successor of Sneferu. The other two were constructed by later kings of the dynasty, Khafre and Menkaure. Probably it was Khafre who built the nearby Sphinx. Everything about the Great Pyramid is impressive. No more massive structure existed until

Temple and pyramid of Khafre, Egypt. *(V-DIA/SCALA)*

the completion of the Grand Coulee Dam in the state of Washington. With a base of 756 feet, the pyramid was originally a little more than 480 feet high. Its mass of more than two million stones covers about thirteen acres. The stone blocks average about two and a half tons each. One red granite slab in the "king's chamber"—one of three at the end of long passageways—weighs fifty tons. The core of the pyramid is of local limestone; the outer covering, now gone, was of higher quality Tura limestone brought from across the Nile and upstream. The granite came hundreds of miles down the river from Upper Egypt. Careful analysis shows at least three changes of plan during construction.

These huge structures were built with long ramps and immense manpower but without the use of wheel or pulley. Herodotus reported an Egyptian tradition that the Great Pyramid required the labor of 100,000 men for twenty years. It is instructive to remember, however, that he, writing in the 5th century B.C., was farther in time from the date of construction of this pyramid than we are from the birth of Christ. Yet engineers today estimate that Herodotus's report was not far off the mark. The historian also says that the Egyptians remembered Khufu and his son as oppressors. Certainly the pyramids give mute testimony of the great power of the pharaohs who built them, of long periods of peace, and, of course, of advanced architectural and mechanical skills.

The pyramids were tombs of the god-king. But they were more. It is not difficult to imagine the thrill that passed through the heart of many an Egyptian when the earliest rays of the never-veiled divine sun touched with brightness the white tips of these graceful structures, heralding another new day. Then he sang the morning song. Moreover, it is likely that most of the work was done during those months when the Nile was in flood—there being little else for the peasants to do.

E. Religion in the Old Kingdom

Deities of the Nile and the Sun

Herodotus noted that the Egyptians were the most religious of all people. The evidence seems to confirm his assessment. Their religion shows all the expected marks of a long evolution. Deities were associated with the heavenly bodies and with animals and insects—from bulls and crocodiles to scorpions and beetles. In a country of a beneficent, never-failing sun and an equally beneficent river and land (along the river), it was natural that two groups of gods should have been emphasized, solar and riverine or land. The Egyptians made some attempts to reconcile these two religious strands, but clearly Egyptian priests did not think it necessary to rationalize completely their religious ideas—or it could be, of course, that what seemed rational to them does not to us.

The gods—who were given anthropomorphic characteristics—were often grouped by twos or threes: husband-wife or husband-wife-child: so Geb and Nut, earth and sky, or the riverine deities Osiris and Isis with their child Horus, who was associated both with the Nile and with the sun. Political unification tended to produce national gods through identification of similar deities. Thus at Heliopolis, Aton, Horus, and other solar deities were somehow equated with Re. Early pharaohs associated themselves with Horus, later ones with both Horus and Re, still later ones with Amon-Re, Horus, and sometimes Aton. Amon was originally an air of god of Thebes. Other major gods included Ptah, craftsman god of Memphis; Apis, the Memphis bull-god; Hathor, the cow-goddess (a mother goddess); and Thoth, the Word of Ptah. There were a host of others.

Emphasis on an Afterlife

Because archaeologists work mostly with tombs, they have learned much about the Egyptians' views of an afterlife. The mastabas, the pyramids, many of their temples, the offerings made to the dead by Egyptians of all ranks testify to the search for a happy afterlife. Despite the idea that

Model of fishing boat and crew taken from Egyptian tomb. *(The Metropolitan Museum of Art, Museum Excavations, 1919-20; Rogers Fund, supplemented by contribution of Edward S. Harkness)*

the deceased might go to a place of the dead, Egyptians thought that a part of the personality, the Ka, the "double" or "vital force" remained in or near the tomb, and consequently must be provided for. It was necessary to keep the body intact and to provide tomb offerings. Those who could afford it were therefore mummified; the tomb was made secure; food offerings were provided both at burial and later if possible; pictures of the deceased inspecting his fields, the harvest, and so on, were painted on the walls of the tomb or shown by scale models. Pictures, images, and even words, it was thought, could substitute for real objects. For the journey to the solar heaven, the dead was sometimes provided with a model boat and crew—or even, as in the case of Khufu and the pyramid builders, with full-size ships. From tomb paintings and models, then, we learn much of Egyptian everyday life.

Egyptians eventually conceived a pleasant "heaven" in the skies and a sort of "hades" of fire and crocodiles under the Nile. Osiris became the judge of the dead. The heart of the deceased, as we may see graphically in several remaining judgment scenes, was weighed against Ma'at, goddess of justice and truth, whose symbol was a feather. (Some of these beliefs evolved after the Old Kingdom.)

Osiris symbolized the resurrection and became judge of the dead because he, too, died and was brought back to life. A famous myth tells of the struggle between Osiris and his brother, Set, who at first was victor. But Isis found the dead Osiris and breathed new life into him. Their son, Horus, avenged Osiris, losing an eye in the fight with Set. There may be an echo of history in this story. Set was from Upper Egypt, Osiris from Lower Egypt. One version of the tale proclaims the risen Osiris as ruler of all. Perhaps the real struggle, ascribed to the gods in the myth, was that for political unity in the Archaic Period. The story of Osiris is perhaps the earliest of the numerous accounts of the dying and reborn god who became a benefactor of humanity. It seems, however, that in early Egypt the hope of an afterlife was reserved for the upper classes. The poor man, in this period, had little to hope for in the afterworld.

The fact that the dead were judged, and that there were separate places for the good dead and the wicked dead, presuppose the development of moral concepts. And, indeed the Egyptians did come to associate morality with religion—by no means a usual thing in human history. The deceased was required to show that he had done no evil. Here, for example, is a much-abridged statement of a nomarch of the Old Kingdom:

> *I gave bread to all the hungry . . .*
> *I clothed him who was naked . . .*
> *I never oppressed anyone . . .*
> *I speak no lie.*[1]

[1] J. H. Breasted, *Ancient Records of Egypt,* 5 vols. (Chicago, 1905–1907), 1:240.

It must not be assumed, however, that these ideas were similar to the Judeo–Christian views of sin and salvation. In fact, by the end of the Old Kingdom, as can be seen in the Pyramid Texts and in *The Book of the Dead* of the New Kingdom, well-to-do Egyptians came to rely more upon magical formulas than upon good deeds for their positions in the afterworld. It remained important to them to make as solid an arrangement as possible for continuing food offerings for the dead. Still, in their emphasis upon morality and religion, and in their well-worked-out views of an afterlife, the Egyptians contributed much to a higher religion.

F. Language, Literature, and Art in the Old Kingdom

Hieroglyphics

It was the Greeks, near the end of the Ancient Period, who gave to the Egyptian system of picture-writing the name "hieroglyphics," which means "priest-carvings," or "sacred writings." By that time hieroglyphs were used almost solely by priests, and usually the picture-signs were sculptured in low relief upon stone. For writing upon papyrus—the very durable paper made by Egyptians from the papyrus reed that grew in abundance along the Nile—the Egyptians used two simplified scripts derived from hieroglyphics: hieratic and demotic. In the hieroglyphic system, a complicated combination of pictographs, ideographs, and phonetic symbols was used. It was not easy for men like Champollion to decipher the writing, even after the discovery of the Rosetta stone, an inscription of 196 B.C. in hieroglyphics, demotic, and Greek.

The writing system included twenty-four phonetic symbols, each of which stood for a single consonant—an embryonic true alphabet. Yet the Egyptians never did anything to simplify the system. In fact, the addition of determinatives, though making the meaning clearer, increased the number of sign combinations. Perhaps the Egyptians did not change their system because for them the visual system itself had become a real art form. The phonetic symbols made it easier for neighboring peoples to use the Egyptian symbols for their own language, and to go on to develop a system basically alphabetic. At the same time, the alphabet was also developing from Mesopotamian usages.

Literature of the Old Kingdom

Time has erased most of the inscriptions and papyri that date to the Old Kingdom. One famous papyrus originally of this period is called *The Instructions of Ptah-Hotep,* a wise old vizier of the Fifth Dynasty. Ptah-Hotep advised young men, with a touch of irony:

> Let not thy heart be puffed up because of thy knowledge;
> Be not confident because thou art a wise man.

For officials, he advised,

> If thou art one to whom petition is made, be calm as thou listenest to the petitioner's speech. Do not rebuff him before he has swept out his body or before he has said that for which he came. A petitioner likes attention to his words better than the fulfilling of that for which he came. . . . It is not (necessary) that everything about which he has petitioned should come to pass, [but] a good hearing is a soothing of the heart.[2]

The establishment speaking!

Other papyri that seem to have originated in the Old Kingdom include a long one relating to medicine, another to mathematics. Both show a knowledge advanced for the age. In his time Herodotus noted that Egyptian physicians tended to be specialists rather than general practitioners, This specialization went back to the earliest times. Surgery, too, was advanced.

Art, Sculpture

Enough has already been said of Egyptian architecture in connection with the pyramids to demonstrate the great achievement in the construction of buildings. But Egyptian sculpture and painting are equally impressive. Both became highly stylized. To many, the stiffness of shoulders and legs in sculpture and the unrealistic means used to portray humans in profile in painting and relief demonstrate a lack of ability on the part of the artists. But such a reaction is a mistake. The Egyptians very early developed certain features of style, and these they canonized and for the most part retained for three thousand years. Their best work shows clearly their superior ability to represent what they wished. Words cannot really prove this point, nor can textbook illustrations. But an inspection of the marvelous remains of Egypt in museums would help verify the artistic greatness of those ancient people.

G. The Decline of the Old Kingdom and the First Intermediate Period

Collapse of an Ordered World

We do not know all the causes of the decline of the Old Kingdom. Probably the later dynasts were personally less effective than their

---

[2] J. P. Pritchard, *Ancient Near Eastern Texts* (Princeton, 1955), p. 412. (Translation by J. A. Wilson.)

predecessors. One major factor, however, was the tendency of the key governmental offices to become hereditary within an aristocratic family. The various nomes tended to become almost independent little feudal monarchies. The decrease in building perhaps evidences a general economic slump. Eventually, the Union of the Two Lands broke up.

With the erosion of authority and economic well-being, some areas plunged into complete disorder. The so-called prophet Nefer-Rohu gives us some idea of the situation in those places:

> This land . . . there is no one who is concerned with it, no one who speaks, no eye that weeps. . . . The sun disc is covered over. It will not shine. . . . The rivers of Egypt are empty, the water is crossed on foot. . . . Everything good is disappeared, and the land is prostrate because of woes . . . .
>
> This land is helter-skelter. . . . I show thee the land topsy-turvy. That which never happened has happened.[3]

Other texts tell of robbery and pillage even of pharaonic pyramids! It is true that these accounts were written during a later period of stability, to contrast that time with the earlier disorder, but the picture is probably accurate enough nevertheless. The old optimism and confidence evaporated. One long, sophisticated poem from this age even elaborates a cynical theme and a longing for death.

Centers of Order Amid Chaos

In a few centers, however, even during this First Intermediate Period, order prevailed. Separate dynasties ruled at the same time over portions of the divided country. One such dynasty was located at Heracleopolis in Middle Egypt, though there, too, dangerous factions tended to arise. The *Instructions for King Meri-Ka-Re,* written by a pharaoh for his son during this intermediate period, warns that if an official is popular, excitable, and an excellent speaker, he should be eliminated forthwith. On the other hand, another famous work from Heracleopolis in the same age shows that Ma'at (justice) still ruled. This work, *Protests of an Eloquent Peasant,* tells of a peasant who was mistreated by a minor official. Perhaps only because of his exceptional eloquence, he was able in a series of speeches to take his story all the way to the king. Ultimately, the offending official was fired and the peasant given his job! Even if this story was but fiction, the warning was clear.

The kings of Heracleopolis were apparently the most powerful in Egypt during the intermediate period. It was the kings of Thebes in Upper Egypt, however, who reunited the land.

---

[3] Pritchard, *ANE Anthology,* pp. 254–255.

H. The Middle Kingdom (c. 2050–1785 B.C.)

Kings of Thebes Achieve Reunification

The reunification of all Egypt was accomplished around 2050 B.C. by a king named Mentuhotep IV of the Theban Eleventh Dynasty. He and a successor of the same name ruled for about sixty years. The Middle Kingdom, though, is practically identical with the Twelfth Dynasty, which was founded by Amenemhet I after a period of disorder. Amenemhet had been vizier of the last Eleventh Dynasty king before he became pharaoh, most likely in 1991 B.C. Amenemhet transferred his capital to a fortified site not far from Memphis in order to maintain more effective control over the two lands.

Eleventh Dynasty kings had been sons of Re in the usual fashion; but Twelfth Dynasty monarchs were sons of Amon, the patron deity of Thebes. He was identified with other, solar deities and indeed was often called Amon-Re. The Middle Kingdom monarchs, however, never established an absolute control over the nobles who ruled the nomes. God-kings they still were, but they had lost something of majesty since Khufu. Perhaps the spectacle of a vizier becoming a divine monarch tarnished the image. Moreover, the feudal, decentralized power and society that had developed from the last century of the Old Kingdom, stubbornly resisted any change.

The Twelfth Dynasty, nonetheless, brought peace, and along with that blessing, a greater social consciousness on the part of officials of all ranks seems to have manifested itself. Words purported to be those of Amenemhet set the tone; he was said to have boasted that "none was hungry in my years, none thirsted then; men dwelled in peace." In instructions to his son and successor, Sesostris I, Amenemhet stressed his care for the poor and the orphaned. But he warned his son not to trust subordinates and he made it clear that he had not been able to gain the loyalty of all. Attempts on his life had soured his outlook. Indeed, it seems that Amenemhet was assassinated.

Prosperity: Trade, Building Construction

Egypt's power and prosperity under the Middle Kingdom were displayed in various ways. Military expeditions, though few, penetrated south as far as Cush and possibly to the northeast as far as Syria, trading expeditions were again sent to far-off Punt, and copper mines in Sinai and gold mines in Nubia yielded their treasures for Egyptian coffers. Much building activity within Egypt gives testimony also to good government with prosperity. The emphasis was not on tombs but on temples and on projects useful to Egyptian agriculture. The great temple complexes near Thebes, so closely associated later with the New Kingdom, were begun in this period. Most useful probably was a vast irrigation project at the Fayum in Middle Egypt.

The Fayum basin, well below sea level, received the waters of the Nile when the river was in flood; when the Nile subsided, however, the water flowed from the Fayum lake (the Greek historians called it Lake Moeris). Amenemhet III (c. 1842–1797 B.C.) undertook huge works that had a double purpose: to reclaim land around the lake for farm production by controlling more precisely the level of the lake, and also to make better and more efficient use of the lake's waters for irrigation during the three months or so when the Nile was low. One single wall that he constructed was twenty-seven miles long. Altogether, thousands of acres of land were made available for farmers and other thousands were better irrigated.

Middle Kingdom Literature

Literary production of the Middle Kingdom period is best illustrated in a work much like a novelette, *The Story of Sinuhe.* Sinuhe was a noble who for some obscure reason fled Egypt at the accession of Sesostris. For many years, he lived with sheiks in the desert to the east and in Palestine. In later life he was permitted to return. Perhaps the most moving thing about the work is the longing of Sinuhe for the amenities of his own land, and his feelings when finally he regained them. He was shaved and bathed and clothed in fine linen. He slept on a bed. A pyramid was constructed for him; he would not have to be buried in a sheepskin after all. The Egyptians found life in their land far more civilized than that in neighboring countries.

Amenemhet III was the last important king of the Middle Kingdom. There followed a period of decline under the Thirteenth Dynasty into a second breakup of the unified land, the Second Intermediate Period.

I. The Second Intermediate Period (c. 1785–1575 B.C.); The Hyksos

As the authority of the Thirteenth Dynasty kings waned—and they certainly ruled all Egypt for a time—an increasing number of Asiatics established themselves in the eastern delta region. Manetho preserves a tradition of an invasion of the Hyksos, a violent irruption from the northeast that swept over all the land. The remains do not seem to bear out his story, however. Probably the Asiatics first managed to set up an administrative segment of northern Egypt as a virtually independent state; then, with help from others from the Phoenicia–Palestine area, they managed to enlarge their territory, expanding as far as Memphis. The Hyksos capital was at Avaris in the eastern part of the Nile delta. Eventually they put all Egypt under tribute as kings of the Fifteenth and Sixteenth dynasties. The term Hyksos means "highland rulers"; literary tradition makes it "Shepherd kings," but this is wrong. Perhaps "Amorite kings" would be more accurate terminology. The Hyksos used weapons that were perhaps new to the Egyptians, including the horse-drawn war chariot and the compound bow. Probably through syncretic identification, the Hyksos worshiped Set (Baal?) as their chief god.

A period of weakness and warfare naturally afflicted the people, and once again, as in the First Intermediate Period, literary remains lament destruction and disorder, though possibly the writers exaggerated. Not only did Asiatics dominate much of the land from the delta, but Nubians moved in from the south and controlled portions of Upper Egypt.

The Hyksos "invasion" and foreign domination in the Second Intermediate Period made a lasting impression on the native Egyptians, and did much to determine attitudes and outlook of the New Kingdom. For the first time, the Egyptians learned to fight—and to hate. When once they regained control, their outlook had changed.

J. The New Kingdom or Empire (c. 1575–1086 B.C.)

Expulsion of the Hyksos

The honor of smashing the Hyksos and of driving them out of Egypt belongs to two sons of Sekenenre, a king of the Theban Seventeenth Dynasty, Kamose and Ahmose. Apophis was the Hyksos ruler in Avaris in the time of Sekenenre. He sent a message to the Theban monarch and declared that the hippopotamuses in the pool outside the palace of Sekenenre bellowed too much at night and disturbed his sleep! Since Thebes was several hundred miles away, it was fairly clear that he meant the missive as a threat. Not only is the message extant, but Sekenenre's mummy survives as well. And from it can be seen that the unfortunate king died a horrible death: there are three holes in the skull. It is not unlikely that Apophis made good his threat.

Kamose, however, took up the cause. An indication both of his problem and of his determination is evident in this hieratic document discovered early in this century:

I should like to know what serves this strength of mine, when a chieftain is in Avaris and another in Cush, and I sit united with an Asiatic and a Nubian, each man in possession of his slice of this Egypt, and I cannot pass by him as far as Memphis. . . . I will grapple with him and slit open his belly. My desire is to deliver Egypt and to smite the Asiatics." [4]

Against Kamose Apophis attempted to make alliance with the Nubians to the south, but his message was intercepted. Kamose defeated the Hyksos and began a four-year siege of Avaris. After a time he either died or was killed and Ahmose, his brother, succeeded. It was he who finally cleared the land of foreign rule and reigned over a reunited Egypt. Despite his relationship to the last rulers of the Seventeenth Dynasty, Ahmose is accounted the founder of the greatest dynasty of the New Kingdom or Empire, the Eighteenth.

The New Kingdom was militaristic, imperialistic, absolutist; in considerable degree these characteristics were a reaction to the Hyksos' domination. A century after the foreigners were driven out, the Egyptian pharaohs, campaigning in Palestine and Syria, still proclaimed their aggressive thrusts as crusades against the Hyksos. A larger professional army was now maintained. The two viziers to the king were now usually generals, their posts primarily military commands. Egypt's kings ruled from Cyrene on the west to Syria and beyond to the northeast, and far into Nubia to the south. Government officials including nomarchs were appointed by the king and controlled by him. Imperial Egypt became the most powerful state in the Near East.

Hatshepsut: First Great Queen

One of the most remarkable rulers of the New Kingdom was the world's first great queen, Hatshepsut (c. 1504–1482 B.C.). Her predecessors after Ahmose, Amenhotep I and Thutmose I, had stabilized the frontiers far beyond the bounds of Egypt proper. Thutmose had campaigned even to the Euphrates River east of Syria. There he no doubt had collided with the Hurrian kingdom of Mitanni (or Hanigalbat). He also pushed imperial frontiers deep into the Sudan. Hatshepsut was a daughter of this great king, who had no sons by his royal wife; a son by a secondary wife, however, married Hatshepsut, his half-sister, and became pharaoh (Thutmose II). He was short-lived, however, and his young son—again by a concubine and not by Hatshepsut—Thutmose III, remained in the background for more than twenty years as his stepmother ruled, first as regent and then as pharaoh.

[4] Paraphrased by Sir A. Gardiner, *Egypt of the Pharaohs* (Oxford, 1961), p. 166.

Model of the Temple of Queen Hatshepsut at Deir-el-Bahri. Note the remarkably modern-looking lines. *(The Metropolitan Museum of Art)*

Since the very concept "pharaoh" was masculine, together with all symbols and appurtenances of the office, artists and scribes were a little confused in portraying the queen and in cutting inscriptions. They sculptured her as a man complete with beard and referred to her in typical fashion as "son" of Amon-Re. To legitimize her position, Hatshepsut claimed to be literally the child of Amon and to have been crowned by Thutmose I himself.

Hatshepsut gave most attention to peaceful pursuits: internal building and external trade were given priority. However, there were some military campaigns during her reign and she herself led one of them. She also had one of the most beautiful temples ever constructed carved into the side of a rocky bluff at Deir el-Bahri near Thebes. Featuring long colonnades on three terraces, the total effect is enormously pleasing to the modern eye. Reliefs show that the terraces were land-scaped with myrrh trees imported from far away, with roots encased in balls of earth. At Karnak, near Thebes, she also added to the complex of temples to the god Amon, patron deity of the capital city.

Thutmose III hated Hatshepsut. When he finally succeeded to the throne he tried to obliterate the queen's name from the land. The hieroglyphic cartouches that spelled her name were chiseled out of her monuments and replaced with his own. Thutmose was much more imperialistic than his stepmother, partly because by this time the frontiers required attention. He made nineteen campaigns into the Palestine-Syria region alone, and subdued the Hurrians, who had gained control of northeastern Syria. He was responsible, too, for beginning a tremendous building program at Karnak—to Amon, of course. Obelisks erected by Thutmose now stand in New York, London, Rome, and Constantinople.

The New Kingdom reached its apogee with the reign of Amenhotep III (c. 1412–1375 b.c.), great grandson of Thutmose III. His power was great and his land was prosperous. Though all the agricultural land belonged to him—through most of history the *fellahin* have been tenants —probably the masses were better housed and better fed than their modern counterparts have often been. As is fitting for a grand monarch,

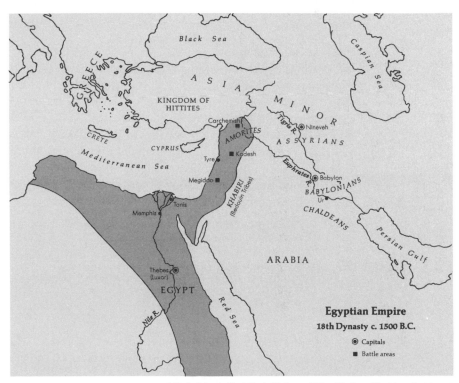

Adapted from **Modell**, A History of the Western World, *volume one.*

Amenhotep erected huge buildings, pylons, and temples; some were at the twin temple centers of Karnak and Luxor, and some were along the magnificent way he constructed between the centers. Statues of himself seventy feet high, which the Greeks called the "Colossi of Memnon," stood in front of his funerary temple on the west bank of the Nile. He also built a huge new palace near Thebes.

Perhaps Amenhotep became too accustomed to peace, or perhaps the age became decadent. His new palace, called "The House of Rejoicing," seems somehow symbolic. Late representations of Amenhotep show him fat and somnolent, and we have solid evidence that the empire was in the same condition. This evidence comes from a site downriver from Thebes, called Tell el 'Amarna. Here, in 1887, a peasant woman found several clay tablets, which eventually, along with others to the number of about 300, found their way into the hands of dealers and collectors for the world's great museums. The tablets were official correspondence, mostly written to Amenhotep and to his son, Amenhotep IV, from the Palestine-Syria region. They tell of a breakdown in Egyptian control in that area, of Hittite kings and local sheiks moving in. The Egyptian rulers, however, did little about it.

The Religious Revolution of Akhnaton

Amarna was in that time Akhetaton, a new capital built mostly by Amenhotep IV (Akhnaton). The names tell the story: Amenhotep, "Amon is satisfied," was dropped in favor of Akhnaton, "beneficial to Aton." Akhetaton means "horizon of Aton." The new city, some distance north of Thebes, was dedicated to the Aton, god of the sun disc. Akhnaton promoted religious revolution, making Atonism the state religion. He dissolved old priesthoods, and closed the temples of the other gods. Amon-Re, hitherto the chief deity of the Empire, was a particular target of suppression. In a famous "psalm" to Aton, attributed perhaps correctly to Akhnaton, the writer declares,

> Thou appearest beautifully on the horizon of heaven,
> Thou living Aton, the beginning of life!
>
> . . . . .
> How manifold it is, what thou hast made!
> They are hidden from the face [of man].
> O sole god, like whom there is no other!
> Thou didst create the world according to thy desire,
> Whilst thou wert alone. . . .[5]

This hymn differs little from earlier ones offered to Amon-Re—also a "universal" deity. And it also demonstrates that imperialism tends to

[5] Pritchard, *ANE Anthology*, pp. 227–229.

Akhnaton and Nofretete. A model in relief from the workshop at Akhetaton (Amarna). *(Courtesy of The Brooklyn Museum, Charles Edwin Wilbour Fund)*

produce a universal religion. The gods of the conquerors are always thought to be more powerful than those of the conquered. Thus the chief deity of Thebes tended to be accepted throughout the empire and to some degree beyond. Akhnaton's hymn, however, differs in its conception of Aton as the "sole god." It seems to suggest monotheism, though on other grounds Atonism appears to have been something less than that. The Aton, earlier portrayed with a hawk-headed human form, was now pictured as the sun disc, and rays from the disc, like streamers, blessed the devotees below.

The priests of Amon had become powerful and rich. To them went official portions of both spoil and tribute. It is therefore suggested that Akhnaton's motives in making Atonism the state religion were in part economic and political—or even personal, perhaps in reaction to a family quarrel. Still, the lengths to which Akhnaton went in the interest of Aton suggest sincerity. Moreover, new forms of art and

61

architecture broke strikingly with the past. The attention given Ma'at (truth) brought realism. The most famous work of the Amarna age is the bust of Akhnaton's beautiful wife, Nofretete, though it is hardly typical. Akhnaton himself is presented as rather ugly, misshapen, effeminate. Some reliefs show a remarkably casual air. Also illustrative of the period are the finds of the tomb of Tutankhamon, son-in-law and successor of Akhnaton. Magnificent and rich they certainly are, but cloying, too, and sometimes overdone.

Tutankhamon—once Tutankhaton—was forced to return to Thebes and abjure the religious revolution of his father-in-law. Amarna, abandoned, became an accursed ghost city, and Akhnaton and all his family were branded "heretics" and "enemies." Tutankhamon, but a child when he came to the throne, died at eighteen. Except for the accident of the discovery of his intact tomb in 1922, he would not deserve mention. His widow, Ankhesenamon, the daughter of Akhnaton, tried to obtain another husband from the great Hittite king Suppiluliumas, but the Hittite scion was killed before he reached Egypt. The Eighteenth Dynasty staggered to a close. A general, Harmhab, who had served under Akhnaton but who had not been a convert to Atonism, at length took charge of the empire. He restored order internally and also recovered some lost territory on the frontiers. Apparently Harmhab had a long and somewhat successful reign, but he had no heir. His successor, short-lived Ramses I, founded a new dynasty in about 1303 B.C.

Restoration Under the Nineteenth Dynasty

The best-known pharaoh of the Nineteenth Dynasty is Ramses II (c. 1290–1223 B.C.). Campaigning vigorously in Syria to restore the old frontiers, he met with some success. We have his boastful account of a desperate battle with the Hittites, who ambushed him at Kadesh on the Orontes River. Only the king's personal courage, he claimed, snatched victory from the jaws of defeat. The frontier was stabilized at that location, however. A few years later he and the Hittite king Hattusilis III drew up a remarkable peace treaty that included such "modern" features as a nonaggression clause, provisions for conditional mutual aid, and an extradition agreement. Both kingdoms were weakened, however, by their long and hard-fought rivalry.

Ramses was perhaps the greatest builder of all the pharaohs. Best known are the huge Hypostyle Hall in the temple of Amon-Re at Karnak and the temple at Abu Simbel. The latter has been sawed into blocks in recent years and raised to a new site at tremendous expense in order to rescue it from the rising waters of the Aswan lake behind the Russian-built dam.

Detail from pillars of the Hypostyle Hall. New Kingdom. *(Through the courtesy of TWA Transworld Airlines, Inc.)*

Invasions and Decline

A series of foreign invasions undermined Egypt's strength beyond recovery at the end of the Nineteenth and during the Twentieth dynasties (c. 1195–1086 B.C.). The invaders came from west and north, by land and by sea, and they included the Danu (perhaps Greeks?), the Peleset (Philistines), and others whose names mean nothing today, such as the Sheklesh and the Weshesh. Ramses III (c. 1192–1160 B.C.) met the invaders and won, but at a terrible cost. Still, he managed to build extensively. His great temple at Medinet Habu is one of the best preserved major structures from ancient Egypt. Despite Ramses' supreme efforts, however, internal affairs were in disorder at the end of his reign. His successors could not retrieve the situation, and the fall of the Ramessides marked the end of the Egyptian Empire.

Many of the dynasties that followed were foreign, and most of these were also weak. Sheshonk I of the Twenty-second Dynasty was rather strong, as we learn from the Hebrew Bible. The Twenty-fifth Dynasty was Ethiopian; the Twenty-sixth, ruling from Saïs, brought a brief renaissance in the 7th and 6th centuries B.C.; and the Twenty-seventh was Persian. After the Thirty-first Dynasty, Alexander the Great established Macedonian rule (the Ptolemies, ending with Cleopatra). Then, from 30 B.C. to the end of antiquity, the Romans held Egypt in their tight grasp.

Books for Further Reading

ALDRED, C., *Akhenaten and Nefertiti,* New York, 1973.

ALDRED, C., *Egypt to the End of the Old Kingdom,* London, 1965.

BOTTÉRO, J., E. CASSIN, J. VERCOUTTER, eds., *The Near East: The Early Civilizations,* New York, 1967.

EDWARDS, I. E. S., *The Pyramids of Egypt,* Baltimore, 1947.

EMERY, W. B., *Archaic Egypt,* Baltimore, 1961.

FRANKFORT, H., *Ancient Egyptian Religion,* New York, 1948.

GARDINER, A., *Egypt of the Pharaohs,* Oxford, 1961.

MERTZ, B., *Red Land, Black Land,* New York, 1966.

MERTZ, B., *Temples, Tombs, and Hieroglyphs,* New York, 1964.

STEINDORFF, G., and K. C. SEELE, *When Egypt Ruled the East,* Chicago, 1957.

WILSON, J. A., *The Culture of Ancient Egypt,* Chicago, 1951.

Other Bronze Age Civilizations:
Aegean, Indus Valley, China

4

The accomplishments of the earliest civilizations gradually diffused throughout the world. Ideas more than material objects spread, took root, and produced not imitations of the original, but distinctive new growths. Thus it appears that the idea of writing spread from Mesopotamia, not the actual cuneiform system. The idea, carried afar, produced Egyptian hieroglyphics, a different hieroglyphic in Crete, and still different writing systems in both the Indus valley (modern Pakistan) and China. And once the concept from Mesopotamia was introduced, the new system in each instance appeared suddenly, without long development. The later techniques for the smelting of copper and the production of bronze seem also to have spread swiftly from their Near Eastern birthplace.

Not all of the great achievements of civilization were disseminated through diffusion. Archaeology and history know of many instances of separate development, often contemporaneous. Pottery-making, for example, seems now to have been invented independently in Europe and not imported from the Near East.

A. Aegean Civilization

Schliemann: Pioneer in Classical Rediscovery

Aegean civilization was unsuspected a century ago. The man who discovered late phases of this civilization in Greece, where it is called the Mycenaean Age, was Heinrich Schliemann, better known for his excava-

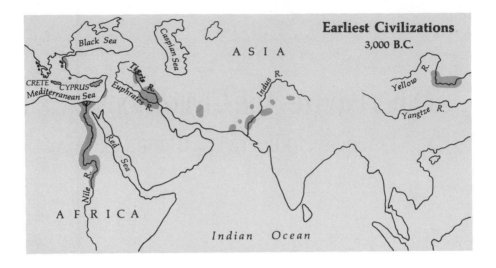

Earliest Civilizations
3,000 B.C.

tions at Hissarlik, ancient Troy, near the Hellespont (Dardanelles) in Turkey. Schliemann was a German of a poor family who had little formal education. Self-taught, however, he became an excellent linguist and a successful businessman in the Low Countries and in Russia. He went to California to see to the affairs of his brother who had died during the Gold Rush, and, by reason of his residence there when the territory entered the Union, he became an American citizen.

Schliemann had dreamed from childhood of seeing ancient Troy and the other sites familiar to him from Homer's *Iliad*. Contemporary scholarship tended to dismiss Troy and the Trojan War as fiction, but Schliemann had faith in Homer somewhat like a fundamentalist preacher's confidence in the truth of the Bible. In retirement in his forties, a world-traveled multimillionaire, Schliemann decided to pursue his dream. He studied philology for a time at the Sorbonne in Paris, terminated an unsuccessful marriage to a frigid Russian woman, and for a second wife chose a seventeen-year-old Greek beauty by whom he had two children, Agamemnon and Andromache. Sophia, his wife, proved to be a great help to Heinrich in his work.

Excavation at the site that Schliemann believed was ancient Troy began in 1870, and the rich discoveries that resulted quickly captured the attention of the world. Schliemann soon convinced all but the most skeptical that he had indeed found the fabled city—though few were as sure as he that he had proved the literal truth of the Homeric story. It is ironic that Schliemann dug right through the city he sought. The richest level, which he thought was the Troy of Homer, 1200 B.C., is now dated back to about 2000 B.C. It was a part of Aegean civilization.

Schliemann also excavated the Greek mainland sites Mycenae and
Tiryns and again turned up marvelous objects such as a king's gold mask
(for Schliemann "the mask of Agamemnon") and a gold cup (naturally,
"the cup of Nestor"). We now know that these objects were older than
Homer's date for the Trojan War, and like Troy, that they too belong
to the Aegean civilization. Even before Schliemann's death it was realized that his and other related finds pointed to a new and great age, a
kind of ancient age of ancient Greece, the knowledge of which had
been lost. But it was left to a young Englishman to work out the form
of this civilization through the study of Schliemann's work and through
his own excavations. This was Arthur Evans.

Sir Arthur Evans: The Excavations at Knossos

The startling finds made by Evans on Crete beginning in 1900 caused
him to spend most of the rest of his life in excavation there. His principal site was the ancient city of Knossos, near modern Herakleion.
There he found a palace that covered more than five acres, with hundreds
of rooms arranged, originally, on four floors. The architecture, rich color,
tapered columns, and terra-cotta drains for flush toilets, impress every
visitor who sees the remains—and Evans' restorations—at Knossos. Pottery found at the site and other art forms, especially frescoes, compare
favorably with contemporary work anywhere. The total effect created
by the frescoes is of life enjoyed to the full, of relative ease and prosperity. Evans also found three systems of writing, a kind of hieroglyphic and
two scripts, which he called "Linear A" and "Linear B."

Knossos was apparently the center of a considerable empire, at
least a commercial empire, for the palace had a tremendous number of
storerooms for oil and other products. Yet the site was not heavily fortified, and there seems to have been little attention given to military
matters. Because the culture centered at Knossos was found to be widespread throughout the Aegean, and because a tradition preserved from
antiquity tells of a Cretan "thalassocracy" or sea empire, it has been
postulated that the kings of Knossos ruled extensive naval dominions.
Other sites of some size have also been unearthed on Crete, with palace
complexes similar to that of Knossos. The rulers of Knossos, therefore,
do not seem to have controlled the whole island, at least not over a long
period. Perhaps Knossos' chief importance lay in its maritime commerce,
and its security depended on a strong navy. Evans named the civilization
after King Minos of Knossos in later Greek legend, dividing it into
Early Minoan (c. 3000–c. 2100 B.C.), Middle Minoan (c. 2100–c. 1550 B.C.),
and Late Minoan (c. 1550–c. 1100 B.C.).

The Aegean: An Advanced Civilization

The Aegean civilization lagged very little behind those in the Tigris, Euphrates, and Nile valleys. The Bronze Age came two or three centuries later, perhaps, but in some ways the culture was as advanced as the others. To the modern taste Kamares ware, for example, a fine, brilliant, polychrome pottery of the early middle period, seems superior to Egyptian or Mesopotamian ware of the same age. A seagoing people naturally visited both the eastern Mediterranean littoral and Egypt, with cultural interchange the natural result. The idea for the hieroglyphic writing probably came from Egypt, and Linear A may be basically a Semitic language. Cretan imports have been discovered in Egypt, especially of the Middle Kingdom and Empire periods, and Egyptian manufactures have been dug up on Crete.

The high period for Knossos, Crete, and the Aegean civilization in general came during the Middle Minoan period, from about 2000 B.C. to about 1550 B.C. The decipherment of Minoan Script B two decades ago forced a rethinking of the probable "history" of this civilization. The problems posed, incidentally, illustrate well the difficulty—one might say the impossibility—of writing history solely from archaeological data. To the surprise of scholars, the script turned out to be Greek. In recent years many tablets written in Script B have been dug up on the Greek mainland, especially at Pylos in the southwest Peloponnese. The current view is that the Achaeans (Greeks) adopted the superior Aegean culture, conquered Knossos about 1550, and in the late Minoan period ruled all or part of Crete. The late phase of Aegean culture on Greece itself is called Mycenaean and will be referred to in Chapter 7 on early Greek history.

Battered by both earthquakes and invasions over a period of several centuries, Knossos and Crete declined, and by 1100 B.C. the island had lapsed into obscurity. Cataclysmic volcanic activity on the Aegean island of Thera probably affected the whole of the eastern Mediterranean. Knossos was shattered by earthquake about 1570 B.C. and burned, probably the result of another earthquake, about 1400. The final invasions of Crete were probably made by the "sea peoples" who destroyed the Hittite Empire and certain Phoenician cities, and who were stopped only at great cost by the Twentieth Dynasty Egyptian pharaohs.

Sites on Thera have been under excavation for the past several years, and have already produced some remarkable remains, including frescoes. Because the island has been rather romantically connected with the lost Atlantis of the myth propounded by Plato, the archaeological work has received much publicity in the press. A great deal is possible at the site, where vestiges of the ancient civilization are buried under many feet of pumice stone and ash. Thera has been called the Minoan Pompeii. The most important relics excavated there, however, belong to a period later than that under discussion in this chapter.

B. Indus Valley Civilization

Another Twentieth Century Discovery

Scholars in the present century have also unearthed another advanced and quite old civilization, that of the Indus River valley. British engineers building railroads in the middle of the last century used brick from one of the largest cities of that civilization, Harappa, as ballast for the roadbeds. Eventually someone noticed that the site seemed antique. Systematic excavation at Harappa and at other sites—notably Mohenjo-Daro—began only in the 1920s and has continued at intervals to the present. The quality of some of the excavation, however, leaves much to be desired.

Tools and other objects belonging to all phases of the Stone and Bronze ages have been found throughout India. True civilization appears suddenly in the Indus valley, however; its remains are superimposed upon a simple Bronze Age village culture and could scarcely have developed from it. Scholars have deduced that invaders must have been primarily responsible for the new civilization, though it is not possible to say who they were. Pakistani archaeologists, however, have recently argued for development of the Indus valley civilization from the indigenous early Bronze Age culture. They note that the earlier culture is geographically almost the same as the "mature" Harappan culture, and emphasize that the early culture is remarkably homogeneous: the pottery, the habitations, the domesticated animals and so on are everywhere the same. They have no explanation, however, for the valley's sudden development into an urban civilization. Carbon 14 dates now indicate that the "Harappan culture" was fully established by 2400 B.C., or soon thereafter, and that by 1600 B.C. it was in decline. (Corrections now being made in Carbon 14 dating will push these dates back in time 200 or 300 years.)

The Indus civilization spread over the entire watershed of the river and its tributaries—a rather extensive area covering about 1,000 miles. Mohenjo-Daro in the northern Sind region is a couple of hundred miles north of Karachi on the coast; Harappa is more than 350 miles farther upstream, on a branch of the Indus called the Ravi, in the Punjab. Most of the territory is in modern Pakistan.

The Indus civilization probably owed something to the earlier developments in Mesopotamia. Archaeology has, in fact, turned up some evidence of cultural interchange between the two regions even before the flowering of the Indus civilization. Seals of various sorts and measurements of length seem to have been derived from western Asia. Weights, however, were different, based on a unit of sixteen. Indus picture-writing used unique symbols, but the idea of writing may well have come from Mesopotamia, as has been suggested. It has not as yet been deciphered, though reports of progress are sometimes publicized. Even if it is deciphered, however, the written materials are not extensive enough to yield much information about the history of the Harappan civilization.

Unity and Uniformity

There is a sameness to the Indus civilization everywhere. Cities and towns are laid out on similar grid patterns; at both Harappa and Mohenjo-Daro there were similar citadels, communal granaries and baths. In some ways the cities were advanced; the street drains, for example, as well as the sanitary arrangements were admirable for the age. Certain art objects, small sculpture, seal reliefs, and jewelry, all pretty much alike, were finely done. The pottery and the bronze tools, on the other hand, were obviously utilitarian and mass-produced.

These elements of similarity plus the demands of the extensive irrigation systems seem to point to planning, to centralized control, perhaps even to absolutism. The sameness persists also in time, so that some scholars have felt a sense of stagnation about the civilization. Cities destroyed by flood were rebuilt on exactly the same pattern as before. Though well-planned, the cities—all of them—presented blank walls to the man who walked their ample streets. Surely it required thousands of slaves, probably state-owned, to bake the bricks and build the huge granaries, kilns, and mills. The writing system also shows no change— no sign of simplification or other advancement during the millennium the civilization endured.

Economic Decline and Aryan Invasion

A period of decline eventually set in, probably caused by changes in the environment. The area apparently became drier; the monsoon rain pattern moved eastward, perhaps in part because men had stripped the land of trees and other vegetation to fire the kilns that baked bricks by the million. Constant irrigation brought salinization of the soil and declining production. Destructive floods, which came every spring from melting snows in the mountains, were compounded by an uplift of the earth's crust near the sea. The result was a pooling of water and a rise in the water table. At Mohenjo-Daro thirty to thirty-five feet of occupation strata now lie below the water table. In fact, the water threatens to destroy the ancient remains, and an appeal was made to the United Nations a few years ago to help preserve the site in a vast effort like that put forth at Abu Simbel in Upper Egypt.

Violent invasion brought the final end of the Indus civilization. Dead bodies were left strewn in the streets of some sites, as at Mohenjo-Daro, where their skeletons have been found. This site, in fact, was apparently abandoned as accursed. The invaders were probably the Aryans spoken of in the Rig Vedas of a later day. They were thus related, at least linguistically, to the rulers of the Mitannians in Mesopotamia and to Greeks and Latins (and many others) farther west. Whatever these Aryans might later achieve, the immediate results for the Indus civilization were fragmentation and decline.

C. Early Civilization in China

Legend and History in Early China

No nation has been more aware of its long past than China. Moreover, there is nowhere a more continuous tradition of political and cultural development. Nevertheless, the Bronze Age and civilization came to China relatively late, as compared with the areas already considered. Chinese literary tradition presents a China already unified under a dynasty of emperors in the 3rd millennium B.C. But no archaeological data have been found to support the tradition, and much of it is obviously mythical. One emperor, for example, is said to have had the body of a dragon and the head of a man. Historians have long since learned that a core of truth can exist behind myth (though myth can never be history); they would not therefore, be surprised if archaeology eventually corroborated the early Hsia Dynasty of Chinese tradition. Numerous Neolithic and Bronze Age sites have been excavated, and distinct Chinese cultures identified and described.

The Shang Dynasty, which was established about 1700 B.C., has been confirmed by archaeology as fully historical, and the king list has been in large part corroborated. As in the Indus valley, a rather high civilization appeared suddenly, without specific antecedents. Unfortunately, many of the "excavations" of Shang Dynasty tomb sites have been mere despoliation for profit, as in western Asia and Egypt. Magnificent, heavy cast-bronze vessels of great variety both in form and decoration grace the great museums of the world. Weapons, too, and even remains of Chinese chariots (sometimes with drivers) buried with royal personages,

Chinese bronze food vessel (*chiu*). Shang dynasty (1766-1122 B.C.). *(The Metropolitan Museum of Art, Kennedy Fund, 1913)*

have been exposed, and help to substantiate the accomplishments of the skilled craftsmen of this age.

Achievements of the Shang Dynasty

The rather large area ruled by the Shang Dynasty, in the central and northern sections of China proper, was located in the Yellow and Yangtze river valleys. The capital, or at least one capital, was found at Anyang in Honan Province in the days of Nationalist China; excavations have continued under the People's Republic. The usual pattern of fortified towns and less advanced rural villages can be seen as elsewhere. It is possible to reconstruct a typical house, and to learn something of the religion of the age. A writing system was employed, which, amazingly, is the direct ancestor of that in use today; some of its symbols can still be recognized in their modern forms. Many of the inscriptions are on flat bones, called "oracle bones," used in a form of divination, and they are still readable.

The most impressive achievement of the early Chinese civilization was in the casting of metals, though the discovery of bronze apparently came late. The techniques achieved within a matter of a few centuries were as advanced as those that required a thousand years to master further west. Moreover, although the Iron Age came late to China, too, when it did arrive the process of casting iron was also developed quickly. Indeed, the iron-casting techniques that evolved in China in the Chou period, which followed the Shang and preceded by several centuries the birth of Christ, are approximately the equivalent of methods developed in Europe in the late Middle Ages.

The end of the Shang Dynasty came about 1200 B.C. According to Chinese tradition, the rulers had become corrupt and so were overthrown. Civilization was continuous, however; cultural progress was not interrupted. The Chou Dynasty, however, lasted beyond the time treated here.

Books for Further Reading

ALLCHIN, B., *The Birth of Indian Civilization,* Baltimore, 1968.
HUTCHINSON, R. W., *Prehistoric Crete,* Baltimore, 1968.
PIGGOTT, S., *Prehistoric India,* Baltimore, 1950.
WATSON, W., *Early Civilization in China,* London, 1966.
WHEELER, M., *The Indus Valley,* London, 1966.

5

Hittites, Phoenicians, Hebrews

A century ago no student of ancient history guessed that the Hittites once ruled a great empire comprising most of Asia Minor, Syria, and the region of the upper Euphrates. Evidence brought up by the spade has now proved that they did. Information on the Hittites once derived mostly from the Hebrew Bible. There the Hittites appear as a minor, tribal group, listed along with the Hivites, Jebusites, Girgashites, and others as competitors with the Hebrews for the control of Palestine. Yet one mention of them in II Kings 7, dated to the last half of the 9th century B.C., suggests that the Hittite kings were men of some power: Israel's Syrian opponents fled because they thought the Hebrews "had hired the kings of the Hittites" against them. We now know that these "kings" were local chieftains who presided over the last remnants of the Hittite Empire, which flourished several centuries earlier.

In the late 19th century, Oxford professor A. H. Sayce collated scraps of information that had been accumulating and suggested that they indicated a Hittite dominion of considerable size. He noted especially certain art forms and finds of an unknown type of hieroglyphic. Serious and marvelously successful excavations began in 1906 with a German expedition led by Hugo Winckler. He chose to dig at Bogazköy, a promising site within the semicircular orbit of the Halys River, about 90 miles east of Ankara in modern Turkey. The ruins were of the ancient Hittite capital Hattusas. Winckler quickly began to find clay tablets by the thousand, the actual archives of the ancient empire.

Unfortunately, Winckler became so excited over his discoveries that he did not adequately superintend the excavations. The clay tablets, lying in orderly rows, were chucked out helter-skelter by workmen who

74

kept no record of their order. One reason for Winckler's excitement was that on the tablets he could read—those written in Babylonian cuneiform —he found diplomatic correspondence that strikingly corroborated and supplemented information already in the historical record. He was especially elated by the discovery of a copy of the treaty made between Ramses II of Egypt and the Hittite king, Hattusilis (see p. 62), the text of which he had already seen in hieroglyphics on the walls of Ramses' temple in Egypt. These discoveries by Winckler and others, continuing and multiplying to the present, have made it possible to learn something of both the history and the culture of the Hittites.

A. The Hittites: A Historical Sketch

Apparently, the Hittites moved into the Anatolian plateau region around the beginning of the 2nd millenium B.C. The name itself offers no clue to their origins, for "Hittite" derives from the name Hatti, given to the region of central Anatolia where they settled. One Hittite religious myth tells of their sun god coming up out of the water, which perhaps implies a previous location west of a large body of water—the Black Sea or more likely, the Caspian? The invaders spoke an Indo-European language, which means that they were linguistically related to Greeks and Italians, among others, some of whom were also on the move at about that time.

The Hittites as a ruling elite set up a monarchy organized politically and socially along tribal and feudal lines. In some ways they were conquered by the conquered: much of their culture was the product of assimilation. In the late 17th century B.C., Hittite kings began to expand south out of Asia Minor. About 1600 B.C. a king named Mursilis carried out a raid as far south as Babylon, helping to put an end to what remained of the empire over which Hammurabi had ruled earlier. But then disputes among the aristocracy over succession to the throne contributed to the empire's decline.

The Hittite Empire, c. 1450–c. 1200 B.C.

Renewed Hittite power at the end of the 15th century B.C. and during the 14th came after a reorganization of the kingship, which was strengthened at the expense of the nobles. Resurgent Egyptian thrusts up into Syria under the kings of the Eighteenth Dynasty helped spark the Hittite revival because the Egyptians weakened the Hurrians in upper Syria. Later, Egypt made an alliance with the Hurrian kingdom, Mitanni, which was centered on the upper Euphrates River. In the days of Akhnaton, however, the Egyptians, bemused with their religious

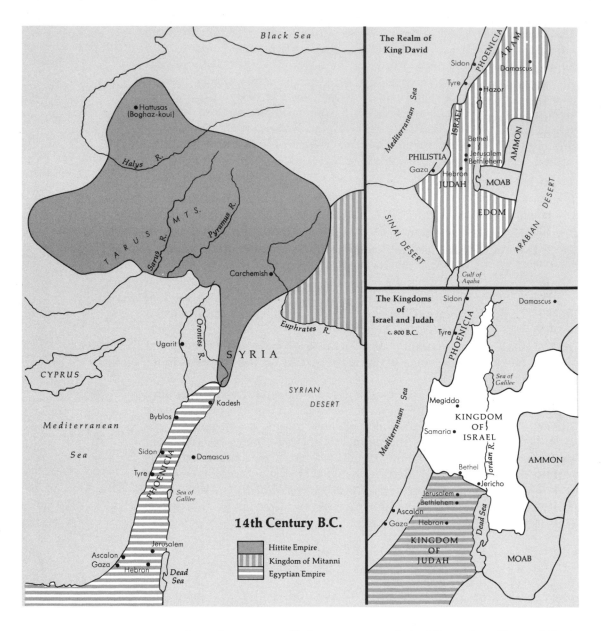

The Realm of King David

The Kingdoms of Israel and Judah c. 800 B.C.

14th Century B.C.

Hittite Empire
Kingdom of Mitanni
Egyptian Empire

struggle at home, gave little support to their Mitannian ally, and Syria was open to penetration by the Hittites.

The imperialist Hittite king who skillfully seized the opportunity to expand at the expense of Egypt and its ally Mittani bore the alliterative name Suppiluliumas (c. 1380–1340 B.C.). In several campaigns he blunted the power of Mitanni and then destroyed it; next he conquered

Syria. His sons became kings of these areas. A smaller Mitanni was re-constituted as a buffer state with Assyria farther east. The widow of Tutankhamon, it will be recalled, appealed to Suppiluliumas for a husband who, she said, would become king of Egypt. Suppiluliumas' correspondence shows that he hesitated, unbelieving, and ordered an investigation. But then it was too late; the son who might have become Ankhesenamon's husband was killed at the borders of Egypt. If he had become king of Egypt, the history of the Near East might read much differently.

Another son of Suppiluliumas, Mursilis II (c. 1339–1306 B.C.), fought hard to hold the empire together. A vassal kingdom of Arzawa in western Asia Minor gave the Hittites continual trouble, and there were incursions from the northeast. Mursilis' son and successor, Muwatallis (c. 1306–1282 B.C.), had revolt on his hands in Syria, where the power of Egypt penetrated once again under the kings of the Nineteenth Dynasty. In a tremendous battle at Kadesh, which Ramses II claimed he won (see p. 62), Muwatallis fought the Egyptian armies to a draw. After a few years' standoff, Hattusilis III (1275–1250 B.C.), brother of Muwatallis, made the permanent treaty with Ramses already mentioned and stabilized the frontier for some years.

The succeeding Hittite kings also faced revolts, however, especially in Asia Minor from Arzawa, now under a vigorous new dynasty, and from Ahhiyawa, which seems to have been an island-based sea power (Rhodes?). It had once been on good terms with the Hittites, even sending royal sons for military training at Hattusas. Possibly the Ahhiyawans were, as some think, Greek: Achaeans. In any event, the Ahhiyawans joined in the great campaigns of the "sea peoples" who struck inland and then south all the way to Egypt. They destroyed the Hittite Empire and all the cities along the Phoenician coast. Egypt, as we have seen, managed to beat off the invaders. Petty kings, usually called Hittite, continued to rule remnants of the empire in northern Syria. But the great days of Hittite power ended by about 1190 B.C.

B. Hittite Culture

The mixed character of the Hittite culture is symbolized in the writing systems discovered by Winckler at Hattusas. There were two systems, borrowed from Mesopotamia and Egypt. There were also several languages: Hittite, from the conquered population, and Babylonian (Akkadian). In language, literature, art, religion, law, and government, the Hittites were borrowers and assimilators. Nevertheless there was, always, an element of originality. Even an untrained eye can quickly learn to recognize the distinctive characteristics of Hittite sculpture, a sort of hybridized collation of Egyptian and Mesopotamian styles—just as it can also learn to see the evidence of external influence.

Technical and Military Innovations

In general terms, one of the most important achievements of the Hittites —at least of peoples ruled by the Hittites—was the advance made in the process of smelting iron. Their smelting process, at first localized in Cilicia late in the period of the empire, introduces the Iron Age. The new techniques, however, came too late to benefit the Hittite armies. Iron weapons could not be made cheaply and at first they were probably no better than good bronze. Not until the rise of the Assyrians were whole armies equipped with iron weapons.

The Hittites did introduce important military innovations, although they learned a few things from the Hurrians, too. In chariotry and in siege tactics, their equipment was the best in the world. They had bigger horses, which could draw large, three-man chariots. And as for siege tactics, it astonished the world when Suppiluliumas was able to take the strongly fortified city of Carchemish in Mitanni in just eight days. They also improved city defenses; gates were redesigned, and the idea of secret exits in walls for counterattacking a besieging enemy was also probably theirs.

Government and Law

In government, the king, though less powerful in the earlier period, was a strong figure in the Hittite Empire. He was not a god, not even the chief priest of the patron deity in the capital, but in state ceremonies he did function at times as a priest and he did become a god at death. Like all Indo-European peoples, however, the Hittites venerated their ancestors, so the fact that the king became a god at death probably does not mean much. The nobles held the key offices, with the most sensitive reserved for men connected with the king. The older feudal system of control of both local government and military procurement was gradually displaced during the empire by a more centralized system.

Mesopotamian influence was especially great not only in language but also in economics. Some cities located on trade routes within the empire were predominantly Babylonian. The law code, discovered in fragmentary form at Hattusas, demonstrates the commercial influence of Mesopotamia. The earliest laws of the Hittites were most concerned with rural problems; later additions to the code provided greater protection for commerce and movable property. Hittite law was somewhat less severe than that of the Semites of Mesopotamia; there was, for example, less use of the death penalty. That Hittite law was less harsh illustrates a principal difference in point of view between the Hittites and the earlier peoples of the Mesopotamian region. The Mesopotamians tried to propound what they thought was the law of the gods. The Hittites considered the law to be a man-made matter.

Religion and Literature

The religion and literature of the Hittites manifest the same combination of inner inspiration and foreign influence. Even Aryan deities from Mitanni were included in the official pantheon. Mesopotamian names for gods—Anu and Ishtar, for instance—turn up frequently. To some degree, it is possible to distinguish groups of gods that correspond to the various population groups of Anatolia. The chief deities of the Hittites were the sun goddess of Arinna, Wuru-semu; the weather god, or lord of the storm, Teshub; and Telepinus, a fertility deity. Teshub was a Hurrian god, and the religion and other elements of Hittite culture are sometimes termed Hurro-Hittite. The mythical story explaining the seasonal cycle was accepted, but with variation. Telepinus simply wanders away and goes to sleep, whereupon life on earth grinds to a halt. It is the lowly bee who eventually finds him and stings him to wakefulness and to a resumption of his duties. Other Hittite literature, except for the diplomatic correspondence already mentioned, includes few documents that are basically historical. In two or three accounts that have been found, however, the reigning king does justify his acts or his accession to power.

Recently, scholars have been stressing the Hittites' role as transmitters of culture. It is possible to see through them the various influences of Mesopotamia in later Western culture. In literature—especially the fertility myths—as in mathematics and astronomy, connections can be seen with later Mediterranean civilization, sometimes specifically, sometimes only generally. In view of the rather close relationship between the Hittites and the Greeks in Asia Minor, it is not unlikely that the role of the Hittites in the sweep of civilization westward was great.

C. The Phoenicians

Civilization and urban life came early to the eastern Mediterranean littoral almost as early as to Mesopotamia and Egypt. An ancient tradition in the Phoenician city of Byblos, twenty miles north of present-day Beirut, claimed that it was the oldest city in the world, and indeed some of the cities in the area show evidence of a continuous history of 7,000 years or so. Certain inland cities, such as Damascus and Aleppo, also have a long history. The peoples of this area developed a civilization most closely approximating that of the Mesopotamians. They, too, were mostly Semitic as was their language; naturally, the people also adopted the cuneiform system of writing that had evolved in Mesopotamia.

At the begininng of the Old Kingdom in Egypt, Phoenicians were already shipping their famous cedar lumber for use in the palaces and tombs of the Egyptian pharaohs and aristocrats. In turn, Egyptian products were sent to Phoenicia. Byblos became the chief center for distribution of Egyptian papyrus outside the country of origin, and in fact the word for book, "biblos" (thus "Bible"), derives from the name of that city. Phoenicians also became early distributors of bronze and other metal products. In the last decade or two, underwater archaeologists have recovered large chunks of bronze in the shape of bull hides, as well as finished bronze pans and implements, from ancient Phoenician shipwrecks of the middle 2nd millennium B.C.

The Homeland

The location of their great cities, of course, helped to make the Phoenicians what they were. Their chief cities, Byblos, Tyre, and Sidon, were not only harbors on the eastern Mediterranean but trading centers on the western curve of the Fertile Crescent. Such a city as Ugarit, farther north in modern Syria, was also a cosmopolitan center, a meeting place for crosscurrents from Egypt, Mesopotamia, and Hittite Anatolia. Connections with the Aramaic cities like Damascus, a few miles inland, also gave the Phoenicians access to important land routes. Their seamen, understandably enough, carried a distillation of culture with them on their journeys west.

The homeland produced certain products that were much in demand. Lumber from the Lebanon mountains, which paralleled the coast in two ranges separated by an interior valley, was widely exported. Metal products have already been mentioned. A superior and very expensive dye, which the Greeks simply called "purple," was laboriously extracted from a species of shellfish.

Navigation, Exploration, Colonization

The Phoenicians sought always to improve the physical conditions of trade: better ships, better navigation, permanent trading stations or full-fledged colonies. And they courageously explored uncharted and far-off regions. In antiquity exploration was desultory at best. The Romans at their height, for example, supported it but little. Here the Phoenicians pioneered.

It was probably the Phoenicians who built the first decked ships, the better to withstand the pounding of the Mediterranean's sudden storms. Most shipping, nevertheless, hugged the coasts. Phoenician navigators compiled logs that described the coastline minutely for their sailors; good anchorages (or, rather, protected beaches; ordinarily, boats were drawn up on the beach at night) and harbors were marked, hazards carefully noted, as were sources of fresh water and supplies.

In exploring and trading, the Phoenicians not only cruised the length of the Mediterranean, they probably coasted north along the Atlantic shoreline as far as Britain and south along the west of Africa as far as Nigeria. There is some evidence of their having visited the Azores. One celebrated expedition in the service of Pharaoh Necho II of Egypt in the 6th century B.C. completely circumnavigated Africa from the Red Sea south and back via the Atlantic. The Greeks refused to believe the story brought back of the sun's movement across the sky on the right hand instead of the left. Our modern conclusion is that the story tends to prove the Phoenicians' claim; it shows that they passed to the south of the equator. The trip reportedly took three years. Other stories of Phoenician expeditions along the western coast of Africa, however, are described so vaguely by the Greeks that one suspects the wily Phoenicians deliberately misled the men who had become their chief competitors at sea.

The rivalry with the Greeks in western waters involved, of course, the products of trade—chiefly precious and semiprecious metals. Agricultural products could not possibly be profitable over a long haul. In exchange for the metals they gave manufactured items of high unit value.

Phoenicians and Greeks also competed in actual colonization of the western Mediterranean. The Phoenicians settled harbor sites and adjacent agricultural land along the North African coast, especially from Tunisia westward. Carthage became their most important North African colony. They were also predominant in southern Spain, western Sicily, and Sardinia. The Greeks were concentrated in southern Italy, eastern Sicily, southern France, and, to a lesser degree, eastern Spain.

The political independence that helped make the Phoenician achievement possible was the chance byproduct of the decline of great empires; there was certainly no unified political federation that spurred them on. The homeland was divided into city-states that sometimes cooperated and sometimes fought with one another in alliance with nearby states. Nor was there really a western empire. Phoenician tended to support Phoenician in the West, as Greek tended to support Greek. But neither of these great peoples ever managed to unite themselves politically. In their homeland the Phoenicians fought redoubtably against the Assyrians and Babylonians as each created an empire, but they finally yielded to both. In the later Persian Empire their ships furnished the fleets that in the 5th century B.C. brought oriental armies into Greece. The high period for Phoenician independent action and influence belongs to the six centuries between about 1200 and 600 B.C.

Disseminators of Culture

Culturally, Phoenicians were carriers more than originators. Their religion is now much more completely known than it was a few decades ago when scholars depended primarily upon information from their Hebrew neighbors. Phoenicians, Hebrews, and other Canaanites had a similar background. The Phoenicians ultimately developed lofty concepts comparable to those of the Greeks, among others, and they frequently centered these concepts around one of the Baals, as Baal Shamin, the Lord of Heaven. And as in other ancient religions, each city had its patron deity. At Tyre, Melkart was the chief god; his consort, Astarte, was worshiped later as Tanit at Carthage, the colony of Tyre. The Greeks equated Melkart with Hercules. The Phoenicians put great stress on ethical values, but they also practiced temple prostitution and human sacrifice, at least in times of great danger. Recent archaeological finds at Carthage confirm what their enemies, the Romans, claimed: that Phoenician children were immolated down to at least 300 B.C., and probably later.

The form of written letters used by the Greeks, later by the Romans, and thereafter by all the Western world, came from Phoenicia. Whether this fact means the Phoenicians should be credited with inventing the alphabet, however, is doubtful—and partly a matter of terminology. Forms of alphabets certainly developed in the area, long before the high period of the Phoenicians, both from cuneiform and from hieroglyphics. But exactly who adapted these systems into the earliest alphabets is not yet precisely known. Recent archaeology has found a cuneiform system at Ras Shamra (ancient Ugarit) north of Phoenicia and dates it to a period soon after 2000 B.C. At that time the Egyptian hieroglyphic was being similarly modified into an alphabet in the Sinai peninsula farther to the south.

There is also the matter of how an alphabet should be defined. The Semites generally did not write the vowel sounds but supplied them in the pronunciation. If, as some eminent linguists hold, there is no true alphabet until vowel sounds are written, then the credit for inventing one must go to the Greeks. Even so, here as elsewhere, the Phoenicians certainly played their characteristic role: they were the transmitters of all sorts of remarkable Near Eastern legacies to the West.

If space in this volume were apportioned solely in relation to the political importance of successive kingdoms and empires, the Hebrews would deserve little more than a sentence in this chapter. On the other hand, if space were allotted in accordance with persistent influence in the modern world, the Hebrews would deserve many more pages than the few that follow. Three of the world's great religions derive from that of the Hebrews: Judaism, Christianity, and Islam. In general, the strongest forces operating in Western civilization today go back to Israel and Greece.

Since the Middle Ages, organized religion and church officers have played a gradually lessening role in politics, society, and the economy of all the great Western countries. The Hebrew approach to life, however—in the West the Judeo-Christian outlook—is still an underlying and integrating force for both individuals and states. Thinking men of the 20th century have often attempted to combine the Judeo-Christian view of life with the rationalist-intellectual view that derives primarily from the thought and method of the great scientists and philosophers of ancient Greece.

To blend a scientific-rationalist approach to human knowledge with any sort of deep religious conviction is not easy. In individuals and in whole societies the effort continues to be made nonetheless—sometimes unwittingly, sometimes deliberately. Results have been erratic. The United States, for example, has at times seemed afflicted with a sort of spiritual schizophrenia as these forces pull in opposite directions. Yet the end result has been beneficial: the American religious ethic has combined with the humanism seen in much of our higher educational structure to ameliorate somewhat the dehumanizing tendencies of science and technology. The human failures of our society are egregious. But if we groan with guilt at our failures and struggle to create a more just society for all, much of the reason for doing so emanates from the Hebrew prophets and teachers.

E. Hebrew History

Origins

The later Hebrews by tradition traced their origins back to the patriarch Abraham. The Bible itself shows that not all the Hebrews of history, even in a very early period, were descendants of this single patriarch.

Nevertheless, it is appropriate to begin with these traditional progenitors. Abraham was said to have come from Ur, which would place him in Sumer (if indeed his city was that Ur) perhaps as early as the 20th century B.C., at or soon after the time of the brilliant Third Dynasty. Most of his relatives, however, lived in the upper Euphrates region about Haran. Recent excavated records of the Kingdom of Mari, on the middle Euphrates, provide us with names in West Semitic (that is, not Akkadian) similar in etymology to Hebraic names in that general area. To illustrate, the people of a region to the north of Mari are there called Benjamites.

Abraham next migrated to Palestine, then inhabited by other West Semites called, in general, Canaanites. He and his nephew Lot are pictured as well-to-do nomads whose wealth was in flocks and herds. Their travels and the manner of life indicated in the Bible, often even in details, fit in well with what is known from history and archaeology of the movements of Semitic peoples in this period and of their manner of life. This does not mean precisely, as is sometimes claimed, that the finds of archaeology have confirmed the Hebrew tradition; the details of the Biblical narrative are impossible to confirm—or to deny. The narrative is, however, basically plausible, even though it was written down at a much later time.

The greatest events of early Hebrew history in the Bible are these: the migration into Egypt of the descendants of Abraham; their fall into slavery; the Exodus from Egypt under the leadership of Moses; and the entrance into Palestine under Joshua after forty years of wandering. It is easy to dismiss the whole narrative as unhistorical because of the supernatural events described as part of the story. Yet again, the substantive material fits well into known history, even though for the first three of the above events there is no evidence outside the Bible.

Exodus

The Biblical account places the length of captivity in Egypt at 400 or 430 years. Exact dating was not a fetish in antiquity, and this figure may simply mean ten or eleven generations (the Hebrews tended to take forty years as a generation). The earliest inscriptional evidence of a people Israel may be the stele of Pharaoh Merneptah found in Palestine and dated about 1220 B.C. The stele seems to mention Israel in connection with an Egyptian campaign there. For this and other reasons the first half of the 13th century B.C., in the reign of Ramses II, seems the most likely date for the Exodus; the wandering and entrance into Palestine come before 1220. If the entry into Egypt had occurred some 400 years before the Exodus, that would place the migration in the period of the Hyksos occupation of Egypt. Further, if the Hebrews were a part of that mixed group called the Hyksos, it can easily be seen how one of their number, Joseph, might rise to a position of importance in the government. The rise of a pharaoh who "knew not Joseph" would refer to the period after the expulsion of the Hyksos and would explain the fall of the Hebrews into servitude

Excavation of the sites that marked the invasion of Palestine by Israel yields disappointingly little information regarding the chronology. At Jericho not much remains that is recent enough to confirm the story. The site called Ai in the Bible—said to have been destroyed by the Israelites—was in ruins long before the late Bronze Age and not rebuilt. But nearby Bethel was destroyed about the time of the Hebrew invasion, in the 13th century. Perhaps a confusion of names? Some other sites mentioned in the Bible as destroyed by Israel were indeed razed in the thirteenth century. The most important of these was Hazor, an impressively strong city in northern Palestine. It was more than two centuries before the Hebrews controlled the best, most productive portions of the land.

The Israelites, loosely organized by tribes, during these years controlled only the Jordan valley and the high ground west of it. Leaders called "judges" arose as occasional champions against hostile threats. The most inveterate enemies were the Philistines, who established themselves in the coastal area to the west of a line between Jerusalem and Beersheba. A judge like Samson could only provoke the warlike Philistines. At length the Israelites demanded a king of their own. Samuel, the last of the judges and a prophet as well, picked Saul, who was acclaimed by the tribes of Israel as their first king. The date was about 1020 B.C.

F. The United Monarchy (c. 1020–921 B.C.)

Saul

Saul enjoyed some successes against the Philistines and others. But he was no grand monarch. His capital and his residence were unpretentious, and he had only a few hundred retainers. Efforts to increase his power met opposition even from Samuel; military levies were half-heartedly supported at best. When Saul began to suffer from fits of depression and when his military successes ended, his popularity vanished. Finally, about 1000 B.C., he and his sons were killed in battle by the Philistines at Mount Gilboa on the great plain called Jezreel or Esdraelon in north-central Palestine.

David

David was Saul's successor. In the latter years of Saul's reign, David had been the focus of opposition to the old king. And, indeed, the prophet Samuel declared that God's favor had been transferred from Saul to the young warrior. David, as a consequence, was outlawed by Saul. But as a charismatic leader whose reputation in war stood high, he was the logical successor. Israel still needed a victory over the Philistines, and David soon gave it to them. He captured the ancient Canaanite city of Jerusalem and made it the capital of a united kingdom. Other Canaanite centers in Palestine were then absorbed. David also expanded Israel's influence and control to the north, east, and south—a feat made possible largely because of the weakness of the great powers. Besides all of Palestine, David came to control the Negev and Sinai desert region to the south. He took tribute from the Philistines, and from the people of Moab, Edom, and Ammon, all of whom lived east of the line of the Jordan, the Dead Sea, and the dry Arabah valley that connects the sea with the Gulf of Aqabah. Other Transjordanian lands and southern Syria were also under his aegis. Considering the times, Israel had become a major power.

Solomon

The apex of the Kingdom of Israel came in the brilliant and prosperous reign of Solomon, son of David (c. 961–922 B.C.). Solomon was later renowned for his wisdom, though to some it might seem unwise for a king to have a harem of 300 wives and 700 concubines. His reputation for wisdom came perhaps from the fact that he started a collection of wise sayings, the Proverbs. The wives, many of them, were the result of diplomatic alliances; the most important probably was the daughter of a pharaoh of Egypt.

Solomon emphasized trade and commerce. He dominated the principal routes into Arabia, and sat astride the roads from Mesopotamia to Egypt. He smelted copper in many places as an object of trade. The once-publicized mines at Ezion-geber in the Negev now appear not to have been worked in this age, though the mine shafts discovered in 1974 not far distant may have been worked by Solomon. Sometimes in conjunction with Hiram of Tyre, Solomon sent out shipping fleets to East Africa, Cyprus, Cilicia, and perhaps as far west as Spain. The story of the Queen of Sheba (in Yemen) coming to visit Solomon with sample goods is not at all unlikely.

Solomon was also a great builder. With timber from Phoenicia, he built a huge palace, called "The Forest" because of the amount of cedar used in its construction. More than a residence, it housed state offices. Much smaller, but significant both politically and religiously, was the Temple to Yahweh that he constructed at Jerusalem. Since the time of David, Jerusalem had become the religious center of the Hebrews as well as a political capital. Phoenician workmen poured the great pillars that stood before the temple and they aided in the art work. Solomon also erected strategic forts, though he undertook few military campaigns. Hazor, Megiddo, and Gezer are three of the more important installations from which he held sway over his own territory and made it secure from attack. His expensive military establishment was organized about a core of chariotry. Horses came from Cilicia, the chariots from Egypt.

Solomon's standing army, his building projects, his political establishment, his wives, all were expensive. Despite a bustling trade and successful commercial ventures, there was never enough money. And the measures that centralized his authority tended to loosen the old tribal ties. Even the priests, though supported by the king, were displeased with the degree of control he exercised—and with the various pagan influences that emanated from his harem. At his death the seeds of revolt lay ready to sprout.

G. The Divided Monarchy (c. 921 B.C.): Israel and Judah

The Northern Kingdom: Ahab and Jehu

When Solomon's son and successor, Rehoboam, refused to grant his people relief from the burden of government, the northern part of the kingdom seceded, and Rehoboam found himself unable to do anything about it. From that time until its destruction, the northern kingdom, Israel (or the Kingdom of Samaria when that became its capital), was separate from Judah (the Kingdom of Jerusalem). The two sister states cooperated closely at times, but they also battled each other, too.

The northern kingdom, Israel, was more populous and more prosperous because it had jurisdiction over the productive plain of Jezreel and a nearby market in the cities of Tyre and Sidon. Israel was often condemned by the Yahwist religious leaders. Its Phoenician connections and the larger Canaanite element in its population brought religious lapses in the view of the southern priests and prophets. Their harsh judgments, however, have sometimes been mitigated by the different standards of the historian.

The best-known king of Israel was Ahab (869–850 B.C.), son of Omri and husband of Jezebel, a Tyrian princess. Jezebel naturally supported the Baals of her homeland, Phoenicia, and incurred the hatred of the Yahwists, whom she persecuted. Ahab is pictured by the Yahwists as weak and unscrupulous. But by chance, Assyrian records give a different account of Ahab's ability. He led an alliance of Israel, Tyre, and Damascus that was so powerful that for a time it halted the advance of expanding Assyria. Ahab's effort, however, and his military campaigns in Transjordan (for example, against Moab) bore heavily upon the populace. Economic decline was soon followed by a struggle for the throne after Ahab's death.

Jehu (842–815 B.C.) finally seized the throne, killed all the blood relatives of Ahab, and restored the Yahwist religion. Israel, however, was never again as strong as it was under Ahab. Jehu paid tribute to Assyria. Some of his successors were prosperous enough, but in 722–721 B.C., after a coalition of Israel and Damascus was crushed by Assyria, Shalmaneser V and Sargon II destroyed Israel and razed its cities including Samaria, the capital. By deporting the Hebrews from Israel and replacing them with men from elsewhere in the empire, the Assyrians changed the demographic character of the region and permanently weakened whatever bonds still held the two groups of Hebrews together. The Jews of later history derive mostly from the southern kingdom.

The Southern Kingdom: Hezekiah and Josiah

The Kingdom of Judah endured until 587 B.C. as a more or less independent entity. At the time of the fall of Israel Judah was allied with Assyria, and the Assyrians considered the little state part of their empire. A few years after the destruction of Israel, Judah, under King Hezekiah (715–687 B.C.), revolted. The Judeans were encouraged by a resurgent Egypt (then under an Ethiopian Dynasty, the Twenty-fifth), by rebellion elsewhere in the Assyrian Empire, and by Hebrew reformers hoping to escape the religious influences fostered by the Assyrians. Besieged by Sennacherib, Hezekiah was forced to return to the fold and pay heavy tribute, but Jerusalem itself was not taken. A later king, Josiah (640–609 B.C.), was also a religious reformer. Lauded in the Hebrew Bible for his efforts, Josiah was able to effect reforms chiefly because the Assyrian Empire was disintegrating. Hebrews rejoiced when the Assyrian capital Nineveh fell to the Babylonians and Medes in 612 B.C. But Josiah was killed when he tried to stop an Egyptian force from coming to the aid of the remnants of the Assyrian Empire.

The Babylonian Captivity

The victory of Babylon over Assyrians and Egyptians in 605 did not, however, bring freedom to Judah. On the contrary, Jerusalem was soon taken by the Babylonians, and a revolt brought violent repression in 597 B.C. and again in 587 B.C. On both occasions large numbers of Jews of the upper classes were carried off to Babylonia. In 587 the last king, Zedekiah, was forced to watch the execution of his sons; he was then blinded and also sent captive to Babylon. Jerusalem was destroyed and looted. Palace, temple, walls, were razed to the ground.

In Babylon most Jews managed to retain their identity and their religion. As we know from a Babylonian document, Zedekiah was apparently well treated. Yet, understandably, the Hebrews were pleased when Cyrus, King of Persia, defeated and took Babylon in 539 B.C. Cyrus and later Persian monarchs allowed the Hebrews to return to Jerusalem and to rebuild it, but Judah remained part of the empire of Persia and was not independent. When in 332 B.C. Alexander the Great of Macedonia took over Palestine in the process of conquering the Persian Empire, Judah came under his control. After his death Palestine was ruled by Macedonian dynasts who were the successors of Alexander, first the Ptolemies of Egypt and after 200 B.C., the Seleucids of Syria.

H. The Evolution of the Hebrew Religion

Religion and History

The Hebrew religion did not develop in a vacuum. It must, therefore, be studied as a part of history. In fact, one of the great strengths of Judaism, as well as of Christianity and Islam, is that it is a religion rooted in history rather than in myth. Yet it should not be assumed that great developments can always be explained by a study of surrounding events, in some way analogous to ecological studies in science. One does not "explain" Moses, Jesus, Mohammed, or for that matter, Socrates and Plato by scrutinizing the society that produced them. Nonetheless, by examining their society one does understand them better.

In a very early period, the religion of the progenitors of the people Israel was that of other West Semites. Like any polytheists they kept certain strongly held beliefs. When they migrated, however, they tended to accept the religion of the new land. Thus the Israelites were doubtless affected, religiously, by their stay in Egypt. One naturally looks, for example, for some indication of influence of Akhnaton's religious views upon Israel. But the differences are greater than the similarities— for example, once the Hebrew leaders had settled on a single god, they did not at all identify him with the sun—and most scholars think there was little if any direct influence.

Moses and Monotheism

The Hebrew Bible underscores the leadership of Moses in the wilderness of Sinai during the catalytic events that made Israel a people and

at the same time established the exclusive worship of one god, Yahweh.[1]
It was said that through Moses God made a covenant with the tribes
of Israel. In return for their loyalty and worship of him alone he would
be to them a special deity, and bless them in various ways. Such a contract relationship between men and God has been compared with the
amphictyonies of the Greeks, such as the Delphic Amphictyony to the
god Apollo. The comparison may be useful, but it is certainly not exact.
The idea of a covenant relationship with God for each Hebrew and for
the nation as well is one of the most emphasized concepts of the Bible.

Whether the religion of the Mosaic period should be called
monotheism is doubtful. Perhaps a few leaders were monotheist; certainly
most Hebrews even long after the Exodus were not. Some scholars describe the religion of Israel at that time as a species of monolatry, or
henotheism; that is, the Hebrews worshiped one god only but did not
deny the existence of others.

The Reforming Prophets

A great period in the development of the Judaism of history came with
the age of the reforming prophets—after the middle of the 8th century
B.C. Amos was perhaps the first. Isaiah came a little later. In the time
of the Babylonian conquests and captivity, Jeremiah and Ezekiel were
also leading prophets. There had been "prophets" at least as far back
as Samuel. Samuel had a group of followers, apparently more or less ap-
prentices, who with their successors were called "sons of prophets." They
"prophesied" mostly ecstatically. Amos, curiously, declared that he was
neither a prophet nor the son of a prophet, though he said he spoke in
the name of God.

The reforming prophets were very much involved in politics,
simply because the religion was also. Israel was a kind of theocratic state;
political and religious leaders supposedly cooperated together in the
name of God to guide the people. Amos predicted the fall of Israel to
Assyria—which did not make him popular in high places. When some
twenty years later Isaiah, with the Assyrians at the gates of Jerusalem,
argued that Judah could not possibly win, he was considered bad for
morale, to say the least; some said he was being treasonous. Jeremiah
predicted Jerusalem's fall to the Babylonians during the last siege; he
was imprisoned and otherwise mistreated.

---

[1] In Hebrew, the name is written with four consonants, YHWH. The name was
considered too sacred to pronounce, and since the vowel sounds were never written,
the knowledge of them was lost. In early English translations of the Bible, vowels were
supplied by using those from the word Adonai (Lord; this word was regularly substi-
tuted for YHWH wherever it appeared) and the name then spelled "Jehovah." Modern
scholars ordinarily use the spelling "Yahweh," as probably more accurate.

These prophets made God preeminently a god of history—or, perhaps more to the point, a god *in* history. Israel fell, they declared, because as a group its people broke the covenant with God. The Assyrians were thus not merely the conquerers of Israel, they were actually the "rod of God's wrath." The deliverance of the city of Jerusalem in the time of Hezekiah reinforced these views. It caused some Jews to believe that their faith in God made the city impregnable to any foe, including the Babylonians. But the prophets saw Judah's corruption, her paganism, her spiritual prostitution. These, they said, would eventually bring on her the wrath of God by the hand of the Babylonians.

The Religious Influences of Exile and Restoration

Once in exile, however, the prophets preached the forgiveness of God upon repentance, and the hope of a future restoration and golden age. Somehow the actuality of restoration, however, never measured up to their magnificent phraseology, especially that of the "Second Isaiah" as the latter chapters of the Hebrew book are often called. In consequence, many Hebrews felt that the real restoration was still to come. And it was to be accompanied with the restoration of the House of David, with religious revival, and with the outpouring of God's blessings upon his favored people. Later sects, the Essenes and the Pharisees, placed particular emphasis on the leadership of the Anointed One, the Messiah, in effecting this restoration.

The great reforming prophets concentrated on an ethical transformation. Mere sacrifice and ritual could not please God, they maintained. Only ethics in action could do that. God for them was truly the sole god. He was the god of the Assyrians and the Babylonians also, whether or not they realized it—though not in the special sense that he was god of Israel. In these several ways, then, the developed religion of Israel was distinctive: it combined a strict monotheism with lofty ethics; in it God was ruler of the destinies of *all* men. This meant that in some usually explicable fashion, God was the guiding force behind human history.

The period after the Babylonian exile brought the restoration of the Yahwist religion in Judah. The temple was rebuilt and the liturgy restored. The stress laid upon racial-religious purity tended to place the Jews in religious and cultural isolation. Still, they had been influenced by the religious crosscurrents encountered in exile. Dualistic concepts (Satan as well as God), the idea of a cosmic struggle between the forces of light and darkness with ultimate victory for the forces of order, the teaching regarding a resurrection—much of which is evident in the recently discovered Dead Sea Scrolls—are all usually taken as evidence of Persian-Zoroastrian influence.

I. The Hebrew Bible as Literature

Organization

Quite aside from religion, the Hebrew Bible contains what is by far the most remarkable collection of history, poetry, philosophy, and romance to come out of the ancient Near East. The collection of books in the Hebrew Bible is divided into three main sections: the Torah (Law), the Prophets, and the Scriptures or Writings. The Torah consists of the Pentateuch, five books attributed to Moses but in the present form put together at a later period and from several more or less parallel accounts. The Prophets are subdivided into the Former and the Latter. The Former Prophets are the historical books, Joshua, Judges, Kings, and Chronicles; the Latter Prophets are again subdivided into Major and Minor groups. The Writings include books compiled over a long period of time (Psalms, Proverbs) and the later works. Thus, for example, Daniel is listed as Scripture rather than with the Minor Prophets.

Law

The law code or the Torah has some unique features. Many of its provisions show Babylonian influences; some sections, for instance, are worded in a fashion closely similar to the code of Hammurabi. But there is a greater humanitarianism evident than in earlier law codes. Special sections provide for the welfare of widows, orphans, and even slaves. Lending money at interest (to fellow Jews) was prohibited; the taking of collateral was permitted but limited. In contrast with earlier codes, no distinction was made between classes. Of course, any student even of recent history knows that when some individuals are powerful and others are weak there is often a broad gap between theory and practice in the application of law.

Philosophy

The Book of Job deserves a special comment because it deals essentially with a question that has always troubled man: Why does evil exist? The date of Job is disputed; the picture of life it presents could easily belong to a very early period, but its position in the Bible, its theology and sophistication argue for a late date. It has been called a drama without action. As the consequence of encounters between God and Satan, God permits the Devil to afflict Job in order to test his faith. Job loses children, wealth, and health. The reasons for Job's suffering become the chief subject of discussion between Job and friends who come to visit

The Dead Sea Scrolls in the Shrine of the Book. *(Israeli Government Tourist Office)*

him. They expound learnedly the view that Job is being punished for his sins, and advise him to repent. Job denies that he has sinned, and in the process eventually becomes almost the accuser of God—who finally enters the controversy and rebukes them all. God emphasizes the unknowable wonders of creation and man's comparatively insignificant knowledge. Ultimately Job is restored to health, wealth, and children. The question of the existence of evil in a world controlled by a beneficent god is answered in this way: God does not cause evil but permits it for his own inscrutable purposes, one of which is to improve men.

The Book of Ecclesiastes is a remarkable volume of literature also. Written by one Koheleth (or "the Preacher," traditionally thought to be Solomon though the book is late for his authorship), this work astonishes readers by its mechanism, its determinism, and its pessimism. Man's purpose is to endure; what he thinks is pleasure is transitory and vain. As for the possibility of life after death, the writer is profoundly pessimistic.

> *There is no man that lives always, or that hopes for this:*
> *A living dog is better than a dead lion.*
> *For the living know that they shall die,*
>   *but the dead know nothing more*
> *Neither have they a reward any more:*
> *For the memory of them is forgotten.*

It is possible, perhaps, to find a bit of optimism in the last verses. At death, the spirit does "return to God, who gave it."

The Septuagint

A Greek translation of the Hebrew Bible, made in Egypt between about 300 B.C. and 100 B.C., has been extremely influential. Called the Septuaginta—abbreviated LXX because seventy scholars are supposed to have participated in the translation—this version included books omitted from the Hebrew canon. Some of the extra books are important historically: the two Books of the Maccabees, for example, tell of the Jewish struggles for independence from Seleucid control in the 2nd century B.C. Jerome, translator of the Latin Vulgate, the official Bible of the Roman Catholic Church, used the canon of the Septuagint; Protestant Bibles now usually follow the Hebrew canon and omit the extra books.

Books for Further Reading

ALBRIGHT, W. F., *From the Stone Age to Christianity,* New York, 1957.

ALBRIGHT, W. F., *The Biblical Period from Abraham to Ezra,* New York, 1963.

BRIGHT, J., *A History of Israel,* Philadelphia, 1959.

DE VAUX, R., *Ancient Israel,* 2 vols., New York, 1965.

FINEGAN, J., *Light from the Ancient Past,* Princeton, 1959.

GURNEY, O. R., *The Hittites,* Baltimore, 1961.

HARDEN, D., *The Phoenicians,* New York, 1962.

LLOYD, S., *Early Anatolia,* New York, 1967.

MACALISTER, R., *The Philistines,* Chicago, 1911.

WRIGHT, G. E., *Archaeology and the Bible,* Philadelphia, 1962.

Later Oriental Empires:

Assyrians, Chaldeans, Persians

6

In the last millennium before the present era, successive large empires dominated the Near East. Persia, the last of these, was the largest. In human history the largest political units have been most successful in establishing peace, order, and prosperity. Ideally, then, it might be thought that up to the limits of effective exercise of control, the larger the empire the better. But as our study of the Greeks will show, certain other aspirations of the human soul are apparently best served when governmental units are small—even if their smallness results in wars, privation, and insecurity.

As conquerors, the Assyrians, Chaldeans, and Persians—and perhaps all others who ever attempted to govern an empire—found their most difficult task to be that of maintaining control over local government. The Assyrians tried stern coercion, deliberate and calculated terror. Leaders of revolts were impaled on stakes, skinned alive, or tortured in other indelicate ways, all of them publicized by the Assyrians. Assyrian kings supposed that such punishment would deter other would-be rebels. But what it reaped was a harvest of hate that became too great a burden. Finally, revolts in the subject monarchies revealed that Assyria was only a shell, that widespread loyal support no longer existed, not even in Assyria itself. When that occurred, the empire fell.

Chaldea in many ways followed the Assyrian imperial system. The Babylonians centralized authority and punished rebels repressively. But to little avail. The Chaldean Empire, too, though compact and blessed with good communications, crumbled with surprising ease.

The Persian Empire made notable political innovations. Satraps (governors) were put in charge of satrapies (provinces), replacing local

95

kings or potentates. In an enormous undertaking, roads were built or improved. A post system enabled royal messengers to move swiftly over long distances. Because the Persian Empire stretched more than 3,000 miles on an east-west axis, communications were vital. Perhaps more important, Persian rulers were religiously tolerant and economically liberal. Yet this empire also weakened and fell through decay from within followed by invasion from without. Perhaps it was simply too large, for it tottered to its end more from dead weight than from the blows of the relatively small army of Alexander the Great.

Modern archaeology has added significantly to our knowledge of these three empires, but in main outline their history was already known through the Bible and through Greek sources, especially Herodotus. Herodotus' *Persian Wars* weaves a fascinating tapestry of fiction and fact. His visits to Mesopotamia and to Egypt make sections on these nations vividly real.

A. The Assyrian Empire (c. 858–612 B.C.)

The Setting

Assyria's location on the upper Tigris River meant that it was intimately involved in everything Mesopotamian from culture to politics. Assyrians were Semites, closely related to the Babylonian Akkadians. The empire of Sargon of Akkad embraced Assyria around 2300 B.C. Somewhat later, kings of the Third Dynasty of Ur dominated the land. Shamshi-Adad (c. 1815–1782 B.C.), an Amorite like Hammurabi, seized control of Assyria and made it a leading kingdom, expanding its influence into the middle and upper Euphrates regions. After him, the Babylonian Hammurabi claimed control of the kingdom. Still later, the Hurrian rulers of the Kingdom of Mitanni dominated Assyria. When Suppiluliumas and the Hittites defeated Mitanni, Assyria, now free, once again rose to prominence. The cyclical pattern continued, however: the kingdom was strong in the 14th century, weak in the 13th, strong again in the 12th.

Early Expansion

Tiglath-Pileser I (c. 1115–1077 B.C.), an energetic and fierce conqueror, became the prototype of the typical Assyrian ruler. His own records testify that he devised deliberate and brutal terror as a fixed policy. But he also, like some of the later Assyrian kings, stood between civilization and chaos. He crushed a semibarbarous invasion from the northwest, and he extended his dominions as far west as Phoenicia, some of whose cities paid him tribute. But the empire then lost its strength, as did all of Mesopotamia, for reasons not well known.

Winged Lion: guardian of the palace Gate from the Palace of Ashur-nasir-apal II. *(The Metropolitan Museum of Art, Gift of John D. Rockefeller, Jr., 1932)*

In the 9th century, under Shalmaneser III (858–824 B.C.), Assyria once again waxed strong, driving west toward the Mediterranean and south to Babylon. As we saw in the sections on Hebrew history, Shalmaneser found himself checked by the alliance of Israel, Damascus, and Tyre. The check was temporary, however. He severely punished Damascus and soon brought Syria and Israel, too, under tribute.

Assyria's long, exhausting efforts to retain control of Babylon, then under Chaldean kings, was probably a mistake. Assyria's greatest military effort should have gone against its chief enemy in the north, Urartu, a kingdom centered about Lake Van. When Assyrian kings were preoccupied with the struggle against Babylon, the kings of Urartu bit off large chunks of Assyrian-dominated territory. For a time Assyria was able to maintain a valiant effort on all fronts. Under Tiglath-Pileser III (746–727 B.C.), Shalmaneser V (727–721 B.C.), and Sargon II (721–705 B.C.), Urartu was reduced in part, rebellious Babylon rewon, and troublesome Syria and Israel again subdued.

Imperial Heights

Assyria reached its height under Sennacherib (705–681 B.C.) and his son Esarhaddon (681–669 B.C.). Babylon again rebelled and was callously sacked, and Elam, east and south of ancient Sumer, made submission.

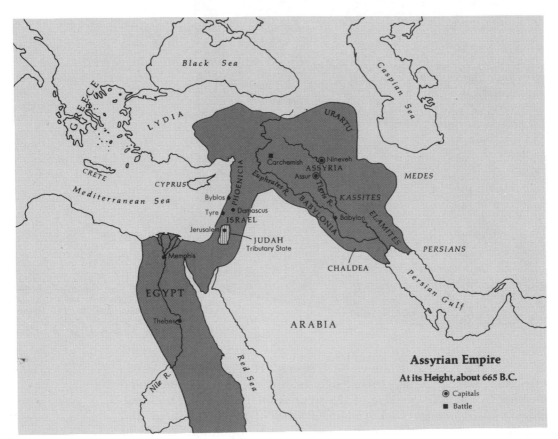

Adapted from Modell, A History of the Western World, volume one.

Esarhaddon briefly occupied Egypt after routing the army of its Ethiopian rulers. At that point the Assyrian Empire included all the Fertile Crescent plus Egypt, Elam, Media, and territories in Armenia and Asia Minor west to Cilicia.

When the son of Esarhaddon came to the throne, Assyria seemed almost invincible. This son, Assurbanipal (669–626 B.C.), proved competent and intelligent, but though he strove mightily, and usually with success, he could not hand down intact to his successors the empire he inherited. Egypt was the first loss: a vigorous new dynasty asserted Egyptian independence. A great and costly campaign barely kept Elam under control. Babylon continually raised rebellion and was practically independent at Assurbanipal's death.

Finally two vassal kings, Nabopolassar of Babylon and Cyaxares of Media headed up a conspiracy that besieged and destroyed Nineveh in 612 B.C., a date that marks the end of Assyria as a power. What remnants of it remained were obliterated despite Egyptian support in a battle at Carchemish on the upper Euphrates, in 605 B.C. by Nebuchadnezzar of Babylon.

B. Assyrian Culture

Relief Sculpture

In art, architecture, literature, religion, and law, Assyrian culture was part and parcel of that of the general Mesopotamian region. Yet somehow the Assyrian achievement is often distinctive, demonstrating a freshness and originality even if within accepted patterns. These striking qualities are best seen in art, more particularly in the relief sculpture, of which an astonishing amount remains. The Assyrian ideal, brutal and masculine, stands out in the portrayals of both men and animals. Disciplined ranks of soldiers courageously attack walled cities; hunted lions charge to certain death. The Assyrians were the Spartans of the Near East. They admired strength, toughness, discipline, endurance, and loyalty.

The sculpture portrays more than brutality, however. Something magnificent is symbolized in the dying lioness, hindquarters paralyzed by cruel arrows, that still faces her enemies and snarls defiance. This element of pathos comes through even more touchingly in the scene of the hunted wild ass that at the risk of her life drops out of the fleeing herd as she looks back anxiously toward her colt, which is unable to keep up. Yet the hard ruthlessness is nearly always there. In one relief Assurbanipal and his wife eat peacefully in a vineyard, but close by on a tree hangs the head of the Elamite king who tried to revolt.

The best relief sculptures were dug up at Nineveh, last of four capitals of Assyria (the others: Assur, Calah, Dur Sharrukin). Several of the later kings lavished their resources upon Nineveh, none more than

Assurbanipal. Many of the sculptures he commissioned are in the British Museum. It has been estimated that if the bas-reliefs from Nineveh were placed in a line they would stretch for nearly two miles. There were twenty-seven gates, all strongly fortified, guarded by massive composite creatures in stone. It was at Nineveh also that Assurbanipal collected his library, again demonstrating that Assyrians were more than hunters and warriors. We shudder when we see the sculptured panels showing men tied asprawl to four stakes, being flayed alive. Such savagery is the dark side of the Assyrian character. But it had virtues as well. The picture of Assyria as a parasitic kingdom living off crushed and cowed subjects is inaccurate and unfair. The Assyrians were probably no more brutal than most others in their time. Darius the Great of Persia, who has no particularly evil reputation, nevertheless once impaled 3,000 Babylonian leaders when he put down a revolt. But because the Assyrians publicized their brutality, their repute is low.

Religion

Assyrian religion was typically Semitic, much like that of the earlier Akkadians. The chief god was Assur, rather than Marduk as in Babylon. Ishtar was venerated in Assyria as throughout Mesopotamia. When Assurbanipal campaigned in Elam, he discovered a statute of Ishtar that had been carried away from the city of Uruk about 1,500 years earlier; piously, he restored it to the ancient Sumerian site. It was to Ishtar as well as to Assur that Assurbanipal prayed for vengeance upon the Greek ruler of Lydia, Gyges. Gyges had been in alliance with Assyria against the barbarous Cimmerians, but he had broken the treaty; when Gyges was killed in battle, the Assyrian king gave due thanks to his gods.

Architecture

In architecture, Assyrians introduced no outstanding new elements. Yet restorations of their walls. gates, and buildings are always impressive. Their use of stone must have given them a feeling of permanence that was lacking in areas where the building material was chiefly mud brick. This readily available limestone made possible the reliefs that adorned buildings and walls. The massive, human-headed winged lion and bull-god sculptures that stood sentinel at the gates of Assyrian cities must have helped any onlooker to feel, not merely to be aware of, the might that was Assyria.

Assyrians were excellent administrators who kept careful records and modern historians are among the beneficiaries. Surviving annals give a clear though one-sided picture of military campaigns and territorial acquisitions. The basis for Near Eastern chronology through several centuries derives from Assyrian *limmu* lists of important leaders, including the kings in their first regnal year. In recent years, for example, Hammurabi has been more accurately dated through a collation of Assyrian and other records.

Assyria's Lasting Reputation for Violence

The world will probably continue to view Assyria through eyes like those of the Hebrew prophet Nahum, who called Nineveh that "bloody city." He—understandably enough—exulted at the news of its destruction.

> *Nineveh is laid waste*
> *Who shall bemoan thee?*

Byron vividly echoes the same attitude. His lines,

> *The Assyrian came down like a wolf on the fold,*
> *And his cohorts were gleaming in purple and gold,*

describe Sennacherib's descent on Jerusalem. No imperial power in any age can expect to be loved by its victims. Even so, quite aside from ideals, can small nationalities ever be free? If the Assyrians had not dominated

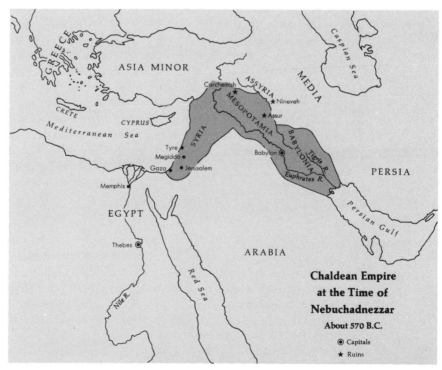

Adapted from *Modell,* A History of the Western World, *volume one.*

Judah it might have been the more barbarous Cimmerians. Moreover, the destruction of Nineveh did not mean freedom for Judah. Kings like Assurbanipal deserve to be remembered for more than their military exploits. And Nineveh was much more than a "bloody city."

C. Chaldea or Neo-Babylonia (626–539 B.C.)

The Magnificent City

Chaldean Babylonia calls to mind, usually, either Nebuchadnezzar's armies carrying away captive Jews of ravaged Jerusalem or the grand city, Babylon, described by a bedazzled Herodotus, sprawling in magnificence alongside the Euphrates. The Greek historian exaggerated a bit the extent of the city. When her chief excavator, Robert Koldewey, led a German expedition at the site several years before World War I, he found nothing quite so extensive as the fifteen-mile-square city that the ancient traveler described. What does remain is impressive enough. The Ishtar Gate, decorated with griffins and other figures in brightly colored glazed tiles, is truly remarkable—sufficiently remarkable, for Koldewey to carry it off to Berlin, where it stands, reconstructed, in a special huge room of the Berlin Museum.

Nabopolassar (625–605 B.C.), as we have seen, aided in the siege of Nineveh. He lived long enough to learn that his son and successor, Nebuchadnezzar (605–562 B.C.), had crushed the last remnants of Assyrian power at Carchemish. All the Syria-Palestine region was swiftly brought under Babylonian control; even the island fort-city Tyre gave submission. Babylon maintained its alliance with Media, and Nebuchadnezzar married a Median princess. Babylon was rich. The best agricultural land and the most important trade routes of the Fertile Crescent lay in her dominions. Certain Babylonian industries, principally textiles and metals, flourished. Nebuchadnezzar could and did play the role of the grand monarch.

Nabonidus: Last Great King of Babylon

The last king of the Chaldean Empire was Nabonidus (555–539 B.C.). For some reason it seems he encouraged Cyrus, King of Persia, to rebel against the dominant Medes—a ploy that proved to be a mistake. Persia soon grew stronger than Media and turned on Babylon. When Cyrus' armies appeared before Babylon in 539 B.C., the great city fell without a fight. Perhaps most Babylonians preferred Cyrus over Nabonidus as their king.

Possibly the Jews in Babylon were also pro-Persian. The author

Detail of the Ishtar Gate at Babylon, Nebuchadnezzar's day (restored). *(Staatsbibliothek preussischer Kulturbesirz, Berlin)*

of the late chapters of Isaiah names Cyrus as chosen by God. One of Cyrus' first acts was to pass an edict to permit Jews to return to their homeland. Without question, the Jews hated the Chaldeans, as the anti-Babylonian emotion displayed in the Book of Daniel testifies (though as we now have it the book is of later date). Belshazzar, crown prince of Babylonia, arrogantly and impiously made sacrilegious use of the vessels from the Temple even as the enemy surrounded the seemingly impregnable city. Then appeared the handwriting on the wall, which, interpreted by Daniel, prophesied impending doom. Jews remembered the holocaust at Jerusalem and the bitterness of captivity. As *Psalm* 137 sets forth their feeling so vividly:

> *O daughter of Babylon, you devastator . . .*
> *Happy shall he be, who takes your little ones*
> *And dashes them against the rock.*

The Babylonians' disaffection with Nabonidus seems to have been connected with his religious policy. The king apparently tried to make Sin, the moon god, the chief god of the empire, displacing Marduk, patron deity of Babylon. Nabonidus' mother was high priestess of Sin at Haran on the upper Euphrates, and the king made his daughter chief priestess to the same god at Ur and at the same time spent a huge sum restoring Ur's ziggurat and temple. He also announced plans to rebuild the temple at Haran on a magnificent scale, though he was never able to effect them because of opposition in Babylon. Nabonidus, moved by some deep conviction, not only attended to Sin; he neglected Marduk. Our evidence includes complaints against him in Babylon that for years he had failed to conduct the new years' celebrations to Marduk.

Nabonidus' motivation and intent cannot be known. He may have felt that the empire was too Babylon-centered, that Marduk was not a universal enough deity to serve as chief god for the whole empire. Sin, on the other hand—or at least a god identified with the moon—was worshiped everywhere. Curiously, Nabonidus withdrew from Babylon and for ten years lived in the Arabian desert, leaving his son Belshazzar to act for him. But Nabonidus was not, as he is sometimes pictured, in scholarly retirement or semimonastic retreat. He was planting colonies in Arabia along important trade routes. The Persian threat in 539 B.C. brought him back to Babylon, but he was unable to rally the people. It is even speculated that he himself opened the gates of the city to Cyrus. However it happened, Cyrus was welcomed as a liberator by the Babylonian citizens. Cyrus took care to be properly installed as King of Babylonia by Marduk, and he meticulously and promptly celebrated the new year's festivals.

The Art and Architecture of Nebuchadnezzar's Babylon

Nebuchadnezzar embellished Babylon and made it a showplace of the age. He built the Hanging Gardens, one of the Seven Wonders of the ancient world, it was said, to please his Median wife; languishing in the flat, hot Babylonian plain, she was unhappy away from her homeland of hills and mountains. Basically the gardens were an artificial plateau irrigated on top by a continuous chain-type pump. The structure, part of a large palace, was faced with stone, a rarity in Babylon, rich as the city was. Probably the gardens were said to be "hanging" because at a distance from the city the greenery on top seemed to float in the air, unsupported. Important too was the ziggurat, with its temple of Marduk, lofty enough even centuries earlier to give rise to the story of the Tower of Babel. The citadel, also faced with stone, loomed above one corner of the city. The Ishtar Gate opened to a Triumphal Way leading to the precincts of Marduk; the gate and the walls flanking the avenue were decorated with colorful griffins and other creatures on a blue background, all in enameled brick. The city walls, more massive than those at Nineveh, were girdled with a moat filled with water from the connecting Euphrates River. The river even ran under a portion of the wall. One story of the city's fall had Cyrus divert the entire river into an irrigation reservoir so that his army could march under the wall. With the fall of the city in 539 B.C., the empire collapsed—swallowed up in the huge and ever-expanding Persian Empire.

D. Empire of the Medes and Persians (612–330 B.C.)

The Rise of Media

Most people today remember the Medes and the Persians from either the visions of the Four Empires in the Book of Daniel or, more likely, from the Greek accounts of the great battles with the Persian invaders at Marathon, Salamis, and Plataea. The wars with Greece were important enough to the Medes and Persians, but hardly so crucial as they were to the Greeks. From the viewpoint of the Persians, most of our textbooks have overemphasized these wars. Yet for Western civilization the conflicts acquire great significance because the Greeks themselves became the intellectual leaders of the civilized world. The Greco-Persian collision is often described in detail for another quite simple reason: we know more about this portion of Persian history because the Greek historians wrote about it. In this chapter we shall attempt a balanced sketch. Persia's wars with the Greeks will be given greater emphasis in the section on Greek history.

The Medes and the Persians lived in a plateau region ringed by mountains, the Medes south of the Caspian Sea, the Persians farther south, east of Elam. The Elburz Mountains just below the Caspian rise as high as 18,000 feet; to the west, overlooking the Mesopotamian plain, is the considerably lower Zagros range. Most of the land of the Medes and Persians was (and is) semi-arid—suitable more for pasture than for agriculture, though in some areas enough water was found to irrigate crops. The Medes raised the best horses in the Near East; everywhere flocks and herds were their standards of wealth. As might be expected of a people made up mostly of nomads, the clan or tribe was the chief social and political unit in an early period. Both Medes and Persians spoke an Indo-European language. Though the areas they dominated were racially mixed, their ruling class seems to have been Aryan, related to the invaders who destroyed the Indus River civilization around 1500 B.C., and to the Hittites and some Mitannians.

E. Political History of the Medes and Persians

Rise of Media

Media was probably unified as a kingdom under the impact of both barbarian invasions and Assyrian raids. The Assyrians valued the horses of the Medes, and after the middle 8th century B.C. they dominated much of the region and established a kind of typical vassal kingdom. The Median monarchs in their turn gained ascendancy over the Persians to the south—who were also ruled by a king but now vassal to the Median rulers. Both Medes and Persians were thus loosely subject to Assyria.

Cyaxares (c. 633–585 B.C.) transformed Media into a real power. As we have seen, he joined with Nabopolassar of Babylon to destroy Assyria in 612 B.C. While Babylon consolidated her hold on the Fertile Crescent, Cyaxares seized the former Assyrian dominions to the east of the upper Tigris and to the north from Lake Van westward into Anatolia. He also controlled some new territory to the east of Media, but how much is uncertain. Median expansion into Anatolia brought war with the King of Lydia, who also was attempting to take advantage of the Assyrian demise. A celebrated eclipse of the sun in 585 B.C.—later claimed to have been predicted by Thales, a Milesian Greek—caused the opposing armies to halt at this sign of displeasure from the gods and a peace was negotiated that set the common boundary between Lydia and Media on the western sweep of the Halys River.

Media Subordinated; The Persian Empire and Cyrus

In 550 B.C. Astyages (585–550 B.C.), the son of Cyaxares and a comparatively weak ruler, was deposed by the Persian king, Cyrus the Great. Cyrus was King of Persia from 559 B.C. and of the whole empire from 550 to 529 B.C. The Medo-Persian Empire thus suddenly became the Persian Empire. This dynasty of Persian kings is termed Achaemenid because it was founded—several generations earlier—by a king called Achaemenes.

We have little beyond unreliable Greek sources to explain why

Cyrus turned on Astyages. The Persian is presented as the noble hero, Astyages as the cruel scoundrel. But ambition is as likely an explanation as any. Though Cyrus used force to assert his hegemony over the whole empire, no major war apparently took place between Persians and Medes; the army of Astyages, it seems, simply deserted to the Persian.

Greek historians, especially Xenophon in his *Cyropaedia (Education of Cyrus)* presented Cyrus as the enlightened paragon. What we know from his deeds confirms a degree of tolerance and enlightenment, but mostly he was a warrior. His first acquisition was the Kingdom of Lydia. Its king was the legendary Croesus. Reportedly encouraged by the Delphic Oracle in Greece, he tried to expand east across the Halys River on hearing of the disorder within Medo-Persia. But Cyrus moved west with his army, defeated Croesus, who soon died or was killed, and then took over all of western Asia Minor (548–546 B.C.). Many Greeks in this region thus became Persian subjects. In subsequent years Cyrus conquered huge chunks of territory in Iran eastward to the edge of the Indus valley. And, as we have seen, at last he took over Babylon and the Fertile Crescent in 539. Cyrus was killed while campaigning northward in an effort to add Armenia to the empire.

Cambyses

Cambyses, son of Cyrus (529–522 B.C.), wished to perpetuate the image of the king as conqueror. He therefore invaded and annexed Egypt, and received as well the submission of Cyrene on the Mediterranean west of Egypt. Herodotus gives Cambyses an especially bad image, portraying him as cruel, alcoholic, and disrespectful of the Egyptian gods. In some details this picture is demonstrably false, though there may have been defects in his character. The king died or was killed while hastening home to put down a revolt.

As our sources have it, the revolt was the work of a Magian priest, Gaumata, who claimed to the Bardiya (or Smerdis), the brother of Cambyses. Cambyses, however, had already killed Bardiya. Several noblemen eligible for the throne, including Darius, joined together to defeat the false Bardiya. Herodotus tells a delightful and no doubt fanciful story of what followed. The noblemen agreed to ride their horses to a certain field at dawn and that man would be king whose horse neighed first. The cunning groom of Darius took the nobleman's stallion to the field the preceding night and introduced him to a willing mare. When the horse therefore arrived at the field the next morning his romantic memories caused him to neigh wildly. Whereupon Darius was acclaimed king. One learns more about Herodotus than about Persian history from this tale.

We have Darius' own account of the revolt and his accession, on the famous cuneiform Behistun inscription mentioned in Chapter 2.

Darius claimed that Gaumata seized the throne in the absence of Cambyses, that the latter died naturally, and that he alone, with the aid of the god Ahura Mazda and a few other Persians, was able to slay the false Bardiya and keep the kingship in the family. (Darius was from a parallel branch of the Achaemenid family.) There are skeptics who suspect that the Bardiya Darius killed was the real son of Cyrus.

Darius the Great

Darius (521–486 B.C.) felt that he, too, must be the warrior-king. He therefore expanded into the Indus region on the east and into Europe on the west. His armies crossed the Bosporus by a bridge of ships in 513 B.C. Much of Thrace and Macedonia, with their valuable gold and silver mines, was annexed. A move to subdue the Scythians north of the Danube nearly resulted in disaster, but overall Darius could report a highly successful campaign.

Darius the Great's imbroglio with the Greeks began in 499 B.C. with a revolt of the Ionians—Greek inhabitants of the western shore of Asia Minor. Causes for the revolt surely related to social, political, and

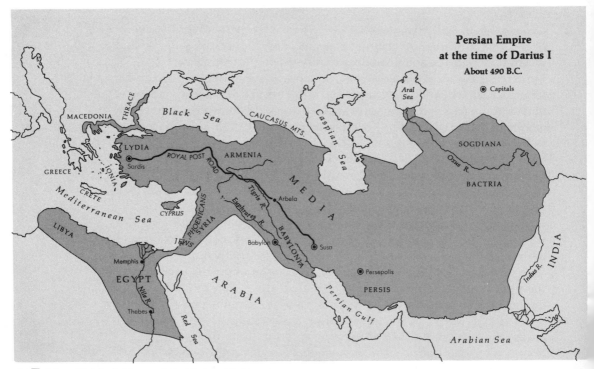

Adapted from Modell, A History of the Western World, volume one.

economic changes then affecting all the Greek cities. Some support came to the Ionians from the Greek mainland; Athenians helped the Milesians to burn Sardis, for example, the Persian administrative center in Asia Minor. As a consequence, Darius decided to punish the mainland Greeks, Athens in particular. His first expedition, moving along the north Aegean by land and sea, was aborted because of the terrible storms that battered his supply fleet. The second expedition, in 490 B.C., came to grief at Marathon. The Persians captured several islands that had been trouble spots, however, so for Darius the Greek campaign was no ignominious failure. Still, the setback called for future action—which Darius never lived to undertake.

Administrative Organization

Darius gave much attention to administration and it was he who set up the provinces called satrapies, governed by appointed satraps. Civil authority was in their hands, but not military; the military districts did not correspond to the boundaries of the satrapies. Darius was a cautious, suspicious man! In his time, also, communications were vastly improved. The most famous route was the Royal Road that led 1,500 miles from Sardis in Asia Minor to Susa the capital. He set up posts along all the major roads at intervals of a day's journey, thereby making feasible a rapid relay of messages or the swift movement of imperial officials. Because the empire was about the size of the 48 continental United States, only such measures made it possible to hold it together. The Greek historians wrote about imperial spies, the "eyes and ears of the king." They seem, however, to have misunderstood terms that applied to two government departments, though Darius did, of course, take pains to keep himself well informed.

A new capital, Persepolis, located east of the old one and at a higher elevation, was also the work of Darius. Susa was too hot during much of the year. Ecbatana, the old Median capital north toward the Caspian Sea was also an administrative center, but Darius wanted something new and grand. The remains show both Assyrian and Greek influence though there are distinctive features. Curiously, not many foreigners visited the site. Before Alexander no Greek to our knowledge had seen Persepolis. Yet it had the main treasury and it was surely too extensive to have been only a residential palace.

Xerxes and the Later Kings

Xerxes (485–465 B.C.) first occupied himself with putting down a revolt in Egypt that had broken out before Darius' death. After that success he was ready for vengeance upon the Greeks for their defiance of his father.

The great invasion of 480 B.C. probably mustered the largest land army yet assembled by any king, though the Greeks' estimates running into the millions were wildly exaggerated. The defeats of 480 and 479 in Greece and even more, the later defeats on the Asia Minor littoral at the hands of Greek amphibious forces were serious. Indeed, the Asia Minor littoral became for the Persians a kind of running sore. Babylon also revolted against Xerxes but was successfully reduced. Unfortunately, Xerxes compounded his problems by deciding that his predecessors had been too considerate of local mores. His efforts to change that made the Persian kings far less acceptable in a number of quarters.

Among the later kings to the end of the empire were Artaxerxes I (465–424 B.C.), whose chief worry was another revolt in Egypt, abetted by Athens; Artaxerxes II (404–359 B.C.), who was nearly deposed by his brother Cyrus, with the help of more than 10,000 Greeks; and Darius III (336–330 B.C.), defeated and displaced by Alexander the Great. Darius III was in some ways the most pitiable of all. In fact, the quality of kingship from Darius the Great onward seems to have deteriorated with each accession. Major causes for decline, besides bureaucratic dead weight, incompetence, and the normal difficulties of holding together so disparate and widespread a mass of people as those living in imperial Persia, seem to have been mostly economic. Too much was spent on palaces and harems. Above all, too great a percentage of the precious metal taken in taxes was simply melted into bullion and stored in the king's treasure houses. The consequent shortage of hard currency had a depressing effect.

F. Persian Religion and Culture

In terms of their later impact, two Persian contributions to civilization were primary. The first was the idea of One World, of the unification of all "civilized" people; the second was Zoroastrianism. The Greeks caught the vision of One World but did not successfully implement it. The idea was again dominant in the days of Rome; the poet Vergil, for example, expressed it eloquently. It may also be seen in the works of the Christian apostle Paul. In the medieval age it was the spirit of the so-called Holy Roman Empire. And in the early modern period it remained a potent concept, influencing the actions of many a king.

Zoroastrianism

The Zoroastrian religion was immensely influential, also. Zoroaster (Persian Zarathustra) himself remains a shadowy figure. Many scholars have decided to accept the first half of the 6th century B.C. as the time in

The ruins of the entrance to the Palace of Darius.
(Iran Information and Tourism Center)

which he flourished, but there is some evidence that would place him earlier. The chief source of information about this Persian religion is the sacred book of the later Zoroastrians, the *Zend Avesta*. A proper understanding of it, however, requires at least as great a scholarly effort as has been put into the study of the Hebrew Bible. The language itself is not well understood, many words are obscure in meaning, and even the order of the book is a matter of dispute.

111

The Sacred Books

The *Zend Avesta* was written down only in the Sassanian period, in the 3rd century A.D. The earliest part is the *Yasna,* in which are found seventeen *Gathas* or hymns. These are usually thought to be the writings of Zoroaster himself. Unless interpreted allegorically, they imply a certain naiveté and a rather rural life for the prophet. The work indicates that the prophet endured a period of persecution, but was finally given protection by a ruler named Vishtaspa.

In many ways Zoroaster's role in Persia is analogous to that of the reforming prophets in Palestine. Like them he preached social justice and taught theology. Like them he claimed inspiration from his god, Ahura Mazda. Zoroaster spoke of a cosmic dualism, of a struggle between the forces of good, centered in Ahura Mazda, and those of evil, headed by Ahriman. Ahura Mazda was god of light, order, righteousness, and truth. Ahriman stood for darkness, chaos, injustice, and the lie. So great is the focus on Ahura Mazda, however, that some see Zoroaster as virtually a monotheist, though the developed religion in Achaemenid times remained basically polytheistic. In a later time, Ahura Mazda was no more than chief of the gods of light. The later religion also acquired priests: the Magi, who took over the religion. In Zoroaster's lifetime, they probably opposed his views.

Man in the Cosmos

Man's role in the cosmic struggle assumed great significance. Each person was to choose sides in the struggle; naturally the prophet taught that one should fight on the side of Ahura Mazda.

> *Contemplate with clear mind the two ways*
> *Between which every man must choose for himself; . . .*
> *Now in the beginning the two spirits which are as it were twins*
> *Are the one good, the other evil,*
> *In thought, word, and deed. And between these two*
> *The wise make a good choice, but not the foolish.*[1]

Zoroaster and his followers wove strands of existing religious beliefs into a new theological fabric, but many of the old elements remained. Worship of fire and earth and of certain of the older gods continued. Mithra, for example, son of the sun, became a chief helper of Ahura Mazda. Still later he was the focus of a related but separate religion, Mithraism. Zoroaster seems to have taught of a final judgment, the "bridge of separation," and spoke of saviors—who may only have

[1] *Yasna* 30; from A. C. Bouquet, *Sacred Books of the World* (Baltimore: Penguin Books, 1954), p. 117.

been right-thinking rulers. His later followers, however, came up with a more precise set of eschatological beliefs based on millennia. The world was to last 12,000 years arranged in quarters of 3,000 years each. The first period was a golden age. The second saw the outbreak of warfare between the dual gods. At the beginning of the third came Zoroaster, to help tilt the balance in favor of the Good. The last was to be a new golden age.

Zoroaster influenced not only Persians and other orientals, but also Hebrews and Christians, among others. One of Plato's pupils refers to him, and it is possible that the great philosopher himself received some of his celebrated ideas from the prophet's view of the nature of man.

This example of the influence of an eastern religious leader upon the greatest mind of the Greeks serves to reemphasize the extensive and continuing impact of the ideas and ways of ancient Near Eastern civilization upon Western civilization.

Books for Further Reading

BRIGHT, J., *A History of Israel,* Philadelphia, 1959.

CONTENAU, G. *Everyday Life in Babylon and Assyria,* New York, 1966.

CULICAN, W., *The Medes and the Persians,* New York, 1965.

FINEGAN, J., *Light from the Ancient Past,* Princeton, 1959.

FRYE, R., *The Heritage of Persia,* Cleveland, 1963.

LLOYD, S., *Foundations in the Dust,* Baltimore, 1955.

MOSCATI, S., *Ancient Semitic Civilizations,* New York, 1957.

OLMSTEAD, A., *History of the Persian Empire,* Chicago, 1948.

SAGGS, H., *The Greatness That Was Babylon,* New York, 1962.

CHART 3 The Mycenaean and Hellenic Periods

PERIOD	THE MYCENAEAN AGE (LATE HELLADIC PHASE OF AEGEAN CIVILIZATION)
c. 1600– Late Bronze Age 1100 B.C.	Flourishing period for Mycenae, Tiryns, Pylos, other royal cities both on the mainland and the islands. Eruption of volcano on Santorini (Thera); decline in nearby cities including those on Crete. Over a period of time, destruction of Mycenae, other Aegean cities.

EARLY IRON OR "DARK" AGE

c. 1100– 800 B.C. 800– Period of Renascence 600 B.C.	Petty kingdoms, agricultural states, dominated by aristocrats;tribal organization; the military dominated by the cavalry. Many Greeks migrate to the west coast of Asia Minor. Extensive colonization to the North Aegean, Black Sea regions, and to North Africa, South Italy, Sicily, South France, East Spain; competition with Phoenicians in the western Mediterranean. Development of trade, rise of trading and artisan classes. Rise of the polis. Development of the heavy infantry phalanx. Sparta a relatively advanced state; Messenian wars; gradual transformation into a militarized society. First tyrants; Gyges in Lydia, Cypselus and Periander in Corinth.

	ATHENS	SPARTA	OTHER
600 B.C.	Cylon attempts tyranny. Draco's law code. Solon's reforms. Peisistratus. Cleisthenes.	Military aristocracy. Further expansion in Peloponnese.	Corinth, other Greek cities also strong trading centers. Thales, Pythagoras.
500 B.C.	Persians defeated at Marathon. Persians defeated at Salamis. Athenian leadership of Greeks; Delian League founded. Period of Pericles' leadership. Sophocles, Euripides, Herodotus. Building of Parthenon. Anaxagoras, the Sophists.	Formation of Peloponnesian League. Leader of alliance against Persia; defeat Persians at Plataea. Period of Spartan isolation.	Ionian revolt against Persia. Persian invasions of Greece. Heracleitus, Parmenides. Many Greek states join Persians, others in Greek alliance.
		PELOPONNESIAN WAR (431–404 B.C.)	
400 B.C.	Aristophanes, Thucydides. Defeat, end of empire, 30 tyrants. Restored democracy; death of Socrates. New Confederacy. Plato, the Academy. Rebellion; end of second federation. Isocrates. Demosthenes' speeches against Philip of Macedonia. Aristotle, Lyceum. Athens defeated with Thebes at Chaeronea; left a free state.	Period of dominance of Greece. Defeats by Thebans: Leuctra, Mantinea.	Corinth, other Spartan allies disaffected; Persia supports alliance against Sparta. King's Peace. Ionian Greeks under Persia. Period of Theban dominance of Greece. Epaminondas. Rise of Macedonia under Philip II. Intervention in Sacred War. Macedonian victory at Chaeronea. Corinthian League the means of Macedonian dominance; garrisons in Corinth, Thebes.

Greece:
The Hellenic
and Hellenistic Periods

The ancient Greeks were history's most brilliant people. In an astonishingly short span of time they scaled the heights in many fields of human knowledge and endeavor. In philosophy, literature, drama, poetry, history, art, architecture, sculpture, and science, human annals can show no equal of their accomplishment. They made notable advances also in the military arts and in government, where they were great innovators.

Yet the Greeks also turned their genius to fruitless, even destructive endeavor. Their soldiers were so good that for centuries they constituted the core of any army in the whole eastern Mediterranean, as well as of many in the west. But because they were fiercely independent in their small city-states, they fought each other endlessly. Though at one crucial time they drew together and were able to defend themselves against mighty Persia, they could not defend themselves against their own natures.

The Greeks theorized brilliantly on government, experimented with direct democracy and even with representative systems and federal alliances, but in the end they were unable to achieve lasting political union. So, they fell piecemeal to Macedonia and finally to Rome. Still, as a conquered people they continued to show their genius in literature, the arts, and even government. Several of Rome's successful governmental systems—in commercial law, for example—were indebted to Greek developments. Many Greeks served in the highest offices in the heyday of the Roman Empire. Moreover, the predominantly Greek eastern half of the Roman Empire survived when the West fell. Known as the Byzantine Empire, it endured a thousand years after Rome and the western provinces fell to the Goths, the Franks, and the Vandals.

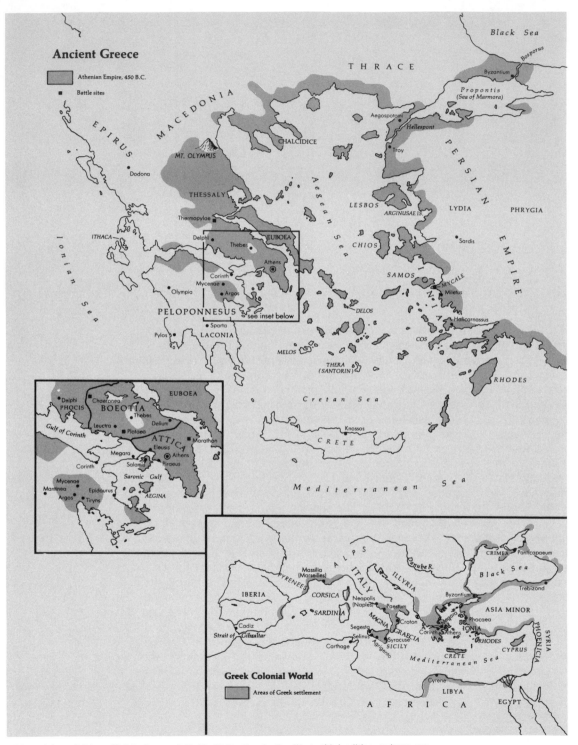

Ancient Greece

Athenian Empire, 450 B.C.

■ Battle sites

Black Sea

THRACE

Propontis (Sea of Marmora)

Byzantium

Bosporus

MACEDONIA

CHALCIDICE

Aegospotami

Hellespont

Troy

PERSIAN

EPIRUS

MT. OLYMPUS

Dodona

THESSALY

LESBOS

ARGINUSAE IS.

LYDIA

PHRYGIA

Thermopylae

Aegean Sea

Sardis

Delphi

Thebes

EUBOEA

Athens

CHIOS

EMPIRE

ITHACA

Corinth

Mycenae

Argos

SAMOS

MYCALE

Miletus

Olympia

I O N I A

see inset below

PELOPONNESUS

DELOS

Halicarnassus

Sparta

Pylos

LACONIA

COS

MELOS

RHODES

THERA (SANTORIN)

Cretan Sea

Knossos

CRETE

Mediterranean Sea

Inset (lower left):

Delphi

PHOCIS

Chaeronea

BOEOTIA

Thebes

EUBOEA

Gulf of Corinth

Leuctra

Plataea

Delium

ATTICA

Marathon

Megara

Eleusis

Athens

Corinth

Salamis

Piraeus

Mycenae

Saronic Gulf

Mantinea

Epidaurus

AEGINA

Argos

Tiryns

Inset (lower right):

Greek Colonial World

Areas of Greek settlement

ALPS

Danube R.

CRIMEA

Panticapaeum

Massilia (Marseilles)

PYRENEES

ITALY

ILLYRIA

Black Sea

IBERIA

CORSICA

Neapolis (Naples)

Trebizond

SARDINIA

Paestum

Byzantium

ASIA MINOR

Cadiz

MAGNA

Croton

Phocaea

IONIA

Strait of Gibraltar

Segesta

GRAECIA

Corinth Athens

RHODES

PHOENICIA

SYRIA

Selinus

Syracuse

SICILY

CRETE

CYPRUS

Carthage

Agrigento

Mediterranean Sea

Cyrene

A F R I C A

LIBYA

EGYPT

Adapted from Brinton, Christopher, and Wolff, Civilization in the West, *third edition, volume one.*

The Earliest History of Ancient Greece

Between the Greece of Herodotus and Thucydides and the earlier Aegean civilization there lay a cataclysmic break, bridged only by folk memory and, in a few places, by the eloquent testimony of massive ruins. The break was in many ways complete. A new system of writing and other new cultural equipage had to be developed. In a direct way the Greece of Pericles seems to owe little to Greece before Homer; yet it is clear that the influence of the past was pervasive, even if it was almost subliminal and expressed in myth rather than in history. We must therefore scrutinize more closely these early antecedents of classical Greece.

Only in the last century have we learned much about the Aegean civilization that flourished in the mid-2nd millennium B.C. The story of that civilization and of the discoveries of Heinrich Schliemann has been told in Chapter 4. In this chapter we shall consider only the Greek phase of Aegean culture, termed Mycenaean—from Mycenae, the first principal site excavated in this area (also by Schliemann) after 1876. The stream of relevant archaeological information continues to come in, from a multitude of other digs. One of the more significant excavations has been that of Carl Blegen at Pylos, in the southwestern Peloponnese. There he found the remains of a palace, with archives written in a script (Minoan Script B) found earlier by Sir Arthur Evans on Crete. Deciphering of the script by Michael Ventris and others, as already mentioned, showed the language itself was Greek. Thus we know that the Mycenaeans, or at least the dominant class in Mycenaean times, were Greeks. The Mycenaean age, then (which is the last phase of Aegean civilization on the Greek mainland), is of more than incidental interest in the story of the rise of Greece to greatness. But we must first consider the physical setting.

A. Geography of Greece

General: Topography and Its Influence

The two peoples most influential in charting the course for Western civilization, the Jews and the Greeks, came from tiny lands. The entire area dominated by Greeks during the period of their highest achievements, including the islands and the coastland of Asia Minor but excluding overseas colonies founded after 800 B.C., would equal no more than the land area of one of the moderate-to-small U.S. states.

The Greeks live intimately with both the mountains and the sea. The valleys, though relatively small, are quite fertile; when well watered, their deep soil is very productive. But most of the land is mountainous, and probably no more than 10 percent is easily cultivable; another similar segment can be terraced for cultivation or used for pasturage. The rest included, in an early period, some forested uplands that later became bare and eroded.

The mountains reach a height of almost 10,000 feet at Mount Olympus in Thessaly and more than 8,000 feet for Mount Parnassus at Delphi. Generally they are disposed in ranges running northwest to southeast. South of the great rift forming the Gulf of Corinth they form a backbone for the Peloponnese. From there, to the east and south, they sink into the Aegean, where their peaks form the Cyclades Islands. Beyond the Cyclades are the Sporades—Rhodes is the largest of this group—so that in calm summer weather the island-strewn sea provides easy access to the mainland of Asia Minor.

Curiously, therefore, geography tended to isolate the Greeks, on the one hand, and to force them out into the sea and so to far places, on the other. The system of rugged mountains and interior valleys cut up their land into compartments suitable for the development of small states, jealous of their independence. But proximity to the sea, good harbors, and the island stepping-stones led to intercourse with the outside world. These diverse tendencies affected the growth of Greek civilization in diverse ways.

Specific: The Compartmented Regions

Now a look at the major land areas of Greece. South of the Gulf of Corinth lies the Peloponnese; connected with the rest of Greece only by the isthmus in the northeast, this large landmass is almost an island. The narrow entrance into the Peloponnese was controlled by the city of Corinth with its lofty citadel, the Acrocorinth. To the south lay Argos, the chief city of the Argolid, with its fruitful plain controlled in Mycenaean times by Tiryns and Mycenae. In the southeast Peloponnese was

Laconia, the territory of ancient Sparta. This city, on the river Eurotas, sprawled below the snowcapped peaks of the Taygetus range. In the southwest Peloponnese was Messenia, with a rich plain coveted by the Spartans. Pylos in the extreme southwest was important only during the Mycenaean age. In the northwest, Olympia, in the rather rugged territory called Elis, was known for its Olympic games and its Temple of Zeus. Achaea along the gulf on the north and Arcadia in the center complete the geography of the Peloponnesian peninsula. Both these areas are composed predominantly of hills and mountains, with small valleys.

Traversing the isthmus to the north, one first entered the territory of Megara, which controlled the northern exit from the isthmus and the Peloponnese. Around the Saronic Gulf to the east lay Attica, a not-too-well-watered plain surrounded on the landward sides by mountains. Eleusis, home of the mysteries of Demeter, and Athens occupied prime sites. Nearby, in the bay, lay the island of Salamis, and farther out in the Saronic Gulf was Aegina. Northwest of Athens, across Mount Cithaeron, Thebes with its productive plain was the chief city of Boeotia. Just off the coast to the northeast was the large island of Euboea. To the west a road led through the territory of Phocis to the oracle of Apollo at Delphi, magnificently situated on the flank of Mount Parnassus, slightly inland from the Gulf of Corinth. Farther west, extending to the Ionian Sea, lay Aetolia. Northward along the west coast was Epirus, where an oracle of Zeus was located at Dodona. The Ionian Islands opposite Aetolia and Epirus included Ithaca, reputed home of Odysseus, and Corcyra (modern Corfu). Except for Thebes, these are all rugged areas as well.

North of Delphi is Thessaly, but the road led northwest from Thebes, around Mount Parnassus and through the narrow coastal pass at Thermopylae. Thessaly had the largest plains in Greece, which produced the greatest quantity of cereal grains. Horse breeding was important here, too. Farther north toward Macedonia the road passed through the beautiful Vale of Tempe, just beyond storied Mount Olympus. The three fingers of the Chalcidice probe out into the north Aegean just beyond Thessalonica. Farther east lay Thrace and the straits separating Europe from Asia Minor. Along the tongue of land called the Chersonese (modern Gallipoli Peninsula), the straits were called by Greeks the Hellespont; the channel leading into the Black Sea was the Bosporus. After the Greeks settled the coast of western Asia Minor (1000 B.C. and after), the areas along the eastern Aegean littoral were named after the local dialects: Aeolis, east of the important island of Lesbos; Ionia farther south, with the islands of Chios and Samos offshore; and Caria in the southwest. The island of Rhodes is just south of here.

Greece, then, was small but tremendously varied. Greeks lived in compartmented districts, yet were thrown inevitably into common endeavors because of similar problems and the proximity of the sea. They found themselves challenged, but not overwhelmed, by a sometimes tough environment. Geography did not in any primary way determine the course of Greek history, but its role was nonetheless great.

B. The Mycenaeans

Mycenae: Aegean Civilization on the Mainland

The earliest infusion into the Aegean area of an Indo-European, Greek-speaking people occurred late in the 3rd millennium B.C. or early in the 2nd. These newcomers were called Achaeans. Widespread destruction marked their coming, as the archaeological sites show. During the next several centuries these Greeks, who became the Mycenaeans of history, learned from the conquered peoples even as they extended the area they dominated. By 1600 B.C. their wealth and culture rivaled that of the Minoans on Crete.

An ancient tradition regarding fabled Mycenae, "rich in gold," was essentially substantiated by modern excavators, beginning with Schliemann in 1876. The National Museum in Athens prominently displays the gold masks, cups, jewelry, and other objects he found in a circle of shaft-graves within the ancient city walls. Schliemann at first thought he had found the grave of Agamemnon; but we know now that the objects date from about 1500 B.C., or three centuries before the time of that Homeric hero. Subsequent excavators found, among other things, a second grave circle outside the walls, also rich in content and belonging to a period about a century earlier. Since no more impressive finds have been made elsewhere of this mainland-centered civilization, it is not inappropriate that Mycenae has given its name to this period. The Mycenaean age, then, is the late Helladic phase of Aegean culture in the area of Greece proper. Mycenae did not, however, rule the entire area; apparently a number of kingdoms existed there. Mycenaean power was minor in a world dominated by such empires as those of the Egyptians and the Hittites.

Centers of Mycenaean Culture

Mycenae, Tiryns, Pylos, and other Mycenaean sites were not cities in the true sense; they were chiefly royal residences and citadels. The fortification walls at Tiryns are up to forty feet thick, and the lintel of the famous Lion Gate at Mycenae is estimated to weigh twenty tons. It is rather puzzling that so high a level of culture could be reached with so little in the way of urban life. A partial explanation is that the culture was adopted, imported along with artists and architects from other centers of Aegean civilization. Some of the tombs are impressive. Called *tholos* tombs, the finest of them are built up of overhanging tiers of rock into corbeled "beehive" domes. Largest is the so-called Treasury of Atreus at Mycenae, which has a dome about forty-five feet high and almost as wide.

The remains of the Mycenaean cities testify to a rather strong, centralized government; the kings must have been relatively rich. The Linear B tablets tell us the king's title: *wanax*. The later term for king, *basileus,* described a subordinate in charge of one of the lesser towns. The army commander was perhaps second only to the king. Priests were important, along with the heads of the various bureaus of government. There seems to have been a quite complex bureaucracy. An amazing variety of artisans are attested in the tablets—doubtless, along with peasants and soldiers, composing an extensive class of free citizens. At the bottom of the social order, as usual, were serfs and slaves.

About 1400 B.C. many of the island centers of Aegean civilization were destroyed, apparently by a terrific volcanic eruption on the island of Thera (Santorin). At Knossos—probably by then under Mycenaean control—earthquake was followed by fire, and the city never really recovered. Mycenaean influence now reached new heights and penetrated to new areas. Byblos in Syria, for example, has yielded large quantities of Mycenaean ware. Mycenaean pottery has turned up also at Tell el Amarna, the site of Akhnaton's capital far up the Nile in Egypt. Mycenaean traders exchanged their wares even in the western Mediterranean.

On the volcanic island of Santorin itself, excavations have been underway since 1967, often attended with considerable publicity. Some of those involved have speculated that the remembrance of the great eruption there and the total disappearance of towns—and to some extent of civilization—on Santorin and other nearby islands such as Crete might have given rise to Plato's legendary tale of lost Atlantis. Such speculation has naturally aroused public interest. The excavations have gradually peeled off the thick layers of ash and pumice stone to reveal some impressive remains, including fine frescoes from the period. Perhaps this site will indeed prove to be the Pompeii of Greece, as it has been termed.

The End of Mycenae: Invasion or Drought?

During the late 14th and the 13th century B.C. Mycenaean civilization declined; and after about 1200 B.C., there was a general collapse. Part of the city of Mycenae outside the walls was destroyed. All the area, in fact, relapsed into a state of near-barbarism in a rather mystifying way.

Knossos was finally destroyed about 1100 B.C. The cause of this general decline has usually been ascribed to the Dorian invasion told of in the literature. Speaking a dialect of Greek, but less civilized than their Achaean predecessors, the Dorians, it was thought, destroyed the major cultural centers especially in the Peloponnese, where they settled. This blow or series of blows was believed to have brought down Mycenaean civilization.

Recently it has been suggested,[1] however, that the Dorians did not play such a role at all and that they came in, as peaceful immigrants, later than has usually been thought. The cause of the Mycenaean decline is laid, instead, to long drought caused by a small shift in the trade winds that bring Greece her rainless summers. The land, thus, it is argued, was abandoned; there was no invasion. The Dorians simply repopulated the land when the rains returned. According to this theory, the few sites known to have been destroyed, such as Pylos, probably suffered at the hands of starving marauders. The great drought also, it is suggested, caused the decline of the Hittite Empire and the displacement of peoples who about 1200 B.C. ravaged the eastern Mediterranean cities and attacked Egypt.

The drought theory is plausible; moreover, it is true that the archaeological evidence from the Peloponnese does not specifically support an invasion. Still, it is hard to see how the drought—which did not affect the country as a whole but only parts of it—could have brought about so complete a cultural breakdown. Men even forgot how to write. Perhaps the most satisfactory reconstruction of events will combine both drought and Dorian invasion: a country weakened internally by the desiccation of the land was struck by Dorian invaders, who likely lived on the fringe of the more civilized area and took advantage of the situation. Because of the drought the Dorians could no more prosper in the drought areas than had their victims; thus they moved on with other roving groups to join in the destruction of Cretan and mainland sites. Centuries later, after the rains returned to the deserted regions, these peoples came back—the legendary "return of the Heraclids."

C. The Dark Age (c. 1100–800 B.C.)

The eclipse of Mycenaean civilization was succeeded by centuries of darkness. Archaeology can show no important new construction for the intervening era, and there is little evidence of economic activity, none of intellectual activity. The Mycenaean territories lapsed into cultural isolation. The very isolation that characterized the "Dark Age," however, made for eventual cultural unification; this was one positive result of the period.

[1] Rhys Carpenter, *Discontinuity in Greek Civilization* (Cambridge, 1966).

After about 1000 B.C. there was a slight quickening in cultural pace. A new form of pottery appeared called Geometric and soon, as archaeologists have discovered, was widely circulated—which implies some revival of trade. Men began to venture farther on the sea. Recovery, however, was to require centuries.

In the aftermath of this disaster to civilization, whether owing to the elements or the Dorian invasion, came the great migration across the Aegean to the eastern islands and the mainland of western Asia Minor. This area became permanently Greek in population, and its inhabitants often shared the history and accomplishments of the mainland Greeks. All Greece, as well as the Aegean littoral and islands, became racially and culturally homogeneous.

Even in isolation, Greece was never completely cut off from the Orient. Two major cultural developments underline this. First, the Iron Age came to Greece, and doubtless this knowledge of ironworking derived from Asia Minor or Syria; as we know, the Hittites first produced the metal in quantity. Second, near the end of this epoch, the Greeks adopted the Phoenician alphabet. The need for a system of writing perhaps made itself felt first on the commercial level.

Literary Lamps

The Dark Age is illuminated—but only a little—by two sorts of surviving literary material. Greek myths are preserved in various writers; many of these surely go back to this or an even earlier age. Since some of these myths have been shown to contain elements of fact, it is sometimes assumed that judicious analysis of almost all the myths can yield historical data; however, this is a fallacious assumption. Archaeology or reliable history must first lay a foundation before any building blocks drawn from myth can be used. Some myths, even those which seem based on historical event, may be purely imaginative invention.

The second sort of literature that casts some dim light on this dark period is the Greek epics of Homer, the *Iliad* and *Odyssey*. The problems involving date, composition, authorship, validity of content for use as historical data, and the like are tremendously complex, as shown by the voluminous modern literature relating to these matters.

In general, Homer's descriptions seem best to fit the period after the Mycenaean age, though he has some accurate information of the earlier time (as when he describes a long shield used then but not in the later period). He tells of a society dominated by a warrior aristocracy whose kings were first among equals. These kingdoms seem petty and poor compared with Mycenae, their economy being almost altogether agricultural. The chief gods were already the Olympian twelve. Perhaps Homer was more important as a maker of history than as a source of historical information. The *Iliad* and *Odyssey* became the great school-book of Greece for centuries. Alexander the Great carried copies of them with him on his prolonged campaigns. These poems are still judged the greatest epics of all time.

Indirect Illumination

Another way of learning more about the Dark Age is to study the conditions of society and the state at the end of the period and to infer from them what changes had occurred not long before. In this way, one perceives that somehow the petty monarchies gave way to aristocratic oligarchy and that the old warfare involving individual combat between warrior-leaders was superseded by an aristocratic cavalry as the chief fighting force. A tradition in Athens suggests that one of their kings, when unable to lead the army at a critical time, was given a general as his assistant. Soon the kingship in that state became elective—at first for ten years, then annually. By this time the real power in Athens was in the hands of an administrative officer, called the *archon,* and the commanding general, or *polemarch.* The king, or *basileus,* was no longer very important. The influence of the aristocratic families was exercised especially through the tribes, whose power (since much of the land was held by them) was economic as well as political and judicial.

D. Currents of Change (800–600 B.C.)

At a quickening pace, the Greek world was transformed after 800 B.C. Trade brought increasing contact with the outside world, and there followed a period of colonization and emigration. New classes of men whose primary interest was commerce or production of export commodities strained the traditional fabric of society and the state. Military developments also helped to bring down the old order and structures.

Colonization and Emigration

Hesiod, a Boeotian poet of the 8th century B.C., may perhaps help us to understand the impulse toward emigration and settlement in far countries that arose at this time. His poem *Works and Days,* a plebeian view of life on the farm in his day, presents a rather grim picture of unremitting labor for little gain. It may have been poverty and over-population, then, which drove Greeks of his time to the sea. Basic raw materials of all sorts were in short supply. The mountains had already been denuded of their forests, so that even lumber was needed; grain, wool, and hides often had to be brought into the land also.

Two sorts of colonies were established: some were basically trading stations, which collected goods for shipment to the homeland; others were larger-scale settlements, usually located on good agricultural land. The latter type developed into independent city-states much like those at home. Most of the colonies were founded by individuals, though sometimes a whole city of mainland Greece or elsewhere joined in the effort and became a "mother city" (*metropolis*). However founded, the overseas colonies were not controlled from Greece; no empire resulted from this substantial emigration. Ties were maintained with the mother cities, but these were mostly commercial and religious, not political.

The areas colonized, both from Greece and the Greek areas of western Asia Minor, included the north Aegean, nearly all the shores round the Black Sea, sites on the Ionian and Adriatic seas, south Italy, eastern Sicily, southern France, eastern Spain, and the area of Cyrene, west of Egypt in North Africa. By far the largest number of colonists went to the west, which became a kind of frontier region for Greeks. In southern Italy, which the Romans called Magna Graecia (Great Greece), the cities of Tarentum, Croton, Sybaris, Rhegium, Cumae, and Naples, as well as Syracuse in eastern Sicily, grew until they were among the most important Greek cities anywhere.

Trade must be two-way: if basic materials are to be imported, something must be exported. The Greek states developed for export the best pottery in the world, plus wine, olive oil, and other products. The new emphasis on produce and manufactures for export caused changes in the economy and society that were of the greatest importance, which will be discussed later in this chapter.

The Rise of the Polis

Of the concomitant changes marking the period 800–600 B.C., one of the more important was the rise of a new sort of state, the *polis*. The city-state—as the term is usually but inadequately translated—was the most typical Greek institution. Centered about a single city, the polis was a genuine community, where the focal city gave its citizenship to all in the area and was itself the political, economic, social, cultural, and religious hub of the state. The restricted size of the polis brought a broad participation in the affairs of state and thus made possible an emphasis on the individual, which in turn led to the progress associated with significant human achievement. In a state of this scale, everyone could know almost everyone else (certainly, that is, those worth knowing). But the polis fostered the intense particularism, rivalry, and internecine warfare that also, unfortunately, were typically Greek. Nevertheless, the great thinkers Plato and Aristotle could envision no more satisfactory kind of state in which to create an optimum balance between order and freedom and yet make possible a high degree of human fulfillment.

Military Changes

Citizens of the United States often tend to forget that all power in a state ultimately depends upon the military or its civilian equivalent, the police. Citizens of Latin America are rarely allowed to forget it! To put it another way, the military establishment of a state usually reflects the society in some important fashion. Occasionally, however, some technical change in the military compels a change in the armed forces, which leads inexorably to changes in the state itself. That is, the army then tends to change society to reflect military reality. In this age such a military change did involve political and social changes.

Warfare in this period came to be dominated by the *hoplite,* or heavy-armed infantryman, fighting in phalanx formation. In the age of the Trojan War, individual combat between hero figures had predominated; then came a period in which aristocratic cavalry formed the core of a state's armed forces. Now, however, the battle ranks of the phalanx required large numbers of men armed with shield (*hoplon*), helmet, breastplate, greaves, and thrusting spear. It became necessary to use every man who could afford this equipment and, ultimately, to enfranchise all such men. The result was a broadened oligarchy, but hardly democracy, for not many men could buy such expensive arms. Yet this military change tended to reduce the power of the old aristocratic families and was in some places a step along the road toward democracy.

A good example of the results of the change may be seen in Sparta. The Messenian wars of the late 8th and the mid-7th centuries B.C. made it imperative to modernize the army—which meant increasing its size to include every possible hoplite. Soon after, all hoplites were enfranchised. At that point, Sparta was surely one of the most liberal states in Greece, in several ways. But here the Spartans froze the military-political development (perhaps "fossilized" would be a better term). The state became a rather rigid oligarchy, which we shall consider later in greater detail.

Changes in Class Structure

The wealth and power of the older aristocracy lay in the land. Society was basically rural and many social, political, and juridical matters were dealt with through the tribes, which were dominated by the great families. With the rise of colonization and trade, with its import-export emphasis, and the development of the polis, the power of the aristocracies began to decline. This was not a decline in wealth, since many landholders cultivated crops for the export market and had the necessary capital to plant olive groves and vineyards. But the landed aristocracy could exercise little control over traders and manufacturers—the emerging middle class—and the artisans now working away from the farms, who soon began to develop into another, wage-earning class. The tribes grew less important; many of the aristocrats themselves acquiesced in a lessened control of the tribes over land in favor of private ownership, since raising olives and grapes required capital investment and special care.

The evolving new groups did not fit into the existing sociopolitical structure and had no part in it. Their needs were different. The merchants, for example, required protection at sea from piracy, laws relating to contracts, and the like. Similarly, the lower-class laborers who worked in pottery shops or shipyards did not fit in and found that the old order paid little attention to their needs. These groups therefore were an unstable element in aristocratic states and tended to support any new structure that would weaken the old system—if the change ministered to their own problems, that is.

The Rise of Tyranny

Leaders called *tyrants* arose; such men—often aristocrats themselves—attacked the entrenched power of the aristocracies in the interests of the newer groups, and were in turn supported by them. They eventually seized power in extraconstitutional fashion and ruled somewhat like modern dictators. The first man to be called tyrant by the Greeks was Gyges of Lydia, who overthrew the previous Lydian king in the middle 7th century B.C. Soon after, Cypselus overthrew the aristocratic Bacchiadae in Corinth and ruled for three decades; he was succeeded by his son Periander. In the mid-6th century B.C., Peisistratus of Athens rose to power through the use of mercenary soldiers.

Tyrants generally supported trade and commerce, sent out colonies, established systems of coinage and weights and measures, issued new laws, and looked out for the interests of the middle and lower classes. The word "tyrant" originally did not carry a negative connotation, for all except the aristocrats initially approved of their work. But whenever absolute power is concentrated in the hands of a single person, the time inevitably comes when an unworthy man abuses that authority in his own interest. This happened in Greece during the "age of tyranny," and soon the word began to acquire its present unsavory connotation.

The tyrants played the role of destroyers of the old oligarchies; but they also made possible further political development. Once the tyrants were in turn thrown out, many Greek states elected to proceed toward democracy. There were sporadic returns to aristocratic rule, as at Corinth; but, no longer bound to the land, the aristocrats there generally looked after the interests of all classes better than most other oligarchs.

Typically, then, from Homeric times to the 5th century B.C., political development in Greece proceeded from monarchy to aristocracy to tyranny to some form of democracy. It should be stressed, though, that scracely any state in Greece was ever really "typical."

Books for Further Reading

ANDREWES, A., *The Greek Tyrants,* New York, 1963.

BOARDMAN, J., *The Greeks Overseas,* Baltimore, 1964.

CARPENTER, R., *Discontinuity in Greek Civilization,* Cambridge, 1966.

FINLEY, M. I., *Early Greece: The Bronze and Archaic Age,* New York, 1970.

FINLEY, M. I., *The World of Odysseus,* New York, 1965.

HUTCHINSON, R. W., *Prehistoric Crete,* Baltimore, 1962.

NILSSON, M., *Homer and Mycenae,* London, 1933.

PAGE, D., *History and the Homeric Iliad,* Berkeley and Los Angeles, 1959.

PENDLEBURY, J., *The Archaeology of Crete,* London, 1939.

SAMUEL, A., *The Mycenaeans in History,* Englewood Cliffs, N.J., 1966.

STARR, C. G., *Origins of Greek Civilization,* New York, 1961.

TAYLOUR, W., *The Mycenaeans,* London, 1964.

VERMEULE, E., *Greece in the Bronze Age,* Chicago, 1964.

WEBSTER, T., *From Mycenae to Homer,* New York, 1964.

Sparta and Athens:
Order or Freedom?

8

A writer of fiction could scarcely conjure up two states exhibiting greater contrast than Athens and Sparta in their heyday. Sparta chose order, stability, a controlled society; Athens chose freedom, kaleidoscopic and creative change, sometimes catastrophic individualism. Antecedents played a part in their development: the Spartans were Dorian, and the Athenians were Ionian. Still, the two peoples spoke dialects of the same language, worshiped the same gods, and lived less than one hundred miles apart, in straight-line distance.

A. Early Sparta

In the Mycenaean age and in Homeric times, Sparta was, like the other Greek states, a monarchy. The story of King Menelaus and Helen begins there. Later, when the none-too-brilliant light of history finally casts dim illumination upon the scene, Sparta was still a monarchy, but there were two kings, with greatly restricted powers. Elected officials had greater domestic authority, and a council and the assembly had strong positions as well.

The Spartans traced their developed state back to a great reformer and lawgiver, Lycurgus. A cursory reading of the early paragraphs of Plutarch's life of Lycurgus, however, shows clearly enough that even in antiquity he was a shadowy figure. It is possible to doubt he ever actually existed, though the soundest scholars are not quite that skeptical. Another Spartan tradition made the governmental reform the response to an answer of the oracle of Apollo at Delphi, called the Great Rhetra. Although the oracle's cryptic sentence can hardly have served as a con-

129

stitution, it might have supported some proposed scheme or a controversial recent change. At any rate, we know the general outlines of the reforms and the major reasons for them.

In the 8th, 7th, and part of the 6th centuries B.C., Sparta was not the culturally deprived, repressive place it later became. Poets, sculptors, and vase painters of great artistic ability lived and worked there. More than any other single factor, it was Sparta's imperialism that inexorably changed the city and shaped its future course. Messenia, to the west, possessed a productive plain that Sparta coveted and took, thereby precipitating a long war. When it drew to an end in the late 8th century B.C., Sparta had already made some military and political changes. As we have noted, all the hoplite class, desperately needed in the fighting, was enfranchised. A second Messenian war in the following century, similarly long and hard, produced further political changes, such as the elected *ephors* becoming the chief magistrates. At this point, Sparta was a relatively liberal oligarchy.

Imperialism and Its Consequences

Along with a degree of political liberalization, however, came a set of conditions that gradually fossilized the state. The Spartiates—full citizens—were a distinct minority, forming perhaps only about 3 percent of the population of the expanded state. To retain control over the subject peoples, they had to band themselves into a military caste exercising rigorous discipline. Their whole purpose in life became the conservation of their own privileged position, but in the name of stability. Every Spartan thus became a professional soldier and nothing more. His education was designed to make him a soldier, and his duty was to the system—or the state, as he would have put it. Trade and commerce were to be discouraged because they would produce uncontrollable change. When philosophy and free education were later embraced in Athens, these ideals became anathema in Sparta—too dangerous. The result for Sparta was indeed order; there were but a few serious revolts over several centuries. But its price was the loss of individual freedom, not only for the subject peoples but for the Spartiates as well.

Government and Society

In developed form, the government of Sparta included two kings of separate family, whose duties at home were primarily religious and advisory. They led the army on campaign and thus were also rather important in foreign affairs. The chief executives at home were the five

Spartan Soldier. *(Courtesy Wadsworth Atheneum, Hartford, Conn.)*

annually elected ephors. A council of elders called the *gerousia,* made up of twenty-eight men over sixty years of age plus the kings, debated matters as it programmed the work of the assembly and served judicial functions. The assembly of all full citizens, or Spartiates, voted without debate on matters presented to it. The ephors were elected by the assembly, along with the elders of the gerousia. The constitution was thus a mixed one, including democratic, aristocratic, and monarchical aspects.

Besides the Spartiates, other major social classes were the *perioeci* ("dwellers around"), who were free but not citizens, and the *helots,* or state serf-slaves who formed the largest group of all. The helots worked plots of publicly owned land that were assigned to the Spartiates, who lived off the produce. These helots, located mostly in eastern Messenia and vastly outnumbering their rulers, were a continual danger to the Spartans. If they should revolt, the threat they posed was not merely military; it was economic and social as well. Yet it is notable that, in times of crisis, the Spartans did not hesitate to arm both the perioeci and the helots.

Most of the full-status Spartans lived off the proceeds from the public lands. Beginning in their seventh year (or as we would say, at age six), when they left their homes permanently to live in training barracks, Spartan boys—like the adult Spartiates supported by the helots —gave full attention to their education. They learned military arts and military virtues: discipline, obedience, toughness, endurance. At age twenty they entered the army. They could now marry but must still live in their communal barracks and contribute to its support; only at age thirty could they live with their wives. This, too, was the age when they got the right to vote in the assembly. If they were fit, they served in the army until age sixty.

Spartans did not completely ignore such cultural activities as music, but theirs were old-fashioned martial tunes and dances. Religion they took very seriously; an important festival was not to be interrupted. Most important were the rites to Artemis Orthia.

The system inculcated a pride in self and city that is not altogether to be disparaged. Spartans, sure of their superiority, for centuries proved they were the best soldiers anywhere. On one occasion when an Athenian twitted a Spartan by saying there were a good many Spartans buried on Athenian territory, the Spartan replied, "There are *no* Athenians buried on Spartan territory." That is, no Athenian army —or for that matter, any other alien force—had reached Sparta in human memory. The Spartans actually gloried in their rough clothing and tasteless food. A visiting Sybarite, after he had eaten a Spartan meal, exclaimed, "Now I know why Spartans are not afraid to die!"

Formation of the Peloponnesian League

Perhaps because the minority of Spartiates felt no need of additional territory, or because they felt they could not exercise adequate control over more helots, Spartan policy changed during the 6th century B.C. A defeat or two played a part in this change as well. Spartan imperialism continued within the Peloponnese, but in a new form. Defeated states— first Tegea, then Mantinea, Orchomenus, and others—were forced into alliance with Sparta herself dominating the system. This alliance system was made most effective by the Spartan king Cleomenes I (c. 519–c. 487 B.C.).

King Cleomenes I not only brought most of the Peloponnese into the Spartan alliance; he also intervened in Athens and Aegina; moreover, he defeated Argos, Sparta's most inveterate enemy in the Peloponnese. Though he was ambitious and capable, Sparta's complicated political system at last defeated him. At one point he was frustrated by the dual king, at another by the ephors. Even the members of the Peloponnesian alliance, led by Corinth, defied him successfully on one occasion when he wished to intervene again in Athens (though the later victory over Argos ended that piece of unruliness). Herodotus relates that Cleomenes attempted to bribe the Delphic oracle to support charges he had made against the dual king, and that he eventually became mad and committed suicide.

B. Early Athens

The Athenians preserved a tradition regarding their political development which probably is in a fundamental way accurate—though not in its details—and which is also rather typical of the evolution of many other Greek states in the same period. The Athenian monarchy was diminished in power at a time of crisis, when the king's power to lead the army was turned over to another official, the *polemarch*. At some later time, this office became elective. Royal administrative powers went next, to the *archon eponymos,* another elective official, after whom the calendar year was named. Finally the kingship itself became elective, first for ten years, then annually, like the other two magistracies. The *archon basileus* (king-archon) retained primarily religious and ceremonial functions. There were also an advisory council, the Areopagus, and an assembly of the full citizens. At some point, six other archons called *thesmothetae* were provided for; their functions were judicial. There was thus eventually a board of nine archons.

Though Athens was ultimately the greatest sea power among the Greek states and, of course, a leader in maritime commerce, this was not the case during the pioneer 8th and 7th centuries B.C. Toward the end of that period, certain disturbances in the now-unified city-state (polis) indicate some degree of economic and social unrest. About 632 B.C. a nobleman named Cylon attempted to make himself tyrant. He failed and fled. His followers were executed. During the affair the leaders in this purge, members of the Alcmaeonid family, were said to have violated the sacred right of sanctuary, since the condemned had taken refuge at the altar of Athena. The family was afterward considered, by its enemies at least, to be accursed. This attempt at tyranny, even though unsuccessful, implies the rise of a group who might oppose the entrenched aristocrats. Similar implications may be seen in a written law code drawn up under the archon Draco about 621 B.C., which was notorious for its harshness (hence the adjective Draconian, signifying a barbarous severity). The death penalty was instituted for numerous civil infractions, even for petty theft. The need for a code indicates that the old tribal system was breaking down.

Solon

The first great constitutional reformer of Athenian history was Solon, elected archon for the year 594 B.C., a liberal aristocrat given broad power to shake up government and society. His acts and his own words, preserved in poems he composed in defense of his measures, indicate clearly that it was a time of deep economic distress and incipient revolt. Athens was ripe for tyranny, and Solon's task was to stave it off by compromise. Though there is considerable information regarding his year in office, it is certain that Solon did not do all that is attributed to him in the sources, and much else about his career is doubtful—even the date of his archonship.

One change that Solon assuredly accomplished was to rearrange the social classes, for political purposes, on a timocratic basis; that is, political classification was made according to wealth, not by birth. This inevitably reduced the power of the aristocrats and corrrespondingly increased that of non-aristocratic but well-to-do landowners, as well as of the relatively tiny but growing group of tradesmen, who could now serve along with the others in the highest offices. At the bottom level, Solon increased the number of full citizens who could vote in the *ecclesia,* or assembly. A new *heliaea,* or people's court drawn from the assembly, heard appeals from decisions of the archons. Middle-level groups were given the right along with the upper class to serve in the *boule,* or Council of 400 (according to Aristotle), which functioned as a steering committee for the assembly.

Solon naturally had to deal with the economic situation. He redeemed men who had been sold into slavery for debt and voided mortgages (probably all of them) in which a human being's freedom was collateral. Though urged by many to do so, he did not seize and redistribute land holdings. He did encourage foreign artisans to settle in Athens. His new system of weights and measures and his new law code—less harsh than Draco's—were perhaps beneficial to the rising group of traders and merchants. Despite these liberal measures, Athens continued to be rocked by troubles. In the ensuing decades, official archon lists twice record a state of *anarchia,* when no archons could be elected, doubtless because of civil disorders. Ultimately Athens did experience the tyranny Solon had tried to forestall.

Peisistratus

Athens' first tyrant was Peisistratus, a noble who sought the support of the poor farmers of the "Hill" (perhaps this familiar term at first referred to a geographical sector east of Athens). Eventually he also gained the support of most of the city poor and of the "Shore" (a group which included some merchants and traders). The "Plain," however, dominated by the landed aristocracy, mostly opposed him. After an initial failure to take power about 562 B.C., Peisistratus was tyrant more or less continuously from 560 to 527 B.C., except for two periods of exile, briefly early in his tyranny and then for ten years (556–546 B.C.).

Peisistratus had a flair for opportunistic publicity. He was thought to have faked the dramatic beating that persuaded the Athenians to give him a personal bodyguard—which he then used to seize power. He married the daughter of one of the major noble families to gain badly needed support. On his return after his first expulsion, proclaiming that the goddess Athena herself was sponsoring his resumption of power, he entered the city in a chariot with a tall, beautiful girl of stately proportions who was clad in armor. His ten-year exile was spent on his own estates in Thrace. From his silver mines and timberland, he acquired enough wealth to hire a band of mercenaries, mostly from Argos; his second return, thus, was something of an invasion.

Peisistratus was careful not to exercise power too nakedly. If he made constitutional changes, they were comparatively minor (though some attributed to Solon may actually be credited to him). He courted popularity in his building program and in his support of public festivals, including the first of the great theatrical contests (in 534 B.C., won by Thespis), which were to make Athens the drama center of the world.

Much of what Peisistratus did was made possible through the expenditure of his substantial personal fortune in the public interest— that is, the income from his silver mines in Thrace. It is often overlooked that one reason for the Peisistratid decline in popularity was the loss of these mines by his successors in 513 B.C. to Darius of Persia. The important silver mines at Laurium, within Attica, were exploited to an extent by Peisistratus, but the rich finds there came only in the 5th century B.C. The tyrant did impose a new land tax, which bore most heavily on the aristocracy. It seems, too, that he seized and redistributed some private land.

At Peisistratus' death in 527 B.C., his two sons, Hippias and Hipparchus, assumed their father's role. Hippias was the political leader, and Hipparchus the patron of the arts. An attempt to assassinate Hippias went wrong, and instead Hipparchus was killed. The would-be tyrant killers were hardly idealists (a homosexual affair was said to be involved); nevertheless, the pair—Harmodius and Aristogeiton—became heroes, and a 5th-century sculpture by Polycleitus helped to perpetuate their heroic image.

Hippias afterward grew suspicious and vengeful. Economic distress caused by loss of the family silver mines must have hurt. In the end, it was the Spartans under King Cleomenes, conservative but opposed to tyranny, who sent troops to expel Hippias, about 510 B.C. The fleeing tyrant took refuge with the Persians and later accompanied them on invasions of his native Greece.

Cleisthenes' Reforms

The ejection of the tyrant of course signaled the return of aristocratic oligarchy. Unfortunately, the aristocrats were divided into bitterly opposing groups: one was led by Isagoras, and the other by Cleisthenes, an Alcmaeonid. The latter leader and his faction had done most to get the tyrant expelled. After the Temple of Apollo at Delphi had burned, he contracted to build a new one. He threw in such extras as a marble front, which were not called for in the contract. The grateful oracle, it was said, began to add to every answer given to any Spartan the words "But first, Athens must be freed." Perhaps King Cleomones did not need such a spur. At any rate, Cleisthenes was unwilling to see Isagoras and his party installed in power by the Spartans. To thwart them, he courted the lower-class supporters of the Peisistratids and thus gained power. Like Solon, he made major changes in the constitution.

Cleisthenes did not foolishly attempt to turn back to some sort of pre-Solonian oligarchy. His greatest concern was to set up governmental machinery that would not further polarize the classes. He therefore made the *boule,* now enlarged to a Council of 500, a more important body, chosen in a balanced fashion from ten newly created, artificial tribes. These were created with local districts, the *demes,* as the basic residential units. Each tribe contained some demes largely dominated by aristocrats, some by the middle class, and some by the lower classes. Fifty persons from each of the ten tribes, chosen by a combination of election and lot, made up the *boule.* Demes were represented in the *boule* according to population—a sort of proportional representation.

This Council of 500 served as the chief deliberative body and steering committee for the assembly comprising all citizens, and it furnished numerous officials. Foreign affairs and most internal matters came under its jurisdiction. The Council of 500 was divided into ten *prytaneis* of fifty men each. One prytany was always on duty, with each serving for the tenth part of the year. The chairmanship changed on a daily rotation. Since one could sit only two years on the council—and those not in succession—a large number of persons were thus able to serve on this important body. The citizens in this way learned the workings of the government. Athens was not yet a complete democracy, but Cleisthenes' innovations took a long stride in that direction.

The nine archons, still the chief executives of the state, were elected only from the top classes as before, so that wealth was still a prerequisite for this office. Moreover, much power remained with the council known as the Areopagus, composed of ex-archons. And it must not be forgotten that votes can be controlled by the powerful.

It was perhaps Cleisthenes who also established a new procedure, ostracism, so called because votes were written on *ostraka,* or potsherds. The purpose was to prevent the return of tyranny by making possible a general balloting for the banishment of overpopular leaders. Some scholars have thought this institution belongs to a later period because it was not actually used until 487 B.C., but it could at first have served its purpose simply as a deterrent. It worked this way: each year the assembly voted whether to have a special secret balloting for ostracism. If one was held and if a quorum of at least 6,000 citizens voted, the person receiving the most votes had to go into exile for ten years. Ostracism became a factional tool, of course, but it was not used excessively.

Later reforms based on the constitution of Cleisthenes may be mentioned here for the sake of convenience, though they belong mostly to the years after the Persian Wars. Army organization was soon based on the ten new tribes, and officials called *strategoi* were elected as commanders of the tribal army units. The ten *strategoi* could be reelected year after year. In the 5th century B.C., when Athens had an imperialistic policy and was often involved in war, it was inevitable that these officials, especially any one *strategos* who could dominate the group, should become the chief officers of the state. This was markedly so after about 487 B.C., when the archons began to be chosen by a procedure including drawings by lot. In 462 B.C., certain judicial powers of the Areopagus were taken away and put into the hands of the popular courts, which became more important. The third-class citizens became eligible for election to the top offices about the same time. By the time of Pericles, it seems that any citizen even of the lowest class—in fact, though perhaps not by law—could hold any office except that of treasurer.

Except for the fact that slaves, women, and foreign residents did not have the rights of citizenship, by the mid-5th century B.C. Athens had become a rather thoroughgoing, direct democracy in a unique way that set her apart from other states.

C. Critical Years: The Persian Wars

The Persians often must have found their Greek subjects in Asia Minor exasperating. Like their brothers across the Aegean, these Greeks wished to move with the times, away from oligarchy, perhaps by way of tyranny, and toward some form of democracy. The Persians belatedly went along with the change to tyranny; they doubtless observed that tyrants can be controlled even more effectively than oligarchs. Eventually the Persian overlords accepted some sort of democracy. A truly democratic state must, by definition, be free, however. The Ionian revolt, which broke out in 499 B.C., was said by Greek sources to have been instigated by Aristagoras, a tyrant of Miletus under the Persians who fell into disfavor; but the inherent Greek drive toward freedom must have been a significant factor in the rebellion.

Once the revolt broke out, Aristagoras sought help from other Greeks. King Cleomenes of Sparta listened sympathetically to his request; but when he learned that the Persian capital, target of a proposed expedition, was three months' march into the interior of Asia, he told Aristagoras to get out of town. The Athenians did send twenty ships, and the men from these ships joined a raiding force that captured and sacked Sardis, a Persian administrative center. Later, when the Persians put down the revolt and in turn sacked Miletus, the Athenians reproached themselves for not having sent more help to their fellow Ionians.

Persian motives for invading Greece proper soon afterward were one part a desire for revenge, one part the wish to prevent similar revolts in the future, and one part simply a continuation of their usual imperialistic policy. A first invasion force, proceeding by sea along the northern Aegean coast, came to grief when storms heavily damaged the Persian fleet in 492 B.C. The Persians had to call a halt, but they had already successfully occupied additional lands along the northern Aegean littoral.

Marathon (490 B.C.)

Persian invaders came again by sea in 490 B.C., this time directly across the Aegean. They took an island or two and then made their base on Euboea, just across from Attica. Soon they debarked an army on the Plain of Marathon, in Athenian territory and only twenty-six miles from Athens itself. The Greeks knew of the threat; they were never without general information on Persian movements, even in Asia. No well-organized defensive arrangements had been made, however. Cleomenes had held Sparta to an anti-Persian policy, and the Peloponnesian alliance could mostly be counted on for aid, even though Athens was the chief target. A runner sent by the Athenians to Sparta brought a promise of help, but a religious festival then in progress was not to be interrupted. The Spartan troops were soon sent north but arrived too late to fight alongside the Athenians. Meanwhile the Athenians, with the help of the Plataeans, faced the enemy at Marathon, blocking the road that led to Athens. A complication developed when the Persians decided to use their superior fleet to bypass the Athenian army. They began to embark a portion of their army, including all their excellent cavalry. While the remainder of their force stayed at Marathon to pin down the

Athenians, the Persian ships would sail around Cape Sunium and perhaps take the ill-defended capital. The plan implies that in Athens there were Persian sympathizers—or at least sympathizers of the cause of the ex-tyrant Hippias, who had accompanied the Persians.

One of the Athenian generals, Miltiades, persuaded the rest to fight, even though the remaining Persian force still greatly outnumbered the Greeks. The disposition of troops and the manner of attack show that the Greek generals understood very well the nature of the two quite different armies. The Persians were light-armed and depended mostly on missiles; the Greek hoplites were heavy-armed and depended on spear thrusts at close quarter. The advantages of the light-armed troops were mobility and flexibility; hence the Greeks extended their battle line dangerously thin to prevent their being outflanked. The wings were kept strong, however, and the weak center was held back somewhat. Then the Athenians attacked at a double-quick pace, no doubt to keep casualties from arrows and other missiles at a minimum as they closed in. The hoplites were able to pin the Persians and Medes back against the sea and won a resounding victory. Casualty figures reported by Herodotus were 6,400 Persian dead, as against 192 Greeks. (Some of the latter's graves have recently been found.)

The victorious army next hurried back to Athens to meet the threat from the sea, and the Persians then called off their faltering expedition. They could still claim important gains in the Aegean islands. They would not attempt to avenge their loss for ten years; but the Greeks, who could not know this, expected an avenging Persian expedition to be sent as quickly as it could be organized.

Themistocles and the New Military Policy

During the decade that intervened between the two major Persian invasions of Greece, a man of an obscure but noble family, Themistocles, made use of democratic processes to rise to power. He ostracized some of his opponents, including the moderate aristocrat Aristeides. Perhaps influenced by the fact that hoplite forces tended to be dominated by oligarchical leaders, but also recognizing that Athenian weakness at sea had almost brought disaster in the Marathon campaign, Themistocles pressed for a completely new military strategy. Athens should, he thought, emphasize sea power at the expense of the army and take a defensive stance on land. He perhaps engineered a small war—a renewal of a prolonged conflict, actually—with the neighboring island of Aegina to gain his point. After the small Athenian fleet was defeated, his proposals to spend the profits from Athenian silver mines near Laurium on ships, port facilities, and fortifications were adopted. By 480 B.C., therefore,

Athens had constructed many new ships and had a navy of about 200 vessels, mostly triremes of the latest design.

Since the rowers of the naval ships were lower-class, both the navy and the imperialism based on it came to be connected particularly with the democracy. Themistocles' strategic policy was similarly identified with his party, and as long as Athens remained an important power in Greece it was generally followed. Perhaps this rise to power of a brilliant man born of a family of no importance under the oligarchy illustrates, as well as anything, the strengths of democracy.

The Hellenic League

The Persians were prevented by revolts, internal problems, and the death of Darius from mounting another invasion before 480 B.C. Preparations for this were extensive and required several years. The Greeks, who had of course learned of the Persian mobilization, made more organized preparation this time to meet the threat. The Peloponnesian alliance served as the nucleus for a defense organization; Athens and perhaps a few other states now allied themselves with it, to form the Hellenic League. The Spartans therefore provided the leadership for the combined force, even for the fleet, which was dominated by the Athenians.

Xerxes' Invasion:
The Razor's Edge (480 B.C.)

The polyglot army that Xerxes put together for the great invasion of 480 B.C. may well have been the largest single army ever collected until modern times. Greek scouts were overawed. Herodotus reported an estimate for the total force, including service personnel but excluding camp followers, of· more than five million. There were terrifying reports of whole streams and lakes drunk dry by men and horses. Although the wide-eyed Greek scouts doubtless exaggerated, the actual figures, even if only a tenth of Herodotus' estimate, were still overwhelming.

This vast horde crossed the Hellespont on a bridge of ships; it numbered far too many troops to be transported any distance by a fleet. There was a combat fleet, and hundreds of supply ships as well, for no army of that size could live off the land in the fashion that was usual in antiquity. Vast baggage trains trailed the marching troops. The army moved ponderously across Thrace and Macedonia, down into Hellas. Before it, most Greek cities in the areas occupied offered earth and water in submission to the Persian monarch. Other states farther south, even Argos in the Peloponnese, "Medized" meekly.

Greek Efforts to Halt the Persians:
Thermopylae and Artemisium

A decision was made by the Hellenic League to try to stop the Persians at the Vale of Tempe, a pass from Macedonia into Thessaly, in order to keep the Thessalians and their valued cavalry safely on the Greek side. But Xerxes' immense forces used other passes, and the Greeks had to abandon the area to the enemy without a fight. To the south, however, where the main road from Thessaly enters Boeotia through a narrow pass along the sea at Thermopylae, a small Greek force under King Leonidas of Sparta opposed the Persian hordes. Just offshore, the Greek fleet, with its nucleus of new Athenian triremes, took up its station off Cape Artemisium, at the northern tip of the island of Euboea.

The 300 Spartans (each doubtless accompanied by helots), with about 5,000 Thespians, Thebans, and others, held off the Persians for a time at Thermopylae, until a Greek guide showed the invaders how to outflank their position. King Leonidas was aware of the danger but, true to the Spartan ideal, elected to fight to the end. Most of the other Greeks were ordered to retreat, however. One of the monuments later set up at Thermopylae seems to symbolize Greek restraint, as well as Spartan concepts of virtue: "Go, passing stranger, and tell the Lacedaemonians that we lie here, obedient to their word." The Greek fleet also was forced back by superior numbers. The Persians, however, suffered greatly from the elements: fierce storms destroyed a large number of their ships.

The Battle of Salamis

As the Persian horde swept through Boeotia, the Athenians withdrew from their city and abandoned it to the enemy. It was a hard decision. They had asked the advice of Apollo from the Delphic oracle and had received a terrifying warning to flee. When they persisted in seeking a more heartening answer, the oracle somewhat tempered its advice: the Athenians were told to trust to wooden walls. Themistocles persuaded them that this meant their fleet. The noncombatant population was therefore evacuated, to the island of Salamis, just offshore in the bay, and to other locations. The Greek fleet took up a position in the bay, while the Athenians on Salamis could only watch in dismay as the enemy sacked and burned their city.

The Spartans were now pressing for all Greek forces to withdraw within the Peloponnese, behind a wall being constructed across the Isthmus of Corinth. They urged that the fleet move south also. Themistocles, in order to induce the invaders to attack, we are told, secretly informed the Persians of the Greek intent to withdraw. Xerxes decided to do so and had a throne set on a high point where he could watch the fateful panorama in the straits below. The numerically inferior Greek ships outmaneuvered the Persian vessels—mostly Phoenician —in the narrow waters and won a resounding victory. The Greek naval force rammed and sank many of the enemy ships. In his tragedy entitled *The Persians,* Aeschylus tells how the Greeks killed Persians thrashing about in the water by battering them with the butts of their spears. Herodotus adds that most of the enemy forces could not swim. Though his defeat was not decisive, since much of his fleet and all of his land army were intact, Xerxes, furious and fearful for his own safety, concluded that no more could be done that year. With most of his army, he returned as he had come, while a considerable Persian force was left behind in Thessaly under his general Mardonius.

Plataea and Mycale (479 B.C.)

The largest single army ever raised by the Greeks in antiquity assembled during the early months of 479 B.C. The Spartans were still inclined to defend only the Peloponnese, at the fortified isthmus, but the Athenians threatened to go over to the Persians unless the Greek army moved north, so that Sparta was finally forced to agree. The Greek force which took up positions some time later at Plataea on Mount Cithaeron, northwest of Attica, numbered about 100,000 according to Herodotus (probably including supply personnel) and surely was not much smaller than Mardonius' army.

After several days of preliminary maneuvering and skirmishing, the Spartan commander Pausanias decided on a minor pullback to escape the attacks of the strong Persian cavalry. At dawn, seeing only the withdrawing rear guard, the Persians attacked. The main body of Spartans quickly moved forward to a strong position and split the Persian line. Then the Greeks charged, killed many, and sent the rest reeling. The Athenian hoplites, the second-strongest contingent on the Greek side, met the Theban allies of the Persians and defeated them. But the chief glory in this victory went to the Spartans. Although Herodotus presents the whole situation as fortuitous, it may have been at least partly planned by the Spartan command. The Persian remnants now withdrew into Asia, never to return. Greece had been saved.

This victory was, actually, a double triumph for the Greeks. On the very same day that the battle of Plataea was fought, as the Greeks reckoned it, a second decisive battle at Mycale in Asia Minor brought added disaster upon the Persians. Much of their fleet was destroyed, along with substantial ground forces, by the Greek fleet and marines. Several of the Aegean islands passed from Persian control at this time, and it did not seem unreasonable that the Greeks might even go on the offensive against mighty Persia.

As it happened, Greeks in the West, on Sicily, also won a great victory in these years. Over a period of two or three centuries, the Carthaginians had backed their fellow Phoenicians in western Sicily in competition with the Greeks, who held most of the eastern part of that island. In 480 B.C. the Carthaginian general Hamilcar brought a large army to Sicily, which was challenged and decisively defeated at Himera in north-central Sicily by Gelon, tyrant-general of Syracuse.

The combination of victories against odds, by land and by sea, in the east and in the west, proved tremendously exhilarating to the victors. Greeks, it seemed for the moment, could do almost anything they put their minds to. A new atmosphere of confidence and enthusiasm invigorated the Hellenes.

D. Delian League to Athenian Empire

Sparta Fails as Leader of All Greece

Just after the twin victories of Plataea and Mycale, Sparta had opportunity to assume the leadership of all Greece in a great counteroffensive against the Persians. Pausanias was willing and led a Greek force that expelled the Persians from some towns in the north Aegean area. Sparta also requested Athens not to rebuild her walls and suggested that other cities' walls be demolished. Sparta herself did not have encircling walls. Themistocles fooled the Spartans: he sent an embassy to discuss the matter and at the same time put all able-bodied citizens to work rebuilding the Athenian walls in great haste, while the ambassadors stalled the negotiations. The Spartans subsequently accepted the accomplished fact.

Spartan ephors always tended to fear extended foreign involvement. When they heard rumors that Pausanias had assumed the airs of a Persian potentate, they recalled him and appointed a nonentity in his place. Soon the replacement too was recalled, and Sparta virtually abdicated the leadership of the general Hellenic coalition. When some of the other allies asked Athens to assume the leadership role, it willingly did so.

Founding of the Delian League

The new confederation, formed in 488/487 B.C., was in truth the brainchild of Themistocles, who had made Athens the foremost sea power in the Aegean. But it was the moderate aristocrat Aristeides who actually brought the organization itself into being, and another aristocrat, Kimon, the son of Miltiades, was its first vigorous leader.

Though theoretically an alliance among equals, the Delian League was dominated by Athens from its inception. Its headquarters was on the island of Delos (hence the name), but Athens furnished all the important officials, including the commander-in-chief, and most of the naval power. The treasurers also were Athenians. Many of the league members were to regret they had all tossed red-hot pieces of iron hissing into the sea and had sworn to abide by the alliance until the iron should float.

Under Kimon's generalship, the League was notably successful. All the Greek states in the Aegean area were freed from Persian domination, and most joined the League. About 468 B.C., a high point in the counteroffensive occurred at the battle of Eurymedon, in southern Asia Minor, where the Persian fleet and army were decisively defeated. The very success of the Delian League, however, brought problems. When the Persian threat receded, some members wanted to withdraw. Kimon established a principle of "no secession" and used military power to enforce this decision. He also arranged that some states, including two which had rebelled, Naxos and Thasos, would no longer furnish contingents of ships and men, but money only. This practice was more convenient for many small states, but it left them entirely at Athens' mercy. The amount of their contributions could be determined by Athens alone, and collections were made under threat of force. The league was growing into an empire, with imperialist coercions.

Sparta at first acquiesced in the formation of an Athenian-led league, probably because the Athenian leaders in charge were rather conservative aristocrats (Aristeides and Kimon), whose basic philosophy called for cooperation with Sparta and other non-allied Greek states in a common offensive against the real enemy, Persia. As the league developed into empire, however, Sparta seems to have made preparations to intervene, perhaps intending to aid Thasos when that city rebelled and was besieged by Athenian forces after 465 B.C. But then Sparta was hit by a destructive earthquake, followed by a helot revolt; so weakened, she was forced to ask for help from her allies. When Kimon led an infantry force from Athens to help, however, the Spartan leaders spurned his assistance. This snub brought a political reaction in Athens, and on his return Kimon was ostracized for a decade.

The Leadership of Pericles

The exile of Kimon meant also a change in party dominance. Democratic leaders Ephialtes and Pericles now assumed leadership of the state and the Delian League. Democratic political reforms we have alluded to earlier were put into effect. Pericles, frequently elected *strategos,* was the architect of domestic and foreign policy.

Pericles continued the offensive against Persia and engaged in risky—at length, disastrous—campaigns into Egypt, to aid a revolt there against the Persian king, who was then Artaxerxes. But he also undertook to create a land empire, based on alliances with mainland Greek states, which directly challenged Sparta's basic position. These allies included Boeotia (except Thebes), Phocis, Thessaly, Megara, Argos, and others. This adventuresome policy brought war with Sparta and her allies at the same time that a tremendous effort was being exerted in Egypt. The Athenians lost on both fronts though without a complete disaster. They lost most of their mainland allies, but Athenian control over the remaining Delian League members in fact tightened. When a Persian fleet threatened to enter the Aegean, the Delian League treasury was moved to Athens, and league members were charged a percentage for the protection of that city's tutelary goddess. Moreover, once peace was again established, Pericles felt free to use at least some Delian League funds for purely Athenian purposes.

Other policies of Pericles grated on the allies of Athens also. Athenian colonies called cleruchies (from *kleroi,* plots of land assigned to colonizing citizens) were sent out to various allied territories, beginning with the Chersonese. The land on which these Athenians settled was purchased by the mother city, but only through a reduction in the subject region's tribute, not by direct payment of funds. The settlers retained their Athenian citizenship and served almost like garrison troops in their new homes, thereby consolidating Athenian domination. It rankled, also, that any protest against the tribute levied on the subject states (at the height of the Delian League there were about 300 of them) could be decided only at Athens, before an Athenian court. Athenian weights and measures were made the required standard; and Athens, to its economic benefit, dominated the minting of all coins.

Rebuilding of Athenian Temples

After about 445 B.C. Athens was at peace with both Persia and Sparta. Perhaps as a means of giving work to unemployed sailors or simply to embellish the city, Pericles, serving as *strategos* year after year, proposed to rebuild the temples on the Acropolis destroyed by the Persians thirty-five years earlier. He had previously suggested that other Greek states assist in this restoration, but without response. Surplus tribute funds from league members and income from other sources, especially the silver mines, provided the necessary capital.

The Parthenon, the Temple of Athena on the Acropolis, begun in 447 B.C., was of course the most important structure built during the age of Pericles. Its chief architect was Ictinus, and its chief sculptor was

The Parthenon, Doric style temple of Athena on the Acropolis, Athens. The most celebrated temple of antiquity. *(Built 447–443 B.C.)*

Pheidias, who also sculptured the chryselephantine (gold-and-ivory) statue of Zeus for the temple at Olympia, considered one of the Seven Wonders of the Ancient World. He placed a similar huge statue of Athena in the cella of the Parthenon and did most of the frieze sculpture, much of which is now in the British Museum. The magnificent Propylaea, or temple-like entrance to the Acropolis, was also built by Pericles (finished about 432 B.C.), along with an odeum (music hall) near the Acropolis. During the Peloponnesian War, after the death of Pericles, the Temple of Athena Nike and the Erechtheum (with its splendid caryatid porch), both on the Acropolis, and the so-called Theseum (the best-preserved temple at Athens), erected near the Agora below the Acropolis, were all constructed.

The Brilliance of Periclean Athens

The physical setting, beautiful even in ruins, is still impressive; but even more astonishing is what we know of the intellectual atmosphere of Pericles' Athens. In the years around 440 B.C., Sophocles and Euripides were writing tragedy; Socrates, then in his twenties, may already have

146

been teaching; Herodotus (originally from Halicarnassus) was writing his *History;* Protagoras and other Sophists were lecturing to eager young men; Pheidias and other celebrated artists went about their work. At no other time in the history of mankind has such a galaxy of intellectuals and artists been concentrated within so small a political entity during such a short period. Intellectuals from other cities were drawn to Athens as if by a magnet. About the time Pericles died, Xenophon and Plato were infants or soon to be born, and Thucydides was a grown man.

Even lower-class Athenians could take advantage of the opportunities of their city, become prosperous through the tribute of empire. Many of her citizens, holding the numerous offices, were on the public payroll. The democracy employed hundreds of jurors *(dicasts);* numerous other citizens served in the fleet. Citizens were eligible, also, for a small payment from a special fund *(theoricon)* that made it possible for them to attend the great theatrical spectacles put on at Athens. And, of course, stipends for public office made it possible for relatively poor men to serve.

It was indeed a brilliant age; but there were dark spots. To some degree, Athenians as a group lived off the labor of their subjects, and many citizens kept slaves. Women did not have very high status and played mostly a subordinate, domestic role. Even the system of salaried public office, without which democracy is impossible, was attacked as a questionable use of state funds by Pericles to build a political machine —a kind of early patronage system. There is some justice in these various attacks, which even today appear occasionally in newspapers and magazines. But whatever Athens' weaknesses in this glorious era, they were more than compensated by its strengths. Nothing can quite tarnish the brilliant luster that history has given to Periclean Athens.

Books for Further Reading

BOARDMAN, J., *The Greeks Overseas,* Baltimore, 1964.

BURN, A. R., *Persia and the Greeks: The Defense of the West,* London, 1967.

EHRENBERG, V., *The Greek State,* New York, 1964.

EHRENBERG, V., *From Solon to Socrates,* London, 1968.

FORREST, W., *A History of Sparta, 950–121 B.C.,* London, 1968.

FORREST, W., *The Emergence of Greek Democracy,* London, 1966.

HIGNETT, C., *A History of the Athenian Constitution,* Oxford, 1952.

HUXLEY, G., *Early Sparta,* Cambridge, Mass., 1962.

JONES, A. H. M., *Athenian Democracy,* London, 1957.

KAGAN, D., *The Great Dialogue: History of Greek Political Thought,* New York, 1965.

MICHELL, H., *Sparta,* London, 1952.

RHODES, P. J., *The Athenian Boule,* Oxford, 1972.

ZIMMERN, A., *The Greek Commonwealth,* New York, 1932.

9

Hellenic Failure:
Recurring War

A. The Peloponnesian War (431–404 B.C.)

In retrospect and in the light of the usual trends in human history, there seems to have been something almost inevitable about the Peloponnesian War. When geography and circumstance throw together two approximately equal powers, they usually contend for supremacy. And when the two states are as unlike as Athens and Sparta, this tendency is even stronger. Athens symbolized all that was liberal, or even radical: freedom (at least for Athenians!), individualism, willingness to try out new ideas. Sparta stood solidly against these things and nurtured conservative ideals: order, stability, obedience. The Spartans were suspicious of anything novel. They were slow to act, however, and it was Athens that forced the ultimate confrontation.

The moving spirit behind that Athenian policy was Pericles. Though he continued to be elected to the *strategia* every year, his position just prior to the war was not so strong as before. He had to fight unpopular little wars to keep the Delian League members in line. His political enemies combined to attack him viciously, sometimes sniping at him through his friends. The sculptor Pheidias was accused of embezzling precious materials; the outcome of the trial is not known, but he went into exile. Aspasia, the beautiful and intellectual woman from Miletus who was a sort of unofficial second wife to Pericles, was accused of impiety. Pericles' friend the philosopher Anaxagoras was charged with atheism. Still, Periclean rhetoric generally controlled the Athenian assembly, and the power politics the "Olympian" espoused became state policy.

148

Athenian presence in western waters always disturbed the Corinthians, chief allies of the Spartans in the Peloponnese. When Athens chose to intervene in the interest of Corcyra, an island in the Ionian Sea once colonized by Corinth, the challenge to the Corinthian sphere of influence was clear. Potidaea, another former colony of Corinth located in the Chalcidice, at the northwestern corner of the Aegean Sea, had become a member of the Delian League. When Potidaea later rebelled against Athens' continued domination, Corinth sent aid. Megara, a small state at the Attic end of the isthmus just opposite Corinth, at one point left the Peloponnesian League over a dispute with Corinth and joined the Athenian alliance. Later it left Athens and rejoined the Peloponnese alliance. In retaliation, Pericles decreed that Megara could not trade with any member of the Delian confederacy. This was a severe economic blow to Megara, which joined with Corinth in demanding a meeting of the Peloponnesian League, at which it persuaded the Spartans to send an ultimatum to Athens. Pericles in turn convinced the Athenians to reject any compromise, and soon the prolonged and ruinous war was on.

The First Stage (431–421 B.C.)

Pericles seems to have felt that a full-scale war with Sparta and the Peloponnesian League was inevitable, and that it might as well come while he was still around to lead it. Certainly Athens was more nearly ready for the conflict than Sparta was. Despite the enormous cost of beautifying Athens and, more recently, of the siege of Potidaca, there were still 6,000 talents in the Athenian treasury; and the fleet of Athens was invincible. The strategy was to be that spelled out by Themistocles much earlier, with some modifications: Athens was not to attempt to defeat the Peloponnesian army, which was probably unbeatable on land, but was to rely mainly on its navy. When the enemy invaded Attica, all its citizens were to withdraw within the walls of Athens or the Piraeus, or inside the "Long Walls" (about five miles long), which in recent decades had been constructed to connect Athens with her port. The outlying land would not be defended. Supplies would be shipped in from overseas possessions. Income from the silver mines, from tribute, and from customs duties in various places was to sustain Athens for the long haul.

Sparta, on the other hand, did not have the economic resources even for long campaigns, much less for a long war. Yet Sparta had men and dependable allies.

Tyche—Fortune—dealt Athens an early, severe blow. The expected invasion came, led by the Spartan king Archidamus II. The Athenians took refuge within the walls as planned, and they allowed their land to be ravaged. The scene was repeated the following year. Then plague struck the crowded city. Within a few months a considerable percentage—possibly a third—of the populace had died. Though Athens fought on and made an apparent recovery, the state was never so strong again. One of those who died during this time (429 B.C.) was Pericles himself. Athens never found another Pericles. A tanner named Cleon rose to leadership, and his chief political opponent was the general Nicias, a conservative aristocrat.

One campaign of 425 B.C. somehow symbolizes this war. The Athenian admiral Demosthenes decided to seize the harbor and spit of land at Pylos in the southwestern Peloponnese, as a way station for naval squadrons and a base for raiding Spartan territory. The Spartans reacted by sending an army to the area, so near to the lands worked by helots. For some months the two forces fought over this spit of land and a neighboring island (Sphacteria), which were both so poor they had no permanent inhabitants. At length the Athenians, under Cleon now, not only won but even took a number of Spartans as prisoners. True, the Spartans were isolated on the island and almost starved to death, but the idea of Spartans surrendering under any circumstance astonished the Greek world. Cleon's reputation stood high; therefore when he recommended that the Athenians refuse to negotiate a peace that Sparta would probably have accepted at this point, he carried the day.

The Spartans found a vigorous general of their own, Brasidas. He realized that Athens was most vulnerable in the northern Aegean area, where its fleet could not bar the entry of the Peloponnesian army. The fighting thus came to focus on Amphipolis, where Cleon brought Athenian troops to oppose Brasidas. In the ensuing battle (422 B.C.) both of these leaders were killed, and the Athenian commander Nicias soon negotiated the peace treaty named for him (421 B.C.). Unfortunately it did not really settle any of the problems that had caused the war, and though intended to endure fifty years, it lasted only eight.

The Second Stage (415–404 B.C.)

The resumption of war was in part the work of another Athenian leader, Alcibiades. This youthful charmer learned from his teacher Socrates everything except his main message—virtue—and had all the abilities to be another Pericles, except for integrity. He persuaded the Athenians to undertake a risky and ultimately disastrous adventure in the west, in Sicily. Just as back home, Greeks in Sicily were divided along Dorian-Ionian lines. When Athens got an appeal for help from Ionian Segesta against Dorian Syracuse, Alcibiades persuaded the citizens not only to give aid but also to attempt to conquer Sicily for Athens. In doing so, Athens would become too powerful for the Peloponnesians.

Alcibiades, unfortunately, at the last minute was charged with profaning the Eleusinian mysteries in a drunken burlesque at a party and was deposed from leadership of the expedition (415 B.C.). Fearing the death penalty, Alcibiades fled—to Sparta. He charmed his way into the confidence of the Spartan leaders; he advised them to resume the war, to send aid to Syracuse, to appeal for help from Persia, and to establish a permanent base within Attica. His advice helped Sparta to win the war. In Sicily, the Athenian expedition laid siege to Syracuse but gradually lost the initiative to an augmented defense force led by the Spartan general Gylippus. Athens strained her resources and sent more ships and men. Through a combination of ill fortune and bad generalship, these forces were bottled up and then destroyed during an attempted retreat. Allied troops were either sold into slavery or eventually redeemed by family or friends, but the Athenians were killed outright or otherwise done to death. This was a terrific blow, from which Athens never quite recovered.

In spite of this disaster, Athens rebuilt her fleet and actually won several important naval victories against the Peloponnesian fleet, which was now financed by Persia. Some Athenian allies, especially those nearest Persia, now began to revolt, with Persian and Spartan aid. In Athens there arose a strong opposition to the democracy because of the losses at Syracuse. Alcibiades left Sparta (it was said that he left the king's wife pregnant) and went on to Persia, where he persuaded the Persians not to help Sparta too much. They would, he said, simply exchange Athens for Sparta as their chief opponent in the Aegean.

Alcibiades now entered into negotiation with some Athenian leaders, first at the base at Samos and then in Athens. He intimated that if Athens were to replace the democracy with an oligarchy he might find it possible to get the Persians to switch sides—all important, since their money was financing the Peloponnesian navy. A conspiracy was formed, a chief opponent was assassinated, and soon Athens became an oligarchy, for the first time since Solon. Still, moderates such as Theramenes retained positions of leadership, and on Samos the democrats maintained control. After a time, when it became apparent the Persians would not support Athens, and after the Athenian navy regained a degree of control over the Aegean, the democracy was restored. Alcibiades played a role in the naval successes. As a reward for this, he was absolved of the sentence and the curse that had been placed on him. Once again he was elected to the *strategia* and given command of the main fleet. At last, however, when the Persians again were bankrolling the Spartan naval forces, Alcibiades lost a major naval battle. It was not his fault—he was absent, and his lieutenant fought against his orders; yet since Athenians had the occasional habit of executing or exiling unsuccessful commanders, Alcibiades fled to a refuge in the Hellespont. After the war the Persians procured his assassination.

For Athens, the decisive defeat came in 405 B.C., when their fleet was destroyed at Aegospotami (Goat's River), on the Hellespont. Soon after, the Spartan admiral Lysander put Athens itself under siege, with a naval blockade this time, and in a few months starved the Athenians into surrender.

B. Spartan Dominance

A New Order for Athens and the Former Members of the Delian League

In the aftermath of these defeats, Lysander and the leadership of Sparta naturally dissolved the Athenian empire. In every "liberated" state, oligarchies were put in control. Decarchies (ten-man boards) supported by Spartan harmosts, who were commanders of garrisons, ruled the "liberated" states. These oligarchical boards exiled or otherwise got rid of their most likely enemies, the democratic leaders.

The Spartan allies, especially Corinth, who had contributed much to the conduct of the war were unhappy with the peace settlement. As they viewed it, Athens was treated too gently; moreover, it was Sparta that gained most of the booty as well as the tribute and continuing hegemony. It was another source of dissatisfaction that the Greek states in Asia Minor were virtually abandoned to the Persians— as the price Sparta paid for renewed Persian support in the later years of the war. As we shall see, however, Sparta was later to attempt to renege on that agreement.

At Athens, the ruling clique comprised thirty, rather than ten, oligarchs. These thirty were supposed to set up a rather broad oligarchy, but they believed no such government could endure while the democratic leaders lived. The ensuing reign of terror accounted for the execution of hundreds of their possible opponents. They well earned their nickname, the "Thirty Tyrants."

A reaction inevitably came. An exiled moderate politician, Thrasybulus, took refuge in a frontier fortress and began to build up a military force. He soon moved on to Piraeus and fortified this important position. The oligarchs attempted to stop him but failed; they then called on the Spartans for aid. It was sent, but the leader was King Pausanias, who disapproved of Lysander's policies. He noted, quite correctly, that those policies were alienating most Greeks from any feeling of loyalty to Sparta or sympathy for its aims. Thebes and Corinth, in fact, had refused to support the expedition. The King superseded Lysander and allowed a compromise. The democracy was restored in Athens (403 B.C.), and amnesty was granted to all oligarchs, who were also given permanent asylum at Eleusis.

Compared with prewar Athens, the restored democracy, however, was a weak state. The population had probably been halved, or even worse. The Athenian empire was gone, and so was the navy. The Long Walls had been torn down. Economically, the city was stricken. Only the beauty of the Acropolis and the Agora nearby, some shreds of the intellectual structure—and memories—remained of the glory that had been.

Sparta Attempts to Lead
a Pan-Hellenic Crusade

The end of the Thirty Tyrants at Athens was followed by the elimination also of many of the decarchies throughout the Aegean, in what was now the Spartan—no longer the Athenian—empire. Sparta maintained in theory the principle of sovereignty for her allies but, in practice, often domineered over them. If Spartans were to become truly leaders of a unified Greece, they must organize a crusade against a common enemy. This could be none other than Persia, which had begun to impose its will on the Asian Greek states. King Artaxerxes II, on his part, had reason to move against the Greeks in general, and especially the Spartans, because of a recent expedition against him—the famous "March of the Ten Thousand."

The Greek mercenaries who comprised the Ten Thousand were in the service of the Persian king's brother Cyrus, who in 401 B.C. attempted to seize the throne from Artaxerxes with the aid of the Greek soldiers. The latter were in ample supply because of the recent end of the Peloponnesian War. Cyrus' expedition was well documented by the historian Xenophon, who participated in it. The army marched deep into the interior of the vast empire and met Artaxerxes' army in battle at Cunaxa, far down into Mesopotamia. The Greeks won the battle with almost no losses, but unfortunately for them Cyrus was so anxious to kill his brother that he recklessly exposed himself and was slain. With their royal paymaster dead, the Greeks had little reason to stay in hostile territory. Under guise of a parley, the Persians treacherously killed the Greek generals. The Greek soldiers then elected new ones and escaped in a desperate march that took them to the Black Sea. Many of the survivors joined the Spartan expedition in Asia Minor, to which we shall return.

A Spartan expeditionary force under Thibron had arrived in Asia Minor in 400 B.C. His successor Dercyllidas accomplished little. The Spartan king who next led this expedition was Agesilaus; surprisingly, for a Spartan, he was wizened and crippled; yet he was quite competent. His campaigns in 396 and 395 B.C. were models of deception and achieved more than might have been expected, given the rather small size of the Greek—and Spartan—contributions to the army. But the Persians were not to be counted out easily.

The Corinthian War (394–387 B.C.)

Persian diplomacy and Persian money, combined with the unpopularity of Sparta's hegemony, stirred up a war against the Spartans in Greece itself, and in 394 B.C. King Agesilaus was recalled from Asia Minor. A coalition of Athens, Thebes, Corinth, Argos, and other states fought indecisively with Sparta for several years. Athens used Persian help to regain some naval power and rebuilt the Long Walls. Sparta won the chief land engagements, but the Athenian general Iphicrates, in a portentous battle, used light-armed troops to destroy an entire Spartan regiment in 390 B.C. Lysander was killed in an early engagement.

   When peace came at last (387/386 B.C.; called the Kings Peace), it was virtually imposed by Artaxerxes, with the connivance of Sparta. Persia gained most from the war: an end to Spartan aggression in Asia Minor and control of the Greek states there. Sparta gained a few more years as the dominant power in Greece.

Renewed War (378–371 B.C.)

Sparta reaped great unpopularity throughout Greece because of her agreement to leave Ionia to the Persians. Sparta's Greek allies were put off also by Spartan interference in their internal affairs and by the tendency of Spartan leaders to treat them more and more as subjects. One of Sparta's generals seized an opportunity to put a garrison in Thebes in support of the oligarchic faction, which drove out the democrats. A similar attempt to put a garrison in Athens' port, Piraeus, alienated the Athenians. After Theban democrats regained control of Thebes in a coup and expelled the Spartan garrison, a new coalition was put together to end the Spartan dominance; Athens and Thebes were the chief allies.

   Athens was able to form a second Athenian confederacy (378/ 377 B.C.), much like the old Delian League, but with safeguards for the allied states against possible Athenian domination. Thebes also strengthened its position in Boeotia and dominated a reconstituted Boeotian League. When Thebes also began to expand outside Boeotia, Athens grew cool to the alliance and sought a peace conference. This conference included representatives from many Greek states, and a real effort was made to end the constant war and repression. Unfortunately, when Epaminondas, the representative for Thebes, attempted to sign for all members of the Boeotian League, Agesilaus would not permit it, and the Theban delegation walked out of the conference. The others signed anyway and left Thebes to the tender mercies of Sparta.

C. Theban Dominance (371–362 B.C.)

Victory over Sparta at Leuctra

As everyone at the peace conference had anticipated, the Spartans quickly mobilized an army and marched north to deal with Thebes. The results, however, were wholly unanticipated. For the first time in memory, a main army of Sparta was defeated and driven from the field at the Battle of Leuctra, in 371 B.C. By keeping Thebes at war for years, Sparta herself had helped to forge the army that defeated her. Two Theban leaders deserve mention as architects of victory. Epaminondas, serving as *boeotarch* in the generally democratic Theban state, supplied the tactical genius. Pelopidas, a dashing and sometimes rash warrior, had helped to train the army, especially the elite Sacred Band of 300 picked men who played a key role in the battle.

The tactics of Epaminondas were unusual enough to be worth a note. Normally, Greek armies depended upon a strong right wing to crush the opposing left. This seemed necessary because of the tendency of the troops to close to the right as they advanced, with each man seeking the protection not only of his own shield but also that of the nearest man on his right. The generals chose to use rather than try to counter this tendency—hence the strong right. Before Leuctra, however, Epaminondas vastly strengthened his left wing and actually withheld his right from battle, since it was made up of allies who might not be dependable. The Sacred Band and the other men on the left were fifty shields deep, compared with the twelve shields of the Spartans. As the startled Spartan commander attempted, just before the battle, to strengthen his right, a cavalry charge threw his ranks into disorder, and the Thebans were suddenly upon them in overwhelming force.

The Humiliation of Sparta

Disastrous defeat is demoralizing for any state; but for Sparta, with her whole society organized on a military basis, the blow was especially severe. King Agesilaus, who was not at Leuctra, put down with difficulty a rebellion of young men at home. He and the ephors then reviewed the stringent laws that disgraced anyone who retreated from a battlefield.

It was then announced that the laws should "sleep" for one day; otherwise all the survivors would have been cashiered. Plutarch says—on what information we do not know—that those at home whose relatives fell at Leuctra rejoiced and that those whose relatives survived felt disgraced, regardless of the official decision to let the laws "sleep."

  Epaminondas now invaded Laconia itself—the first such invasion since the Dorians had occupied the Peloponnese—but was prevented from taking the unwalled city of Sparta proper by energetic defense measures and a fortuitous flood of the Eurotas River near the city. Epaminondas helped organize a new Arcadian League as rival to Sparta in the peninsula, with headquarters at Megalopolis. Moreover, he freed Messenia, with its hordes of helots. Sparta's power went into a decline that was permanent, except for a brief period of resurgence near the end of the following century.

Theban Ascendancy and Decline

The only possible contender with Thebes for the premier position among the Greek states at this point was Jason of Pherae. He began as tyrant of that city, located in Thessaly, and by a combination of genius, force, and threats of force, he had in recent years made himself ruler of all Thessaly in a typical sort of alliance. He appeared with an army just after the Battle of Leuctra and mediated a temporary truce that permitted the Spartans to retreat to the Peloponnese. Certainly his ambitions would soon have brought him to a confrontation with the Thebans, even though the two leagues were on friendly terms. In 370 B.C. he planned some important military venture; some thought he even intended to seize the treasure of the Delphic priests to use it to finance a large-scale conquest. But he was assassinated, and no significant figure was found to take his place. Much of his territory was soon under the control of the Thebans.

  The power of Thebes rested chiefly in her leaders: Epaminondas, the cool and competent general, and Pelopidas, the impulsive but equally competent tactician. Epaminondas was austere, reportedly something of a philosopher. His views were liberal. He could hold the top office of *boeotarch* no more frequently than every second year, however, and thus his recommendations were not always followed. Thebes generally used the army instead of persuasive leadership to force its rule upon others. It therefore became just another aggressive city-state, muscling its coercive way to the top.

  Thebes' control outside Boeotia extended to Thessaly and even Macedonia. At one point a young Macedonian of royal family was brought to Thebes as a hostage; later he would be King Philip, father of Alexander the Great. Pelopidas had much to do with success in this area, but unfortunately he was killed in a rash charge against superior numbers in Thessaly. The very success of Thebes ensured a coalition against that city. Athens joined Sparta and others in an anti-Theban alliance. Though landlocked, Thebes even built a navy in an attempt to counter Athens' power at sea. Sparta gradually strengthened her position in the Peloponnese, and Thebes found it necessary to intervene there twice more.

Epaminondas led the final thrust into the Peloponnese, where he hoped to regain control without a fight; but this was not to be. At Mantinea, in Arcadia, he was brought to battle in 362 B.C. Astonishingly, through a series of maneuvers before the battle, he succeeded in again surprising the allies with precisely the same tactics he had used at Leuctra. The Thebans swept the field, in what would have been a great victory had Epaminondas himself not been killed. Before he died, he learned that others he considered capable of assuming command had been killed, too; he therefore counseled that the Thebans make peace and return home.

The Thebans could no longer aspire to the leadership of all Greece. The Athenians perhaps did, and once again began to tyrannize over the members of their reconstituted confederacy. But a rebellion in 357 B.C., abetted by the enemies of Athens, left the state much weakened. Another would-be leader, the small state of Phocis on the borders of Delphi, plunged into meteoric political adventure for a few short years. After a dispute with the priests of Delphi, the Phocians virtually took over the oracle. In the inevitable "Sacred War" that followed, waged against some members of the Delphic amphictyony, the Phocians made use of the Delphic treasure to hire mercenaries and for a time were astonishingly successful. Ultimately, Phocis was defeated by Philip II of Macedonia, who used the alleged religious war as an opportunity for massive intervention in Greek affairs.

D. Macedonia Rises to Dominate Greece

The king who made Macedonia the chief power of the Greek peninsula was Philip II (r.359–336 B.C.). He became head of state when he was about twenty-three, first as regent for his nephew Amyntas and then, quite soon, as king himself. The two years Philip spent as a hostage in Thebes during its years of ascendancy were decisive in shaping his career. He learned more of military matters than of the philosophy he studied in Epaminondas' house. An eminently pragmatic person, he saw that what Macedonia really needed was a better army.

Macedonia had many enemies, and there were formidable obstacles to any rise to significance for it. The country was more rural than Greece to the south, and tribal influences were still strong. Macedonia had been effectively unified only in the late 5th century B.C.—but as a monarchy, not as a city-state. Illyrians to the west, Thracians to the north and east, Thessalians to the south, and Athenians, who had strong interests in the entire northern Aegean area: all these would oppose any powerful development of Macedonia.

Philip's Reorganization of the Army

All the Greek states by this time relied heavily on mercenary troops, especially archers, slingers, and other light-armed specialists. Philip used them, too. But in a period when the Greeks used fewer and fewer citizens in their armies, Philip was able to make Macedonians the core of his phalanx and to keep them in service on a year-round basis. Recently acquired silver and gold mines made possible this heavy military expenditure. To instill group loyalty, the units were organized by tribe. A longer thrusting-spear than was normal in the south made his phalanx quite formidable. More close-order drill was needed, but this was no problem. In addition, Philip—having learned this, among other things, from Epaminondas—developed a very strong cavalry contingent, which he used to break the opposing line of battle and throw it into disorder—much the way Epaminondas did at Leuctra and Mantinea, but with even more decisive impact.

With this army Philip soon defeated the Illyrians and Thracians, despite Athenian support for some of the latter group. He expanded to the sea east of the Chalcidice. In that area he captured Amphipolis and renamed it Philippi. Near this city were more of the rich gold and silver mines that gave Philip at least 1,000 talents a year—the financial sinew he needed for his aggressive policies. His power soon was felt toward the south, also, as he expanded into Thessaly.

Philip Intervenes in the Sacred War;
Demosthenes' Opposition

As we have seen, the Phocians, fighting against certain members of the Delphic amphictyony, won several quick victories and soon pressed north into Thessaly. The Thessalians called on Philip and Macedonia to aid them (353 B.C.). After an initial defeat, the next year Philip was able to drive the Phocians out of Thessaly. He hoped to use the Sacred War, by playing the role of defender of Apollo and the Delphic oracle, to gain a powerful position in central Greece. Temporarily, however, he was

Demosthenes, greatest of all Athenian orators. Best known for his famous *Philippics. (Alinari-Scala)*

unable to proceed into Phocis proper. A group of allies, including Athens, sent troops to the pass at Thermopylae and blocked him. Philip returned home to Macedonia and to further campaigning against Thrace and other neighboring areas on the north and west. Macedonia's territory, wealth, and power were increasing rapidly, and soon Philip felt capable of moving against the Chalcidian League (around Chalcidice), the most important city of which was Olynthus. Athens had long had an important interest in the area.

The most indefatigable opponent of Macedonia in the days of both Philip II and Alexander after him was that greatest of all Athenian orators, Demosthenes. In a series of famous orations delivered over a period of about a decade, his famous *Philippics,* the Athenian thundered against the Macedonian. The first came in 351 or 350 B.C. Demosthenes

159

tried almost in vain to arouse the Athenians to their old glory. In one way the orator seems, in retrospect, to have been prescient, patriotic, and courageous; but in another way, he seems more a man who lived in the past, who was attempting to call the Athenians to a war they could not sustain and had no chance of winning—perhaps a bit out of touch with reality.

When Philip turned upon Olynthus in 349 B.C., in his three Olynthiac orations Demosthenes urged the Athenians to intervene, even though Olynthus had been allied with Philip against Athens only a short time before. Athens did send help to Olynthus (more mercenaries than citizens), but the aid was too little and too late. Philip diverted the Athenians by promoting a revolt in Euboea against its pro-Athenian leader. In 348 B.C. Philip was able to destroy Olynthus. The whole campaign illustrates Philip's consummate if somewhat unscrupulous methods: he took advantage of money, weather, diplomacy, trickery, bribery—as well as of his military power—to achieve his goal.

By now most Athenian leaders, including Demosthenes, his inveterate orator-enemy Aeschines, and Eubulus, the cautious and moderate financial expert, recognized the necessity for peace. An embassy under Philocrates (Demosthenes and Aeschines were also members) traveled to Macedonia and negotiated a peace in 346 B.C. Athens and Macedonia became allies; the effect of the peace was to abandon Phocis to Philip. The Macedonians soon reduced Phocis, thereby ending the Sacred War. Philip was given the vacant place on the amphictyonic council and, in fact, a few months later was allowed to preside over the Pythian festival at Delphi.

Demosthenes and other Athenians, perhaps feeling guilty over the fate of Phocis and with good reason mistrusting Philip, began to have second thoughts. Demosthenes now delivered a second *Philippic* (343 B.C.), in which he charged that Philip intended nothing less than the destruction of Athens and he called into question the justice of some of Philip's recently acquired holdings in the northern Aegean. Philocrates, the chief negotiator of the peace, was charged with treason and went into exile. Demosthenes next initiated one of the most famous trials in all the classical world, a proceeding in which he impeached his rival Aeschines. The latter was acquitted, however. The published orations of the two, with their bitter charges and countercharges, in a biased way provide much of the information we have for this period. The works of Isocrates, another great orator—or rather, publicist, for his speaking voice was poor and others presented his orations—who saw Philip as a possible savior of Greece from itself, present additional information, quite different in tone.

In succeeding years Demosthenes continued his campaign to

create an anti-Macedonian alliance. His third *Philippic* came in 341 B.C. Philip's continuing expansionist tactics caused friction, but specific incidents in the deteriorating relationship were as much the fault of Athens as of Philip, who seemed genuinely to respect the great cultural traditions of that city. Philip's moves against the straits of the Bosporus and the Hellespont, so important to the Athenian grain supply, did much to bring Athenians around to the views of their great orator. Other Greek states also began to side with Athens.

Battle of Chaeronea (338 B.C.); The Corinthian League

The crucial point came when Philip prepared to intervene in another Sacred War, against Amphissa, which like Phocis earlier had a dispute with the Delphic priests. Demosthenes was able to get even Thebes to join with Athens to stop the southward thrust of the Macedonians. At Chaeronea, before Thebes, in 338 B.C. the Macedonian army crushed the allies, and Macedonia soon dominated practically all Greece. The Theban sacred band fought valiantly to the last man. The Athenians, including Demosthenes, fled the battlefield.

Except for Thebes, the Greek states—Athens especially—were lucky to receive treatment no more severe than a forced alliance with Macedonia. Philip's leniency was perhaps in part owing to the advice given him by the aged Isocrates, who had long hoped for a great leader, not a tyrant over Greece but a statesman and unifier.

Philip, at any rate, took little vengeance except on the Thebans. Demosthenes escaped punishment. The Macedonian king did force the Greeks into an alliance called, conventionally, the Corinthian League, whose member states were to remain autonomous. There was a league council and a league army, but no central taxation. Philip was to be the *hegemon* (guide, leader) of both the political structure and the army of this alliance. Macedonian garrisons were to be stationed at key points in Greece: Corinth, Thebes, Chalcis, and Thermopylae. More than a means of curbing the recalcitrant Greeks, the league was also to be the instrument of a unified Greek crusade against Persia under the leadership of Philip. Perhaps the hand of Isocrates may be seen here, too. The liberation of the Greeks in Asia Minor from the Persian yoke was a popular cause.

King Philip, however, was not destined to lead the cause. As he made preparations for the campaign, he was struck down by an assassin (336 B.C.). It was his young son and heir Alexander who would eventually lead the crusade against Persia.

Books for Further Reading

ADCOCK, F. E., *The Greek and Macedonian Art of War*, Berkeley and Los Angeles, 1957.

BURN, A. R., *Pericles and Athens*, New York, 1949.

CASSON, L., *Ships and Seamanship in the Ancient World*, Princeton, 1971.

FERGUSON, W. S., *Greek Imperialism*, New York, 1913.

FINLEY, J., *Thucydides*, Cambridge, Mass., 1952.

FREEMAN, K., *Greek City-States*, New York, 1950.

FROST, F., *Greek Society*, Lexington, Mass., 1971.

GLOVER, T. R., *From Pericles to Philip*, New York, 1917.

JAEGER, W., *Demosthenes: The Origin and Growth of His Policy*, Berkeley and Los Angeles, 1938.

JONES, A. H. M., *Sparta*, Cambridge, Mass., 1967.

KAGAN, D., *Outbreak of the Peloponnesian War*, Ithaca, 1969.

LAISTNER, M. L. W., *A History of the Greek World, 476–323 B.C.*, London, 1936.

Cultural Heights

10

The diverse inventiveness of Greek genius produced only disaster in political matters. The same genius, when expressed in science, philosophy, literature, art and architecture, produced the most astonishing flowering of culture known to history. These developments are discussed topically in this chapter. In this sort of survey, integration of these cultural topics into the flow of political history would result in unhappy fragmentation. The reader should keep in mind, nonetheless, that these achievements were often closely related to the great stream of mundane events, in order to view the discussion in proper historical perspective.

Any discussion of Hellenic culture must center upon Athens. We shall see, however, that science, philosophy, sculpture, and architecture flourished earliest on the Ionian coast of Asia Minor; this was at all times an important center for culture, along with Corinth, Syracuse, and other city-states. In a quite early period, even Spartan ceramic ware was superior to that of Athens, as was the more renowned Corinthian ware. But as artists in Athens (who may have been mostly *metics,* or alien residents) developed the black-on-red technique ("black-figured") to the ultimate, and then the red-on-black ("red-figured"), that city took the lead in production of fine pottery. With the prize festivals, Peisistratus established Athens as the center for drama, and Pericles encouraged philosophy, art, and architecture. Athens thus became preeminent in almost all facets of intellectual and artistic achievement.

163

Attic lekythos, red-on-black ("red-figured") as developed by Athenian artists. Hunter with dog. Fifth century B.C. *(Boston Museum of Fine Arts)*

A. Early Science and Philosophy

Thales and the Early Milesians

What traits of mind, what influences of environment, could cause one lone man, perhaps for the first time in history, to attempt to see and explain the world solely on rational grounds? Such a man was Thales of

Miletus, who flourished in Ionia soon after 600 B.C. No question of human causation can ever be fully answered, even by the individual involved himself, let alone by a historian some 2,500 years removed from the events. But the location of these happenings seems significant: Miletus was situated in Asia Minor, near the terminus of the great Royal Road that reached deep into Persia. Sea trade also occupied many Milesians; contacts with the older, more sophisticated civilizations of Asia were therefore numerous.

Thales' surviving fragments reveal nothing of his motivation. Two Greeks of a somewhat later period made it clear that what may come first in such an innovative learning process is shock, when a man discovers he has been taught much that is not true. This realization often comes, in turn, when a man looks out upon a wider world than that in which he was reared. Xenophanes of Colophon, founder of the so-called Eleatic school of natural philosophy, realized that the gods of Homer and Hesiod must be poetic invention when he learned that other people invented gods with traits like their own. The Ethiopians, he said, made their gods black; Thracians made theirs redheaded. He went on to theorize that there must be only one god, nothing like men, a being capable of seeing, feeling, thinking of all and eternally unchanging. Hecataeus of Miletus, geographer and proto-historian, about 500 B.C. traveled to Egypt and was shocked to learn that the priests there considered Greek ideas about the gods crude and puerile. Men of such inquiring minds, then, learned not only to mistrust what had been handed down to them by the ancients but also to doubt even the evidence of the senses.

Thales and his successors launched on a great adventure of the mind: through logical analysis alone, and ignoring the many-layered accumulation of myth, legend, and superstition by which men formerly explained the mysterious universe, they contemplated what is (being) and how it came to be and how it changes (becoming). Thales saw unity in what is, and he concluded that the unity must be one of substance. This basic substance, he decided, was water. The notion of a basic substance was pursued by several of Thales' successors. This idea is not so naïve as it might first appear, when one troubles to think about it.

Thales is supposed to have made his reputation by a spectacular prediction of the solar eclipse that took place in the spring of 585 B.C. He must have had astronomical records from either Mesopotamia or Egypt available to him. Astronomers today doubt he could have predicted the exact time of an eclipse on the basis of information then available; perhaps he merely predicted an approximate time, or perhaps he made a lucky guess.

Pythagoras (c. 580–500 B.C.)

Pythagoras, a generation younger than Thales, was also an Ionian Greek, born on the island of Samos, off Miletus. As a mature man, he emigrated to the West Greek colony of Croton in southern Italy and there made his mark. Pythagoreans emphasized numbers and their relations—or mathematics—as the key to the understanding of what is, rather than a theory of primal substance. Everyone knows one of Pythagoras' discoveries in geometry: as transmitted by Euclid, the so-called Pythagorean theorem is in daily use in building construction. Pythagoreans stressed harmony, which in music was shown to rest on a mathematical basis. Numbers, therefore, could be a practical guide in human affairs and could provide a mystical key to understanding the universe. The world, this school thought, was spherical—because a sphere is perfect.

Some Pythagoreans led ascetic, almost monastic lives and espoused.the Orphic religion, with its belief in transmigration or cycles of reincarnation of souls (or perhaps Orphism borrowed this from the Pythagoreans). Pythagoreans in southern Italy attempted to impose their austere code of conduct upon whole city-states. This brought a violent reaction in the 5th century B.C.; such puritanism was not for the average Greek. Nonetheless, Pythagoras influenced Plato, among many others, and there was an occasional resurgence of Pythagorean thought even in the time of the Roman Empire.

Heracleitus and Parmenides:
Polarization and Compromise

Two other natural philosophers, Heracleitus, an Ionian of Ephesus, and Parmenides of Elea in southern Italy (late 6th–early 5th century B.C.), brought to a climax the arguments on the nature of being, or reality, and of becoming, or change. Heracleitus said that change, a kind of constant flux, is the only reality; no such thing as *being* exists. That is, everything in the universe is either coming into being or passing out of being. He did see some logical unity in change, and this principle of rational order he called *logos*. His most famous aphorism was that "You can't step into the same river twice." The most famous comeback to this reported, probably facetiously, was that one of his debtors refused to pay him back on the grounds that Heracleitus wasn't the same person who lent the money and he was no longer the same person who borrowed it! Heracleitus thus rejected absolutes.

Parmenides took precisely the opposite view. There is no such thing as change, he said—only being. He completely mistrusted the evidence of the senses. Logically, he argued in his celebrated analysis, *not-*being cannot be; moreover, whatever is, is at once, completely and eternally. All apparent change is illusion. For him, the universe was a perfect body, that is, a sphere, and the earth was also a sphere set in the middle of the universe.

Compromise views were put forward. The best-known of these pluralists was Empedocles of Agrigentum, in Sicily, who lived in the mid-5th century B.C. He argued that there are four basic elements—fire, water, earth, and air—which never change, as Parmenides had said, but which constantly appear to change through their varying combination or dissolution, as Heracleitus had argued. Empedocles was a remarkable person, at times followed by thousands of disciples, who heeded his words as if inspired. Said to have healed the sick, he was thought to be in the final incarnation before union with deity.

Ionian by birth but Athenian by adoption, Anaxagoras, the friend of Pericles, held that there are an infinity of elements, which can come into or pass out of existence. In this same vein were the atomists, the best-known of whom was Democritus, a generation younger than Anaxagoras and perhaps once his pupil. He postulated an infinite number of atoms rushing through space, coagulating in vortices to form an infinite number of worlds. Either he or later atomists postulated also, a kind of geological and biological evolution.

The Sophists

The Sophists were a diverse group of philosophers who "brought philosophy down to earth" and became professional teachers of young men in Greece. Speculations about the cosmos they rejected as unprofitable or not relevant and turned to questions of how man ought to behave on earth.

In general, the Sophists were subjective in their outlook. This is best expressed by Protagoras, who was also a friend of Pericles in Athens, just before the Peloponnesian War. "Man is the measure of all things," he said, "of things which are, that they are; and of things which are not, that they are not." This quotation is much discussed; it appears to mean that he felt that man has no grounds for judgment but his own perceptions and his own mind. Followed to its logical end, this view would support relativism in morals, justice, and all other issues.

Gorgias of Leontini, in Sicily, who as an old man came to Athens during the Peloponnesian War, emphasized rhetoric and other practical virtues in his school—for which he charged very high tuition. He was totally skeptical of any possibility of real knowledge. "Nothing exists," he said. "If anything does exist, we cannot know it. If we could know it, we could not communicate it." Many of the sophists were apparently cynical and argued specious cases: for example, that justice was simply the interests of the stronger. Socrates and Plato opposed such skeptical, relativist teaching vigorously.

Socrates. *(Scala Fine Arts Publishers, Inc.)*

B. The Great Age of Philosophy

Socrates (469–399 B.C.)

Socrates surely ranks as one of the most influential persons in the history of Western civilization; yet we do not know him well. He left no writings, and we learn of him chiefly through the works of Plato and Xenophon. But Xenophon had only a shallow perception of his teacher; Plato nearly always used Socrates as the chief character in his dialogues, and it is difficult to separate Socrates the protagonist from Plato in these creations.

Socrates was a stonemason who made an indifferent living for his family. No wonder his wife Xanthippe had a reputation as a nag. He taught an important array of pupils; besides Plato and Xenophon, Alcibiades and Critias were among them. But unlike the Sophists, he taught without pay. Moreover, his teaching was infused with a high moral purpose: education, he insisted, had the improvement of the individual as its sole purpose. His didactic method was unusual. He felt that knowledge was already somehow immanent within each person and needed only to be elicited. He therefore used a question-and-answer method to lead his students to see for themselves. The same sort of system was also used by him in debating with others, with ironical effect, and the great teacher made enemies when he demonstrated publicly that many self-declared experts did not know what they were talking about.

Socrates' great emphasis was on virtue, which he felt could be elicited from every man. Wrong behavior was simply ignorance. For example, persons who commit murder may understand that it is "wrong" to do so, but at the moment of their crime they believe that, at this place and time, it is right for them. Socrates taught, and strictly adhered to, the principle that it is never right to do wrong. Curiously, he declared that he was sometimes guided, in a negative way, by an inner voice, a *daimon*.

Socrates' trial and subsequent execution took place in the disillusionment following the Athenian loss of the Peloponnesian War. In this vengeful atmosphere, he was accused of introducing strange gods and of corrupting the youth of Athens. If we can believe Plato, he ignored these charges and instead chose to defend his whole life and purpose. Perhaps the real reason for such crude accusations was that Alcibiades and Critias turned out so badly after having been instructed by Socrates. The jury that convicted him did not expect he would die as a result. He had the right of suggesting an alternate sentence, which was usually exile; instead, he said they really ought to reward him, not penalize him, but if they insisted, he would pay a small fine! The jury was so irritated it confirmed the death sentence. Socrates could still have escaped (his friends arranged to bribe the jailor), and probably even his accusers would have preferred that he go into exile. However, he insisted that all his life he had taught that one should obey the laws and that it is never right to do wrong. How could he now turn his back on his own teachings? He drank the hemlock and died a martyr to his own cause.

Plato (c. 429–347 B.C.)

By common consent, Plato is the greatest philosopher in the Western tradition. Some of his work in systematic thought seems so much like musings from an ivory tower that one forgets how much he was influenced by events of his own day and by his efforts to confront contemporary problems. The failure and defeat of Athenian democracy, the dismal performance of oligarchy at the time of the "Thirty Tyrants" (some of whom were friends and relatives, for Plato was of the Athenian aristocracy), the execution of his beloved teacher Socrates, and the continued bloodletting in Greek politics all affected his thinking.

Socrates had taught his pupils to go to the root of any problem, to look for its essence. Plato did not attempt, piecemeal, to consider the world's ills; he sought for ultimate reality and the manner in which men might learn of that and attempt to perfect themselves and their institutions. His theory of Ideas is at the center of his philosophical thought. In this usage, the word "idea" is a transliteration from the Greek and does not mean "idea" in our modern sense at all, but rather signifies "form." Plato taught that the world of sensation is part illusion; reality lies in a separate world perceived only through the trained mind. Thus beauty, for him, was a thing in itself; things that are called beautiful are so only as they partake of the true or ideal form, Beauty. Other such forms include the four cardinal virtues: wisdom, restraint, bravery, justice. The highest of forms, almost like a monotheistic deity, was the Form of the Good. Plato was influenced by Orphism and believed (perhaps from Socrates) in the immortality of the soul.

The historian, of course, is interested in the great philosopher's ideas on government, a topic Plato treated in several of his dialogues, including the greatest of all, *The Republic.* The search for the best form of government, for Plato, was essentially the search for Justice. He argued the necessity that kings should become philosophers—or philosophers, kings. He outlined educational curricula, in which he eliminated Homer and all such "nonsense." The Greek polis was the ideal size for his perfect state, which was a single community. His society comprised two main classes, the workers and the guardians. Some of the latter would also be the rulers of the state. This upper class would be an elite of superior persons properly educated. They would possess all things in common; marriage would be eliminated; their children would be reared under the tutelage of the state. This sort of Utopia has been much imitated in literature, but seldom in practice.

In his later dialogues, Plato argued for a mixed constitution. He attempted to put his views into actual practice in Syracuse, which he appears to have visited three times, during the reigns of Dionysius I, his son-in-law Dion, and his son Dionysius II. Unfortunately the philosopher's counsel seems to have had little impact upon the government there.

At Athens Plato established the Academy, where he lectured for most of his mature life. The Academy, along with the Lyceum later established by Aristotle, endured until the Christian emperor Justinian shut down both schools some 900 years later.

Aristotle (384–322 B.C.)

Best remembered as the pupil of Plato and the teacher of Alexander the Great, Aristotle ranks close behind Plato as an important philosopher in his own right. He is notable for common sense, a respect for the common views of men, a keen ability to analyze and classify, and exhaustive thoroughness. Aristotle was much more interested than his master was in physical research, and his works are much more diverse. A mere list of the subjects of his works (which, unlike Plato's, are far from complete) is impressive: he wrote on physics, botany, biology, geology, astronomy, politics, logic, poetics, metaphysics, ethics, and other topics.

Rather typically, when Aristotle began to investigate government, he researched the constitutions of 158 states, including Carthage. His analysis, also typical, seems impeccable; there are good forms and bad forms, distinguished by whether those ruling do so in their own interests or in the interests of the people as a whole. Basically, there are governments that consist of one person, of a few, or of many—three each of good and bad forms:

Good forms	*Bad forms*
Monarchy	Tyranny
Aristocracy	Oligarchy (or plutocracy)
Constitutional government	Democracy (or mobocracy)

Though this is an oversimplification (and Aristotle also oversimplified), it is an impressive and deceptively simple analysis. Aristotle himself rather favored the constitutional government, with checks and balances and a large, stable middle class.

Aristotle rejected Plato's theory of Ideas and held that his ideal pure forms were just universals. In many ways Aristotle was a reconciler of opposing views and, in fact, strongly emphasized that extremes were likely to be the worse alternative, while the mean was generally the better position.

C. Poetry and Drama

Poetry cannot, within the limits here, be given the treatment it deserves. Homer's great epics have already been mentioned in other contexts; the work of Hesiod, a Boeotian poet of plebeian views who was contemporary or nearly so with Homer, also has been a source of information. Another early poet was Tyrtaeus (7th century B.C.), whose martial lines and rhythms put backbone into the Spartans at the time of the Messenian wars.

One of the greatest lyric poets of all time, the earliest-known notable female poet, was Sappho of Lesbos (late 7th–early 6th century B.C.), who also ran a sort of finishing school for young ladies on that island. Even in translation the surging, tender emotions of Sappho come through: "The moon has set, and the Pleiads; it is midnight. And I lie here—alone."

A different sort of poet was Pindar of Thebes (518–438 B.C.), whose values were aristocratic and who sang the glories of the victors at the great athletic festivals. He was not eulogizing individuals so much as applauding dedication, courage, and agonizing effort.

The greatest Greek poetry is found in the drama. Growing out of festivals to Dionysus, god of wine, the early performances were poetry recitals with chorus. At Athens, after Peisistratus first offered a prize in 534 B.C. (won by Thespis that year), the dramatic performances were supported by the state. Scripts were screened by a board, and the best plays were backed financially by prominent citizens assigned that duty and were presented in official contests, with prizes for winning entries. Possibly as early as Pericles' day, as noted previously, a special fund (theoric fund) established with profits from the silver mines paid small amounts to poorer citizens to permit them to take time off to enjoy the dramatic presentations.

Aeschylus (c. 525–456 B.C.)

A convenient way to remember the approximate ages of the three greatest Greek tragedians is to use the date of the Battle of Salamis (480 B.C.) as a focus. Aeschylus was present at the battle and described it in his play *The Persians;* Sophocles, fifteen or sixteen years old, led the chorus of young men who celebrated the victory; and Euripides was four or five years old at the time.

Aeschylus added a second actor, which made possible a true dialogue, with the chorus playing a background role. In *Agamemnon,* for example, the chorus represents the townspeople. This play, one of the conventional trilogy, was based on the tale of Agamemnon, his wife Clytaemnestra, and their children Iphigenia, Electra, and Orestes. The story itself was familiar to the audience: it occurs at the end of the Trojan War, yet the atmosphere at Mycenae was foreboding. Clytaemnestra had become alienated from Agamemnon, because he had offered Iphigenia as a sacrifice to enable the Greek fleet to sail off to war, and she had taken as a lover Aegisthus. When Agamemnon returned, with Cassandra (who knew everything that was to happen, though no one believed her forecasts), he was killed by his wife and her lover. Aeschylus' sonorous, lofty language spells out the message of proud men come to grief at the hands of Zeus, of wrong following upon wrong down through the generations. His audience knew that just as this was not the beginning of sorrows, neither was it the end: "This is no mere drizzling shower. Fate now is whetting Justice's heavy sword on a new whetstone. . . ." All great literature deals with universals. This play, like all the rest of the greatest Greek tragedies, somehow touches every reader (or hearer) and impresses upon him the common tragedy that is the ultimate core of every human life.

Sophocles (c. 496–406 B.C.)

No other tragedian won more first prizes in the Athenian competitions than Sophocles, who added a third actor and painted scenery. His play *Oedipus Tyrannus* (or *Oedipus Rex*), perhaps the best-known and most widely performed ancient tragedy, tells the story of a man who was predestined by an oracle of Apollo to kill his own father and marry his own mother. His parents and he himself took desperate measures to prevent these events from coming to pass, but in vain. Yet the play's message is not merely that man is a tool in the hands of Fate or the gods, for Oedipus says, "Apollo brought these ills to pass; But the right hand that dealt the blow was mine" (referring to the killing of the man who he later discovered was his father). The whole play has all the suspense of a murder mystery. The chief investigator, King Oedipus, not only is himself the murderer but also, unknowing, is the husband of his own mother. Tension builds as, step by step, the evidence falls into place and finally brings Oedipus face to face with the horrifying truth. *Antigone,* deservedly, is perhaps second only to *Oedipus* in popularity. It is a story of the duties of religion and family loyalty confronting loyalty to the state and society. Examination of such universal problems makes Greek tragedy timeless and enduringly meaningful.

Euripides (c. 485–406 B.C.)

Much less lofty, but just as meaningful, are Euripides' plays. He won few first prizes, but more of his plays have survived than those of Aeschylus and Sophocles together—which says something for his later reputation. One of the most interesting of his tragedies is *The Bacchae,* which tells the story of the introduction of the wild rites of Dionysus, in which the Bacchae or Maenads worked themselves into a frenzy (or the wine god did it for them) and afterward ran to the woods, where they tore to pieces the first living thing they saw and consumed it raw. In the play a young king who has heard scandalous things about what transpired during the Dionysian rites attempts to stop the quickly spreading rites by going into the woods in pursuit of some Bacchantes, including his own mother. But he is found there and torn to pieces. His mother carries his head back to the city, thinking it is the head of an animal. In the most electric moment of the play she comes to her senses and recognizes what she holds. The message, as so often in Euripides, is ambiguous: Did he mean to suggest it was useless to fight against the gods? or did he criticize traditional concepts of the behavior of the gods? Certainly the latter intention is possible, for Euripides was influenced by the Sophists.

Aristophanes (c. 450–c. 385 B.C.)

Though we know the names of several writers of the Old Comedy of the 5th century B.C., the only extant plays of this type are those of Aristophanes. Full of allusions and open references to contemporary conditions, they are immensely valuable to the historian, but their exaggeration and distortion make their comment difficult to assess. The comedy is bawdy, sometimes obscene, but also at times serious and even lofty.

Aristophanes opposed the Peloponnesian War. His early plays expressing that opposition were allowed to be presented even as the war went on. *The Acharnians* presented the viewpoint of Attic farmers whose lands were ravaged by the Peloponnesians. *The Knights* made an open attack upon the Athenian democratic leader Cleon, who in the play is bested by a sausage seller who overmasters him by better application of demogogic techniques.

In *The Clouds,* Aristophanes' best-known and perhaps best play, Socrates and the Sophists were lampooned. Socrates runs a "thought factory" with doubtful intent; two of his pupils want to learn how to swindle people better. The play did perhaps damage the great philosopher's reputation. Socrates himself thought so.

Lysistrata is a celebrated tale in which the women of Greece decide to end the war by withholding sex from their husbands until they make peace. In *Ecclesiazusae,* women take over the government and set up a communistic system. This and *Plutus,* the last play of Aristophanes now extant, are quite different from the earlier plays, with little reference to the real world and no insult to any living persons. Sometimes referred to as Middle Comedy, they belong to the period of disillusionment following the Peloponnesian War.

D. Religion

Modern students of ancient Greece sometimes note the rationalism of the philosophers, the ridicule of the gods implicit in Homer and explicit in Euripides and Aristophanes, and the attitudes of intellectuals such as the great historian Thucydides and conclude that religion was no longer of any real importance to the Greeks. This is a mistake. The greatest of the philosophers were quite religious; the last thing Socrates did was to ask a friend to offer a cock to Aesculapius, god of healing, to satisfy a vow he had made. Plato was very nearly a monotheist. The charge of impiety, still a serious accusation even in enlightened Athens, could bring exile to friends of Pericles, indictment (by Cleon) of Euripides, death to Socrates, and the threat of death to Aristotle. The Greeks were not so arrogant as to think that, because they had learned a bit about the physical world, they had proved the nonexistence of deity.

Religion was inextricably bound up with ordinary life and with the state in ancient Greece. Thus, for example, proper reverent treatment of gods, temples, and images was involved in simple patriotism; to offend deity was to threaten the state. That is why it was so serious a matter when someone defaced the Hermae just as the Athenian expedition embarked for Sicily in 415 B.C.

On the other hand, no Greek religionist ever claimed that he alone had found the true way. The Greeks in general had no received dogma, not even about the origins of the gods. They had, then, no heresy; toleration came naturally to them, except when they saw some threat to traditional institutions or the state. Greeks had no priestly hierarchies; their temples were served by lay priests. Perhaps in a few instances, the priests were professionals, such as those of Apollo at Delphi.

The Twelve Olympians

The Olympians appear already fully developed in Homer, composite deities with long traditions. Zeus was the great sky-god of the Indo-Europeans, wielder of thunder and lightning, Nordic but associated also with Crete, where he was said to have been born and to have died! Yet like the rest he lived on as an immortal. Associated with the bull, Zeus was a god of justice and a symbol of humanity. Athena, patron deity of Athens, was a war-goddess, but also a goddess of wisdom and crafts. As Athena Parthenos, she was the virgin-goddess. She was associated, appropriately, with the owl. Apollo—who along with Aphrodite was on the side of the Trojans in the Trojan War—was a war-god, a god of law and right, and the god of purity of young men, connected especially with Delphi and Delos. Equally complex were the other Olympian deities: Hera, Hestia, Hephaestus, Poseidon, Artemis, Ares, Demeter, and Hermes, the messenger of the gods. Also important was Heracles (Hercules), a symbol of man-become-god as the result of great labors in the interests of others. Alexander the Great and certain of the Roman emperors later would consciously imitate him. Dionysus, god of wine, was sometimes included among the twelve Olympians in place of Hestia, goddess of the hearth.

Oracles held an important place in the religious activity of the ancient world. One of renown was that of Ammon at the Oasis of Siwah in Egypt; almost all others of importance were Greek. Among them were those of Zeus at Dodona and at Olympia; that of Asclepius, the god of healing, at Epidaurus; and the most famous of all, that of the Pythian Apollo at Delphi. Questions were addressed to the oracles through various mechanisms, and responses came in varying ways. At Dodona, answers were interpreted from the rustlings of a sacred oak. At Epidaurus, sick persons slept in the temple and hoped for something —perhaps even a miracle—that might bring healing. Doubtless the priests there were experts in medical science; Greek physicians were much sought after in the ancient world. At Delphi the Pythia, or priestess, heard the questions as she sat in a transport of ecstasy, possessed by the god, on a tripod said to be located over a fissure that was the navel of the earth. Her responses were interpreted by priests, and the answers were delivered to the questioner in verse form.

Enough has already been said about Delphi to emphasize this oracle's great importance in the political, social, and cultural life of Greece. The responses of the Delphic oracle, as we have seen in the case of its opposition to the Athenian tyranny, could be quite politically motivated; inevitably the oracle took sides in the great struggles within Greece. The amphictyony, or religious league formed to protect the oracle, was itself much involved with interstate politics. But the oracle also was much concerned with moral questions and upheld high standards. Carved on the front of the great Temple of Apollo were two aphorisms symbolizing the Greek outlook on life at its best: "Know thyself" and "Nothing too much."

The popularity of Delphi at its height reflects, of course, the wisdom of the responses given there. Part of its attraction surely related to the magnificent site, on the flank of Mount Parnassus, overlooking the Gulf of Corinth. The great games held there every fourth year (Pythian Games) were almost as popular as the better-known ones at Olympia. Those at Olympia, founded in 776 B.C., were initiated almost two centuries earlier than those at Delphi.

Delphi and the other Greek oracles predictably declined as Greece itself did. Plutarch and other later Greeks discussed with some nostalgia the decline of the oracle at Delphi. The operation continued, nevertheless, until the Christian emperor Theodosius closed it down in 390 A.D.

The Mystery Religions

Orphism was a mystery religion. The Orphics generally believed in cycles of reincarnation to higher or lower levels, according to behavior in any particular life. So little remains of its lore because the knowledge leading to higher levels was secret (hence the term "mystery"). Orpheus himself, the legendary sweet singer, was a kind of prophet; Dionysus was the god of this cult.

Eleusis became a center of a mystery cult in connection with the myth of Demeter and her daughter Persephone, who was carried off to

Delphi, on Mount Parnassos. The theatre and remains of the temple to Apollo. In the temple was the Omphalos, the "navel of the world." *(Alinari-Scala)*

the underworld by Hades. Since Demeter was goddess of grain and fertility, the earth did not bring forth its fruits while she wandered in her sorrow. At Eleusis, the Attic Greeks claimed, she first partook of some barley water and began to return to her former self. The Eleusinian rites were, of course, secret but somehow involved the barley water, a grain of wheat, a washing or purification, and the hope of a life beyond this. So humanistic a man as the Roman Cicero, when initiated into the mystery rites in the 1st century B.C., was impressed by them.

E. History

It is often said that true history begins with the Greeks. This may seem a puzzling assertion, since many earlier documents, from Sumerian clay tablets to the Bible, are basically historical in nature. History as a category of literature and as a discipline, however, does have its beginning

177

with the Greeks. In this sense, history is the systematic investigation of a specific topic, with the selection of material to be included made according to the purpose of the study.

Herodotus (c. 485–c. 425 B.C.)

The "Father of History," as Herodotus is called, has left us his chronicle of the Persian Wars, which is not only the first real work of "history" (the word itself, used by Herodotus in his opening sentence, in Greek means research) but also the oldest extant Greek prose. Poetry was the earlier vehicle for conveying information in written form, even by such a figure as Solon when defending his acts as archon.

Herodotus came from Halicarnassus in Asia Minor; he may have been a travel lecturer, and some of his work seems to incorporate lecture material. The work is nevertheless unified and structured toward goals that are literary as well as strictly historical. Herodotus wrote interestingly, even delightfully, and his writings include much that moderns tend to dismiss as legendary, mythical, or fantastic. Yet he was by no means gullible, for he often remarks something to the effect that this is what they say but he doesn't believe it. His interests ranged widely: he included information that was geographic, social, economic, religious, and psychological as well as political. Much of what we know of Persia and Egypt in the decades before Herodotus comes from the accounts of this historian. He managed to be remarkably objective, even toward the Persians, the chief enemy of the Greeks in the period of his research. Some later critics consider him biased toward Athens, where he lived and wrote during his middle years.

One might wish that Herodotus had included more "solid" information in place of some of his more dubious tales or that he had done a little more research in connection with the actual campaigns of the Persian War; but keeping in mind that he was something of a pioneer, we realize that this achievement was indeed tremendous.

Thucydides (c. 460–c. 403 B.C.)

Thucydides, by common consent, was the greatest historian in antiquity and one of the greatest historians of all time—certainly one of the most influential. An Athenian, he lived and was educated in the Periclean age, served as a general in the early years of the Peloponnesian War, and wrote his history of that war while in exile as a result of an unsuccessful military campaign. His work (which extends to 411 B.C.) shows the influence of the skeptical Sophists and, in structure, the influence of the forms adopted by the great dramatists. What he had to chronicle, after all, was a great fratricidal tragedy.

In contrast to Herodotus, Thucydides had almost nothing to say of the influence of religion or oracles or of the intervention of the gods; his approach was strictly rational. He discussed remote and immediate causes of the war and looked for underlying influences, just as a modern historian would. When reading Thucydides, one feels that here was a great mind at work—objective, rational, methodical, and above all believable.

Thucydides' greatest fault was that he gave conclusions, often with little indication of supporting evidence. We have to trust him. In Herodotus it is often possible to decide, on the basis of information he himself included, that he was mistaken and that the truth must lie in another direction. This sort of independent analysis usually is not possible with Thucydides' work. In fact, the large gaps in Thucydides concerning religious, social, and economic matters make one fearful at times—even while admiring his obvious great competence as a historian —that he allowed his mental set to keep from his readers data they might judge important to the truth.

It is even possible to suspect that, since Thucydides was tremendously clever, he may very subtly have conveyed impressions, under cover of apparent objectivity, that are not objective at all. This could have been done in the speeches, for example, which are so well done they are often accepted as the exact words of the speaker. How many times have even modern historians quoted Pericles—when, in fact, they are quoting Thucydides? Though the latter himself tells us in the introduction what his general policy was in regard to the speeches, we have absolutely no way of knowing whether, in any instance, Thucydides was trying to give the actual content of a speech as he heard it or as someone else heard it whom the historian had interviewed—or whether he is simply presenting sentiments he thinks "appropriate to the occasion." Unfortunately, Thucydides' imitators, especially in antiquity, followed him in this practice. The speeches are very important in conveying a sense of immediacy; the reader almost feels he is there. Still, they may tell us more about Thucydides' own great ability than about history.

Xenophon (c. 434–c. 355 B.C.)

Though a student of Socrates, the Athenian historian Xenophon had no great depth of mind, as his works well show. He was quite influential, nevertheless, because he wrote well and because he was widely read. Doubtless the most significant of Xenophon's works was his *Anabasis*, the story of the march of the 10,000 Greek soldiers hired by Cyrus into the interior of Persia. Xenophon himself was elected one of the commanders before the arduous retreat toward the Black Sea. *The Anabasis* underlined the vulnerability of the great empire. Alexander the Great was to read and be impressed by this story.

Xenophon also wrote the *Hellenica,* a continuation of Thucydides' narrative down to the Battle of Mantinea in 362 B.C. Though only a shadowy imitation of his great predecessor's work, it helps greatly to fill in an otherwise obscure period. Xenophon also wrote eulogistic works on Agesilaus, king of Sparta, and on Cyrus the Great of Persia. The latter book, called the *Cyropaedia,* was considered useful reading by Cicero centuries later. Xenophon wrote about the constitution of Sparta, on the teaching of Socrates, and on other practical topics such as cavalry tactics. Readable, useful to a degree, and third-rate is the general modern judgment of Xenophon's body of work.

Books for Further Reading

BROWN, T. S., *The Greek Historians,* New York, 1973.

GLOTZ, G., *Ancient Greece at Work,* Reprint, New York, 1967.

GUTHRIE, W. K. C., *The Greeks and Their Gods,* Boston, 1965.

GUTHRIE, W. K. C., *Socrates,* Cambridge, 1971.

GUTHRIE, W. K. C., *The Sophists,* Cambridge, 1971.

HAMILTON, E., *The Greek Way,* New York, 1930.

JAEGER, W., *Aristotle,* Oxford, 1934.

KITTO, H. D. F., *The Greeks,* Middlesex, 1957.

MURRAY, G., *Five Stages of Greek Religion,* New York, 1955.

NORWOOD, G., *Greek Comedy,* New York, 1931.

NORWOOD, G., *Greek Tragedy,* New York, 1920.

PARKE, H. W., *Greek Oracles,* London, 1969.

SELTMAN, C., *The Twelve Olympians,* New York, 1960.

SNELL, B., *The Discovery of the Mind,* New York, 1960.

TAYLOR, A. E., *Plato,* New York, 1927.

TAYLOR, A. E., *Socrates,* New York, 1933.

WEBSTER, T. B. L., *Life in Classical Athens,* New York, 1969.

Alexander the Great

11

Individuals, it often seems today, have little impact on history. Presidents and premiers struggle with problems not of their making, often with small success. To the modern observer, events appear to control men. The world careers on blindly in a kind of inexorable, staggering course toward nobody knows what goal. It is instructive, however, to note the weighty influence of some leaders of the past—leaders whose achievements are not to be explained solely in terms of environment or upbringing. Alexander the Great is one such figure.

So great were the changes Alexander initiated that historians give a different name to the period after him: the age in the Greek world before Alexander is called Hellenic; that after him is called Hellenistic. Though the term Hellenistic is usually applied specifically to the period after Alexander's death, it seems most logical to use it for the age beginning in 334 B.C., when Alexander, the Macedonian king, crossed the Hellespont and began his fateful invasion of the Asian mainland.

A. Alexander's Conquests

Young Alexander Takes Control

Philip II of Macedon had groomed Alexander to command by taking him along on military campaigns, leaving him as regent in his absence, and even making him second-in-command, in charge of the cavalry, at the crucial Battle of Chaeronea (338 B.C.), when his son was only eighteen years old. In the following two years, however, increasing tension had built up in the family. Philip's relations with Alexander's fiery

CHART 4 Alexander the Great and the Hellenistic Age

PERIOD	MACEDONIA	OTHER
336 B.C.	Philip assassinated. Alexander takes over, becomes head of Corinthian League, defeats Thebes, destroys Thebes.	
334 B.C.	Begins campaign against Persia. Granicus, Issus, sieges of Tyre, Gaza, occupation of Egypt. Visit to oracle of Ammon.	Sparta leads rebellion against Macedonia; suppressed by Antipater, Macedonian general.
331 B.C.	Gaugamela; end of Persian Empire. Campaigns in the East; defeat of Porus; return to Babylon. Plans for further campaigns.	
323 B.C.	Death of Alexander; Perdiccas and Antipater regents. Antipater defeats Athenians et al. in Lamian War. Death of Antipater; struggle for control, Polyperchon, Cassander. Death of Philip III, Olympias, Roxane, Alexander IV.	Demosthenes leads another rebellion, Lamian War; defeat; suicide. Ptolemy satrap in Egypt, Antigonus in Asia Minor; his son Demetrius at Athens and the islands; Seleucus satrap of Babylon; Perdiccas not able to control. Ipsus; Antigonus killed. All major Successors now call selves kings.
300 B.C.	Continued struggle for throne; death of Cassander; later rulers include Demetrius, Pyrrhus, Lysimmachus, Seleucus, Ceraunus.	In theatre, New Comedy: Menander and others. Zeno founds Stoic school of philosophy; Epicurus founds Epicurean school of philosophy. Battle of Corupedion.
281 B.C.		

PERIOD	MACEDONIA	GREECE	SYRIA	EGYPT
280 B.C.	Antigonus Gonatas establishes Antigonid Dynasty.	Formation of Achaean, Aetolian Leagues. In Sparta, Agis and Cleomenes try to restore the old order. Aetolians ally with Rome against Philip V, and against Rome with Antiochus. League dissolved. Polybius, other Greeks taken hostage to Rome.	Seleucus I assassinated. Antiochus I.	Ptolemy II king. Height of power under Ptolemies II and III. Alexandria a great city. Aristarchus, Eratosthenes at Museum. Six Syrian wars during this entire period.
200 B.C.	Philip V makes alliance with Hannibal against Rome. In a second war, defeated by Rome. Perseus; war with Rome, defeat. Macedonia, 4 republics. Fourth war with Rome; becomes a Roman province.		Antiochus III; conquests. War with Rome, defeat. Antiochus IV; forced out of Egypt by Rome. Religious imperialism, trouble with the Jews under the Maccabees.	Loss of Palestine to Antiochus III.
100 B.C.		Achaeans rebel against Rome. Corinth destroyed, all Greece subordinated. Athens joins Mithradates; sacked by Sulla, Romans. Achaea a separate province.	Pompey annexes Syria as a Roman province.	Low prices of wheat bring economic crisis. Caesar in Egypt. Antony, Cleopatra defeated. Egypt a Roman province.

Tetradrachm of Alexander the Great. Presumably an engraving of the young king, horns on his head in the style of Zeus-Ammon. *(Hirmer Foto Archiv, Munich)*

mother, Olympias, had never been ideal. He always had other women. She was intense, passionate, and attracted to the exotic and unusual, as in religion. Philip at length chose to make a second marriage (legal in Macedonia), to the daughter of one of his chief lieutenants. Taking concubines was one matter, but this formal marriage was quite another. Thereafter Olympias was completely estranged from her husband. At the wedding the new father-in-law proposed a toast that the union might result in a legitimate heir to the throne. Alexander, who was present, stood up and threw his goblet at the man. "What do you think I am," he demanded, "a bastard?" Small wonder that, when Philip was soon after assassinated (336 B.C.), some thought that Olympias and Alexander were implicated; but there is no evidence of that. Alexander vigorously tracked down and executed the murderers.

Alexander quickly took over the reins of government. After he had moved south and been accepted in Philip's place as commanding general of the League of Corinth, he announced his intention of proceeding with his father's planned invasion of Asia. But the news of

Philip's death had brought troubles in various areas. Alexander, not yet twenty years old and still untried, soon proved equal to the challenges in campaigns against the Thracians to the northeast and then against Danubian barbarians to the north. A campaign against Illyria to the west was necessary; there his forces fell into a topographical trap, but he extricated them by adroit maneuvering.

Now a rumor reached the Greek cities to the south that Alexander was dead. Demosthenes, of course, was quick to try to organize a drive for freedom from Macedonian dominance; but Alexander moved very swiftly—it had already become one of his trademarks—and was at Thebes before a coalition army could be put together. He defeated the Thebans and took the city. As an object lesson it was destroyed, except for the temples and the house that had belonged to the poet Pindar. Again Athens escaped Macedonian wrath, and once again Demosthenes was lucky to keep his life and freedom.

Invasion of Asia:
Battle of Granicus (334 B.C.)

Alexander's attack on the massive and still strong Persian Empire was something of a confident gamble. Macedonia's finances could not support a long campaign; quick victories were necessary. The Hellenic fleet of about 160 ships was numerically inferior to that of the Persians, which was chiefly Phoenician in its makeup. The Greek army was large by Hellenic standards, but diminutive compared with the hordes that Persia could field, given time. Alexander had less than 40,000 men, including cavalry and specialized units. About half of these were Macedonian, and the rest were allies. The Greek infantry was the best in the world, but the Persians too would have thousands of Greeks in phalanx in any army they raised. Perhaps the Macedonians were superior enough to give Alexander the edge here; but since they were fighting against superior numbers and far from home, one must say that the odds were not on Alexander's side.

The crossing of the Hellespont was itself surprisingly easy. Philip had sent Parmenion, one of his senior generals, across with an army two or three years before. Though hard-pressed, Parmenion still held a bridgehead in Asia Minor. The Persian commanders, who must have known of Alexander's movements, did not mobilize their navy to oppose the crossing. Alexander himself, playing the new Achilles, went to Troy to make a landing. There, symbolically, he threw a spear into the sand and sacrificed to the specter of King Priam, who had been slain by the son of Achilles. Even at this early date, Alexander saw himself as no mere man; at the very least, he cast himself in a heroic mold.

The Persian commanders elected to oppose Alexander at the

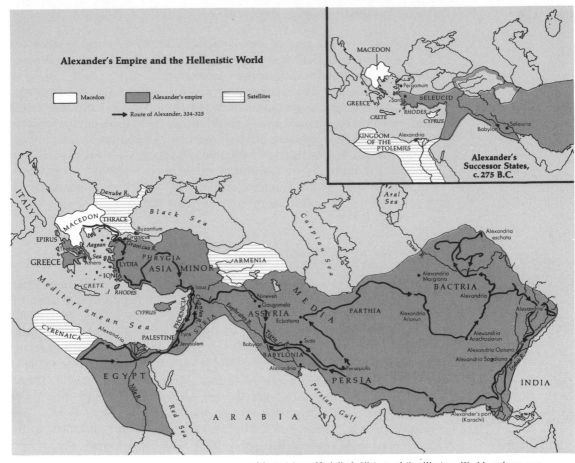

Alexander's Empire and the Hellenistic World

Macedon   Alexander's empire   Satellites
Route of Alexander, 334-325

Alexander's Successor States, c. 275 B.C.

Adapted from Modell, A History of the Western World, volume one.

Granicus River. To attack, Alexander would have to cross the stream and storm the banks on the opposite side. Rejecting any suggestion of caution, Alexander launched his attack as soon as his forces were set. He led the heavy cavalry of his right wing in a headlong, oblique (diagonal) assault that disarrayed the opposing forces enough to permit his infantry to make its crossing. Then, with the opposing center held fast, he used his cavalry to roll up the line from the now-exposed flank. Rashly and impetuously, Alexander charged into the melee himself, and would have lost his life but for the quick action of one of his lieutenants, "Black" Cleitus. Among those slain on the Persian side were thousands of Greek soldiers, who were looked on as traitors to their homeland. Surviving Greeks were put to work as slaves in Macedonia. One of Alexander's characteristics was a willingness to learn and to change. And he soon changed his attitude toward Greek mercenaries who had fought for the Persians; in fact, he enlisted some in his own army, though he did not use them in key units such as the phalanx.

By the end of that year, the whole western half of Asia Minor was in Alexander's hands; once liberated from Persian rule, the Greek cities there perhaps joined the Corinthian League. Macedonians replaced Persians as satraps in most western regions. The supplies and money captured made it possible for Alexander to go on with his campaign as planned. He wintered at Gordium, where he is reputed to have cut—rather than untied—the famous Gordian knot (of which it was said that he who learned its secret would someday rule Asia).

From Issus to Egypt (333–332 B.C.)

The world waited for the great battle that was sure to come in 333 B.C., when the fully mobilized army of Darius III of Persia would meet the somewhat augmented forces of Alexander. The clash came in late fall at Issus, on the Mediterranean shore just south of the mountain passes leading from Asia Minor into Syria. Darius had superior forces but allowed himself to be brought to battle on a field too narrow to make maximum use of his numbers. Again Alexander, leading the heavy cavalry on the right wing, smashed the forces opposite and then rolled up the line. It did not help Persian morale much when, Darius, conspicuous in his chariot, fled before the contest was fairly decided. In the confrontation of personalities, Alexander won hands down. Darius even abandoned his wife and daughters; captured by Alexander, they were treated with studied courtesy.

That winter and most of the next year were spent in reducing the port cities that gave Persia her troublesome naval superiority. Tyre required a siege of seven months; Gaza, three. The main sector of Tyre was situated on an island; Alexander at length decided to build a mole out to the island and did so, under great difficulties. Not until he achieved naval supremacy in the locality, however, did the city fall. The captured populace of these cities was either killed or sold into slavery.

Jerusalem and Judea seem to have gone over to Alexander's camp peacefully. Egypt too surrendered to Alexander without a struggle. Alexander sacrificed to Apis, the bull-god of Memphis, and was made king with the traditional coronation. In fact, he always sacrificed to local deities and was quite scrupulous in his treatment of priests. He seems to have believed strongly in oracles and soothsayers, one of whom had accurately predicted the date he would take Gaza and had warned him it would be a dangerous day for him personally—and he was wounded in the fray.

Some biographers, both ancient and modern, have made much of the psychological effects of a trip Alexander made to the oracle of Ammon (the old Amon god of Thebes) at the oasis of Siwah, in the western desert of Egypt. Quite probably the priests there hailed Alexander as "son of Ammon," which would translate into Greek as "son of Zeus," since the Greeks identified Ammon with Zeus. Except for the Persian dynasty, all the kings of Egypt for two thousand years had been "sons of Ammon." Certainly the priests of the oracle told the young king whatever else he wanted to hear.

The first of the cities named Alexandria was established in a strategic location on the Nile delta to serve as the Greek administrative capital; this ultimately became the most important city of Egypt. Alexander eventually established eighteen cities bearing his name—which indicates a healthy ego.

Gaugamela—The Decisive Battle (331 B.C.)

Near the end of 332 B.C., when Tyre and Gaza had fallen, Alexander received a communication from Darius offering a negotiated peace. Darius would pay 10,000 talents as ransom for his family and would cede to Alexander all the land west of the Euphrates. At a council meeting,

Mosaic of Alexander fighting Darius in battle, found at Pompeii. *(Alinari-Scala)*

Parmenion suggested that, if he were Alexander, he would accept the terms. Alexander's much-repeated reply was that, were he Parmenion, he probably would. Only death would put an end to Alexander's imperialist quest.

Late the following year Alexander's army crossed the Euphrates, next the Tigris, and then turned south. At Gaugamela his troops encountered the main Persian force, the largest army yet. This time it was the Persian generals who chose the battleground: they took up their position on a broad, flat plain. They hoped to make maximum use of their numerically superior cavalry and immense forces. They had cleared the ground for their scythed chariots, with which they hoped to cut up the array of the Hellenes. This battle, above all, tested Alexander's generalship and the mettle of his men.

Alexander accepted the fact that his army would be outflanked and arranged for defense not only on the flanks but also at the rear. The chariots would be taken care of by the light troops that screened the phalanx if possible; those who reached the main battle line were to be allowed to dash through quickly opened corridors to the rear ranks, where other light troops would handle them.

Alexander approached the enemy while moving obliquely to the right, which forced the Persians to move also—but less skillfully. A gap opened near their center. Ignoring the already fierce cavalry skirmish on his flank, Alexander charged the gap with his heavy cavalry, followed by the phalanx, and with this bold tactic won the battle. His oblique advance had made things difficult for Parmenion on the left wing, however; furthermore, a gap opened in the Greek phalanx when the left was unable to advance at an equal pace with the right. The Greek line was penetrated at this point, the left wing was surrounded, and the camp was taken. Thus Alexander could not pursue Darius when he fled, since it was necessary to keep his own troops from disaster. But the news of the crushing defeat of the Persian center spread, and the rout became general. Eventually Alexander captured the Persian camp and, a little later, its base of operations farther south. His victory was complete, but Darius still lived.

Alexander spent a little time at Babylon; on a sentimental impulse, he had several thousand of his troops begin to rebuild the dilapidated remains of the ancient city, but he soon left the task unfinished to press on. At Susa he saw spoils that Xerxes had taken from Athens a hundred and fifty years before. He wintered at Persepolis, where, for some curious reason, the palace of Darius and Xerxes was burned. Perhaps this was meant as a symbol of the fall of the Persian Empire, but more likely it was simply an accident—after all, it belonged to Alexander now. At Susa and at Persepolis also, Alexander came into possession of the main Persian treasury, with vast quantities of gold and silver. He was rather prodigal with it, both in gifts and in other expenditures. So much of the raw metal was coined and put into circulation that, over the next quarter-century, prices in the entire eastern Mediterranean area were inflated by about 100 percent.

Alexander, the Great King

Early the following year, Alexander and his army were once more on the move. Unable to organize effective opposition so soon, Darius again fled, only to be killed by one of his own lieutenants, the satrap Bessus. Alexander could now take over the titles, as well as the office and accouterments, of the dead monarch.

But the campaigning went on. The army, now somewhat smaller and including native contingents, moved east and northeast in the next four years and penetrated as far as the area of modern Pakistan. Across the Indus and some of its tributaries they marched, sometimes against bitter opposition but finally always victorious.

A battle at the Hydaspes River, a branch of the Indus farther to the east, is of interest both as the most desperate Alexander ever fought and as that which best confirms his great ability as a general. The east bank of the river was held by Porus, the region's king, with a force larger than the Macedonian, including 200 elephants and 300 chariots. No direct crossing was possible against these powerful defenders. After passing days and nights of deliberate false alarms, Alexander quietly led a major portion of his army by night to an uncontested crossing several miles upstream, while one of his generals remained to hold the bank opposite Porus as usual. Alexander, superior only in cavalry, managed to lure the enemy cavalry into a preliminary battle and threw it back upon the center, with Porus's elephants and infantry, just as the phalanx arrived on the attack. Meanwhile the rest of his army made the river crossing and attacked from the rear. Still, the victory was a near thing, in considerable part because of the bravery of Porus. Alexander captured him but later confirmed him as king and even enlarged his kingdom. Porus afterward remained a faithful ally.

By then (326 B.C.), Alexander's army was tired of the eternal campaigning that took it ever farther from home. Though many of the soldiers doubtless were replacements, there was a veteran core that had marched all the way from Macedonia and fought in all the major battles. The straight-line distance was 3,000 miles; in all, these men had walked at least 10,000 miles during eight years of campaigning. It is not surprising that one day when Alexander ordered his troops to continue the march eastward, they refused. Alexander sulked in his tent to show his displeasure, but the mutiny did not end. The King at last gave in but decreed the army return by another route; so they marched down the Indus Valley, to return westward part by land and part by sea.

One incident that occurred on the march down the Indus seems very revealing of Alexander's character and of the army's feelings also. When a small walled town of the Mallians refused to surrender, Alexander ordered it taken. Two ladders were constructed to scale the walls. When the command to attack came, his men were reluctant to climb the ladders. Alexander himself went up first, accompanied by two aides, and fought his way atop the walls. Looking back, he saw that his men still were not following; so he leaped down inside! Suddenly the Macedonian soldiers realized how serious the situation was and stormed up the ladders in such numbers that both broke. By the time they had mended them and rescued Alexander, he was seriously wounded, with an arrow piercing a lung. For many days after, it was doubtful whether he would live or die.

Perhaps this wound shortened Alexander's life. The march home across southern Iran, mostly desert, was a terrible nightmare for most of the army and even worse for the camp followers, and cannot have improved the King's health. Yet, once back at Susa and Babylon, Alexander began to plan future conquests while at the same time reorganizing his imperial administration. After a year's rest (324 B.C.) for the army, he would undertake a great campaign into Arabia; later he would gain more complete control of the Black Sea area. In the more distant future would come, possibly, ambitious campaigns against Carthage and other powers of the western Mediterranean. But, weakened by his wounds and fever as well as by dissipation, Alexander died in June of 323 B.C. at Babylon—not yet thirty-three years old.

B. Alexander's Goals and Ideals

It is amazing what different pictures are presented of Alexander by his numerous modern biographers, all of whom of course rely on the same basic body of evidence. The diversity of their views is greatest when they attempt to evaluate Alexander's motives and aims.

Alexander's View of Himself

It has already been mentioned that Achilles was Alexander's hero and that he sought consciously to imitate him. From the beginning he claimed descent from Heracles, the great example of the man-become-god. After his visit to the oracle of Ammon in Egypt, he began to claim a position as the son of Zeus; in fact, Olympias is said to have encouraged him in this, by telling him that Philip was not his father. Alexander went so far as to send messages to the Greek states asking them to acknowledge his deity. In most states the populace shrugged its shoulders collectively in response and said, "Why not?"

Along the way farther east from Ecbatana, Alexander began to require his subjects to practice *proskynesis,* prostration of the body when approaching his presence. He called himself by the Persian title "Great King" and even began to wear Persian dress. He made considerable use of Persians in high position and, when he reorganized the army in 330 B.C., started training natives as fighting men and eventually used some even in the heavy-infantry phalanx.

All this conduct displeased his own men. In fact, one of Alexander's continuing problems was the strong feelings against absolutism among Macedonians of all levels. Alexander's pretensions provoked more than one conspiracy against himself. One involved Philotas, the son of Parmenion, and the senior general himself was executed on mere suspicion of involvement. Another apparently involved Callisthenes, the nephew of Aristotle, one of a corps of scientists, engineers, and historians who accompanied the army on the great Asian campaign. The rank-and-file Macedonians objected most to the equal treatment accorded some of the "barbarians," and only slightly less objectionable to them were Alexander's pretensions to deity and the *proskynesis.* Alexander exempted the Macedonians from all such requirements. Still, down to the last days of his life, he had difficulty in conciliating his troops on these matters.

What of this evidence for Alexander's view of himself? How does it all add up? Alexander had a tremendous job to do. He could not do it merely as king of Macedonia; he must make something more of himself. Nor could he function to his fullest potential as *hegemon* of the Corinthian League. It might have been all right to settle for that after his first campaign, but a league official could neither administer the world's greatest empire nor unify it. And surely Alexander's chief goal was just that—to organize this empire and to function as its monarch. He had to be king of all his far-flung subjects, not only of Greeks or Macedonians. These aims surely explain his new titles and seeming pretensions.

Alexander's Ideals

It is impossible to discover any of Aristotle's influence in Alexander's ordering and administration of the new empire. Alexander wished to be acceptable to all his subjects, and this may explain much: his attempts to deify himself, his adoption of exotic native dress, and his use of natives in high position and in the army.

Did Alexander believe in a true brotherhood of men and strive

for that? Did he believe in "one world" only in the sense that he wished
to conquer and rule it all, or did he somehow in a humanitarian and
symbolic way wish to create a brotherhood of man? Alexander did
encourage his men to marry native women in the conquered lands; it
was said that at Susa in 324 B.C. he had 10,000 marriages celebrated at
one time between his men and native women. While this was most
likely meant as a regularization of existing irregular alliances, Alexander
may have felt that children of mixed parentage would be loyal to him
and to his new regime. He himself married both the Bactrian princess
Roxana and a daughter of Darius. In many ways Alexander tried to
demonstrate that the peoples of Asia he ruled were more to him than
mere barbarians, but whether any lofty humane ideal inspired him or
whether he was prudently trying to unify his dominions in order to
control them we cannot know.

C. Alexander's Impact on the World

Immediate Impact

The bringing down of the Achaemenid dynasty of Persian kings and
its replacement with Greco-Macedonian rule, of course, changed conditions drastically for almost everyone in the eastern Mediterranean regions. Greeks and Macedonians had triumphed over the barbarians and
proved their right to dominate. The opportunities for these Hellenes
now exceeded anything they might once have imagined. Soldiers and
politicians, merchants and traders, all could now advance and prosper.
Even Greek intellectuals, patronized by Alexander and his successors,
had new vistas opened to them.

The subjugated Asian peoples were not oppressed by Alexander.
As we have seen, he made at least some use of them even in high office and
in the army. Merchants and traders among the native Asians must have
prospered along with the Greeks. The precious bullion the Persian
monarchs had hoarded was coined and put into circulation, with a
quickening economic effect over the entire area. No official policy of
restraint or discrimination prevented Asians from sharing in this economic growth, though Greeks perhaps often managed to gain favored
status.

Long-range Impact

Alexander shook up the Greek world along with that of the Asians. In
his wake, Greeks were forced to rethink their politics, their society, their
religion, and their culture; but they were likely to remain unchanged at

home and to accept new views only in overseas posts. The parochial city-state mentality persisted in Greece proper. Perhaps Greece could never have been truly unified, even by Alexander and even if he had lived three or four decades more. Abroad, however, where Greeks ruled as a superior class, the typical political unit became the one Alexander had established: an absolute, divine monarchy.

The great migration of Greeks, who took along with them the Greek language and Greek literature, art, and architecture changed the world and produced the Hellenistic age. Throughout the Near East, Greek became the lingua franca. Everywhere there developed a class of natives who were thoroughly Hellenized, and thus were looked on with favor by their rulers, though perhaps sneered at contemptuously by their more conservative countrymen. The capitals of the Hellenistic kingdoms grew into cosmopolitan centers of great size. These tremendous urban centers, especially Alexandria in Egypt and Antioch in Syria, became not only political capitals but also centers of diffusion for Greek culture.

Greeks were, in turn, tremendously influenced by Oriental ways. That is, as Moses Hadas has emphasized,[1] the age after Alexander was one of fusion as well as diffusion. In many ways, but most notably in religion and philosophy, the Greeks themselves learned from their subjects and were gradually changed.

It has been suggested that Alexander oxerextended the resources of the Greco-Macedonian world. There were simply not enough Hellenes to furnish the manpower necessary to consolidate the tremendous empire he had conquered. Even a fusion of races could not soon have made it possible for this great state to endure, or even for the fragmented successor states to endure for long. In consequence, it is argued, Alexander weakened the Hellenic world itself and opened it to eventual Roman aggression and conquest. Whether this judgment is valid, it is difficult to say.

Alexander's greatest legacy was his vision of a united world. To a degree, at least by the time of the early Empire, the Romans were actuated by the one-world view Alexander had created. The idea, in Roman dress, survived the fall of Rome, and in some ways this vision has endured into modern times. The youthful Napoleon's Near Eastern adventures were to a degree inspired by Alexander's ambitious vision. The various one-world hopes and dreams of the present century, though no longer based on a single great unified empire, nevertheless are in part heir to the one-world view inspired by Alexander. In short, it would be hard to point to any other individual in world history (in a political role) who has been more influential than Alexander the Great, the charismatic conqueror who died before completing his thirty-third year.

[1] *Hellenistic Culture: Fusion and Diffusion* (New York: Columbia University Press, 1959).

Books for Further Reading

BURN, A. R., *Alexander the Great and the Hellenistic World,* New York, 1962.

CARY, M., *A History of the Greek World from 323 to 146 B.C.,* London, 1932.

EHRENBERG, V., *Alexander and the Greeks,* Oxford, 1938.

GREEN, P., *Alexander the Great,* New York, 1972.

GRIFFITH, G. T., ed., *Alexander the Great: The Main Problems,* New York, 1966.

OLMSTEAD, A. T., *The History of the Persian Empire.* Chicago, 1938.

PEARSON, L., *The Lost Histories of Alexander the Great,* London, 1960.

ROBINSON, C. A., *Alexander the Great,* New York, 1947.

STEIN, A., *On Alexander's Track to the Indus,* London, 1929.

TARN, W. W., *Alexander the Great,* Cambridge, 1948.

WILCKEN, U., *Alexander the Great,* New York, 1932.

The Successor States

12

The far-reaching empire of Alexander fell apart at his death. There was no logical successor, and he had made no arrangements for the succession. Perhaps he refused to believe that he too could die. His half-brother, Philip III Arrhidaeus, unfortunately was of moronic intelligence. Roxana had been left pregnant, and a short time after Alexander's death she produced a son, Alexander Aegus.

The officers and cavalry of the army, representing the nobility of Macedonia, favored making the young Alexander king, though a long and doubtful regency would be necessary. The common soldiers, however, who in Macedonian fashion constituted an assembly, favored making Philip Arrhidaeus king. (Probably it was not generally known just how low the prince's I.Q. was.) By way of compromise, therefore, the two were made joint rulers, and a council of generals was named to act as regents. Chief among these were Perdiccas, one of the senior generals with the main army, and Antipater, who had been in command in Macedonia since 334 B.C., when the army left for Asia.

In a relatively short time a power struggle began. For decades a number of generals, some of them very competent, fought for the right to be the new Alexanders. Olympias, the mother of the dead Alexander, played a role, by championing the cause of young Alexander IV, Roxana's child. But he, Philip Arrhidaeus, Olympias herself, Roxana, and even another child claimed to be a bastard of Alexander, became pawns in a lethal game that saw them all dead within a few years.

The struggles of Alexander's successors, inconclusive and prolonged, raged over personal goals—survival or self-aggrandizement. Whatever idealism may have motivated Alexander (such as, perhaps, his vision

195

of a one-world brotherhood) was lost to his successors, who had no time to consider such impractical and unattainable dreams. One result of this was to widen the gulf between the Greeks as a master race and their subjects. But, as we shall see in the next chapter, on an intellectual level the ideal of brotherhood was still emphasized and widely propagated.

The political history of the Hellenistic age is so scrambled and complex that it seems not only fruitless but also impossible to give even a general sketch of it. This chapter will therefore attempt to indicate only typical patterns and record a few important events. Actually, the most significant political movement in the period was the gradual encroachment by Rome, which continued until all the great Hellenistic powers were absorbed into the Roman Empire. This topic will be discussed more thoroughly in the subsequent chapters on Rome.

A. Greece and Macedonia

The Period Immediately After Alexander's Death

Even while Alexander was alive and winning his greatest victories, Sparta had led a rebellion against Macedonian dominance in Greece (331 b.c.). Antipater, Alexander's lieutenant in Macedonia, put down the rebellion. The Athenians had been tempted to join the Spartans and, under the leadership of Demosthenes and others, remained ready to join any anti-Macedonian alliance that had a chance of success. News of the death of Alexander, therefore, ignited another attempt to throw off the Macedonian yoke.

This war was a serious threat to Antipater. It was called the Lamian War because much of the activity took place around Lamia, a fortified city in southern Thessaly controlling the major route from central Greece. Athens had built up its sea power and had some of the latest types of vessels, quadriremes and quinqueremes. A mobilization of the resources of several imperial satraps, however, made it possible to defeat Athens at sea and eventually to invest the Attic capital itself and force its surrender. The other allies had mostly given up earlier. This time Demosthenes and several other leaders who were notoriously anti-Macedonian were marked for death. Demosthenes fled and, when about to be captured, took poison. During this time Aristotle also left Athens; his connections with Macedonia made him most unpopular, and he was charged with impiety. He is reported to have said as he departed that he could not allow Athens to sin twice against philosophy.

So long as he lived, Antipater, though much disliked, managed not only to keep the Greeks in proper subjection but also to hold the throne for the co-rulers, Philip III and young Alexander IV, the son of

Roxana. On Antipater's death, however, everything changed. His successor, at his own recommendation, was Polyperchon. But Antipater's son Cassander chose to dispute power with Polyperchon, intending, it would seem, to rule himself. He gained the support of many Greek states by proclaiming the principle that all these states should be free; and he got the support also of Antigonus, a powerful satrap in Asia Minor.

At this point Olympias intervened from her homeland in Epirus. She took over Macedonia briefly, in the interest of her grandson Alexander, and had Philip III assassinated. But then Cassander appeared with an army and drove out Olympias and her forces. Eventually he captured her and had the army condemn her to death in 316 B.C. Cassander was now the unrivaled ruler of Macedonia. Not until 310 B.C., however, did he kill the young Alexander and his mother Roxana.

Greece and Macedonia in the 3rd Century B.C.

Cassander controlled Macedonia until his death in 297 B.C. In the usual fashion he attempted to dominate all Greece, partly through the League of Corinth. He was opposed in this effort by a son of Antigonus, Demetrius Poliorcetes (the Besieger), who was trying to make himself king over all the empire of Alexander. This new contender, who conducted operations in the islands and in Greece proper, made his headquarters at Athens and was for a time accorded divine honors and in effect made tyrant. Demetrius succeeded brilliantly in gaining influence and alliances among the Greek states, while his father had a major part in the struggle for Asia. However, in 301 B.C. the Battle of Ipsus in Asia Minor changed the situation. Antigonus and Demetrius faced a formidable coalition: Cassander; Seleucus, satrap of Babylon; Lysimachus of Thrace; and Ptolemy, satrap of Egypt. All these local rulers were calling themselves kings by now. Antigonus was killed at Ipsus, and Demetrius' power was much reduced as a result of their defeat by Lysimachus and the others. The Athenians refused to receive him; perhaps they were repelled by the way he had lived so dissolutely in the Parthenon on the Acropolis.

Demetrius' fortunes revived, however, when he made an alliance with Seleucus, who now saw Ptolemy of Egypt as his chief enemy. Demetrius seized Macedonia from Cassander's younger brothers, who were fighting over the kingdom, and resumed his efforts to control all Greece. About 287 B.C., he was driven from the kingdom by King Pyrrhus of Epirus, who is better remembered for his invasion of Italy a few years later, and by Lysimachus, one of the Alexandrian successors, who ruled Thrace. Lysimachus then became king of Macedonia.

A second major battle (there were many lesser ones) among the successors, at Corupedion in Asia Minor in 281 B.C., ended Lysimachus' reign and his life at the hands of Seleucus, who proclaimed himself King of Macedonia. Shortly after, however, Seleucus was assassinated by a renegade son of Ptolemy, called Ptolemy Ceraunus, who also ruled Macedonia briefly. Finally, Antigonus called Gonatas (the Knock-Kneed), a son of Demetrius I and grandson of Antigonus I of Syria, the general of Alexander, gained the throne of Macedonia to establish the Antigonid dynasty there. He had to fight against a Gallic invasion that devastated much of Greece and Asia Minor. He was also temporarily displaced by Pyrrhus when the latter returned from his ill-fated Italian venture; but by 272 B.C. Antigonus Gonatas was firmly established in Macedonia, where the Antigonid dynasty then endured for about a century.

Two federal-style leagues were constituted in Greece during the mid-3rd century B.C. and played an important political role for several decades. The Aetolian League exercised its power to the north of the Gulf of Corinth and ultimately reached to the Aegean. The Achaean League flourished in the Peloponnese. Both of these federations had league officials, league assemblies, and league armies. Neither was dominated by a single state as earlier leagues had been. Both played a part in reducing Macedonian power over Greece.

The city-states that had been so powerful in the classical period were now comparatively weak. Thebes, rebuilt after its destruction by Alexander, was again reduced by the Aetolian League. Athens led still another rebellion against Macedonian dominance in the middle of the century and found the attempt ruinous. Thereafter Athens played no further important role in world politics but remained a cultural, university center.

In the latter part of the 3rd century B.C., Sparta enjoyed a bit of a revival. The city had declined since classical days, and even its legendary ideals had been eroded. The love of money, ancient writers declare, infected many of the Spartiate class, which was much diminished in numbers through profligacy and extravagance. Some Spartiates sold or somehow lost their allotted public lands and, impoverished, were then unable to contribute their share to the public barracks. Such Spartans lost their first-class citizenship and were classed as "inferiors." Much of the Spartan wealth was now in the hands of women.

Two kings, Agis IV and Cleomenes III, who ruled Sparta between 244 and 221 B.C., attempted to carry through a revolution that was really conservative in nature. They wished to restore what they thought was the constitution of Lycurgus. Accordingly, they cancelled some debts, seized land and redistributed it to an enlarged body of Spartiates, and reinstituted the old training.

As the old Sparta had been dominant in the Peloponnese, so

must the new. This meant conflict with the Achaean League. King Cleomenes at first defeated the league and seemed on the point of raising Sparta to its old eminence. But then the chief leader of the Achaean League, Aratus, reluctantly called in Macedonia to aid against Sparta. Giving up Corinth to occupation by Macedonia was the price paid for this support. The situation was ironic, for some decades earlier Aratus had made his reputation by expelling a Macedonian garrison from Corinth. Cleomenes was defeated by the combined forces in 222 B.C. at Sellasia, a few miles north of Sparta.

This did not quite end Sparta's ambitions. Under the tyrant Nabis at the beginning of the 2nd century B.C., Sparta was still a power to be reckoned with. Nabis attempted to continue the conservative restoration of Cleomenes III and also to restore Spartan dominance over the Peloponnese. He succeeded in gaining control of Argos and other territories. But later in his reign (207–192 B.C.) Rome effectively restricted Nabis's power, and finally the Aetolians procured his assassination. Eventually Rome swallowed up Sparta along with the rest of Greece.

Macedonia and Greece Fall to Rome

Philip V of Macedonia (221–179 B.C.) was at once one of the most competent and the most unfortunate of the Antigonid kings. As usual for Macedonian rulers, he felt he must dominate all Greece and exercise a major influence in a larger sphere encompassing all the Balkan Peninsula. About the time he came to power, the Roman Republic intervened on the eastern shore of the Adriatic to eliminate some pirate nests there. Philip considered this an intolerable incursion into his sphere of influence and therefore allied himself with Hannibal during the Second Punic War. The Romans retaliated first by making alliances with the Aetolians and other of his adversaries and then by declaring war on Macedonia itself once Hannibal had been defeated. The Macedonian phalanx fell before the Roman legions at Cynoscephalae in Thessaly in 197 B.C. Philip was not treated severely by the Romans, however, and all the Greek states were declared by Rome to be free. The Romans felt the Greeks should all be duly grateful for this generosity, and thereafter they resented any action by a Greek state that might be construed as against Rome's best interests. The Aetolians, who had fought with the Romans at Cynoscephalae, were bitterly resentful because they were not allowed to occupy large chunks of Macedonian border territories as a reward.

Rome forced a third Macedonian war on the son of Philip, Perseus (r. 179–167 B.C.), who, they felt was preparing for war against Rome. By this time both the Greek leagues were in disfavor at Rome. After a Roman victory over Perseus at Pydna in 168 B.C., Macedonia was made over into four separate republics. An unsuccessful rebellion in

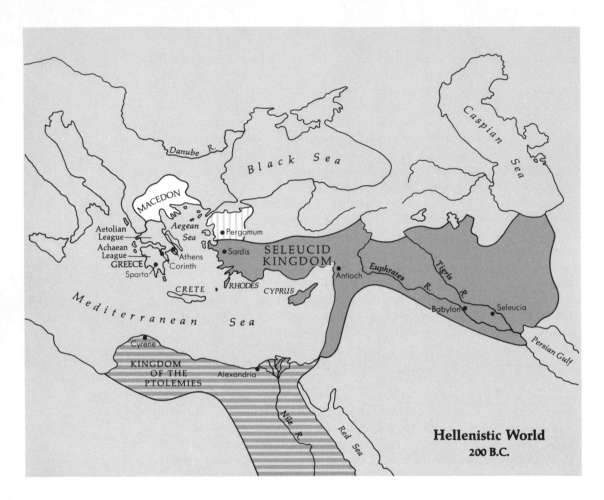

Hellenistic World
200 B.C.

149/148 B.C. was followed by the conversion of Macedonia into a Roman province. The Aetolian League had already been dissolved by Rome following the Syrian War, discussed later in this chapter. The Achaean League also rebelled against Roman influence in 148 B.C., and in the war which followed Corinth was destroyed as an object lesson. Greece outside Macedonia (later called Achaea) became in effect a Roman province also, though it was not officially organized as such until the time of the Emperor Augustus.

B. Syria, Pergamum, and Egypt

Syria under the Seleucids (301–63 B.C.)

The founder of the Seleucid dynasty of Syria was Seleucus I Nicator, one of Alexander's generals. From a position as satrap of Babylon, he gradually extended his power until all the empire eastward to the Indus came under his control. In India, however, a remarkable native king, Chandragupta of the Mauryan dynasty, withstood Seleucus. They came to an understanding by which Chandragupta was confirmed sovereign over all the provinces in the vicinity of the Indus and Seleucus got war elephants (by tradition, 500 of them). He used these battle animals in struggles in the west against Antigonus and Lysimachus. He profited from both the major battles mentioned earlier, Ipsus (301 B.C.) and Corupedion (281 B.C.). By the latter date he was actually in control of, or in a position to control, all Alexander's dominions except Egypt and India. But then he was assassinated by Ptolemy Ceraunus and was succeeded by his son Antiochus I. Most subsequent rulers of the dynasty were named either Seleucus or Antiochus.

The sixth in the Seleucid line was Antiochus III (r. 223–187 B.C.), eventually surnamed "the Great." His predecessors had not been able to keep all the territories ruled by Seleucus I, and Antiochus III made a serious effort to recover them. His greatest successes came in the east. In the west the chief enemy of Syria was Egypt, for the Ptolemies held the Palestine–Lower Syria region, along with other territories in Syria and Cilicia. Antiochus gained control of all these, though not easily. His first major effort against Egypt in 217 B.C. came to grief; only in 200 B.C. did he succeed in defeating the forces of young Ptolemy V and in annexing the disputed lands.

A second Seleucid opponent of note was the Attalid kingdom in western Asia Minor, the Kingdom of Pergamum. (See page 208 for a discussion of the city of Pergamum.) Though it was established on an independent basis somewhat earlier, the true founder of this monarchy was Attalus I (r. 241–197 B.C.). Only a period of weakness in Syria made the creation of this kingdom possible, and its every expansion was at the expense of at least the pretensions of the Seleucids and was a challenge to them. Antiochus the Great never got around to destroying Pergamum, but its kings were acutely aware that he might undertake such reprisal at any time. Eumenes II (c. 195–159 B.C.) of Pergamum helped to persuade the Romans to intervene in Asia against Antiochus, whose power he much exaggerated to them.

The reasons for the clash of Rome with Syria were several. For one, Antiochus had given asylum to Hannibal when that enemy of Rome fled to the East soon after the end of the Second Punic War (201 B.C.). For another, in attempting to regain all the territory held by Seleucus I, Antiochus moved into Thrace, and Rome professed to be perturbed by any such invasion of Europe. Third, Antiochus was allied with the Aetolians, who had become anti-Roman after Macedonia was let off easily following Philip V's defeat in 197 B.C. And then, as we have said, Eumenes II played a role of intriguer.

Antiochus III actually took an army of several thousand men to

Greece. But neither he nor the Aetolians mobilized anywhere near the number of men each had promised. Rome declared war and crushed the allied force at Thermopylae in 191 B.C. Then the Roman army crossed into Asia Minor, where with the aid of Eumenes' cavalry it defeated Antiochus' main army. The Seleucid king had to give up all territories in Asia Minor, pay a large indemnity of 15,000 talents, reduce his fleet, and get rid of his war elephants. He died a short time later, still trying to raise money to pay the heavy installments of the indemnity.

From this time on, Syria declined. A son of Antiochus III, Antiochus IV Epiphanes (r. 175–164 B.C.), made a great effort to stem this decline. He fought successfully against Egypt, only to be forced out of that country by a warning from Rome. He tried to unify his diverse dominions with a syncretic religious policy. This perhaps was successful in some places; but at Jerusalem, where the Syrian monarch sacrificed pigs and set up his own statue in the Temple precincts, it produced rebellion, led by anti-Hellenist Jewish conservatives. The Jewish feast of Channukah in December celebrates the date in 164 B.C. when, under the leadership of the Maccabees, the Jews purified the Temple. Meanwhile Antiochus campaigned against another revolt to the east but died, reputedly mad, before he could recover the situation.

The Seleucid dynasty endured, though continually beset by dynastic strife, rebellious subject peoples, and economic troubles, until 63 B.C. In that year Syria was made a province of Rome by Pompey the Great, almost as an afterthought. While conducting a war against Mithradates of Pontus to the north, Pompey noted the power vacuum to the south and simply moved into the area, almost without opposition. So ended the second of the great Hellenistic monarchies. Palestine became a client state of Rome; as for Pergamum, when the last of the Attalids died in 133 B.C., his will made Rome heir to the kingdom. Rome first had to fight a small war to convince the Pergamenes that the will was valid, and thereafter Pergamum became a Roman province called Asia.

Egypt under the Ptolemies (305–30 B.C.)

The first Ptolemy, another of the Macedonian generals of Alexander, was named satrap of Egypt after the death of Alexander. As Ptolemy I Soter, he soon began to act independently, like a monarch ruling his own kingdom, and in 305 B.C. he openly proclaimed himself king. His conduct in the early years brought efforts by Perdiccas to discipline him, but Ptolemy was able to hold the naturally protected Egypt against that general, and later against Antigonus as well. He seized Cyrene, and during the maneuvering before the Battle of Ipsus (301 B.C.) he occupied Palestine and Lower Syria as well. He had given Seleucus I refuge from

Ptolemy I, Lagos (Soter);
tetradrachm of Ptolemy II.

Antigonus at a critical moment and had also lent Seleucus forces to reconquer his satrapy, Babylon. Thus Seleucus did not attempt to dislodge Ptolemy after Ipsus, when he gained full control of North Syria and most of the rest of Alexander's empire.

Egypt reached a height of power in the first half of the 3rd century B.C., under Ptolemy II (r. 282–246 B.C.) and Ptolemy III (246–222 B.C.). It seems that it was really the second wife of Ptolemy II, Arsinoë II, who organized the strong and aggressive policy of the king. She was also his sister. This was only one of a whole series of brother-sister marriages that characterized the Ptolemaic dynasty, and Arsinoë was only one of a series of strong-minded women who helped make Hellenistic history. Egypt's power now extended north along the Phoenician coast and into the Aegean.

Ptolemy III continued this aggressive drive. However, Antigonus Gonatas of Macedonia defeated the Egyptian fleet in the Aegean; and a few years later Antiochus III of Syria, as we have seen, began to push the Ptolemaic forces out of their positions along the eastern Mediterranean coastline. Even when the Ptolemaic kingdom was reduced to Egypt proper, Cyrene, and a few islands (after 200 B.C.), however, Egypt remained strong.

Internal problems followed one of Egypt's great victories, that over Antiochus III of Syria in 217 B.C., at Raphia, along the coast of what is now the Gaza Strip. The young Ptolemy IV was at this time under the influence of native ministers, who armed the indigenous populace in putting together the army that defeated the Seleucid force. As a consequence of this participation, native Egyptians aspired to higher posts and even tried to expel the alien Macedonian dynasty. One of the rather meager sources of information for this period is the famed Rosetta Stone. It tells of the building of a temple on which construction was halted numerous times because of internal disorders. Much is sometimes made of the fact, too, that the first known worker-organized work stoppages that can properly be called strikes occurred in Egypt during the Hellenistic age.

Friendship with Rome saved Egypt from Antiochus IV in 167 B.C., as we have seen. But a little later, a profound economic depression —drastically low prices for Egypt's major export, wheat, followed by several successive bad crop years—made it impossible for Egypt ever to recover its strong position of the 3rd century B.C. The quality of its rulers seems also to have declined from this time on.

In one significant respect, Egypt under the Ptolemies differed from the other two major Hellenistic monarchies. Its economy was controlled down to the last detail by the government, in a system somewhat comparable to state socialism. It was nothing new in Egypt, of course, for the Pharaoh to claim title to most of the land; this was true even in remote antiquity. The Ptolemies, however, also placed tight controls on imports and exports. Numerous monopolies were either directly operated by the state or were granted as special privileges or for monetary consideration to individuals. The chief imports so controlled included olive oil, wine, and lumber. The chief exports, wheat and paper, were closely controlled as well. So completely was every economic activity monitored that natives even had to buy permits each day they fished in the Nile.

On the plus side, some of the Ptolemies spent considerable sums to improve the irrigation systems, as for example, in the Fayum area. As we shall see in the next chapter, Ptolemaic rulers sometimes also spent large sums for the benefit of scholars, schools, and libraries. On the minus side, the enormous revenues furnished opportunity for grandiose foreign ventures to some of the dynasts, who used Egypt simply as a base of operations. For the native populace, Macedonian rule was an episode; they did as they have always done—endured.

Everyone knows the last ruler of the Ptolemaic line, Cleopatra VII, who will be dealt with further in the later chapters on Rome. Ambitious and competent, she had great plans that might well have come to fruition had she not backed the loser in a major civil war in Rome. Octavian (later to be Emperor Augustus) could not forgive Cleopatra her support of Antony, whom she had married. He therefore invaded Egypt, and the ill-fated lovers committed suicide. The last of the great Hellenistic monarchies thus fell to Rome, in 30 B.C., and became another of the provinces.

Books for Further Reading

BEVAN, E. R., *The House of Seleucus,* London, 1902.

BEVAN, E. R., *Jerusalem Under the High Priests,* London, 1912.

BEVAN, E. R., *The Ptolemies of Egypt,* London, 1927.

BURN, A. R., *Alexander the Great and the Hellenistic World,* New York, 1962.

BURY, J. B., *The Hellenistic Age,* Cambridge, 1925.

CARY, M., *A History of the Greek World from 323 to 146 B.C.,* London, 1932.

LARSEN, J. A. O., *Greek Federal States,* Oxford, 1968.

LARSEN, J. A. O., *Representative Government in Greek and Roman History,* Berkeley and Los Angeles, 1955.

MACURDY, G., *Hellenistic Queens,* Baltimore, 1932.

PETERS, F. E., *The Harvest of Hellenism,* New York, 1970.

TARN, W. W., *Hellenistic Civilization,* New York, 1952.

TARN, W. W., *Hellenistic Military and Naval Developments,* Cambridge, 1930.

13

Hellenistic Culture:
Currents and Crosscurrents

One might imagine that balance-of-power politics and the frequent wars among the Hellenistic powers caused such constant turmoil that the creative mind could not function. They did not. These wars were dynastic struggles fought with professional armies. The entire populace was not involved in the way the people of Athens and Sparta were caught up in the Peloponnesian War. The actual theaters of conflict experienced much depredation and destruction, but battles seldom touched the great centers that served as the capitals for Hellenistic monarchies. Intellectual activity was almost uninhibited, and even commerce was seldom seriously affected.

A. The Great Cities of the Hellenistic World

Just as the cities produced the first civilizations in an earlier era, so the Hellenistic cities were cultural centers of fusion and diffusion, synthesis and syncretism. These cities, the largest the world had yet seen, were the natural creations of absolutist monarchies. Great centralization of power required great concentration of administrative offices, soldiers, arms and armament, businesses, warehousing facilities. Necessarily, there followed a similar concentration of population.

Alexandria

Egypt, with her centralized government and highly centralized economic system, developed the largest capital city, Alexandria. Located in the Nile Delta on a site with an excellent harbor, it was also connected to

206

one of the branches of the river by a canal. Egypt's low and undifferentiated coastline made it difficult at times for ships at sea to locate the harbor. The Ptolemaic solution was a lighthouse nearly 400 feet high on the harbor island of Pharos—one of the Seven Wonders of the Ancient World. The lighthouse was only one of the wonders of Alexandria. It was the most cosmopolitan of cities as well as the largest; perhaps a million inhabitants crowded into its quarters by the end of the Hellenistic period. It was the city with the largest Greek and the largest Jewish populations in the world, and its broad streets were planned on a rectangular pattern. A letter preserved on papyrus in Egypt's dry sands, written by a woman who had just moved to the city, complains to a country relative that the city's broad streets made shopping too difficult: one's feet were tired all the time!

The patronage of the early Ptolemies made Alexandria a leading cultural capital. The library, the largest in ancient times with at least 700,000 volumes, drew scholars like a magnet. The Museum (home of the Muses) supported research and teaching of enormous importance. To be head of the Museum at Alexandria was to hold the most important academic position in the world—with the possible exception of leadership of the Academy and the Lyceum in Athens. The foremost scholars in both cities were likely to be more than purely philosophers; they were scientists as well—men of broad interests and attainments.

It was at Alexandria that Jewish scholars produced the Greek translation of the Hebrew Bible, the Septuagint. This collection, which contained extra books called the Apocrypha, was much used by Hellenized Jews and even by Palestinian Jews, though the latter subsequently rejected the Apocrypha. Many of the quotations in the Christian New Testament are from the Septuagint. When Saint Jerome translated the Bible into Latin—the Vulgate, which is still the official Bible of the Roman Catholic Church—he used the arrangement of the Septuagint.

Antioch, Pergamum

The sprawling Syrian Empire spawned a number of important cities, among them Seleucia on the Tigris. The chief administrative center, however, was Antioch on the Orontes River in Syria. Situated on an easily defended site, Antioch was one of a complex of four cities founded in Syria by the Seleucids, each, like Alexandria, planned on a grid pattern. It too was cosmopolitan, with native, Jewish, and Greek quarters. Like Alexandria it was something of an intellectual center, with library, museum, and gymnasia. Two of the new cities were ports, the busiest being Laodicea. The other inland city, Apamea, was chiefly a military base.

The greatest city in Asia Minor was Pergamum. At the beginning of the reign of Attalus I (mid-3rd century B.C.) it was only a hill fortress from which Attalus made a reputation by defying invading Gauls—the Galatians. Much of the Attalid income, derived from a relentless tax system and the export of parchment, fine textiles, and pitch, was put to the enrichment of this capital. Its most famous edifice was the altar of Zeus, excavated in the present century and taken to Berlin. It also contained several gymnasia and celebrated temples. The library at Pergamum grew until it was second in size only to that at Alexandria. There were, of course, other notable cities in Asia Minor, in particular Ephesus with its huge temple to Artemis, and Halicarnassus. This last city was the site of another of the Seven Wonders, the Mausoleum built in the middle of the 4th century B.C. for King Mausolus.

B. Science

The significant—sometimes astonishing—advances in basic and applied sciences, medicine, mathematics, and mechanics during the Hellenistic period can only be indicated here. The work of a few of the most eminent figures must be permitted to symbolize the whole.

Aristarchus of Samos (c. 310–230 B.C.)

Many otherwise well-informed persons today believe that all men before Columbus thought that the world was flat. Greek thinkers after Pythagoras, however, conceived of the earth as a sphere, perhaps primarily because they considered the sphere a perfect figure. A pupil of Plato, Eudoxus, attempted to reconstruct the entire universe mathematically. He gave special attention to the planets—a word derived from a Greek word meaning "wanderers" because, as compared with stars, planets do not remain in relatively fixed positions. Eudoxus and some contemporaries postulated an earth revolving upon its axis every twenty-four hours.

Aristarchus of Samos, working at the Museum in Alexandria, went further in his theories than Eudoxus. He conceived the system that bears the name of Copernicus, who lived 1,800 years later. That is, he thought that the sun was much larger than the earth and that the earth, along with the planets, revolved about the sun. The chief objection to this view was that the stars did not seem to change positions, as they would (and do, imperceptibly) if the earth moved in an orbit. Aristarchus replied, it seems, by arguing for a much larger universe than anyone suspected. His figures for the size of the sun and its distance from the earth fall short of reality (311 times the earth's mass and 18 to 20 times the distance from the earth to the moon), but his errors were due solely to the lack of instruments for precise measurement. Unfortunately, his views were not generally accepted, partly because it did not occur to him that the whole universe is moving and that therefore the planets' orbits are elliptical.

Eratosthenes of Cyrene (c. 275–195 B.C.)

Eratosthenes, head of the library at Alexandria, was almost as versatile as Aristotle. He was nicknamed "Beta," which indeed implied that he was second best, but then he was second in so many areas that it became a backhanded compliment. Eratosthenes worked out a historical chronology widely accepted in antiquity. Most striking of his other achievements was his measurement, with considerable accuracy, of the circumference of the earth: he missed by only a few hundred miles. Again, as in Aristarchus' work, the system was perfect and only the measurements were faulty. Eratosthenes computed the difference in the declination of the sun's shadow at two cities in Egypt on the day of the summer solstice. The two cities, he thought, were in exactly the same latitude. The resulting angle, converted into a fraction of a circle, needed only to be inverted and multiplied by the distance between the two cities to give him the correct figure.

Archimedes of Syracuse (c. 287–212 B.C.)

The achievements of Archimedes surpass even those of Eratosthenes, who was his friend. It is ironical that Archimedes is best remembered for certain practical engineering devices—inventions he considered trifling. His greatest accomplishments were in mathematics; indeed, he was quite possibly the greatest mathematician of antiquity. Some of the problems he solved would now be demonstrated by analytical geometry or integral calculus. He did much work in relation to cylinders, spheres, spirals, and conic sections. His predecessor, Euclid, whose work on the *Elements of Geometry* was much less original, is better remembered as a mathematician.

Whatever Archimedes thought of it, his practical work deserves to be remembered, nevertheless. He discovered the principle, named after him, that an object immersed in water is lighter by the weight of the water displaced. His discovery evolved after King Hiero of Syracuse asked him to determine whether a certain metalsmith had cheated him. The king feared that the smith had used different proportions of gold and silver than were given to him to make an elaborate crown. Archimedes was able to demonstrate that the smith was honest. Hiero was also much impressed when Archimedes, using either levers or pulleys (he worked out the principles of both) launched a huge ship the king had built; one of the largest constructed in antiquity, it must have displaced at least 4,000 tons. Archimedes also designed a revolutionary screw pump to make irrigation from the Nile River easier. And at the siege of Syracuse by the Romans in 212 B.C. he made bigger and better war machines —grappling cranes, missile throwers—than had yet been used. He was killed by a Roman soldier when Syracuse fell, reportedly when he shouted at the man not to disturb the figures he had drawn in the sand for study.

Industrial Revolution in 200 B.C.?

The practical inventions of Archimedes and others in the Hellenistic Age are impressive. Water power, harnessed in various ways, operated machinery. Even a slot machine, which operated by the insertion of a coin, was developed. Hero, an Alexandrian scholar, discovered more than one way to make mechanical use of steam. There is little doubt, in fact, that, the technological knowledge then existed to initiate an industrial revolution 2,000 years before it actually occurred. Much work would have been required in metallurgy and in the manufacture of instruments, for example, but it could have been done. What primarily prevented it from occurring was the cheapness of human labor, especially slaves. Only profitable operations endure and prompt the further improvement of machinery. As so often in history, though, one is led to speculate how different the world might have been if men like Archimedes and Hero had sparked a continuing revolution in labor-saving devices.

The crucial role of slavery as an impediment to mechanical and economic progress in antiquity has been denied by some modern scholars, but without sufficient reason. It is true that learned men like Archimedes scorned the practical side of their work, and it is equally true that the Ptolemies and other patrons subsidized science as a matter of intellectual curiosity. Nonetheless, the availability of cheap labor was the main reason the industrial revolution did not begin about 200 B.C.

C. Philosophy

Cynics and Skeptics

Several schools of philosophy were established in the Hellenistic era, including those of the Cynics and the Skeptics. The founder of the Cynic school was Antisthenes, a pupil of both Socrates and Gorgias the Sophist. It was said that Antisthenes and Plato disliked each other cordially, and for approximately the same reasons. Antisthenes thought Plato a rich snob; Plato thought the other a flaunter of poverty, for Antisthenes taught the absolute unimportance of everything except virtue. Birth, rearing, money, property, even convention and good manners were nothing.

A cynic far better known than Antisthenes was Diogenes of Sinope, who spent most of his life in Corinth. Diogenes dramatized the Cynic beliefs through his style of life. He reduced his needs to the minimum, lived in a barrel, and ate with a single dish and spoon whatever anyone gave to him, uncooked. Legend has it that he carried a lighted lantern "looking for an honest man," and that he gave Alexander his comeuppance when the young king arrived in Corinth. He asked Diogenes what the philosopher would have from him. Diogenes demanded that Alexander get out of his sunlight. Alexander is reported to have said then that if he were not Alexander he would be Diogenes; more likely, it was perhaps fortunate for Diogenes that he was an old man at the time. Diogenes' frequently shocking behavior probably made him something of a tourist attraction. But he was well enough liked by the Corinthians; when some rowdy boys once broke up his barrel, local persons took up a collection for a new one.

Skepticism was advocated by the leaders of the Academy, a century or two after Plato. Those heads of the "Middle" Academy like Carneades in the 2nd century B.C. who propounded their views of the impossibility of perception of truth surely would have pained the founder of the school. Plato had fought against similar ideas in the Sophism of his own day.

Stoicism and Epicureanism

Two great schools of philosophy developed in the Hellenistic Age: Stoicism—named from the porch (*stoa*) in Athens where its Cyprian founder, Zeno, taught—and Epicureanism, named for its founder, Epicurus, an Athenian from Samos. Both Zeno and Epicurus were teaching in Athens by 300 B.C. Both philosophical systems had a great impact over a long period. Stoicism influenced many Roman leaders and helped to mold Roman institutions, especially legal ones. Christian views, of a later time, of course, bear a marked similarity to Stoic ones.

Both Stoicism and Epicureanism were concerned primarily with helping individuals decide how they should behave in a world they never made; that is, their emphasis was on ethics. Zeno and Epicurus were, quite understandably, reacting to the world Alexander left as a legacy. Both developed a materialistic view of the universe, with an accompanying cosmogony. But in ultimate ways the two systems were vastly different.

Stoic Beliefs

Zeno, and more especially his successors Cleanthes and Aratus, propounded beliefs that were as much religious as philosophical. The one-world view fostered by Alexander's conquests meant for them the basic equality of all races of men under the universal and benevolent dominion of a Father-God. The materialistic universe they envisioned, though cyclical in nature, was nevertheless guided by God—or Zeus or Mind or Providence—in rational ways often hidden to men. These Stoics were not really monotheists, though they frequently talked as if they were. One unfortunate consequence of their religious emphasis was an often quite superstitious belief in divination and in astrology, the pseudoscience of the influence of the stars on human destiny.

Man's position in the Stoic's universe was distinctly subordinate. The individual must accept his lot without complaint; he must not cry out against Destiny (hence the modern meaning of "stoic"). He should play his assigned role with dignity and courage. Things that seem evil, even disease and death, are not really so; man must always keep in mind the rational nature of the universe. Mind, not the emotions, must rule the individual. The suppression of emotions such as anger and bitterness seems to us laudable, but Stoicism also taught the suppression of the finer emotions such as mercy and love. To be a Stoic was not easy. Self-control, the greatest virtue, was to be supplemented with temperance, modesty, and honesty. Stoics did argue, however, that men might work to improve their lot and that of their fellows. Public service, they taught, was noble and enriching. The true Stoic was a good citizen and when opportunity afforded a good magistrate or judge. The Good Man who accepted his Destiny, who saw God in all that is and in all that he experienced—this was the Stoic, and in the Stoic conception, a happy man.

Epicurean Views

Epicurus lived and taught in a pleasant garden withdrawn from the world —a fact that seems to symbolize all of Epicureanism. The universe, he said, is material and mechanistic; it came to its present state by chance evolution. The gods, if they exist (Epicureans were not Atheists exactly, but behaved as if they were), Epicurus believed, live apart from men and have nothing to do with them or their lives. Man's chief goal in life must be to seek his own happiness. This he could best do by recognizing the basic evils of the world and of the mass of men and by withdrawing from public affairs to whatever retreats he might find with others of similar views.

Like the Stoics, Epicureans who followed Epicurus believed in a high personal code of ethics, for Epicurus taught that no man could be happy unless he was also virtuous. The philosophy itself, however, which is basically selfish in nature, attracted many who interpreted the conclusions of Epicurus to mean that one should "eat, drink, and be merry." It is difficult to know just how influential Epicureanism was. Not a great many specific followers of the philosophy are known, but its influence seems to have been quite pervasive.

Both philosophies spread to the Roman west. Possibly Caesar and certainly Lucretius stand out as Epicureans of the 1st century B.C. The younger Cato, Seneca, and Marcus Aurelius are among the longer list of noted Roman Stoics.

D. Religion

The tendency toward a species of monotheism was not confined to the Stoics. Any period in which there is considerable trade and intercommunication among people of distant areas manifests this trend—through the identification of the different principal deities—toward syncretism. The conquests of Alexander and the thinking that accompanied it, of one world and of one people of the world, gave impetus to monotheistic thought. Perhaps the growing familiarity with the Jewish religion, with its well-developed monotheism, may also have contributed something to the trend. Large, absolutist states, however, have their own built-in impulses toward a universal, if not monotheistic, deity, especially if the ruler manages to associate himself with the dominant god, as Egyptian pharaohs had done from far antiquity.

Syncretism: Sarapis

As the chief deity of their kingdom, the Ptolemies chose a god neither wholly Greek nor wholly Egyptian, Sarapis. The name apparently came from a combination of two ancient Egyptian gods, Osiris, god of the underworld and judge of the dead, and Apis, the bull god of Memphis. The attributes of Sarapis were universal: he too was judge of the dead, but he blessed men in all ways and was considered a creator. His greatest temple was naturally, in Alexandria. Just as naturally, the temple was in the Greek style. The worship of Sarapis and the construction of shrines to him spread over the Mediterranean, following the trade routes. One important temple was built at Delos, for example, and by the 1st century B.C. his devotees were to be found at Rome. Thereafter, the popularity of Sarapis began to fade; he was partially replaced by another old Egyptian deity, the goddess Isis.

In the great days of Egypt two millennia earlier, Isis had been the wife of Osiris and mother of Horus, one of the riverine deities who was also associated with fertility and motherhood. In the Hellenistic age Isis, along with Sarapis and several other eastern deities, developed into a universal god who was worshiped throughout the Mediterranean in Roman days. Identified by the Greeks with Aphrodite (earlier with Demeter), Isis was also the goddess with whom Cleopatra chose to be identified, probably in a pattern set previously by consorts of the Ptolemies. She was especially important to women in pregnancy and childbirth and also to travelers. An extant prayer addressed to her reads like one that might have been composed by a Jew or a Christian. In it, Isis seems omnipotent, benevolent, merciful; exclusivism, however, necessarily one element of real monotheism, is absent.

The King as God: Antiochus IV of Syria

The priests of any well-organized religion are always men of some power and influence, not only religious but economic and social. Kings and other heads of state have thus often believed that for their own protection religion must be closely supervised or controlled. In the Kingdoms of Egypt and Syria in the Hellenistic era, the association or even identification of the king with the chief deity was considered vital to sound statecraft.

The Syrian king Antiochus IV (175–164 B.C.) tried to make his diverse empire more unified by artificially syncretizing religion. (See also p. 202.) All the major deities were to be considered as one; thus, the Jews' god, Yahweh, was to be identified with the Syrians' Baal Shamin and the Greeks' Zeus, and so on. Antiochus took the surname of Epiphanes, which with "Theos" understood means "the god made manifest," and completed the godhead by including himself in its identification. Apparently, statues of himself were to be erected at every major religious site in the kingdom, and worship accorded the king in this way.

Most peoples of the empire no doubt accepted the identification with a shrug as nothing new. The Jews, however, rebelled under the Maccabees against both their own hellenizers and the king. Antiochus never did regain control of the area before he died, so the Jews for the most part retained their independence until the Romans asserted control over Palestine.

Judaism itself became widespread, chiefly through the emigration of Jews to Alexandria, Antioch, and other cities of the Hellenistic east, and, eventually, to Rome as well. The religion remained everywhere the strict monotheism it was in Palestine, but it was influenced in its outward forms by the cultures of various areas. The very term "synagogue," which describes the local organization typically used by the Jews of the dispersion, is Greek.

Other Oriental Religions

The Asia Minor-Syria region exported its own forms of religion to Greece and the western Mediterranean during the Hellenistic Age and the Roman period that followed. The goddess Cybele is typical of this influence. Called also the Great Mother, the Mother of the Gods, or the Great Mother of Pessinus (from the town in Asia Minor where the mythical stories about her centered), Cybele ranked almost with the Twelve Olympians from a rather early period. Yet she gained even more adherents in Hellenistic times.

The reasons why Cybele and other oriental deities grew in importance were perhaps related to the religious needs of the common people. These needs were not satisfied by the cold, formal rites to the state deities or the parochial local gods. The worship of Cybele began in Rome in 204 B.C. under the tutelage of two of its leading noble families. There Cybele became a sort of upper-class goddess, and her spring festival was one of the most celebrated in that city.

Cybele's priests were self-emasculated *galli*. Her rites were sometimes emotional and orgiastic. At Rome they were somewhat more dignified but still noisy, as we learn from the poets. The most important characteristic of the Cybele and similar cults was that of "mystery." Participants in the mysteries were given promises of blessings in this life and privileges in the next.

E. Literature

Much of the more significant literary work of the Hellenistic Age was philological in nature, especially that at Alexandria. There scholars collected the great works of the past and established definitive texts, expunging and emending with skill. They wrote critiques and commentaries, compiled dictionaries and bibliographies. Unfortunately, most of their labor was lost in antiquity. Even so, had not an Alexandrian scholar discovered a moldering part of Aristotle's library, we would be even poorer today in the treasures of the past.

History

Two great writers compiled oriental histories: Manetho and Berossus, both hellenized natives of Egypt and Mesopotamia, respectively. Their works survive only in fragments, but it is obvious that they helped to keep alive much that would otherwise have been irretrievably lost.

The greatest Greek historian of the age was Polybius. Large sections of what survives of his *Histories* deals with Rome, but the account as written embraced the Graeco-Roman world. Substantial fragments illuminate such crucial periods as that in which the Ptolemies and Seleucids fought for control of Egypt, 220–200 B.C. Polybius was especially well qualified to write of all the Mediterranean. He was a Greek who lived at Rome for a number of years, and was friendly with Romans who held high positions. He himself had previously held office in the Achaean League. In addition to traveling throughout his Greek homeland, Polybius visited Spain and North Africa. His theory of cycles in political evolution, which modified Plato's and Aristotle's conclusions, is interesting. He thought the most stable and enduring constitution, like the Roman and the earlier Spartan, should contain a balanced mixture of the elements of monarchy, oligarchy, and democracy. However, the soundness of such a constitution, he thought, would at last be undermined when one element—most likely the democratic—overshadowed the others.

Poetry

Some of the best poetry of the age was written by the great Stoic teachers, Cleanthes and Aratus. Their hymns of praise and prayers to Zeus as God rank with the great psalms of the Hebrews. And it was probably this age, incidentally, in which some poet of the Hebrews was producing the Song of Songs.

At Alexandria, the pastoral idylls of Callimachus and Theocritus (who was born in Sicily), composed in the 3rd century B.C., exercised great influence on the later Latin poets of the Augustan period. Callimachus was also a scholar, and perhaps the first to organize the collection of rolls in the library at Alexandria. Apollonius, who lived some years at Alexandria before retiring to Rhodes after quarreling bitterly with Callimachus, wrote the epic *Argonautica,* which relates in Homeric rhythms the familiar story of Jason's search for the Golden Fleece and his love affair with Medea.

Drama

Many forms of drama continued to be produced in the Hellenistic Age, with Athens, through sheer tradition, still the theatrical center. Of tragedy little remains, probably testimony enough to the general quality. The 3rd century saw the development of the so-called New Comedy, which is much more like the modern forms of comedy than the plays of Aristophanes. The best-known writer of these comedies was Menander.

Not until about thirty years ago did we have a full play of Menander's —when the sands of Egypt yielded one almost entire. But it is a disappointment. Clearly, some of his other works—of which we have considerable fragments—were much better. Again, much of the importance of the author lies in his influence upon later writers in Latin—in this case Plautus and particularly Terence, several of whose plays are extant. The New Comedy was rather frivolous, filled with sex intrigues and impudent slaves, and turning upon plots that often involved fortuitous solutions to not very serious problems. Will the aristocratic young man be able to marry the slave girl he loves? He will, because she turns out to be the long-lost daughter of a friend of the family. The humor depended upon pun-filled dialogue, exquisite timing, and crowd-pleasing actors.

All of which reminds one again of the essential modernity of the Hellenistic Age.

Books for Further Reading

BAILEY, C., *Epicurus,* Oxford, 1926.

BEVAN, E. R., *Stoics and Skeptics,* Oxford, 1913.

BEVAN, E. R., *Later Greek Religion,* New York, 1927.

BROCK, A. J., *Greek Medicine,* New York, 1929.

CLAGETT, M., *Greek Science in Antiquity,* London, 1957.

DIJKSTERHUIS, E. J., *Archimedes,* Copenhagen, 1956.

DRACHMANN, A. G., *The Mechanical Technology of Greek and Roman Antiquity,* Copenhagen, 1961.

HADAS, M., *Hellenistic Culture: Fusion and Diffusion,* New York, 1959.

HEATH, T. L., *Aristarchus of Samos,* Oxford, 1920.

RIST, J., *Stoic Philosophy,* New York, 1969.

SAYRE, F., *The Greek Cynics,* Baltimore, 1948.

THOMPSON, J. W., *Ancient Libraries,* Berkeley and Los Angeles, 1940.

WEBSTER, T. B. L., *Studies in Menander,* Manchester, 1950.

CHART 5 The Roman Republic

PERIOD	ROME	ELSEWHERE
800 B.C.	Rome a tiny village on the Palatine Hill.	Carthage founded by Phoenicians; Greek colonies in south Italy, east Sicily, elsewhere. Etruscans powerful north of Rome.
700 B.C. 600 B.C.	Petty kings; Etruscans gain control, make Rome into an important political and economic center.	Assyrian Empire reaching its height. Fall of Assyria to Medes, Babylonians; Nebuchadnezzar. Babylonia falls to Cyrus and Persians.
500 B.C.	Rome freed of Etruscan kings; becomes a republican oligarchy; period of economic depression, decline follows. Struggle of the orders begins.	Persian Wars with Greeks; Athenian empire. Etruscans decline under attack from Gauls, Greeks, and Romans. Peloponnesian War; Spartan dominance in Greece.
400 B.C.	Romans take Veii, then lose to Gauls; city burned and sacked. Rome achieves dominance over Latin peoples; suppresses revolt; sets up alliance system.	Theban dominance; rise of Macedonia. Alexander becomes king; conquest of Persian Empire.
300 B.C.	Samnite wars; Roman expansion of power in Italy. End of struggle of the orders (Hortensian Law). Wars with Pyrrhus and others lead to Roman dominance of all Italy south of the Po Valley. First Punic War; Sicily becomes a province, then Sardinia and Corsica. Earliest Latinized productions of Greek theater. Occupation of the Po Valley.	The successor states: Ptolemaic dynasty in Egypt Seleucid dynasty in Syria and much of Near East Antigonid dynasty in Macedonia Attalid dynasty in Pergamum Achaean and Aetolian leagues in Greece.
200 B.C.	Second Punic War; two provinces in Spain; First Macedonian War concurrent; Second Macedonian War follows. Syrian War; playwrights Plautus and Terence. Third Macedonian War. Polybius at Rome, becomes member of "Scipionic circle." Culmination of career of Cato. Fourth Macedonian War, Achaean War, Third Punic War; North Africa and Macedonia provinces. The Gracchi; land and grain laws.	Antiochus III recovers much land previously lost; acquires Palestine from Egypt; loses war to Rome, in alliance with Aetolians; Aetolian League dissolved. Philip V of Macedonia chooses Perseus as successor. Perseus killed; Macedonia four republics. Antiochus IV of Syria; Jewish revolt. Macedonia a Roman province; Greece subordinate. Achaean League dissolved. Attalus III dies, wills Kingdom of Pergamum to Rome; this becomes province of Asia.
100 B.C.	Marius; Jugurthan and Celtic Wars; Saturninus. The Italian War; Italian and Latin allies enfranchised. Mithridatic War; civil strife in Rome. Sulla's return; civil war; conservative reforms. Reforms mostly scuttled; Third Mithradatic War, height or Pompey's career; Cicero consul; Catiline. First Triumvirate: Caesar, Crassus, Pompey; period of Lucretius, Sallust, Catullus. Civil war between Pompey and Caesar; Pharsalus, Pompey dies. Assassination of dictator Caesar; renewed civil war; Second Triumvirate against Brutus and Cassius. Octavian victorious over Antony and Cleopatra.	Cilicia taken over by Rome as a province. Mithradates of Pontus "liberates" peoples subject to Rome in Asia Minor; defeated by Rome. Bithynia also willed to Rome in Asia Minor; Mithradates reacts with war. Cyrene becomes Roman territory. Cyprus taken over by Rome. Parthians defeat Crassus in war and kill him. Cleopatra cooperates with Caesar, then with Brutus and Cassius; forgiven by Antony, marries him; defeated by Octavian, the couple are suicides; Egypt becomes Roman province.
27 B.C.	Octavian becomes Augustus; controls Roman world.	

Rome

History is not always—perhaps not often—specifically useful. (Of course, it is in a general sense valuable!) The history of Rome, however, has been thought useful by hordes of scholars, amateur and professional, and also by politicians and ordinary men who see analogy to the present in the decline and fall of the Roman Empire. For several reasons, the history of Rome suits such comparison better than most other histories. We have been left a fairly detailed account of the rise of a small village on the Tiber to world power and dominion, followed by its agonizing deterioration, accelerating decline, and reverberating collapse. Roman history presents what seems a complete unit, the tale of the entire life cycle of a political organism. The historians Spengler and Toynbee found in it a model when they looked for cycles in history.

But political units, though fashioned by men, are not biological organisms. Seldom exact, analogies are often more misleading than illuminating. This sort of speculative misuse of Roman history does not, however, detract from its enduring importance. Wise men will read with profit how Rome, succeeding where the more brilliant Greeks had failed, managed to govern so well this diverse mass of people and provinces. Rome created a centralized administration held together by a road system unequalled until modern times and built far-flung cities well equipped with aqueducts, basilicas, temples, theaters, and arenas. But after all this astonishing achievement, the Empire lapsed into disquieting decay and dissolution. This decline, too, is profitable and sobering to read.

Earliest Rome

14

A. Geographical Setting

Rome now seems an unlikely spot for the center of a world empire. Italy does not have the resources for a first-rank power in the twentieth century; but by ancient standards, and especially in comparison with Greece, the Italian Peninsula was both richly endowed and strategically located. Greek travelers who visited Italy in antiquity marveled that the land seemed one vast garden. Though the Apennine Mountains form a spine for the 600-mile-long peninsula, they do not compartmentalize the country as do the mountain ranges of Greece; moreover, the rich agricultural areas of Italy are larger than the productive valleys of Greece. Italy yielded iron ore, copper, and precious metals, but its true wealth was more a matter of cropland, pasture, forests, and above all, men to fill the ranks of army after army.

The location of Rome influenced its development throughout ancient history. In the earliest period the city's position on the Tiber about eighteen miles inland gave it both security from piracy and a valuable outlet to the sea. The roads west of the Apennines tended to converge on Rome also, for the lowest point to ford the Tiber was there. The Tiber Island also made it easy, later, to bridge the stream. From remote antiquity, roads had come down along both sides of the Tiber as well. In the next phase, the age of expansion within Italy, Rome's central location and good communications were important. Beyond Italy, the Romans first expanded westward, because in its natural geography Rome faced west. This meant that Rome waxed strong in the West before it turned to confront the sophisticated and powerful Hellenistic states in

Italy
in the 6th Century B.C.

Areas dominated by
Greeks
Etruscans

the East. Still later, when Rome's empire embraced the whole Mediterranean basin, Italy's central position eased the task of governing. It should not be thought, however, that geography alone, in any mechanical way, determined the history of Rome. Physical setting was just one important factor.

From the Alps to the heel of its bootlike peninsula, Italy stretches about 750 miles. It is relatively narrow, however, averaging only about 120 miles in width. On the east is the Adriatic Sea, with Illyria and Epirus lying beyond in ancient times; Greece lies farther to the southeast. On the west the Tyrhennian Sea is marked off by large islands: Sicily at the toe of the boot, and Sardinia and Corsica. The Alps, higher than any mountains in the United States outside Alaska, provide some natural protection for Italy, but there are numerous passes. The Apennines, less lofty, connect with the Alps on the west. Between the Alps and the Apennines nestles the Po Valley, the richest agricultural region of ancient and modern Italy; in the earliest history of Rome, however, it played almost no part.

Important areas along the west coast of ancient Italy included Etruria, located north of Rome and named after the Etruscans; Latium, where Rome was situated; Campania, a quite rich agricultural area farther south; Lucania, just south of Campania; and at the toe of the boot, Bruttium (modern-day Calabria). On the opposite side, the heel of the boot was occupied by ancient Calabria (i.e., Calabria and Bruttium are reversed in modern Italy). North of Calabria, along the eastern, Adriatic coast lay Apulia; in the rough hill country inland southeast from Latium between Apulia and Campania rose Samnium; and farther north along the Adriatic lay Picenum and Umbria.

The climate of much of peninsular Italy is typically Mediterranean: summers are dry and hot, winters are wet and cold. There is somewhat more rainfall than in Greece. In the southernmost regions, desert winds off the Sahara (the sirocco) sometimes desiccate the land. In the north, on the other hand, winds off the Alps can be freezing cold.

B. Civilization Moves West: Etruscans, Greeks, and Phoenicians

The high civilization that first developed in the ancient Near East was diffused gradually—perhaps "percolated" would be a better word—into the western Mediterranean. The Bronze Age arrived in Italy about 1800 B.C.; the Iron Age, about 900 B.C. The Bronze Age in Italy did not rest upon a brilliant urban culture as it did in Mesopotamia. There were urban settlements, and excavation of some of them, as in the neolithic Terremare culture of northern Italy, has furnished evidence of planning and orderly development. (Archaeologists of a century ago were too glowing in their reports, however.) Not until the Iron Age did the western Mediterranean achieve a high culture, largely brought in by traders and settlers. Rome was to be much influenced by these settlers: Etruscans, Greeks, and Phoenicians.

Etruscans

The mystery of Etruscan origins titillates the curiosity of everyone who studies them. Both in antiquity and in modern times scholars have argued the question. Two opposing views get the support of most scholars: some think the Etruscans were an indigenous people, and others hold they came as immigrants to Italy in the early Iron Age, probably from the east, most likely Asia Minor. Herodotus and most other ancient historians thought the latter. Archaeology can now tell us a great deal about the physical world of the Etruscans and the development of their culture, but it has yet to verify their origins. Nor have we learned much about their government and modes of behavior from the quite extensive remains.

Etruscan culture first appeared in Italy in Etruria, a region named after them by the Romans. (Etruscans called themselves the Rasenna.) In the archaeological strata of Etruria this culture is super-imposed immediately over an early Iron Age culture called Villanovan. Scholars who think the Etruscans were indigenous see Etruscan culture simply as a late and distinctive phase of the Villanovan; yet in other areas, Villanovan culture did not develop such distinctive features. It is hard, then, to see how the two groups could have a similar history.

Some facets of Etruscan life seem Oriental. Their distinctive sculpture shows an Oriental cast, and Etruscans are known to have imported art objects from Egypt and elsewhere in the East. Many of their religious practices, especially the reading of omens in the study of animal livers and entrails and their manner of burial, derived from the East. The most frustrating element of the Etruscan enigma is their language, which might help to solve the mystery if it could be read and compared with other similar languages. Since they used, basically, the Phoenician characters already adopted by the Greeks, the words themselves can easily be made out, and even their grammar can be partly discerned. The language may be similar to one used in the Aegean area and in Phrygia, but evidence for this is slight and indecisive.

Etruscan government rested on a loose league of twelve cities, held together more by religious than by political ties. A chief festival was the annual gathering to honor the goddess Voltumna at a site called Volsinii, possibly Bolsena or Orvieto on the modern map. The priest-rulers of each of the twelve cities, who were called *lucumones,* conferred in council under the chairmanship of an official called *rex* and made common plans. Action apparently required unanimous approval. The Etruscans thus were not tightly organized politically, and different cities of the league not only pursued isolated goals but sometimes actually fought against each other.

Etruscan power reached its height in the 6th century B.C. Though never very numerous as a people, the Etruscans ruled over an extended area. They expanded north toward present-day Bologna and then across the Apennines into the rich Po Valley. They competed with the Greeks in southern Italy and won control of Campania, the richest agricultural region of the south. Rome, too, and probably all Latium came under their influence.

The Etruscans were a great trading people. For export they made objects of bronze and iron; the best deposits of copper and iron ore in all Italy lay in Etruria and on the island of Elba, just offshore. Great slag piles remain to testify to the huge amounts of iron produced in the area in antiquity. Important silver-bearing lead deposits were also exploited. Etruria produced an abundance of farm crops, and her great forests were so dense that the Romans feared them for centuries. The Etruscans maintained a merchant fleet and shared with Greeks and Carthaginians the sea trade of the West.

Planned layouts for towns were an Etruscan specialty, as the visible remains show. Settlement sites were shrewdly chosen, and fortifications were carefully designed to fit the terrain. Etruscan architecture is impressive and, again, distinctive. Through archaeological remains, tomb paintings, and reproductions on later Roman coins, we know with some certainty how an Etruscan temple looked. It was more nearly square than the Greek temple and had fewer columns and more decoration especially on gables and friezes. Terracotta antefixes, more elaborate than those on Greek temples, are often found. To the modern eye these temples, as vestiges of antiquity, seem somewhat baroque yet attractive.

The enormous hemispherical vaulted tombs, sometimes completely underground, in which the Etruscan upper classes interred their dead, have yielded most of the Etruscan art that remains to us. The best site for the tourist to inspect these fascinating tombs is at modern Cerveteri (ancient Caere), where the local museum preserves some fine objects salvaged in the vicinity. The Villa Giulia in Rome is the most comprehensive Etruscan museum. There are preserved excellent examples of terra-cotta sculpture, especially on sarcophagi; beautiful examples of Etruscan pottery, somewhat imitative of the best Greek ware but with a distinctive Oriental cast; detached wall paintings, which decorated the tombs in profusion; and the fine bronze ware the Etruscans loved.

The Romans were to learn much and borrow much from the Etruscans. They made use of Etruscan *haruspices,* or takers of omens; borrowed their temple architecture, and even certain deities; and learned from them to make statues of their gods. Elements of Roman government derived from the Etruscans also: names for officials, the Senate, accouterments of office. In the field of entertainment Romans were influenced by Etruscan music, dancing, theater, and contests of various sorts, including —unfortunately—gladiatorial combats. Such influence was greatest and most direct about the 6th century B.C., when Rome was ruled by Etruscan kings, but it continued over a span of centuries. Gaius Maecenas, the friend and counselor of the Emperor Augustus, was Etruscan; and he still maintained the reputation Etruscans had as connoisseurs of sensual pleasure. The Emperor Claudius in his early life studied and wrote on both Etruscan history and language. By this time, however, there was

Detail of a sixth century B.C. Etruscan relief; wood overlaid with bronze. *(The Metropolitan Museum of Art, Rogers Fund, 1903)*

something antiquarian about Etruscan studies, since as a people they had dissolved in Rome's melting pot.

The Greeks in the West

Arnold Toynbee, in his *A Study of History,* argues that the proper unit of historical study is the society or civilization, not individual states. Thus, he listed Rome under "Hellenic society." Whether or not this division is proper, it does underline the undoubted fact that Rome owed more to the Greeks than to any other people, that Roman culture was in many important respects a continuation of Greek culture.

226

The Roman debt to Greece, however, was often not a debt to the Greeks in their mainland home, but to Greeks in the West. Many first-rank Greek philosophers, poets, architects, painters, mathematicians, scientists, and politicians resided in Sicily or southern Italy. Familiar names leap to mind: Pythagoras, Parmenides, Zeno, Empedocles, Gorgias, Archimedes, Timaeus and Diodorus, among others. Western Greeks were traders and explorers; they informed the Romans about geography. Western Greek potters, painters, town planners, and other artists and craftsmen often worked for the Romans. Ultimately the greatest influences did come from Greece itself, for it was there that the greatest thinkers and most of the greatest artists lived.

An increasing number of archaeological sites show that Greeks had penetrated the West already in the Mycenaean age. Homer's *Odyssey* perhaps indicates some continued familiarity with Sicily and southern Italy during the dark age that followed. Beginning in the 8th century B.C., Greeks moved westward in large numbers, as we have seen. Sites on the island of Ischia and at Cumae in Campania were colonized in the mid-8th century B.C., and a large number of important sites elsewhere in southern Italy and Sicily within the following century. Greeks also settled in what is today eastern Spain and southern France. In these new lands they organized city-states like those developed in Greece, fought each other with the same abandon that Spartans, Athenians, and Thebans did, and warred against the Etruscans and Carthaginians as well.

Greek influence reached Rome first through the Etruscans, later through Roman alliance with the Samnites in Campania (still under strong Greek influence), and still later through Roman conquest of southern Italy and Sicily. When, in the 2nd century B.C., Rome's power enveloped Greece and Macedonia, another surge of cultural penetration resulted, and this persisted into the period of the Roman Empire.

Phoenicians

By Greek reckoning, the Phoenician colonization of the western Mediterranean occurred earlier than their own. In moving westward, Phoenicians appear to have been interested mostly in trade, whereas many Greeks simply wanted land for agriculture. Yet the Phoenicians, too, needed an agricultural base and so came to control much land around Carthage, elsewhere along the North African coast, and in western Sicily and southern Spain. Neither Greek nor Phoenician colonies were controlled from the mother city, though religious and commercial ties were strong.

When Tyre and Sidon and other Phoenician home cities were weakened and then conquered by the Assyrians and later the Babylonians, Carthage emerged as leader of the Phoenicians in the West. In western

Sicily, for example, Phoenician colonists looked to nearby Carthage for assistance whenever they found themselves in conflict with the Greeks at the other end of the island. With both a rich trade and a productive agriculture, Carthage was well equipped to lead. Most of the land owned by Carthaginian aristocrats was worked by the native populace; Carthaginian citizenship was restricted, so that the total number of Carthaginian citizens was relatively small. A core of citizens staffed the navy and the officer corps of the army, but most soldiers were hired mercenaries from Libya, Iberia, Greece, and elsewhere. The long heritage of Phoenician seafaring and extensive trade made the navy important in Carthaginian eyes; hence, more care was given to ships and harbor facilities than to the development of a land army.

The government of Carthage was a close-knit oligarchy. The popular assembly had little power; the aristocratic senate had more, but most power resided in an inner council of the senate called "the Hundred" and in a still smaller group, known as "the Thirty." The assembly elected the chief magistrates, called *suffetes,* and also the generals. This mixed constitution was stable, at least as compared with the Greek states in the West, which alternated—sometimes "gyrated" would better describe the process—from oligarchy to democracy to tyranny.

The Carthaginians influenced the Romans most through warfare. They forced the Romans to build a navy and thus to turn to the sea. Carthage gave Rome its most severe tests. Spoils and territory won from Carthage made Rome rich and gave it the base for eventual world dominion. In some specific areas, however, the Romans learned from the Carthaginians in peace. Long before the Romans, for instance, Carthaginians developed plantation-type agriculture. An important book on the subject written by a man named Mago and translated into Latin in the 2nd century B.C. the Romans found quite instructive. In addition, some of the procedures of the Roman system of provincial government were adapted from Carthaginian ones.

C. The Monarchy: Legend and Fact (c. 753–509 B.C.)

As everyone "knows," Rome was founded by Romulus, twin brother of Remus, in 753 B.C. This date was decided upon by Marcus Terentius Varro, a Roman intellectual of the 1st century B.C., on the basis of available data, including that of researchers during the preceding century or two who had concerned themselves with the same problem. Some of this evidence was tenuous indeed. As for Romulus—he may have been invented a few centuries earlier to account for the name of the city. Modern archaeology provides us with some solid information unavailable to Varro; but he, in turn, had access to other important materials that are no longer available. We are forced to rely on the accounts, in particular, of the historians Livy and Dionysius of Halicarnassus, and to winnow as best we can the scanty wheat from their abundant chaff.

The Romans listed seven kings, from Romulus to Tarquinius Superbus, who ruled from 753 B.C. to 509 B.C. Each of these rulers seems rather stereotyped in the accounts. Romulus, one of twin sons of Mars by a vestal virgin, was a vigorous conqueror and assimilator. His successor Numa Pompilius, a Sabine, was a religious and political organizer. Tarquinius Superbus was the prototype of the tyrant, who ran roughshod over the rights of other Romans—meaning, of course, the aristocracy. Although we cannot give strong credence to these stories, the king list itself may be approximately correct.

It is clear from archaeology that Rome was no more than a tiny village on a hill above a ford in the Tiber in the mid-8th century B.C. The celebrated Forum was at this time a burial ground. As the legends said, the earliest settlement was on the Palatine. But these ancient accounts make of Rome much more than it was at a given time. The first pebble-paved streets probably were laid only in the last century of the monarchy. Contrary to the traditional Roman view, it is very doubtful that in this early era Rome dominated the other Latin states in the area. In the days of the later kings, who were probably Etruscans, Rome did develop into an important town; in comparative terms, it would be proper to call it a city. One significant piece of solid evidence is the temple of Jupiter Optimus Maximus, Juno, and Minerva, built in Etruscan style and by tradition dedicated in the year the monarchy ended and the Republic was established. At the time of its construction, and consistently through several later reconstructions, it was the largest temple in all Italy.

The three Etruscan kings made Rome a prosperous city. Etruscan trade and manufactures centered in Etruria, of course; but Etruscans also controlled the rich area of Campania south of Rome. The natural land routes passed through Rome, and its strategic site made the city one of the more important regional centers in the Etruscan system. On the other hand, when Rome eventually asserted her independence, Etruscan trade bypassed the city. The result for Rome was a severe economic decline, which has been attested by archaeology. Romans of the early Republic, for example, could no longer afford expensive imported Greek pottery.

D. The Early Republic
(c. 509 B.C.)

Expulsion of the Etruscan Kingship

A primary cause for the expulsion of the Etruscans, it seems, was a change in military tactics all over Italy, similar to changes which had occurred in Greece even earlier. Armies grew larger and began to depend less on aristocratic cavalry than on heavy-armed infantry. Extremely important to the new tactics was the size of the phalanx; this meant the use of ever-larger numbers of men—mostly commoners, naturally. Etruscan kings who developed such armies necessarily depended less on the nobility. The nobles felt their power and status slipping away and reacted. The expulsion of Tarquin, then, was not so much a patriotic uprising against a foreign tyrant as it was a reactionary effort by Rome's nobles to retain their dominant position in the state. The story of Tarquin's son Sextus raping the fair Lucretia, whose suicide then actuated the heroic Lucius Junius Brutus to free the country, is most likely a romantic invention.

Struggle of the Orders

The Roman aristocrats—patricians, as they were called—could not manage without a large body of infantry any more than could the kings. Using this need as leverage, the Roman plebeians over a period of time demanded concessions from the aristocrats, in what the later Roman historians called "the struggle of the orders." Plebeians gradually got a greater share in government. As Rome expanded in central Italy and gave citizenship to the conquered, the struggle of the orders was refueled by new plebeians. The patrician class was a closed group that could be entered only by birth. Even though some newly assimilated citizens had been aristocrats at home, they became plebeians in Rome. Such men often furnished the leadership for the Roman "plebs" as a whole, agitating for the plebeians' right to hold office and participate in all the institutions of the state.

The struggle of the orders continued intermittently from the beginning of the Republic to about 287 B.C., when the Hortensian Law marked its successful end. At the same time, it should be emphasized, the plebeian class came to include many important and wealthy men. Along with the patricians, those who reached the highest offices formed an expanded aristocracy, the *nobilitas*. In time these *nobiles* guarded their acquired privileges almost as jealously as the patricians of old had done.

In the 5th century B.C. plebeians gained the right to elect ten tribunes of the plebs annually. The chief function of these officials was to protect plebeian rights. Their concern, of course, was most often for upper-level plebeians; few tribunes interested themselves in helping lower class plebeians. Other rights gained in this century were the codification of law (the XII Tables of 451–450 B.C., by traditional dating), the right of intermarriage with patricians, and the right of being elected military tribunes with consular power—officials who replaced consuls in most years between 444 and 367 B.C. The 4th century brought further advance: in 367 B.C. one of the Licinian-Sextian Laws provided that one consul should be a plebeian. By the end of that century, plebeians could legally serve in any elective office. The Publilian Law of 338 B.C. and the Hortensian Law of 287 B.C. gave the two popular assemblies the right to pass laws without prior approval of the Senate, as was previously required.

Government after the Struggle of the Orders

Aside from the moribund curiate assembly, which had been more important under the kings, there were two citizen assemblies in the Roman state: the Assembly of the Centuries *(comitia centuriata)* and the Assembly of the Tribes *(comitia tributa)*. The centuriate assembly elected the chief magistrates, declared war, served as a court in capital cases, and passed laws. A consul usually presided over its sessions. The tribal assembly, which comprised all citizens also, was more democratic than the centuriate assembly. The centuries were organized on the army model into cavalry and five classes of infantry. Voting began at the top and stopped when a majority was reached, so that rich patricians and plebeians usually determined the outcome. In the Assembly of the Tribes, however, placement in the tribes was on the basis of residence, not wealth, and the voting order was determined by lot. Under the presidency of a tribune, the tribal assembly without the patricians—a body usually referred to as the *concilium plebis*—elected the tribunes of the plebs. The tribal assembly also chose other officials, passed laws, and served as a court.

A most important body, with about 300 members during most of the Republic, was the Senate. It was composed of ex-magistrates, who served for life. Its members were appointed by the censors, who could also remove members for cause, such as immoral behavior. The Senate always gave its opinion in the form of advice to the convening magistrate, usually one of the consuls. Its decrees, called *senatus consulta,* were seldom disregarded by the magistrates and therefore usually had the force of law. As Rome expanded into empire, the Senate gradually arrogated to itself the right of assigning duties to the chief magistrates, the power of controlling state money, and (eventually) of controlling the provinces. It gained this extensive power partly because of the great experience and influence *(auctoritas)* its members possessed and partly because it could, when necessary, be in almost continuous session, whereas the citizen assemblies were unwieldly and slow to act.

The chief magistrates, elected annually, were consuls and praetors. The two consuls were the chief executives and frequently served as generals in the army. The praetors within the city were judges; outside the city they too might lead armies. Consuls and praetors had *imperium,* the right of command. Dictators, chosen in emergencies to exercise the power of both consuls for a maximum period of six months, had this same authority. Censors, elected about every five years, took the census, assessed property for taxes, let out government contracts, and assigned men to the Senate, the cavalry, or their place in the assemblies. Like consuls and praetors, censors were elected in the Assembly of the Centuries. The aediles and quaestors were elected in the Assembly of the Tribes. Aediles organized major festivals and supervised trading in the Forum. Quaestors were financial officials. One quaestor was assigned to each general; two city quaestors supervised the treasury and, later, the port of Ostia, with particular attention to the important matter of grain imports.

Social Organization of the Early Republic

Early Rome was basically rural; in society, government, and religion there were tribal vestiges of sorts. One such institution, which not only survived but evolved with changing society, was the patron-client system. Most patricians, and later many plebeians, were patrons to numbers of clients. Patrons looked out for their clients' welfare, especially in connection with the courts. Clients supported their patrons; in early times, they probably did so with weapons, but in the historic period, they responded chiefly through their votes. The patron-client relationship had a religious aspect and was hereditary. This helped the aristocracy to control votes in the assemblies; the timocratic arrangement in the centuriate assembly, of course, made it easier to control the important elections in that body. The nobility thus controlled the offices, the Senate, the assemblies, and also the army, which they led. The social organization simply reflected the realities of power.

The great power and pervading influence of the family was another tribal leftover from remote antiquity. The *pater familias* retained his control over grown and married sons. It is always stressed that his power even allowed him to take the life of any member of the family, but known examples of this can be counted on the fingers of one hand. The great emphasis on family extended into the sphere of religion, leading to ancestor worship at the family hearth, and into politics, where alliances of families were able to control elections.

Early Romans worshipped a multitude of deities. Most were *numina,* powers or spirits; there were *numina* of fountains, streams, woods, pools, crossroads, and so on. The family gods are best known: Vesta, goddess of the hearth; the *lares* and *penates,* gods of the property boundaries and storerooms; and Janus, god of the threshold. Jupiter Capitolinus was the chief deity of the state, and there were state cults of Vesta and Janus also.

Etruscan and Greek influence led the early Romans to identify many of their deities with those of these two more civilized peoples. The Romans now conceived their gods in anthropomorphic style and imported sculptors to create their images. As we have seen, they began to build temples also, first in the Etruscan and later in a modified Greek manner. Jupiter was equated with Zeus, Juno became one with Hera, and Mars found analogy in Ares. Yet in many instances the Romans retained views of their gods or gave them attributes that had no counterpart in Greek conceptions.

Romans had a conviction that they were more religious than those peoples they conquered, especially the Greeks—and they were probably right. The chief priest at Rome, the *pontifex maximus,* was always an important official with duties going beyond pure religion. This and other priestly offices (usually in colleges), as well as the college of augurs, were always filled with laymen, not professionals. Members of another important college of women, the vestal virgins, served thirty years each · and thus were actually professionals, since they had no other major pursuits.

Struggle to Survive in the Early Republic

The expulsion of the Tarquins brought not only economic depression, as we have seen, but also attempts of Etruscan leaders to regain control of the city. The Romans later told much-embellished stories of their heroic efforts to safeguard the new freedom. Horatius, who held off an Etruscan army at the Tiber bridge, and Cincinnatus, who left his plowing to rescue a besieged Roman army, were held up to generations of Roman boys as examples of their ancestors' indomitable courage, which they were expected to imitate.

The early books of Livy emphasize that the new republic was in constant danger from the Etruscans and other nearby peoples: the Sabines, the Volsci, and the Aequi, among others. Some sort of martial cam-

The reverse of this first century B.C. denarius shows the temple of Jupiter Optimus Maximus as it was before the fire and reconstruction after Sulla.

paign was a yearly affair. Even though tradition may exaggerate, it is not unlikely that for most ancient Italian peoples, a summer's campaign was a routine part of the yearly military training for youths. Rome at length made headway against neighboring Etruscan powers. The first important victory across the Tiber in Etruscan territory was the taking of Veii, on a strongly fortified eminence north of Rome. According to tradition, a siege of ten years was required to reduce this Etruscan stronghold, which fell to the forces of another hero type, Camillus, in 396 B.C. (by the traditional dating).

The Romans did not have long to celebrate, for the most serious threat in their early history soon descended upon them. Gauls from central Europe had poured into the Po Valley in recent years, thereby weakening the Etruscans as they drove them out of that area. In 390 B.C. the Gauls (Senones) moved down into central Italy; their chief aim was perhaps to despoil the Etruscan cities north of Rome, and they sought alliance with Rome. But the Romans chose to oppose rather than cooperate with them. The result was a disastrous battle just north of Rome at the Allia, a tributary of the Tiber. Rome itself was then taken and burned, except for the citadel on the Capitoline Hill.

After a time, the Romans scraped together a rich ransom to negotiate the withdrawal of the Gauls. Camillus, who was made dictator, reorganized the army and defeated the Gauls the following year. Then the city was rebuilt. Rome now grew stronger than ever. The later Romans thought their city had dominated the Latins even during the reign of the kings, and that this dominance was maintained through alliances formed in the early years of the Republic. The facts, however, seem to indicate that Roman conquest of the Latins came about only in the middle decades of the 4th century B.C.

Books for Further Reading

BLOCH, R., *The Etruscans,* London, 1958.

BLOCH, R., *The Origins of Rome,* New York, 1960.

GRIMAL, P., *In Search of Ancient Italy,* London, 1964.

HUS, A., *The Etruscans,* New York, 1961.

MACKENDRICK, P., *The Mute Stones Speak: The Story of Archaeology in Italy,* New York, 1960.

PALMER, R. E. A., *The Archaic Community of the Romans,* Cambridge, 1970.

PALLOTTINO, M., *The Etruscans,* Baltimore, 1955.

RICHARDSON, E., *The Etruscans: Their Art and Civilization,* Chicago, 1964.

SCULLARD, H. H., *A History of the Roman World from 753 to 146 B.C.,* London, 1935 (3d ed., 1961).

SCULLARD, H. H., *The Etruscan Cities and Rome,* Ithaca, 1967.

WOODHEAD, A. G., *The Greeks in the West,* New York, 1962.

Expansion in Italy:

Growth into a Republican Empire

15

The reasons why Rome expanded into world empire are of course manifold. For almost any people in antiquity, expansion required no justification. If opportunity presented itself for successful penetration of a region worth the taking, moral scruples rarely hindered. Much of Rome's expansion was of just that sort—opportunistic. Certainly there was no overall blueprint for conquest, no master plan; no one foresaw the end from the beginning. Quite often, it was a matter of one thing leading to another. Alliance against a common foe often brought with it responsibility to aid the ally against a new foe. Possession of new territory brought with it the responsibility to protect it. In any age, when semicivilized areas abut lands controlled by a highly organized power, the latter is drawn into the less-developed areas as if by a kind of power vacuum.

Most of the time Roman statesmen pursued a step-by-step course, solving immediate problems in the forthright, sometimes crude and cruel, Roman way. Principles did guide the Romans: they would never surrender nor negotiate from weakness, but always fight to a successful end; they were as firm (or cruel) as necessary to accomplish the goal; they punished any disorder like rebellion severely.

It must be admitted that in some wars, especially during the late Republic, Roman leaders were motivated by conscious imperialism. "To the victor belongs the spoils" was a concept generally accepted in antiquity. Sometimes Romans fought chiefly because victory would bring profit to individuals as well as to the state. Whatever the reasons, Romans fought often and usually won. Gradually they raised the city on the Tiber to world dominion.

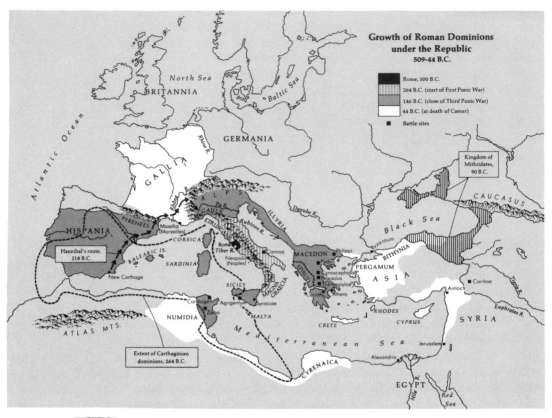

Adapted from Brinton, Christopher, and Wolff, *Civilization in the West, third edition, volume one.*

A. Toward Dominance in Italy

The Latin Revolt (341–338 B.C.)

Rome's relationship with her nearest neighbors, as we have seen, had been forged through struggle and alliance over a rather long period. The "revolt" of 341 B.C., grew out of Latin resentment because Rome's increased strength was changing the real conditions of their alliances. The treaties were no longer between equals; they only ensured Roman domination. Most important was the outcome of the struggle. Once the Romans had won, they cemented ties with these nearby Latin and some Italian states and so set the pattern—comparatively enlightened and enduring—for the later organization of all Italy.

The sensible, restrained settlement of 338 B.C. permitted all the states involved to retain autonomy at home, to continue to elect their own officials, and to collect their own taxes. None of them could make treaties with anyone else, however, and all had to supply troops to serve with Roman armies in the field. The nearest Latin states were actually incorporated into Rome, and their citizens received full Roman citizenship. The *fasti*—lists of officeholders at Rome—soon began to include the names of some of these new citizens, thus proving they had equal opportunity to reach high office; in this way some new citizens even entered the nobility, though they could not become patricians, of course.

Latin states not incorporated into Rome became close and respected, though dependent allies, with rights of trade and intermarriage as well as self-government. Inhabitants of Italian states which had participated on the side of the rebellious Latins were made citizens without the right to vote or hold office at Rome. Though they controlled their own affairs, they were directly subject to Roman magistrates, whereas the Latin allies were not. Within a period of a century and a half, however, these states also gained the vote at Rome.

This wise policy ensured the loyalty of Rome's neighbors in the heart of Italy. The bonds created were to withstand even the terrific stresses created by Hannibal's invasion in the next century. As Rome conquered the Italian Peninsula, the subjugated peoples were given similar treaties and brought into the alliance system on the same strong basis: autonomy in internal affairs at home, treaties with Rome only, and a commitment to serve with Rome's armies.

The Samnites

The most stubborn opponents blocking Rome's rise to dominance in Italy were the Samnites. Kinsmen of the Romans and other Italians, the Samnites mainly inhabited the hill country east and south of Rome; some Samnites lived in Campania, which they had seized when Etruscan control faltered. The Samnite League, in area and population, was perhaps double the size of Rome with her Latin allies. Romans and Samnites made an alliance in 354 B.C., perhaps against the Gauls, who occasionally ravaged Italian cities from Umbria, where they had settled.

The First Samnite War (343–341 B.C.) seems to have been caused by Roman willingness to offend the Samnite hillfolk in order to gain a foothold in Campania through alliance with the plains Samnites (Oscans), who dominated Campania from their capital at Capua. Some of the hill Samnites attacked the Oscans (they were competing for iron-rich border hill country), and Rome came to the rescue. The war was decided in a single battle, obviously a Roman victory, though the ensuing peace was a negotiated one. Rome now held Campania in firm alliance, and her extended power equalled that of the weakened Samnite League.

Both Romans and Samnites fought to keep their own allies in

line in the period immediately following the First Samnite War. Rome's struggle with her Latin and nearby Italian allies is discussed above. At the same time, both Romans and Samnites prepared for a second conflict. Rome irritated the Samnites by planting colonies on the fringes of Samnite territory to strengthen her communications corridor to Campania, and the Samnites encroached on central and southern Campania to strengthen their position against Rome.

The Second Samnite War (c. 327–304 B.C.) severely tested Rome. At the Caudine Forks, a few miles east of Capua, a full-size Roman army of perhaps 10,000 men—Roman historians said 20,000—with both consuls was forced to surrender (321 B.C.). Late in the war the Etruscans joined the Samnites, thus forcing Rome to fight on two fronts. But Rome gained allies in Apulia and elsewhere in south Italy, doggedly persevered, and won a favorable peace. Some territory on the western fringes of Samnium became Roman, and Rome established Latin colonies in Apulia east of Samnium, hemming it in. The Roman strategic position was therefore distinctly improved.

Rome's burgeoning power alarmed all her neighbors and quickly brought on the Third Samnite War (298–290 B.C.). Only the Romans' superior manpower reserves enabled them to win this conflict, since they had to maintain three separate armies, dangerously dispersed, in Apulia, Campania, and Latium, for the Samnites had persuaded both Etruscans and Gauls to ally with them. The Romans won a crucial battle in 295 B.C. at Sentinum in Umbria, which prevented the linkup of all three allies. It was a desperate fight, won only after the Roman consul Publius Decius Mus inspired his flagging men by "devoting" himself—and the enemy!—to the inferior gods; he then plunged to a sacrificial death amid the ranks of the enemy.

In the peace settlement, Rome took some of the best Samnite and Gallic lands. The remaining Samnite states, along with some Etruscan ones, were forced into the Roman alliance system. Roman dominance over Italy was now assured, though the fighting was far from over.

The Pyrrhic War (281–275 B.C.)

The alliances made during the Samnite Wars and the conquest of Samnium itself involved Rome with south Italy. The Greek states there had always contended with each other and with their neighbors, the Lucanians. The most powerful of the Greek states was Tarentum, which three times within the previous century had hired whole mercenary armies to come to Italy from Greece and fight her land battles. In 4th-century Greece, even King Agesilaus of Sparta had led an army in the pay of a king of Egypt; and after Alexander the Great, Greek mercenary armies fought all over the Mediterranean. The Tarentines, then, fearing the growing power of the state on the Tiber and certain that Greeks could be found to fight for their cause, decided to challenge Rome. When a small Roman naval fleet sailed into southern waters, ostensibly to aid the Greek city Thurii against the Lucanians, Tarentum invoked an old treaty limiting the range of Roman ships, then attacked and sank the Roman fleet. A Roman embassy, according to Roman sources, lodged a protest, only to be insulted by the Tarentines. And the war soon was on.

The army brought in by the Tarentines was that of King Pyrrhus of Epirus, across the Adriatic. Pyrrhus, related by marriage to Alexander the Great, was a great but capricious general who was always seeking new adventures before present business was settled. Twice he had the throne of Macedonia within his grasp, but each time he withdrew prematurely. Now he saw a great opportunity; apparently he hoped to control all of southern Italy and Sicily.

Pyrrhus's superior cavalry and his elephants gave him the edge in a first battle against the Romans at Heraclea in 280 B.C. The following year he won a second battle, at Asculum in Apulia. Both battles were hard-fought and indecisive. The Romans may have invented the story of the Greek general's remark that if he won another such battle he was lost, but the term "Pyrrhic victory" still describes a battle won at too great a cost to the victor.

Pyrrhus now took his army off to fight for Greeks in Sicily against the Carthaginians. There also he was successful but found it tiresome to reduce the Carthaginian forts along the western coast. Nor did the Sicilian Greeks, in wild gratitude, declare him monarch of all he surveyed. Meanwhile, Rome was again making headway in southern Italy. Pyrrhus answered the call for help and fought the Romans once more. This battle, at Beneventum in 275 B.C., Pyrrhus lost, though his army was by no means destroyed. He went back to what seemed better opportunities in Macedonia and the Peloponnese. A short time later, just as his troops were successfully storming the Greek city of Argos, Pyrrhus was killed— ironically, by an old woman. She threw a roof tile that hit him on the head and someone with a sword finished him off.

Rome now forced the defeated Greek cities of southern Italy into alliance in the familiar pattern. The only difference was that, whereas most allies furnished troops to fight with the Roman army, the Greeks contributed ships and men to the Roman navy. During this same period the Romans also subdued the remaining Etruscan states, in a struggle that continued until 265 B.C.—a date that marks the end of their Italic phase of expansion. Rome now controlled all of the Italian Peninsula south of the Po Valley through her alliance system.

B. Rome's Greatest Challenge: The Punic Wars

Carthage was a great sea power, concerned primarily with trade. Rome was still a nation of small farmers with only a minuscule navy, reflecting slight interest in seaborne commerce. The two nations had made treaties of alliance on at least three occasions, most recently against Pyrrhus, when he had invaded Sicily. It is one of history's anomalies that within a decade these recent allies were locked in protracted, bitter struggle.

With Rome's growing alliances, however, interests and responsibilities had increased. No longer was this a small state on the Tiber primarily concerned with Latium. The same factors that caused the Greeks to struggle with Carthage over a period of two centuries—mostly in Sicily —could now induce a serious confrontation between Rome and Carthage. A minor crisis at a strategically sensitive spot that both states might wish to control would make this clear.

First Punic War (264–241 B.C.)

The focus of the trouble we refer to was Messina, the Sicilian city on the vital straits between Sicily and the Italian mainland. These straits control the Tyrrhenian Sea, off the western Italian and Sicilian shores. At this point, Messina was in the hands of the Mamertines, Campanian (Samnite) mercenaries formerly in the service of Syracuse, who sometime before had massacred the men of Messina and taken the women for themselves. Young King Hiero of Syracuse attempted to take the city and punish the renegades. The Mamertines called on Carthage for support; then, for good measure, they also called on Rome. Always interested in curbing Greek power in Sicily, Carthage responded. After some delay, the Romans did so also and, by trickery, gained control of the city. Carthage called home its general in command and executed him, presumably for stupidity, and then declared war.

King Hiero first sought alliance with Carthage. Later, under threat of siege, he allied himself with the Romans, an alliance he was to keep for fifty years. Rome soon discovered how hard it was to win a land war in Sicily without control of the seas. With this incentive, the Romans built their first real fleet, equipping the ships with a special boarding bridge nicknamed the *corvus* ("crow"), from its beaklike appearance. This made possible unorthodox tactics involving the use of more infantrymen aboard ship. The Roman fleet defeated the Carthaginian, but its vessels were soon lost to the elements. Throughout the war, a major problem for Rome was to build ships and to find admirals: Roman generals were versed only in land warfare. Carthage's main difficulty was altogether different: to hire enough mercenaries and to find capable generals to lead them.

240

The Romans opened a new phase of this costly war with an invasion of North Africa under the consul Marcus Atilius Regulus in 256 B.C., following the example of an earlier Greek tyrant of Syracuse, Agathocles. Carthage's unpopularity with the African natives who were her subjects made such invasions feasible. Regulus gained local support and defeated a Carthaginian army. Carthage now wished to negotiate peace, but Regulus demanded nothing less than unconditional surrender. The Carthaginians therefore sent out recruiters to collect mercenaries and hired a Spartan general, Xanthippus, to lead them. The next year Regulus was soundly defeated and captured along with most of his army. This event points up a common misconception—that citizen troops were better than mercenaries. The mercenaries were in fact better, but Rome and her allies could muster more men than the Carthaginians could hire.

Members of Regulus's family may later have invented the story of how the general was sent back to Rome with peace terms, which he then recommended that the Senate reject—this in spite of the fact he had given his word that he would return to Carthage, and also in spite of the fact he could expect severe treatment from his captors. The tale has it that he was tortured to death on his return. The story entered the canon of patriotic tales reiterated to every generation of Roman youngsters to teach them hardihood and dedication to the state above all.

Rome had mobilized a fleet of fighting ships and transports and succeeded in saving a part of the army of Regulus. Ironically, the rescue fleet was then almost entirely destroyed in a storm. In this disastrous campaign alone, Rome lost nearly 100,000 men. By 250 B.C. Rome had lost two more fleets with most of the men aboard, partly owing to enemy action and partly to storms. After a lull, Rome managed one last desperate effort, building another fleet of ships of improved design with money scraped up partly by private contributions. A Carthaginan fleet was defeated near Sicily, off Drepana; the fortified cities of western Sicily fell one by one. Suddenly the exhausting struggle was over (242 B.C.). Rome got Sicily and an idemnity of 3,200 talents, to be paid by Carthage in installments over a ten-year period.

The Carthaginians soon were embroiled in a bitter war with their own mercenaries; they had promised them large bonuses but now refused to pay because the war was lost. This mercenary war extended even to Sardinia. When the Romans saw Carthage sending troops to that island, so near the Italian coast, they declared the action a breach of the peace and sent an ultimatum. Carthage could only back down and accept terms. Rome now seized Sardinia and Corsica also and added another 1,200 talents to the indemnity Carthage was to pay. This action of Rome in 238 B.C. naturally infuriated the Carthaginians, and none more than Hamilcar Barca, an effective general who had kept the Romans off-balance in Sicily for as long as Carthage's fleet brought supplies. Hamilcar took his young son before an altar of Tanit, Carthage's chief deity, and made the nine-year-old swear he would always be an enemy of Rome. The son's name? Hannibal.

Second Punic War (219–201 B.C.)

Once the mercenary war was settled at Carthage, Hamilcar Barca led the Carthaginians in a vigorous attempt to restore their prosperity and power. He took an army into Spain, reasserted Carthage's former control there, and expanded north along the eastern coast. He extracted silver from mines in the area and found new ones. When he died in 231 B.C., he was succeeded by his son-in-law Hasdrubal. Ten years later he too was killed, and Hannibal became commander. Perhaps the Barcids ruled Spain as a sort of personal empire, but their success brought them support in Carthage.

The Romans, though preoccupied with other matters in this period, nevertheless were concerned over the Carthaginian conquest of Spain. To a Roman query about this expansion, Hasdrubal answered they were only trying to get enough money to pay the Roman indemnity—a reasonable enough reply. About 225 B.C., however, the Romans were prodded by their Greek allies of Massilia (mod. Marseilles) to curb the Carthaginian expansion. A treaty was drawn up by which the Carthaginians agreed to stay south of the Ebro River. A complication, however, was left unsettled; Rome had another commitment in the area: an alliance with the city of Saguntum, south of the Ebro. From the Carthaginian point of view, if this commitment was made before the Ebro accord, it was cancelled by the treaty; if the alliance was made after the treaty, it was a clear violation of it. (Some later Roman historians felt sensitive enough about this to falsify the location of Saguntum, placing it *north* of the Ebro!)

However it was, Hannibal understood well enough when he attacked Saguntum in 219 B.C. that his action would mean a second war with Rome. Perhaps the time seemed propitious. The Romans had just repelled a Gallic invasion from the Po Valley and were attempting to colonize that region. Thus, all the Gauls in the valley were now enemies of Rome. Moreover, Rome was embroiled in Illyria. Piracy in the Adriatic had brought complaints from allies, and when diplomacy failed to suppress the freebooters, Rome sent military units to do the job. In addition, Hannibal had a large army, trained to a fine edge, and was ready for revenge on the Romans. To get full support from Carthage itself, however, he wanted the Romans to force the issue. Saguntum was just the instrument he needed. During several months of the siege of Saguntum, the Romans mopped up as best they could in Illyria and the Po Valley; then the Roman Senate sent an embassy to Carthage. The two sides could agree only to go to war.

The standard early type of the silver denarius, Rome's major coin during the middle centuries. First struck during the Second Punic War. On the obverse, left, the goddess Roma, on the reverse, right, the gods Castor and Pollux as horsemen.

The Romans planned to invade North Africa again, but Hannibal's famous march changed their plans. In the summer of 218 B.C., with 30,000 or 40,000 men, including some fine cavalry and elephants, Hannibal moved across the Pyrenees and through southern France; in early fall he crossed the Alps and proceeded down into the Po Valley. His army had suffered from the rigors of early snows in the Alps and even more by the opposition of Alpine tribesmen. The latter were not pro-Roman, but they automatically fought any army passing through their territory. A Roman army sent out from Italy had missed Hannibal's army because the Romans thought the Carthaginian objective was Massilia, an ally in southern France. Most of this Roman army then went on into Spain. This decision, to create a second theater of operations there, was decisive for the ultimate victory, but there were long intervening years when it must have seemed a mistake.

In November Hannibal crushed a full-size Roman army at the battle of the Trebia River, where he set an ambush and overwhelmed the unwary Romans. Then he spent the winter in recruiting Gauls. In 217 B.C. Hannibal moved south into central Italy by an unexpected path. In the marshes he contracted a fungus infection and lost an eye. Near Lake Trasimene he won a second major battle. Again, the Romans were ambushed and driven into the lake, where many drowned. After this disaster the Romans chose a dictator, Quintus Fabius Maximus, whose delaying, harassing tactics against Hannibal gained him the surname Cunctator ("Delayer") and the reputation of having saved Rome.

What Hannibal chiefly desired was to break up the Roman alliance system. Fabius tried to prevent this. It was most significant that all of Rome's older allies save one—Capua—stuck firmly with Rome. These allies furnished about half the manpower that made possible the eventual victory.

In the fateful year 216 B.C., two consuls at the head of a reinforced army decided to engage Hannibal in battle once more. At Cannae in Apulia, on ground chosen by Hannibal, a Roman army superior in size to the Carthaginian pushed its way into a tactical trap; most of the Romans, squeezed tightly into a milling mass by Hannibal's superior cavalry, never got into the fight, and most were slaughtered. Rome reported its losses that day at 80,000; actual losses were considerably less, but this was the most severe defeat the Romans ever suffered in their rise to power.

The situation worsened; now Rome's most recent allies in southern Italy went over to Hannibal. The City of Syracuse in Sicily (its ruler Hiero had just died) joined the Carthaginian side. Worst of all, potentially, Philip V of Macedonia, irritated by Roman penetration of Illyria, east of the Adriatic in what he considered his sphere of influence, made formal alliance with Hannibal. Rome's fortunes reached their lowest ebb; but Rome, as always, fought on doggedly. The Senate even refused to ransom the prisoners captured at Cannae.

After Cannae, Rome gradually recovered ground against Hannibal's best efforts. In Sicily, Marcus Claudius Marcellus besieged and took Syracuse (212 B.C.); it was in the capture that Archimedes was killed. On the Italian mainland, Rome was able to besiege and recover Capua, even though Hannibal made a feint to the walls of Rome to draw the Roman army away from the city. A little later, Tarentum fell into Roman hands. Marcellus won two or three unimportant battles against Hannibal himself in southern Italy. The Carthaginian general Hanno even lost his camp at Beneventum. Yet, amazingly, though without adequate reserves and money, Hannibal's mixed army never faltered. There is no mention of mutiny in any of the accounts.

Philip of Macedonia never sent aid to Hannibal. Rome sent a few troops to Greece, made an alliance with the Aetolian League, and won minor successes against Philip's allies. Roman control of the Adriatic prevented more vigorous action by Macedonia; then, too, Philip had other fish to fry.

It was in Spain that the most portentous events took place in these years. Two Scipio brothers, one the father of the great Scipio, fell in battle in 212 B.C. Thereupon, in 210 B.C. Publius Cornelius Scipio (later known as Scipio Africanus Major) was by a vote of the Roman people given the Spanish command, though he was young and had not held the usual offices. Scipio swiftly conquered New Carthage, the main base of the Carthaginians. He had the help of the gods: an unusually low water level left the city's sea walls vulnerable. Scipio attributed his good fortune to a close relationship with Jupiter Optimus Maximus, with whom he had communed in the temple on the Capitol before leaving Rome. By 206 B.C. Scipio had driven all Carthaginians from Spain.

Scipio made only one major error: he permitted Hasdrubal, the brother of Hannibal, to escape the Iberian Peninsula with an army in 208 B.C. The following year, having followed Hannibal's earlier path, Hasdrubal was in Italy. Roman counterintelligence, by intercepting a message, prevented Hannibal from learning accurately of Hasdrubal's movements. In a daring maneuver, the Roman army facing Hannibal left its camp, marched 240 miles in six days, and joined another force opposing Hasdrubal near the Metaurus River in Umbria. The combined armies annihilated the Carthaginian troops (207 B.C.). Hannibal was informed of the catastrophe when Hasdrubal's head was tossed over the wall of his camp. Another effort to reinforce Hannibal by sea led by his other brother, Mago, failed (205–203 B.C.).

Scipio returned to Rome in 206 B.C., in time to be chosen consul for the year 205 and to receive command of an invasion force. Late the following year he crossed from Sicily into North Africa. In 203, Hannibal was recalled by the Carthaginians to undertake the defense of Carthage itself. For more than fifteen years he had suffered no major defeat during his stay in Italy; but in 202, at Zama Regia, Hannibal was defeated by Scipio in a decisive battle. Scipio had the aid of Numidian cavalry; moreover, Hannibal's elephants misbehaved and did more damage to the Carthaginian troops than to the Romans. Yet it was Scipio's flexible tactics that earned the victory. Scipio soon took the rather grandiose surname "Africanus." Carthage had no options left and capitulated.

By the peace treaty drawn up in 201 B.C., Carthage gave up Spain, which Rome soon converted into two provinces, Hither and Farther Spain. Carthage had to reduce the size of her fleet and army and had to pay, over a period of fifty years, an indemnity of 10,000 talents. She also became an ally of Rome—which meant that Carthage could not wage war without Rome's permission.

The Second Punic War against the forces of Hannibal was the most important that Rome ever fought, and Zama was one of the most important battles. Though the battle on the Metaurus River had meant the turn of fortune in Italy, right up to the end of the war it was questionable whether Rome would emerge merely as a survivor of the most serious threat it had ever faced, or as the dominant power in the western Mediterranean. The victory at Zama ensured that Rome would be dominant. As events would soon show, Rome could now dominate not only the West but the whole Mediterranean basin. A loss at Zama would still have left Rome one of the great Mediterranean powers; victory made possible the eventual vast Empire.

C. Roman Penetration of the Eastern Mediterranean

Second Macedonian War (200–196 B.C.)

Rome had concluded a separate peace with Philip of Macedonia in 205 B.C.; yet some Roman leaders felt that Philip's alliance with Hannibal after Cannae was a low blow that merited sterner retribution. Moreover, Rome's Greek allies clamored for action. A Senate recommendation to the assembly for war against Macedonia came in 200 B.C., only a year after the peace with Carthage. The war-weary Romans voted down the motion. A few months later, however, with impassioned oratory a Roman consul assured the assembly that it was not a question of whether there would be war but, rather, whether it would be fought in Greece or, if Rome delayed, in Italy itself. With Hannibal's successes still fresh in their minds, the Romans now voted for war.

Decisive action did not come until 198 B.C. The young consul Titus Quinctius Flamininus persuaded the Achaean League to join the alliance Rome already had with the Aetolian League. The following year, at Cynoscephalae in Thessaly, the Roman legions first met the Macedonian phalanx. With considerable help from the Aetolians, the more flexible legions took advantage of a break in the phalanx and won a resounding victory, which virtually ended the war. Afterward Flamininus persuaded the Senate to adopt a liberal policy for all Greece. Philip was let off with only the loss of recently acquired territory and a small indemnity of 1,000 talents.

Many Greeks feared they had exchanged one master—Macedonia —for another; but at the Isthmian games of 196 B.C., Flamininus announced dramatically that Rome would withdraw entirely, leaving all the Greek states free. This announcement brought such wild rejoicing that the games were canceled. Surviving inscriptions show that some Greeks made Flamininus a god. The Greeks were to learn, however, that Rome expected such beneficence to bring its reward. The Greek states were expected to behave much as client behaved toward patron within the Roman social structure. Overt ingratitude to the Roman was a mark of disloyalty, deserving punishment. But the jubilant Greeks could hardly know this—yet.

The Syrian War (192–189 B.C.)

Members of the Aetolian League were disgruntled by the peace terms. They had expected to profit handsomely from the defeat of Macedonia, since they had been allied with Rome for many years and had fought at Cynoscephalae. Instead, Rome's liberal policy meant little booty and almost no territorial gain for them. Despite Flamininus' fancy phrases, it became evident that Roman influence in the eastern Mediterranean would remain great. The Aetolians therefore sought a way to redress the balance and found it, they thought, in King Antiochus III (r. 223–c. 187 B.C.), the Seleucid ruler of Syria.

Antiochus' prime political and military objective was to rule the largest possible territory—at least all that dominated by his most successful Seleucid ancestors, and possibly all that ruled by Alexander the Great. He had recently taken lower Syria and Palestine from the Ptolemies of Egypt; now he needed a foothold in Europe. He wanted control of Thrace, and perhaps he wanted much more. Certainly Antiochus wished an end to Roman intervention in the eastern Mediterranean. To this end he concluded an alliance with the Aetolians.

This alliance would assuredly mean war with Rome if Antiochus brought troops to Greece. Rome had already given the Syrian king an ultimatum. Probably the chief reason for Rome's concern was Hannibal, for about him some Romans were almost psychotic. Hannibal had stayed in Carthage for a few years after the peace of 201 B.C.); but then he heard—whether correctly, we cannot say—that the Romans intended to demand he be surrendered to them. Therefore he fled and found refuge at the court of Antiochus, where of course he schemed against Rome.

Another element in Rome's opposition to Antiochus was the role of Pergamum. This kingdom in Asia Minor had joined the alliance against Philip in the First Macedonian war (concurrent with the Second Punic War) and had fought with a Greek coalition against Philip and Antiochus, who had begun gobbling up territory in Asia Minor and the Aegean islands toward the end of the 3rd century B.C. Now the Attalid king Eumenes II (r.197–159 B.C.) feared that Antiochus' ambitions included the acquisition of Pergamum; hence he played on Roman fears and fought along with them in the war.

First Rome and her allies defeated the inadequate army assembled by Antiochus and the Aetolians in Greece, at Thermopylae (191 B.C.). Then Rome sent an army into Asia Minor. There, at Magnesia, with great help from Eumenes' cavalry, the Romans crushed Antiochus in a major battle at the end of 190 B.C. The Roman commander was Lucius Scipio, brother of Africanus—who, of course, became "Asiaticus." In the peace that followed, Rome again took over no territory, though Antiochus was deprived of all his lands in Asia Minor. Most of these were given to Eumenes and the Rhodians, whose fleet had helped defeat Antiochus' navy (under the command of Hannibal). The Carthaginian exile fled again and took refuge with Prusias, King of Bithynia, whom he urged to war against Eumenes of Pergamum, Rome's friend and ally. When Rome demanded that Prusias deliver Hannibal up, the great Carthaginian leader ended his life with poison about 182 B.C.

If the Romans took no lands they did take a tremendous indemnity (15,000 talents) and required that Antiochus' fleet be reduced and his elephant corps eliminated. A year later, as he was taking treasure from a temple in an effort to pay off the Romans, Antiochus was killed by a priest.

The Roman army took a tour about Asia Minor, accepting or forcing the surrender of various territories—and accepting "gifts" from the cities as well. Such pacification was needed, however; some Gallic tribes were unstable and warlike. Not only Roman commanders, but also individual soldiers, profited tremendously from this war, especially in the subsequent military tour mentioned. Some later Roman historians dated the moral decline of Rome from these campaigns, with their debilitating spoils.

Third Macedonian War (171–167 B.C.)

Though King Philip cooperated without actually participating in the war against Antiochus, relations between Macedonia and Rome were always strained. Inhabitants of border territories were continually appealing to Rome against Philip's ambitions, and Rome usually ruled against the Macedonian king. During these decades every Greek who had a grievance tended to present his case at Rome. The Romans were contemptuous of what they thought of as sniveling Greeks, but they were flattered too; and it was noticed that the decisions tended to favor those who first appealed to Rome. Thus Rome was constantly involved in Greek affairs.

Philip greatly strengthened his army and his treasury, and the Romans thought he was building up to another challenge. They were offended, also, at Philip's decision on a successor. His elder son Perseus was born of a secondary wife, whereas the younger, Demetrius, was well-born. Demetrius, who had spent some years in Rome as a hostage and had made friends with influential Romans, attempted to persuade his father to follow a pro-Roman course. Perseus, with forged documents, convinced his father that Demetrius was traitorous; Philip thereupon had his younger son executed. Thus, when Perseus succeeded Philip at his death in 179 B.C., he was already in bad odor with Rome. The Romans interpreted his continuation of Philip's policies as proof that he also intended to fight Rome when ready. The Greeks brought numerous charges against Perseus at Rome, and the Romans believed some of them. King Eumenes of Pergamum even made a special journey to Rome to accuse Perseus before the Senate. When Eumenes was waylaid afterward and nearly killed as he journeyed toward Delphi in Greece, the Romans were ready to believe that Perseus had ordered the murder attempt and that the incident confirmed the charges Eumenes had made.

There seems little doubt that Perseus did not want to fight, and that he was forced into an unjustified war. As Rome prepared to declare war (171 B.C.), he offered to capitulate on the same terms given his father after Cynoscephalae; but the Romans would have none of it. From the vantage point of history it often seems that there was a kind of inevitability about Roman victory. But if Perseus had been a little freer with his money and a little more adept at diplomacy, Rome might well have lost—and thereafter might have stayed out of the eastern Mediterranean. However, under command of the consul Lucius Aemilius Paullus, son of the consul of the same name killed at Cannae, a Roman army in a close-fought battle again crushed the Macedonian phalanx, at Pydna in 168 B.C. Perseus was eventually captured and led in a triumph into Rome, where he died or was killed.

Rome still did not annex Macedonia, which was instead divided up into four separate republics. Of course, Perseus' property became spoils for Rome; his treasury, more or less intact, was seized, and his library was sent to Rome, to become the first important one in that city. Paullus also inflicted fit punishment on the Epirotes, who had supported Perseus. Scores of their towns were destroyed, and 150,000 of their men were sold into slavery. Part of the reason for this unwarranted brutality was that the Roman soldiers did not feel they had been given enough loot after the combat in Macedonia. Even without annexation of land, imperialism was quite profitable—so much so that, from this time on (167 B.C.), no Romans living in Italy paid any direct taxes into the state treasury.

Wars Against Macedonia, the Achaean League, and Carthage (149–146 B.C.)

No long explanation is needed for the fourth and last Macedonian war. Division of the country had meant artificial restraints on trade; the silver mines had been closed down. Economically, the country was in ruins. A man who claimed to be a son of Perseus raised a rebellion, which the Romans put down (149–148 B.C.). The commanding general was one Metellus, who naturally then called himself "Macedonicus." Now at last Macedonia became a province of Rome.

The Greek war, waged mostly against members of the Achaean League, came about because the Greeks were goaded beyond endurance by restrictive Roman policies. Rome's troubles with Macedonia and Carthage also made the timing seem propitious. Hence, Roman ambassadors were insulted, and war ensued. As an object lesson, the Roman general Lucius Mummius destroyed Corinth, a center of the revolt (146 B.C.). Greece was not formally organized as a province but was in the same situation, under the tutelage of the governor of Macedonia. A little more than a century later, Augustus organized it into a separate imperial province called Achaea.

The origins of the Third Punic War are more complicated than can be fully discussed here. Scipio Africanus had made an ally in North Africa of King Masinissa of Numidia. At the end of the Second Punic War, Numidian territory had been increased at the expense of Carthage. In the following decades Masinissa often encroached upon Carthaginian territory, and since the Carthaginians could not go to war without Roman approval, they could only appeal to Rome—and Roman commissions usually decided in Masinissa's favor. In 149 B.C. an anti-Roman party gained ascendancy in Carthage in the wake of Masinissa's latest land grab, raised an army, and went to war with Numidia, contrary to the treaty with Rome. Masinissa, of course, called on his ally, and Rome responded. It is well known that some Romans, notably old Cato, already favored war.

When Rome declared war, there was a reaction in Carthage. The men in the city responsible for the policy that had brought down upon them Rome's declaration of war were executed. Ambassadors were sent to Rome to offer a negotiated surrender, only to be told that the consul would see them back in Africa. Once arrived there with an army, the consul called on the Carthaginians to surrender their arms. They surrendered 100,000 sets—which does seem a large quantity, since Carthage had already outfitted a well-equipped army then in the field against Numidia. Once they had given up their arms, the Carthaginians were told to evacuate their city. It was to be destroyed! In revulsion, another overturn brought new leaders to power in the city. The appeasers were executed, Carthage's gates were closed, and her walls were manned. Men and women worked desperately to make arms and equipment; and amazingly, the Carthaginians held out for three years against the much superior Roman forces. The Roman general who finally took and destroyed the city in 146 B.C. was Publius Cornelius Scipio, called Aemilianus because he was a Scipio only by adoption; he was actually the son of the Aemilius Paullus who had defeated Perseus. Like his adoptive grandfather, he took the surname Africanus.

Carthaginians who survived the ruin were transplanted elsewhere in North Africa. The city was leveled, its site cursed and strewn with salt. Some traces of Carthaginian culture lingered on. The territory itself, however, became a Roman province called Africa. Rome's superiority, both in the West and the East, could no longer be questioned.

Yet it should not be implied that all was now peaceful from East to West. The Romans continued to have trouble with the Illyrians on the eastern shores of the Adriatic and for decades maintained armies there much of the time. Spain put the Romans to the test even more for

the Celt-Iberians reacted fiercely against continual Roman encroachment. Guerrilla-type warfare, like running sores, persisted there during
much of the 2nd century B.C. Governors of both Spanish provinces had
to maintain standing armies and were often in the field on campaign.
Several Roman generals lost their reputations in this restless arena.
Much of Spain was pacified by 132 B.C., when Numantia was destroyed;
but the peninsula as a whole was finally conquered only in 19 B.C., more
than a century later.

Books for Further Reading

ADCOCK, F. E., *The Roman Art of War Under the Republic,* Cambridge, Mass.,
    1940 (rev. ed., 1963).

ASTIN, A. E., *Scipio Aemilianus,* Oxford, 1967.

BADIAN, E., *Foreign Clientelae,* Oxford, 1958.

DE BEER, G. R., *Hannibal: Challenging Rome's Supremacy,* New York, 1969.

FRANK, T., *Roman Imperialism,* New York, 1914.

SALMON, E. T., *Roman Colonization Under the Republic,* Ithaca, 1970.

SALMON, E. T., *Samnium and the Samnites,* Cambridge, 1967.

SCULLARD, H. H., *A History of the Roman World from 753 to 146 B.C.,* London,
    1935 (3d ed., 1961).

SCULLARD, H. H., *Scipio Africanus: Soldier and Politician,* Ithaca, 1970.

WARMINGTON, B. H., *Carthage,* London, 1960 (rev. ed., 1969).

16

State and Society:
The Impact of Empire

The Rome of 146 B.C. was vastly different from the Rome of a century
or so earlier, when Rome had dominated all Italy south of the Po
Valley. The Romans ruled the Italian states indirectly, through a kind
of confederacy, but got no income from them. In the intervening period,
Rome fought wars on three continents and came to dominate the whole
Mediterranean littoral. Eight provinces now sprawled from Spain to
Macedonia, from all of which regular tribute flowed to Rome. Earlier in
the 2nd century B.C. this income had been greatly augmented by spoils
and indemnities; as we have seen, Carthage was made to pay 10,000
talents after the Second Punic War, and Syria 15,000 talents after 189 B.C.
Rome had become a world capital, and bustled with general prosperity.
It was an exciting city, too, for in the Roman Forum were made decisions that affected the entire civilized world. The Roman calendar was
crowded with festivals, games, theater, gladiatorial combats, and races.
The city on the Tiber was decidedly the place to be in this era.

A. Social and Economic Transformations

The Upper Classes

The Roman aristocrats who belonged to the "establishment," who held
the highest offices, served on embassies, and sat in the Senate, found
their positions enormously enhanced by the Republic's gradual expansion into empire. Roman officials were the most important people in the
world, with unequaled opportunities for profit and prestige. Consuls
and praetors, once local magistrates whose power was limited by law

and tradition, now ruled provinces with almost absolute authority. Inevitably, such men developed new conceptions of themselves as representatives of the dominant power in the Mediterranean and acquired new standards and tastes in their personal lives. As a matter of course, they acquired finer homes and clothing, personal slaves—in short, luxury and status quite beyond anything known to their grandparents.

The greater benefits now conferred by high office brought increased competition at the polls. A few "new men" reached the top offices as new plebeian families shouldered their way into the select circle of aristocracy, which by now included both patricians and plebeians, for it was an officeholding aristocracy. Family-political alliances of an informal sort were formed around nuclei of older families. Although these coalitions shifted constantly and involved complex personal relationships, their goals were clear: to see that the right persons gained the right offices and were given the best assignments. Sometimes these family-political groups can be identified with continuing policies, but for the most part their sole objectives were the control of elections and offices, and thus the Senate. Among the leaders of such informal factions in the 2nd century B.C. were the Claudii and the Scipionii.

A Rising Middle Class

In most of history the term "middle class" refers to a group of men who have money but who are not aristocrats. In Rome such men came of plebeian families who were nonpolitical and whose members did not often attain high office. By the 1st century B.C., men of upper middle class were usually called equestrians; that is, they owned sufficient property to be ranked with the cavalry contingents of the Roman army. But to use the term "middle class" here is in part misleading, for many equestrians were not middle class businessmen at all; they were landowners who had close relationships with the senatorial aristocracy.

Rome's expansion, the great wars, the vast building projects, commercial opportunities created by Rome's new position—these were the factors which fostered the rise of a moneyed middle class. The contractors who built the ships for Rome's great fleets, supplied its armies, constructed roads, bridges, and public buildings, or bought up slaves and spoils for later sale at a profit almost all prospered and became economically powerful. By the 1st century B.C. many among them were bankers, tax collectors, and moneylenders.

A lower middle class, made up of enterpreneurs on a small scale, flourished also. These men might own a few fishing boats, operate small shops, or build olive and grape presses or other machinery. One of the misfortunes of Rome was the failure of these middle groups in society to continue to grow and flourish. Too many members of the upper middle class became interested only in banking, tax collecting, and moneylending. Many of the rest were ruined by civil war and, ultimately, by competition from the developing Western provinces as well.

Growth of the Latifundia

An important economic change on the rural scene after the Second Punic (Hannibalic) War involved the development of capitalistic agriculture. Upper class Romans were restricted in their economic activity by station, by custom, and in part by law. Land, however, always respectable, was accounted the basic form of wealth throughout ancient times. To those with money, land was available. State-owned land (ager publicus) could be leased. Some, in fact, had been used to pay off war debts contracted when the state borrowed from private individuals during war emergencies. Land also could be purchased, sometimes at low rates, from small owners who left or were forced off their farms. Besides capital and land, a third requirement for the new-style farm was manpower—slaves or tenants. Slaves were available in large quantity during the 2nd century B.C. from the sale of war prisoners. Those used as farm labor came mostly from less-civilized areas such as Spain, Cisalpine Gaul, or Illyria. Supervisors, bookkeepers, cooks, physicians, tutors of children would likely be Greek or Asian.

The object of capital investment is profit. In human terms, this meant that the slaves had to be adequately cared for, but also that the maximum amount of labor was extracted. Some slaves worked in irons and slept in prisons. In economic terms, this system of agriculture meant an emphasis on cash crops, that is, livestock, grapes for wine, and olives. Grain was unprofitable, partly because large quantities were brought in as tribute from the provinces, especially Sicily, and sold by the state and partly because it could not be transported far by land conveyance economically. In social terms, the new latifundia (that is, large landed estates) meant a decline in numbers of small independent farmers, who were replaced by tenants and slaves. In political terms, this latter change tended to destroy the old patron-client system, in which lay much of the power of the aristocrats. The family-political alliances helped to offset the decline of the old system; but these political effects were nonetheless portentous.

The Lower Classes

The reduction in numbers of the small citizen-farmers has sometimes been overemphasized, for this group remained the basic ingredient in

Rome's political, economic, and military systems. Yet all these systems were changed and weakened. Consider the army. Rome did not draft the poorest citizens for military service, but kept the army in the hands of those who had some stake in the existing system. Terrific losses in battle, especially during the Hannibalic War, and the displacement of small property owners by slaves meant a shortage of draftable military manpower. During the 2nd century B.C. the property qualification for military service was drastically reduced; still there were scarcely enough men, for Rome now required soldiers not merely in war emergencies but also for standing armies in the provinces. In consequence, military conscription bore excessively hard on the draft-eligible citizens.

Many propertyless men drifted or migrated to the cities, particularly Rome, and the capital soon was bursting at the seams. The population pressure made it necessary, in 144–140 B.C., to build a new aqueduct for the city and refurbish the two old ones. Since for most of the century Rome was prosperous, a man could find work or go into business in a small way. Ambitious public and private construction and the service needs of the expanding population meant opportunity even for simple day laborers.

A new class thus arose in Rome: *proles,* the Romans called them, day laborers without property. There had always been propertyless laborers, of course, but previously they were scattered in rural areas. As long as times were good, these lower class city workers did well; but they had no reserves. Their lodgings were likely to be miserable, and they were subject to the whims of economic fortune. It is significant, too, that they lost former ties of clientage while retaining the right to vote. This new class of proletarians constituted an unstable mass in the capital. One day its members would starve, riot, and follow demagogues and military leaders in civil commotion. For the time, however, they did not suffer inordinately; their precarious situation was brought home to them only with the economic depression that was to come in the 130's B.C.

B. Intellectual and Moral Change

An emergent world capital eventually is likely to become something of an intellectual center as well. In the 2nd century B.C., however, this development was only beginning in Rome, which in many ways had long absorbed intellectual impulses from other peoples. The Etruscans, Greeks, and Carthaginians had all contributed something to Roman culture. But now, when so many Romans traveled in Greece and the Hellenistic East and when so many Greek pedagogues, scholars, and physicians were imported into Rome proper, a new wave of influence was felt.

Literature

Soon after the First Punic War, Latin translations of Greek dramas were presented in Rome. After a few years dramatists began to modify these plays and put them in Roman dress, so to speak. Ennius (239–169 B.C.), a Greek poet from Tarentum, was brought to Rome and made a citizen. He presented there numerous tragedies based on the older Greek masters. Plautus (254–184 B.C.) and Terence (195–159 B.C.) used Greek plots from the New Comedy of Menander and others, but they were original in their brilliant mastery of the Latin language. Social historians are acutely interested in what they changed from the Greek plays that were their models. No Latin counterparts existed for the Greek *hetaira,* or courtesan; and no Roman *pater familias* would ever put up with the impudent slaves and disobedient sons that appear in the plays. Greek settings were the rule; to put such plays into a Roman setting would have outraged Roman sensibilities. Roman tragedy, some considered quite good by ancient writers, was also produced later in the century, but none of it has survived.

The oldest extant Latin prose is *De Agricultura,* a work of Cato the Elder dealing with all aspects of the new agriculture. This work (also often called *De Re Rustica*) is unpolished and owes very little to Greek stylistic models. It does owe a great deal to the Carthaginian Mago, however, whose work had circulated in Rome in translation for some years.

The history of Polybius (discussed in Chapter 13, on Hellenistic culture) hardly belongs to Roman literature; yet Polybius well illustrates in his own person the Greek influence upon intellectually inclined Romans. The exiled Greek historian lived at the house of the Roman general Aemilius Paullus and helped to tutor his son, who was later adopted into the Scipio family and known as Scipio Aemilianus. Scipio continued to cultivate the company of Polybius and other Greek and Roman intellectuals, creating an informal group now often termed the "Scipionic circle." Besides Polybius, this circle included Panaetius, a Greek Stoic philosopher; Lucilius, the first great Roman satirist; and several others. Lucilius' work is known to us only in fragments, preserved through occasional quotation in later writers.

Philosophy

Romans were exposed to Greek philosophical teaching of all sorts during this period. The skepticism of certain Greek philosophers repelled many Romans, however. Carneades, while on an embassy to Rome about the middle of the 2nd century B.C., horrified conservative Romans by arguing both for and against justice as a knowable and workable concept in lectures given in the capital. Stoicism was much more to their liking; Roman views of public service, personal and civic virtue, and stern self-control gave them a predilection for a philosophy emphasizing these qualities. Panaetius of Rhodes (c. 180–111 B.C.), mentioned above as a member of the Scipionic circle, was a house guest of Scipio for some years. He, more than any other person, introduced Stoicism to the Romans and, to some degree, popularized its doctrine. The greatest influence of this philosophical school, however, was to be during the next three centuries.

Religion

The stresses of the Hannibalic War produced unorthodox religious behavior in Rome, some of which the officials tried to suppress. On the highest levels, however, one religious innovation was welcomed in Rome. The goddess Cybele, said the keepers of the Sibylline Books, (of oracles), if brought to Rome would help it to victory. The priests of the goddess in Asia Minor agreed to send to Rome her effigy—perhaps a meteorite. After a few years the goddess was housed in a new temple on the Palatine Hill.

During the decade 190–180 B.C., devotees of the wine god Bacchus attempted to draw in Roman young people to the orgiastic worship of that god. Conservative Romans brought charges of immorality and even conspiracy, so that the Bacchic rites were sternly curtailed by decree of the Senate. Large numbers of persons, mostly in the Greek areas of southern Italy, were summarily tried and executed on conspiratorial charges.

By the middle of the 2nd century B.C. there was a changed, more relaxed attitude toward religion among some upper class intellectuals. Polybius makes it clear that Romans he knew had come to feel that the state religion was useful primarily to keep the masses in disciplined control. This attitude gradually spread, and by the middle of the next century two consequences were apparent: the governing class was neglecting temples, rites, and the priesthood; the unexpected corollary was a weakening of the constitution itself, of which the state religion was so integral a part.

Morals

It is almost a truism of history that each generation thinks that, in its own day, the world is "going to the dogs." One must necessarily believe that, unless morals have declined in each generation since the beginning of time, such gloomy and pessimistic views are usually wrong. In any contemporary setting it is very difficult to gauge such trends. However, the historian, using hindsight, can sometimes make a more accurate assessment. It does indeed appear now that the greater affluence and widened horizons of Romans in the 2nd century B.C. did cause some erosion of old values and a greater emphasis on material status and possessions.

The Romans whose opinions have been preserved had differing explanations for this worsened moral climate. Some attributed it to the influx of rich spoils from the Syrian War: others saw Greek contacts and Greek influence as the prime cause; and still others thought the defeat of Carthage removed the last strong enemy of Rome, with the unfortunate result that the Roman young no longer cultivated the military virtues.

Two Men, Old and New: Cato and Scipio Aemilianus

Two great Romans, a generation apart in age, will symbolize for us, first, the inertia and strength of Roman conservatism and, then, the dynamics of change.

Marcus Porcius Cato (234–149 B.C.) as a "new man" rose from an undistinguished family to the top offices of Rome—and thereby to a place for his family in the aristocracy. He advanced through sheer ability, displayed most effectively in speeches before the people and in the law courts. He was sponsored by a patrician closely associated with the great Fabius Maximus. As praetor and consul, Cato performed well, but he is best remembered for his use of the office of censor in 184 B.C. and for his long-continued, mostly conservative influence.

Most Roman censors in these decades took stern positions on mores and morals. Cato, convinced it was Greek influence that was eroding the fiber of the Roman young, was the sternest of the lot. As censor he assessed at ten times their real value all luxuries, such items as pretty young slaves, often bought to permit the master to indulge his sexual appetites. He carefully winnowed the lists of members of the Senate and the *equites,* or cavalry. For a moral lapse, he even excluded a brother of the Flamininus who defeated the Macedonians in 196 B.C. Earlier Cato had played a part in the Bacchanalian investigations and the resulting harsh decree. Three years after his censorship he instigated a book burning of Pythagorean writings accidentally discovered and judged subversive.

Cato had only scorn for the "Greeklings" who aped Hellenic ways and worshiped Hellenic philosophy and literature. He felt it impossible to imbibe the culture of the Greeks without picking up their vices as well. When the Academic skeptic Carneades visited Rome on the abovementioned embassy and charmed the young with his lectures, Cato saw that his business was expedited so he would not stay long in Rome. He seems to have been behind passage of a decree requiring all

Greek philosophers to leave Rome. Yet Cato himself knew the Greek language and sent his own son—with much warning—to study in Athens.

In one way, moreover, Cato actually encouraged change. His book *De Agricultura* gave sound advice to those who would buy slaves and organize *latifundia* to grow olives or grapes. He seemed unaware that these slave-operated plantations had deleterious effects on the old Roman constitution.

Scipio Aemilianus (185–129 B.C.), as we have seen, was the grandson of the first Scipio by adoption and the natural son of the Aemilius Paullus who defeated Perseus of Macedonia in 168 B.C. He grew up with privileges of family and prestige that Cato lacked. His career took him to the top offices, but not merely because of family connections. Though Cato and the Fabian family group with which he was associated generally opposed the Scipios, the old orator felt that Scipio the younger was one of the few capable military men and politicians left in Rome. It was Scipio who destroyed Carthage, as Cato had desired and the Senate ordered, at the end of the Third Punic War (146 B.C.). His views on the importance of maintaining the old morality were the same as Cato's. Though he occasionally supported a liberal measure—for example, one of three bills that extended the secret ballot in voting—he supported the *mos maiorum* (ancestral custom) almost as strongly as Cato did.

Scipio and Cato, however, had quite different views about the Greeks. Scipio was to a degree philhellene; that is to say, he admired and embraced Greek philosophy and literature and hoped to see them emulated in Rome. The "Scipionic circle," as has been noted above, included Panaetius, the philosopher who popularized Stoicism in Rome, as well as the Greek historian Polybius and the Roman playwright Terence and the satirist Lucilius.

Of Cato, Scipio, and other Romans of the 2nd century B.C. it may be said that, as in so many other times and places, these men embraced certain elements of change without desiring or perceiving what other transformations would inevitably follow.

C. The Gracchi: Challenge to the Old Order

*Economic Downturn:
An Accumulation of Problems*

The number and seriousness of the long-neglected internal problems at Rome were masked by prosperity for some years. The decline of the small farmer and the growth of the city proletariat produced the obvious difficulty that the number of draft-eligible men was steadily dropping; but the parallel deterioration of the constitution because of the fact that the city *proles* no longer had any real attachment to the ancestral state was not so obvious. The unequal benefits of empire and the growing gap between the status of rich and poor did not seem so acute as long as the poor were not in fact starving. The coming of economic depression, however, did reveal at least partially the depth of the trouble.

The economic depression was caused by several factors. The end of profitable wars and spoils, much of which had been spent in Rome, was one cause. Another was a worldwide grain shortage, which caused prices of this staple to go up. Most important for the city of Rome itself was a slave rebellion in Sicily. Perhaps as much as half the grain supply for Rome came from Sicily, either through tribute or through additional purchases. The slave revolt came at a time when grain prices were already high from scarcity and, moreover, during a period when pirates were quite active. In consequence, the city suffered from an acute grain shortage and soaring prices at a time when these could not easily be rectified.

Tiberius Gracchus, Tribune of the Plebs (133 B.C.)

It would not have been without precedent if an official had proposed that the state make an extraordinary effort to import grain and sell it at a loss to relieve the economic crisis. Nor is it impossible that this was done, at least on a small scale. Young Tiberius Sempronius Gracchus, who took office as tribune of the plebs on December 10, 134 B.C., felt that any enduring solution must also deal with long-range problems and underlying causes. As he saw it, the most serious problems all related to the decline of the small farmer and the large-scale migration to the city. The shortage of men for the draft and the lack of grain grown in Italy itself were both connected with the decline of the small farmer, for owners of the new *latifundia,* profit-motivated, seldom raised grain. Partly in consequence, there was an overdependence upon Sicily for wheat. Gracchus wanted to reestablish the peasant class, protect Rome's reservoir of manpower for the army, and reduce the dependency on Sicilian grain. To these ends he proposed an agrarian law he thought would achieve it all.

Tiberius Gracchus's land law was not revolutionary. It dealt with public land, not at all with privately owned land. Like earlier laws, it limited the amount of public land any one Roman could hold; it also provided for distribution of the rest of the public land (or the best of it) to the Roman poor, on a lease basis. Whatever injustice there was in the law was a consequence of the sloppy way in which the public land had been leased or neglected in the past. Persons who expected to be able to hold their leases indefinitely had poured capital into the land.

In other cases, land that had been proclaimed as confiscated by Rome had never actually been taken over. By the Gracchan law, persons would be dispossessed whose ancestors had lived on their land for perhaps centuries. This situation applied especially to Rome's Italian allies, who were bitter about it. Much land in southern Italy had been confiscated on paper after the war with Hannibal, as punishment for states that had deserted the cause of Rome, but this was never actually taken from the Italian owners. Now, two-thirds of a century later, this land was to be taken over by Rome.

The initial outcry against Gracchus's proposal came primarily from Romans. Quick passage of the measure was prevented by the veto of another tribune of the plebs. Tiberius, sure of his cause and encouraged, it seems, by Blossius of Cumae, a Stoic and democratic theorist who was his adviser, carried through an unprecedented recall election, got rid of the offending tribune, and put another in his place. This, as much as anything Tiberius did, aroused his political enemies. Roman aristocrats always feared as a potential tyrant anyone who offered great benefits to the general public. This recall election seemed to confirm their fears. Most of the aristocracy opposed Tiberius (who was also an aristocrat and had the support of other senators); his bill became law, but only a tiny sum of money was voted to help his agrarian commission carry out its terms. The majority of the Senate remained firmly opposed to the tribune's efforts.

Tiberius pressed on, nevertheless, and used private funds. Then he got an unusual opportunity: Attalus III of Pergamum died in 133 B.C., the year of Gracchus's tribunate, and willed his kingdom to Rome. Tiberius, ignoring the Senate (which usually controlled both finance and the provinces), got a law passed which would have the new province settled by action of the Assembly, not the Senate, and also to use Attalus' treasure in carrying out the agrarian law. On top of this, Tiberius announced he was running for reelection. His enemies considered this illegal. At the time of the elections disorders broke out. The senators heard rumors that Tiberius was demanding a crown. Tiberius was defended before the Senate by the consul, who refused to take action. The chief priest (*pontifex maximus*), however, got together a crowd of persons and assassinated Tiberius and his friends. For centuries Rome had witnessed no political assassination, but officials did nothing about it, since too many important Romans were involved. The chief priest found it expedient to leave the city soon afterward, perhaps because of threats to his life.

The agrarian commission was reconstituted and continued to operate for a time, but owing to persistent complaints of the Italians, Scipio Aemilianus got its power reduced. Some land was indeed distributed to the poor, but not enough to reverse the trends mentioned above —if that was possible at all.

Gaius Gracchus, Tribune of the Plebs (123–122 B.C.)

Gaius, the younger brother of Tiberius Gracchus, eventually took up his brother's cause. The immediate crisis involving the grain supply at Rome had been somewhat alleviated by the end of the slave revolt in Sicily. The condition of the Roman poor was still very bad, however, for grain prices did not come down much and many were doubtless still unemployed. To them, a mass of voters of some consequence, Gaius Gracchus offered hope.

Elected tribune for 123 B.C., Gaius quickly initiated a rather extensive program. This included a restoration of power to the agrarian commission, but there is no evidence that it did much to distribute public land to individuals after this time. Gaius depended primarily upon a price-fixing measure for grain to relieve the hungry. The state would sell the grain received as tribute at a price much lower than the current market—about the market price before the shortage began. He hoped this would force all prices down. Unfortunately, it did not, and the state had to buy grain at high prices and sell it at low prices, with resulting strain on the treasury.

Gaius also constructed granaries, roads, and bridges, with a double intent: to obviate future shortages of food and to give immediate employment to the jobless. Other measures he initiated included colonization on a considerable scale; a change in the tax structure of Pergamum, the new province the Romans called Asia, to produce more income for the treasury; and weakening of the power of the Senate by staffing the jury panels of the permanent courts with equestrians of non-political families, excluding senators and their close relatives.

After serving two consecutive years as tribune, Gaius failed to be reelected for a third year, in a bitter campaign. No sooner was he out of office than his political enemies began to try to annul some of his laws. During his efforts to prevent this, a messenger of the consul was killed by one of Gaius's followers. Gaius and his friends, about to be "railroaded" (they felt) for complicity in the murder, refused to give up and barricaded themselves in a temple on the Aventine Hill. The consul, Lucius Opimius, an old enemy of the Gracchi, collected troops and stormed the temple. Gracchus fled but soon after was killed (121 B.C.).

The Gracchan Heritage

In their brief careers the Gracchus brothers had effected some changes destined to be permanent. Leaders continued to arise who emulated them. Typically they used the office of plebeian tribune, bypassed the

Senate, and proposed popular measures. They were thus called *popu-lares.* Actually, the *populares* did not at any time constitute a true party in the modern sense. Popular leaders mostly used this approach as an alternate route to power. Some of them, however, did benefit lower class Romans, and no doubt some of them sincerely wished to do so. One should not doubt, either, that their opponents, who eventually called themselves *optimates,* sincerely believed that only their own conservative approach could preserve the Republic and that most of the popular leaders were would-be tyrant-demagogues of the Greek stamp.

What the Gracchi most definitely did was to point up the dual nature of the Roman constitution. Magistrates and Senate, tribunes and Assembly—both groups had power either by custom or by law to do many of the same things. Before the Gracchi came to power, the chief officials were the consuls and praetors, and the chief deliberative body was the Senate. The primary assemblies elected the officials but did little else. After the Gracchi, a tribune (or a popular consul) might well be the most important official, able to use the primary assemblies as legislative bodies to bypass the Senate. Before the Gracchi, despite occasional clashes, political leaders cooperated to make the constitution—defective as it was—work. After the Gracchi, the kind of tolerance that is always needed to make any republican constitution work was often lacking. Violence in the Forum became common. Ultimately it led to civil war and the end of the Republic.

Who was to blame for the century of unrest and civil war that followed the Gracchi? The blame lies at so many doors it is futile to attempt to focus on one person or two or on a single group. The oligarchy seems, in retrospect, to have been extrordinarily shortsighted and greedy at times. But the popular leaders also seem, sometimes, to have sought personal power, to have aimed at nothing short of over-turning the traditional state. One thing is certain: we do not have in the Roman Republic a simple contest between democracy and oligarchy, as sometimes portrayed. Nor is it quite true, as is also often said, that the senatorial oligarchy resisted and did not change to meet the needs of empire. It did—but admittedly not enough—and thus it may be true that such an oligarchy could not long govern a far-flung empire.

After the Gracchi, at any rate, things were never the same again.

Books for Further Reading

Astin, A. E., *Scipio Aemilianus,* Oxford, 1967.
Badian, E., *Foreign Clientelae,* Oxford, 1958.
Boren, H. C., *The Gracchi,* New York, 1969.
Brunt, P. A., *Social Conflict in the Roman Republic,* London, 1971.

FRANK, T., *Life and Literature in the Roman Republic,* Berkeley, 1930.

GRIMAL, P., ed., *Hellenism and the Rise of Rome,* New York, 1969.

GRUEN, E. S., ed., *Imperialism in the Roman Republic,* New York, 1970.

GRUEN, E. S., *Roman Politics and the Criminal Courts, 149–78 B.C.,* Cambridge, Mass., 1968.

HILL, H. H., *The Roman Middle Class,* Oxford, 1952.

MARSH, F. B., *A History of the Roman World from 146 to 30 B.C.* (rev. H. H. Scullard), New York, 1963.

McDONALD, A H., *Republican Rome,* London, 1966.

ORMEROD, H. A., *Piracy in the Ancient World,* London, 1924.

SMITH, R. E., *The Failure of the Roman Republic,* Cambridge, 1955.

TAYLOR, L. R., *Roman Voting Assemblies,* Ann Arbor, 1966.

Death-throes of a Republic

17

The violence employed by the opponents of the Gracchi was a two-edged sword. In succeeding decades popular leaders made good use of it against the traditional oligarchy. Small-scale violence became an almost acceptable part of the Roman political scene. One reason for this continuing violence was the lack of an effective police force for the capital. The Romans felt no need for such control. Important persons moved about only with a sizable group of retainers and hangers-on. Lower-class citizens were rather primitively expected to protect themselves or seek the aid of bystanders when trouble arose.

Violence has by-products. In such an unruly age, less "reprehensible" methods of influencing elections and legislation—such as bribery—came to seem harmless, almost proper conduct. Escalating violence and disregard for law brought armed clashes, and finally civil war, on such a scale that the inevitable consequence, no matter which side won, was the end of the Republic. The cynical historian may say that, after all, the fall of the Republic meant only the replacement of one set of oligarchs with another set. But there was a difference: the Republic did at least incorporate certain safeguards against control of the government by paranoid individuals. The form of government which followed ensured that this result would sometime follow.

A. The Jugurthan War and Gaius Marius

Outbreak of the War (112–111 B.C.)

It must have been a surprise to many Romans when they found themselves at war with Jugurtha, King of Numidia. Numidia in North Africa, under the patronage of the Scipios, had been a friend and ally of Rome ever since the Second Punic (Hannibalic) War. Rome had often supported Numidia in border disputes with Carthage. Jugurtha, the illegitimate grandson of King Masinissa, had fought with the Romans as a cavalry officer under the younger Scipio Africanus (Aemilianus), and the latter's high commendation caused Micipsa, then ruler of Numidia, to adopt Jugurtha and give him an equal inheritance with his own two sons. Soon after Micipsa's death, however, the ambitious Jugurtha had one of these heirs, his cousin Hiempsal, slain. Rome's entry into the North African war was a consequence of the struggle between Jugurtha and Adherbal, his surviving foster brother, over their share of the kingdom.

Whatever the problems in Numidia, it was still an independent state, and thus Rome had no legal right to intervene. Its reasons for doing so were at least three. First, Rome was now the next-door neighbor of Numidia, since the former Carthaginian homeland had become the Roman province of Africa. Second, certain longstanding allies of Rome, Italians engaged in trade in Numidia, had for some reason chosen to support Adherbal's cause. Jugurtha apprehended several hundred of these supporters at Cirta in 112 B.C. and massacred all of them. Finally, the whole question was taken up by popular politicians suspicious of the motives of the central oligarchy, and so entered the arena of partisan politics back in Rome. Highly placed Romans were accused of taking bribes from Jugurtha on a lavish scale to influence the outcome. At this distance, we cannot reliably determine the truth of these charges.

Marius and the War

When the fratricidal conflict in Numidia began, Roman officials at first only remonstrated. But when Italian allies were killed, a Roman army sailed for Numidia. Jugurtha "surrendered" to the Roman commander, who left him in control of the kingdom—and not much weaker than before. After the bribery charges and the ensuing investigation (during which Jugurtha was summoned to Rome, and while there inadvisedly arranged the assassination of a cousin who might have made a further claim to the Numidian throne), war was resumed. In command of the Roman forces was Quintus Caecilius Metellus (later surnamed "Numidicus"), who took along Gaius Marius as his legate.

Marius came of a family who had been Roman citizens for only a couple generations. Since none of his ancestors had reached high office in Rome, he was not of the nobility, but of equestrian rank. He had served with distinction in Spain with Scipio Aemilianus and must have known Jugurtha. His official career in Rome had proceeded slowly. He served as tribune in 119 B.C., but was probably the oldest man in the college. After failing to be elected to higher office once, he finally made it —sources say through bribery—to the praetorship.

Marius quarreled with Metellus in Africa and, against the latter's wishes, returned to Rome to campaign for the consulship. "New men" rarely reached the office of consul without powerful sponsorship, but Marius criticized the way in which the guerrilla-type war in Numidia was being bungled and gained office on a "win the war" theme. The Assembly voted (doubtless against the wishes of the Senate) to put Marius himself in charge of the war, superseding in command his former patron, Metellus.

Between 107 B.C., the year of his consulship, and 104 B.C., Marius managed to bring the Jugurthan War to an end. Jugurtha himself was captured, ironically, by the man destined to be Marius' greatest enemy— Lucius Cornelius Sulla. Numidia was reduced in size, and an unambitious king was found for its throne. Marius had again demonstrated his military competence.

Threat from the North: Gallic Migrations

By this time Marius was needed in Italy once more, to face an enemy much stronger and more terrifying than the King of Numidia. As early as 118 B.C. masses of Celtic tribes whom the Romans called Gauls had moved into what is now southern France. The main tribes were the Cimbri and the Teutones. Roman armies trying to support Roman allies against these invaders suffered a series of defeats. A major effort to turn back the migrating tribesmen was made in 105 B.C. under the consul Mallius and the proconsul Caepio. But in a battle at Arausio (modern Orange, in southern France), the Gauls were able to fight the two Roman armies separately and won a tremendous victory. It was said that 80,000 Romans were killed in this debacle. The way was then open for invasion of Italy, but fortunately for Rome the Gauls first went west into Spain. In desperation the Romans turned to Marius, who was elected consul *in absentia* and put in charge of the war when he returned from Africa. While serving as consul five years in a row (104–100 B.C.), he put together a new army and, in two great battles in 102 and 101 B.C, annihilated the barbarians.

Marius reorganized the army in a way that had political consequences that were probably inadvertent. In order to recruit enough Romans in good health and of military age, he enlisted men who had no property. He also reorganized the training and organization of the legions. Significantly, he now tended to become the patron of these thousands of Romans, who had no loyalty to any other patron or even to the traditional state. He is reported to have treated them well, and so one must presume they had something to do with his reelection year after year.

They supported his cause in confrontations in the Forum. Though Marius did not make the most of this newly developed support, he showed Romans what tremendous political possibilities now existed for successful generals assigned to important commands.

Saturninus

An army of propertyless men must be taken care of, both in and out of service. Soldiers who had nothing expected to gain booty, and they wanted a bonus on discharge. Marius prudently saw to it that his men got something out of the war. In order to get the necessary legislation passed to give them land as a discharge benefit, however, he needed political friends. One man willing to help in exchange for political support was Lucius Appuleius Saturninus, who had begun his career in the usual fashion and reached the quaestorship in 105 or 104 B.C. He was put in charge of the grain supply at Rome's port, Ostia. A shortage pushed prices up, and the Senate relieved him of this assignment. Doubtless, this would have meant the end of his elective career if he had not resorted to extraordinary measures.

Saturninus now became a popular demagogue, supporting popular measures—and the aims of Marius—as tribune of the plebs in 103 and 100 B.C. Saturninus passed a law giving Marius' veterans 100 *iugera* (about 63 acres) each in Africa. Another law provided for sale of grain to the poor at a nominal price, much lower than that established by Gaius Gracchus. Saturninus also supported a man who falsely claimed to be a son of Tiberius Gracchus. In the elections of 100 B.C., his followers killed one of the candidates for the consulship, an opponent of Saturninus' own candidate.

This blatant violence was more than the senators could tolerate. They passed the Final Decree, demanding that the consul take action against Saturninus and the culprits. The consul in Rome at the time was Marius. He took Saturninus and several others into custody, and they were shut up in the Senate house. What Marius intended to do with them no one knows; probably he wanted to give them a fair trial. However, a mob, probably abetted by important senators, climbed onto the Senate roof and killed the imprisoned men by hurling the heavy roofing tiles down through the rafters.

Marius now found himself unpopular, though he had acted neither as a popular ally of Saturninus nor as a member of the inner oligarchy—and did not really fit into either category. It has often been said that he was a great general but a poor politician. He retired from office and played a small part in public affairs for several years. The land law for his veterans was not carried through.

Rome's Allies—Their Changed Position

At the time when Rome conquered the Italian Peninsula and formed an alliance system with the Italian states, that system seemed quite liberal. If these Italians were not true equals with Rome, they almost were. Free from internal interference on the whole, they were required only to furnish troops to fight alongside the Romans. By the beginning of the 1st century B.C., however, this relationship had changed vastly. Rome had not deliberately put down her allies; but Rome's new position of dominance in the world and the new opportunities open to Roman citizens meant that, relatively, the position of its allies had worsened. Not only had Italians fought alongside the Romans to repel homeland invaders such as Hannibal; they had also gone off to fight in Spain, Greece, the Near East, and North Africa. Their reward was to see Rome prosper and grow even stronger—and at the same time, subtly and gradually, almost inevitably exercise a tighter control over all Italy.

The Italian allies were particularly irked by the Gracchan agrarian laws, which underlined their inferior situation. When the Roman armies were disbanded and only Roman citizens were given bonuses and land, the Italians seethed; they had helped Rome to conquer and hold the Mediterranean world but did not share in the benefits. After Latins and Italians settled in Rome and were registered as citizens (some had this right), they were rudely disfranchised in 95 B.C., perhaps because their votes had been influencing elections.

The disgruntled Italians talked of rebellion but instead found a champion among Roman politicians. He was Marcus Livius Drusus, tribune of the plebs in 91 B.C. and son of a man who had shown sympathy for the Italians when as tribune he opposed Gaius Gracchus in 122 B.C. Drusus, though oligarchic in sentiment and acting with the support of many senators, passed measures of a popular sort, including a grain law and a colonization scheme. He also promoted measures to benefit the Senate itself and the equestrian class. His motive, it seems, was to build widespread support for the main objective, which was to give citizenship to the whole of the Italian Peninsula. When this measure was at last put forward, however, he lost his support and, soon after, was assassinated.

The Social War Brings Enfranchisement

The killing of Drusus sparked the revolt of the Italian allies. A government was formed—a federation called Italia, with officials comparable to those of Rome. In the early months of the war Roman civilians were killed in large numbers; and as often as not, Roman armies lost to their similarly trained and armed former allies.

Another blow struck Rome at this same time. Mithradates, King of Pontus in Asia Minor, led a rebellion against Roman power in that area, with great initial success. This forced the Romans to engage in a degree of sensible diplomacy in Italy which had been lacking before. In a series of laws the Romans enfranchised, first, all the Latins and Italians who did not join the rebellion; later, all who laid down their arms; and finally, all the Italians. Still, the fighting continued into 87 B.C. If the Romans had been as reasonable earlier, a great deal of bitter fighting and lingering animosity could have been avoided.

Even after the end of the Italian War, the Roman oligarchy, fearing the electoral power of the new voters, attempted to restrict these privileges to a few of the tribes, or to put them into new tribes which would vote last. Popular politicians prevented this and so gained the general support of the new citizens.

C. The War Against Mithradates: Civil War in Rome

Sulla Takes Command

As one of the consuls for 88 B.C., Lucius Cornelius Sulla commanded six legions of troops in the final stages of the Italian War. Since he had demonstrated his military prowess and had experience in Asia Minor as governor of Cilicia, he was named by the Senate to take command of the war against Mithradates. A tribune of the plebs named Sulpicius Rufus, however, felt that Gaius Marius should be given the command. Naturally, politics entered into the matter, for the man who got such an important post would command large numbers of soldiers and might profit both politically and economically.

The dual nature of the Roman constitution was clearly demonstrated here. The Senate traditionally made the command appointments and controlled the provinces. In theory, however, the Assembly could supersede the decrees of the Senate, and had indeed done so once before for Marius, when in 107 B.C. he was given command of the Jugurthan War. Sulpicius convened an assembly—probably a mere fraction of all the people—to pass a law that gave command of the campaign against Mithradates to Marius. Those who tried to prevent the action were manhandled, and at least a few, including a relative of Sulla, were killed.

Sulla considered the whole action illegal and criminal. He fled to his army and led them in a march on Rome itself—the first time a consul had invaded the city with troops. Sulpicius and several others were killed, and Marius fled for his life. Sulla made certain arrangements, including the election of consuls he thought "loyal," and went off to Asia Minor to fight Mithradates.

Overturn in Rome

Early the next year, one of the consuls Sulla had thought safe, Lucius Cornelius Cinna, attempted to pass legislation securing equal voting rights for the new citizens and so precipitated a new civil conflict. Driven out of the capital, he managed to get control of an army, and then recalled Marius from his refuge in North Africa. When Marius joined him, they marched on Rome, expelled Sulla's supporters, and killed a considerable number of presumed enemies.

Cinna and Marius were elected consuls for the next year, 86 B.C. Marius no doubt intended to take over Sulla's command but died on January 13. His successor, Flaccus, raised an army and went east, presumably to replace Sulla. Flaccus was killed in a mutiny by his legate, Fimbria, who then took over the army. Sulla naturally did not accept Fimbria's claims, and Fimbria either could not or did not wish to attack Sulla. The two armies, though wary of each other, for a time cooperated loosely in the war against Mithradates.

Sulla's Victories in the East

Since Mithradates was in control of the sea, Sulla from the beginning felt he could not invade Asia Minor without a fleet. Besides, Mithradates was widely supported by the Greeks, who detested Roman rule. Athens had even made an alliance with him, and her port, Piraeus, was his major naval base in the Aegean. Sulla therefore besieged Athens in 87–86 B.C. When he took the city, he treated the Athenians harshly. Piraeus soon was in his hands also, and Mithradates' ships departed. Two armies that the king sent by the land route to stop Sulla, in 86 B.C., were crushed at Orchomenus and Chaeronea, though in each instance Sulla was outnumbered.

By this time Lucius Licinius Lucullus, Sulla's legate, had gathered together a fleet. Fimbria's army actually crossed the Aegean first and nearly captured Mithradates himself. Soon defeated at sea and confronted by two Roman armies, Mithradates was ready to negotiate peace. Sulla limited the vanquished ruler's navy and took some indemnity, but otherwise he reestablished the prewar boundaries. Sulla's army might then have fought that of Fimbria; but the latter's troops went over to Sulla, and their abandoned leader committed suicide.

Sulla now prepared to return to Rome. He took time to reorganize the province of Asia and punished not only collaborators with Mithradates but the whole populace, which was required to pay five years' back taxes at once (paid to Mithradates) and an additional indemnity. The provincial cities had to borrow the necessary money—from Romans—and were still trying to pay off this debt two decades later.

Sulla's Return: Civil War and a New Order

Cinna served as consul each year while Sulla was gone. With other moderate leaders he tried to prepare for the civil war that now seemed inevitable. When he attempted to lead troops out of Italy, however, he was killed. Other leaders arose in his place, but when Sulla landed in Italy in 83 B.C., they were unable to cope with him. Sulla neutralized the Italians, who tended to support the popular leaders, by announcing he accepted the voting arrangement for new citizens that had been enacted during his absence. Through intrigue, siege, and combat, Sulla's forces won over the various armies feverishly raised by his opponents. The largest battle was at Rome itself, in 82 B.C. at the Colline Gate, where Sulla captured and slaughtered thousands of Samnites. He cowed the Senate, which meekly named him "Dictator for Reconstituting the Republic."

As dictator, Sulla ruthlessly proscribed those who had opposed him. Several thousand persons were killed without trial, in a climax to the escalation of terror alternately mounted by both popular leaders and Sulla. Sulla also revised the constitution; he tried to eliminate its dual nature by taking away most of the powers of the tribunes of the plebs and the popular assemblies. He intended that the Senate should control almost all governmental functions except the elections. He enlarged the Senate, however, bringing into the government men who had not previously participated in the power structure. Sulla voluntarily relinquished his dictatorship in 79 B.C. and retired; he died the following year.

Reverse, denarius of Sulla, showing a triumphal chariot, with the goddess Victory flying above, crowning the victorious general.

A decade of war for Romans—with former Italian allies, with Mithradates, and among themselves—threw the economy into complete disarray. Even the large sums brought back by Sulla from the East or gained from sale of the property of those he proscribed were not enough to restore a balance. It would be years before the province of Asia again produced the volume of tribute it once accounted for. Moreover, the civil war continued in Spain. There one of Marius' officers, Quintus Sertorius, collected troops, made allies of the Iberian natives, and defeated several Roman armies sent against him. In 74 B.C. Mithradates decided that Rome was weak enough for him to make another trial at arms. Part of Rome's problem was the lack of vigorous leadership in the restored oligarchy.

In 73 B.C. trouble broke out in Italy itself, almost serious enough to make Romans forget the challenges to their authority in Spain and Asia Minor. A Thracian gladiator named Spartacus and seventy of his fellows broke out of their barracks at Capua, south of Rome. They defeated the hastily raised local troops sent against them and captured their arms. Spartacus persuaded thousands of the slaves in the countryside to join him and equipped them with arms from dead legionaries. Ultimately he crushed even consular armies with his motley force, which reportedly approached 100,000 at its height. The rebels ravaged large areas from Lucania on the south to the Po Valley in the north.

Inevitably the Roman government collected stronger forces. Marcus Licinius Crassus, placed in command, trapped and destroyed the slave army in 71 B.C. He killed large numbers, perhaps including Spartacus himself; thousands of others he crucified along the roads stretching north toward Rome. A fragment of Spartacus' army escaping to the north had the misfortune to encounter a Roman army under Pompey the Great, returning from Spain. They, too, were annihilated. Fearful slave owners, though somewhat poorer from the loss of their "property," could nonetheless breathe again.

D. New Leaders for a Faltering Republic

Marcus Licinius Crassus (115–53 B.C.)
and Gnaeus Pompeius Magnus (106–48 B.C.)

Crassus had spent his time in hiding in the days when Cinna and the partisans of Marius controlled Rome and Italy, and as the crisis approached, Pompey also disappeared from public view. Both came out of hiding, raised troops, and fought with Sulla in the civil wars. Pompey collected three whole legions. After he successfully carried out the various commands Sulla had given him, the dictator dubbed him Magnus ("The

Great"), the surname he proudly used the rest of his life. Crassus also did well in this conflict; he commanded the victorious wing at the decisive battle of the Colline Gate.

During the years after Sulla's retirement, both these military leaders served in important commands, as we have seen; Pompey against Sertorius in Spain, and Crassus against Spartacus. In 71 B.C. both still commanded armies, and both decided to stand for the consulship. Both were ineligible, probably, by Sulla's laws: Pompey was too young and had never held any elective office at all, yet had been given *imperium* and even celebrated a triumph; Crassus had held the praetorship too recently, perhaps. At this point the two decided to follow Sulla's example, rather than his laws. They got together, though neither liked the other, and threatened to use their armies if they were not permitted the illegality of running for the consulship. To gain votes, they let it be known that if elected they would restore the powers of the tribunes of the plebs. In this way they were elected. As consuls in 70 B.C., then, these former lieutenants of Sulla scuttled the remains of his constitution. The two-track route for political advancement was restored; the potential for constitutional conflict between tribunes and consuls, the Assembly and the Senate, was renewed.

Marcus Tullius Cicero (106–43 B.C.) and Gaius Julius Caesar (100–44 B.C.)

Two other young men, Cicero and Caesar, also entered upon their careers during or soon after Sulla's dictatorship. Both courageously opposed Sulla, though not with arms. In 81 or 80 B.C. Cicero defended Roscius, who stood accused by one of Sulla's freedmen, Chrysogonus. The latter had made a good thing of handling the numerous properties of proscribed nobles, which were sold at auction. Skillfully treading dangerous ground, Cicero won his case and made his reputation.

Caesar from the beginning was a Marian; in fact, by marriage Marius was his uncle. Caesar had married the daughter of Cinna, and he refused Sulla's request to divorce her. To escape the latter's displeasure, both Caesar and Cicero decided to take extended tours in the Hellenistic East until Sulla retired.

Cicero was a sort of popular politician, but his popularity rested on his exceptional oratorical ability, used to gain friends, and in public service, rather than on advocacy of popular measures of the Gracchan type. In 70 B.C., he successfully prosecuted an unscrupulous former governor of Sicily, Verres, and thereafter his rise was rapid. He reached the consulship in 63 B.C., at the earliest age permitted under a Sullan law still in effect. As consul he prevented passage of radical agrarian legislation that had political clientage as its real purpose and, late in the year, suppressed a conspiracy against the state. A bankrupt patrician named Catiline, who had failed three times to reach the consulship, in desperation formed the conspiracy, which eventually developed into armed revolution. Catiline proclaimed cancellation of all debts and even appealed to slaves to join his revolt.

The suppression of this conspiracy was Cicero's finest hour, as he saw it. After hearing rumors, the consul diligently sought and found evidence that made it possible for him to expose the plot before it had gone too far. Acting on a Final Decree of the Senate, Cicero took some of the conspirators into custody and put them to death. Actual military action was then required, the following year, to destroy the nondescript army Catiline had managed to put together. Cicero hoped that this threat to legitimate rule would serve as a salutary lesson to the oligarchs and businessmen whose fortunes were endangered by Catiline, so that they would afterward unite in a more harmonious state. The renowned orator wearied even his friends with his boasts of how he had averted general disaster.

Caesar made his way upward in the popular manner, winning votes through a much-stressed relationship with the late Marius, his uncle, and through the fine games he put on as aedile in 65 B.C. Unlike Cicero, he wanted military command and went to Spain after his praetorship of 62 B.C. He had spent huge sums the previous year to obtain the office of *pontifex maximus* and, before he could proceed to Spain, had to borrow money from Crassus, who was called Dives ("the Rich"), to pay off creditors who had attached his baggage.

Pompey Eliminates Piracy and Crushes Mithradates

Meanwhile Pompey emerged as the dominant figure in Rome. His position, like that of Cicero, fell between the popular one and that of the *optimates;* that is to say, he was somewhat equivocal. He attempted to stay on good terms with the Senate; yet both of the two great commands given to him during the decade 70–60 B.C. came by a vote of the Assembly, over opposition of most of the Senate.

The first of these assignments was an extraordinary command against the pirates in 67 B.C. The Romans had long neglected their responsibility of keeping the seas and seacoasts secure. However, when the pirates threatened Rome's lifeline—the grain supply—and even raided the mainland coastal cities north of Rome, something clearly had to be done. The task was made worthy of the great Pompey by the size of the forces allotted to him: hundreds of ships and many thousands of men. Pompey acted energetically and efficiently, and within ninety days the seas were cleared of the marauders. Mopping up operations were continued in pirate base areas such as Cilicia and the island of Crete.

The second law, in 66 B.C., put Pompey also in command of the war against Mithradates. This war had begun in 74 B.C., when by King Nicomedes' will Rome "inherited" Bithynia, on the border of Mithradates' kingdom of Pontus. Mithradates did not want Rome for a near neighbor; moreover, as we have seen, the troubled state of Rome's affairs encouraged him to think he might now succeed where he had failed before. The consul Lucullus, a lieutenant of Sulla in the first Mithradatic war, was put in charge of Rome's armies. He brilliantly defeated Mithradates and drove him out of his kingdom and into Armenia, his ally.

Yet the war dragged on. Some of Lucullus' troops were kept in service beyond the legal period, and their leader's strict discipline irritated his men. In consequence, part of his army mutinied. Lucullus had to withdraw, and Mithradates was able to reenter Pontus. Meanwhile Lucullus had made enemies at home by his fiscal policy in Asia; he reduced interest payments on loans that dated back to Sulla's confiscatory measures. These loans had been made, of course, by important Roman moneylenders and tax collectors. This damaging combination of mutiny in his army, loss of ground to Mithradates, and influential enemies at home caused Lucullus to lose his command to Pompey.

Mithradates was actually a beaten man. Pompey, with fresh troops, made short work of the war, and Mithradates soon fled to his dominions on the north shore of the Black Sea. A short time later he was dead. Pompey now reorganized all of Asia Minor; he put part of the Pontic lands into the Roman province of Bithynia and secured the allegiance of various client kings in the area.

Pompey went far beyond this. To the south, the old Hellenistic kingdom of Syria had almost distintegrated, with various factions vying for control. Without legal authorization he moved into this power vacuum and took over; Syria became a Roman province. No one back in Rome complained of this illegality, for the new province would bring in much tribute. Pompey also settled a dispute over the high priesthood at Jerusalem, during which he used his army to put down the objections of some of the Jews. Thus Judea became a client state, supervised by the governor of Syria. Pompey added greatly to Rome's prestige and wealth. He too became enormously wealthy—a fact not totally unrelated to his conquests—and had great influence as well, though not so great as he imagined.

Cicero: Vain Hopes for a Harmonious State

The consul for 63 B.C., Marcus Tullius Cicero, was one of the few politicians in Rome who wanted to preserve the Republic and who also understood what sort of policy was necessary to stay its decline. As a "new man," the first of his family to attain the consulship, he considered himself the representative of the equestrian order from which he came—both the second-rank country gentry and the rich and influential tax collectors (*publicani*) and moneylenders who made up this order.

Cicero worked for a "concord of the orders," a harmonious working relationship between the aristocratic ruling class and the equestrian order. As he saw it, such an enlightened coalition would in a paternalistic way look out for the interests of the lower classes, whose support they would both deserve and get. The concord would need the cooperation of a figure as powerful as Pompey. Cicero did not think this would be difficult to manage, since he had supported Pompey for the Eastern command. It should only be necessary that the Senate defer to the "prestigious one."

The leaders in the Senate, however, were of a different mind. The extraordinary commands Pompey held were a threat to the Republic, because they resulted in a tremendous clientage. Accordingly, upon Pompey's return, they determined to bring him to heel. One of these senatorial leaders was a younger man, Marcus Porcius Cato (c. 95–46 B.C.), great-grandson of his namesake Cato the Elder. He attempted to emulate his ancestor's blunt style and was an unbending Stoic. He did not understand that a politician must know how and when to compromise; in consequence, he was a poor politician. (Or perhaps it would be kinder to say he was an unsuccessful statesman.)

Not suspecting that he would have difficulties with the inner oligarchy, Pompey disbanded his army as soon as he reached Italy late in 62 B.C. He celebrated a grand triumph at Rome in the following year. But when he attempted to get the Senate to ratify his Eastern settlement and to find some land for his veterans, he was rebuffed and found himself unable to do anything about it. The Senate also rebuffed the publican company that contracted the taxes for the province of Asia when it asked for a review of an unprofitable bid. Cicero saw the reasons for the behavior of the senatorial oligarchs, but he understood also that the state could not function without the support of the equestrians and powerful leaders like Pompey. He feared that the concord of the orders he had labored over would collapse, and it soon did.

E. The "Triumvirate": Caesar, Pompey, and Crassus

Caesar Puts Together a Coalition

When Caesar returned in 60 B.C. from his governorship in Spain, he wanted three things: a triumph, election as consul, and a juicy new command. Cato and his fellow optimates in the Senate chose to try to block his way, too. They refused to allow him to stand for the consulship while remaining outside the city. He could not enter the city without laying down his *imperium,* thus losing his chance for a triumph. Caesar decided to forego the triumph and stand for consul. He won Pompey and Crassus to his side by proposing what historians now call the First Triumvirate. A contemporary called it a "three-headed monster." With Caesar's organizational genius and popularity, Crassus' money, and Pompey's prestige, the coalition was too formidable for the oligarchy. The triumvirate was strengthened by the marriage of Pompey and Caesar's daughter Julia.

As consul for 59 B.C., Caesar turned away from a hostile Senate and through the popular assemblies got for the triumvirs what they wanted: for Pompey, ratification of his Eastern settlement and land for his veterans; for Crassus, a revision of the tax contracts (and no doubt repayment of some of the loan made to Caesar); and for himself, an extraordinary command—in Gaul—for five years.

In Gaul, Caesar embarked on an imperialistic adventure. Even if one discounts the reports he himself made in the finely written *Gallic Wars,* it is apparent that he did spectacularly well. In fact, his partners in the coalition soon saw that he had got the best of the bargain, and they began to angle for important commands for themselves. To this end, they got Caesar's support and had themselves elected consuls for the year 55 B.C. Then they gave Caesar a five-year extension of his Gallic command; Crassus got a command in Syria, and Pompey in Spain.

Dissolution of the Triumvirate

Crassus wanted to stir up a war with Parthia, a country east of Syria that was troublesome to the Romans, and he succeeded. In 53 B.C. he led a grand campaign across the Euphrates River. The Parthians, however, used their superior cavalry, surrounded the Romans, wore them down, and won a resounding victory at Carrhae. Crassus himself was killed. A young subordinate named Gaius Cassius prevented the Parthian victory from bringing disaster to Syria. One member of the triumvirate was now gone. A little earlier, Julia had died in childbirth, along with her child. Two of the links that held Pompey and Caesar together had snapped.

Pompey had always been jealous of Caesar. The senatorial leaders therefore attempted to win over Pompey and thus break up the remains of the powerful coalition. They had earlier given Pompey another command, the charge of the grain supply, which permitted him to stay in Rome instead of going off to his Spanish province. Now they supported an extension of his commands—but not of Caesar's.

In 52 B.C. when disorders reached an intolerable level in Rome,

Pompey was made sole consul. One cause of public violence was the murder of Clodius at the hands of his arch rival Milo. As tribune in 58 B.C. and later as leader of an organized gang, Clodius served his own and Caesar's purposes through violence or threat of violence. During his tribunate he exiled Cicero for having put citizens to death without trial in his consulship (the conspiracy of Catiline) and sent Cato off to organize a new province, Cyprus. This prestigious pair had seemed to pose the greatest threat to the triumvirate. In their absence, Clodius' gang of ruffians became such a menace to the orderly functioning of the state that many senators supported Milo when he organized another, opposing gang. When Milo murdered Clodius after a brawl near Rome, however, his friends either abandoned him or decided they no longer needed him. Clodius' death produced a grand riot, in which his followers burned down the Senate house as a funeral pyre worthy of their dead leader. Milo was then brought to trial and exiled, despite Cicero's efforts in his defense.

Pompey, now supported by most of the Senate, apparently decided that Caesar must not be permitted to gain more power. Caesar's command in Gaul was approaching an end after ten years. What he wanted now was the right to stand again for the consulship, this time *in absentia*. He did not wish to lay down his command, since this would expose him to a politically inspired prosecution that could bring his career to an abrupt halt. The majority of senators wanted both Caesar and Pompey to lay down their commands and give up their armies; but with Pompey's influence exerted in one direction and Caesar's (through lieutenants such as Mark Antony) in another, the senators were not actually free to act. The only option open to them was the choice of mastery by one of these two powerful men—whichever one might leave the Republic least damaged. Since Pompey seemed safest, they opted to support him. Accordingly, the Senate formally voted to terminate Caesar's command by replacing him. The senators did not permit Antony, as one of the tribunes of the plebs, to veto the decree and, in fact, drove him from the city. They must have expected war.

F. The Civil War of 49–45 B.C.

From the Rubicon to Pharsalus

Caesar's positions in the negotiations before the civil war seem to have been more moderate than those of Pompey and his party. Once he had crossed the boundary of his province at the Rubicon, however, on January 10, 49 B.C., he acted with great speed and vigor. Pompey, handicapped because he did not have complete authority, had to flee Italy. Caesar soon gained the allegiance of troops Pompey had counted on if war came, and even captured the state treasury in Rome.

The greatest threat to Caesar lay in Spain, where Pompey had six legions of troops. In a quick campaign Caesar outmaneuvered and defeated the commanders loyal to Pompey. Acting with leniency toward the troops, he allowed them either to join his army or to leave. Some of them presumably went to rejoin Pompey, who was marshaling men and supplies east of the Adriatic, across from the heel of the Italian Peninsula.

Caesar returned to Rome, arranged to be elected consul to legalize his position, and prepared to pursue Pompey. Since Pompey's fleet controlled the sea, the task was not easy. Caesar and his lieutenant Mark Antony got their legions across the Adriatic with difficulty and at great peril. Immediately, supply lines became a problem for Caesar; assaults on Pompey's strong position at Dyrrhachium were beaten off. During the winter his beleaguered men ate roots and anything else they could scrounge.

In late spring or early summer, seeking food, Caesar moved his legions to the Thessalian grainfields of northern Greece. There, at Pharsalus, the most decisive battle of the war was staged. Pompey's force was somewhat superior in numbers—especially his cavalry—but not in quality of fighting men. Caesar's men held steady under a cavalry attack on their flank, and their clever commander used reserves at a critical point to overpower the opponent's left wing. Pompey himself fled to Egypt, only to be killed by a Roman adviser to the young Ptolemy who thought it would please Caesar. When the latter arrived, he had the man responsible executed. Caesar was the victor, but the war was not over.

Caesar spent that winter in Egypt. He intervened in a dynastic struggle in Alexandria to support the claims of young Queen Cleopatra; this provoked hard fighting for the small body of troops he had with him. It seems he also had a child by the queen. At any rate, she named the son she bore the next year Caesarion. In the spring of 47 B.C., Caesar made a quick foray into Asia Minor, where Pharnaces, the son of Mithradates, had opposed his lieutenants. It was following this victory that he sent back his famous message, *"veni, vidi, vici."* Then he returned to Rome, where his presence was much needed. Antony and another lieutenant, Dolabella, were quarreling over policy, and there were problems galore. Caesar had been named dictator in 47 B.C., to maintain an appearance of legality when his consulship expired, and he arranged to keep both titles for the following year.

Final Battles: Thapsus and Munda

Under the leadership of the younger Cato and others, Caesar's enemies had collected new forces in North Africa. Caesar moved his army across the sea in late 47 B.C., and in the following year maneuvered to force his opponents to fight on ground of his own choosing, near Thapsus. The result was the customary victory for Caesar. Cato committed suicide at Utica after hearing of the disaster. Still the war flared up again. In Spain the sons of Pompey mobilized men and received refugees from Thapsus, so that Caesar had to make yet another Spanish campaign. The battle of Munda (near modern Osuna) in 45 B.C. was a severe test to his forces, but the outcome was the same. Caesar was losing his patience, however, and so were his troops; the slaughter of the losers went on for some hours, and a nearby city they had used as a base was treated harshly.

In 46 and 45 B.C., Caesar celebrated five public triumphs—though none over Roman opponents; that would have been in bad taste. One was over Vercingetorix, the leader of the Gauls in their final rebellion against the Roman conqueror; others were over the Alexandrians, Pharnaces, King Juba of Numidia (who had aided Pompey's faction in North Africa), and finally, against the Spanish allies of the Roman army defeated at Munda. These occasions were crowd-pleasing, for Caesar had long ago learned how to put on a spectacle. He gave 100 *denarii* to every citizen—as much as the average laborer might make in four months' work. Moreover, he was generous with many who had opposed him, including Cicero, who had hesitantly joined Pompey on principle. After Pharsalus the great orator had returned to Italy from Greece.

G. Dictator Caesar

Caesar's New Order

Plutarch, a century and a half after Caesar's death, wrote what many of the Roman ruler's contemporaries must have believed: that the great leader was from the beginning of his career aiming at absolute power. This view is surely wrong. Caesar doubtless did want to become one of the power elite, but he was almost driven to war. Naturally he did his best to win.

Once Caesar grasped power, he embraced it wholeheartedly. There could be no turning back. The old order was moribund, and a new order had to be fashioned. Those who dislike Caesar say he was really at a loss in this constructive aspect, that he planned huge new wars because he didn't know what else to do, that most of his so-called reforms were ill-planned or presented by someone else after his death. Those who admire Caesar present a long list of significant accomplishments they attribute to him. The truth probably lies somewhere between these extremes.

Caesar doubled the number of quaestors, increased the number of praetors, and made other changes in the lists of officials. He greatly increased the size of the Senate—occasionally, of course, putting into it men he owed favors—and also included some recently enfranchised Gauls.

He somehow reorganized the government of the various towns within Italy (any arrangement would likely have been more logical than the hodgepodge that had grown up) and made some changes in provincial government, especially in the collection of taxes, which were needed. He planned and partially carried through grandiose projects in Italy. For Rome, there was to be a new basilica in the Forum and, indeed, a new forum with a temple to Venus, adjacent to the old and named after him the Julian Forum. An artificial harbor was to be constructed at Ostia to give Rome a more satisfactory seaport. Lake Fucinus in central Italy was to be drained, giving many acres of new and valuable farmland. These last-mentioned projects he did not even begin.

Caesar instituted a new calendar based on the solar year, for which he used Egyptian astronomers as advisers. The old calendar had got far out of alignment with the seasons, since the extra (or intercalary)

Caesar, the first living Roman to be honored by having his image appear on coins. *(Alinari-Scala)*

months had not been interpolated in recent years. The result was that 46 B.C. stretched out to 445 days. With the corrections made by Pope Gregory XIII in 1582, Caesar's calendar is still in use all over the world.

When Caesar took over in Rome, 320,000 persons were getting free grain from the state. He was able to cut this figure in half, partly by sending out colonies all around the Mediterranean. Veterans were also sent to such colonies. This policy (not really initiated by Caesar), continued by Augustus and his successors, did much to Romanize the provinces. The Dictator still retained a quite large army. When he was assassinated, plans were well advanced for extensive and expensive military campaigns in Dacia (in modern Romania) and against the Parthians.

The Assassination and Its Aftermath

Caesar was in general personable and amiable. His clemency during the civil wars was notable. Yet, once in power, he did not carefully enough avoid offending the sensibilities of his fellow aristocrats. He remained consul in successive years; he held the dictatorship first for single years, then for a term of ten years, and finally for life. By 44 B.C. his image was appearing on coins—the first living Roman to be so honored—with an inscription proclaiming him perpetual dictator. The story that he was urged to accept the title Rex (king) by Antony but rejected it may have been an effort to reassure the people that he would not claim that title, forever blackened in Roman history by the Tarquins. Caesar controlled the elections and even had them conducted for three years at one time, in order to provide the magistrates and governors who would be needed while he was away on his projected military campaigns.

Caesar, then, was king in all but name. He wore regalia that belonged only to kings and triumphators. He claimed descent from Romulus and from Iulus (Ascanius)—and thus also from Venus and Mars. A priesthood was set up, with Antony at its head, to offer sacrifice to Caesar's *genius*. In view of all this panoply, it is not surprising that a large conspiracy against him was formed, including men who had fought with Caesar in the civil wars (Decimus Brutus and Gaius Trebonius) as well as men who had fought against him and been forgiven (Marcus Junius Brutus and Gaius Cassius). As everyone knows, on the Ides of March in 44 B.C. Caesar was struck down by conspirators in Rome at the foot of a statue of Pompey. This took place at the Senate house built by Pompey, near the theater also built by Pompey in the Campus Martius, not far from the modern Largo Argentina.

The conspirators—or "liberators," as they chose to be called—convinced themselves and hoped to convince others that they had acted from high ethical principles. Therefore they killed Caesar only; Antony, consul with Caesar, was spared, as was Marcus Lepidus, who as *magister equitum* was second in command to Caesar as dictator. The assassins expected public approval and general support, both in the Senate and in the Forum. What they got instead was an ugly reaction that caused most of them to flee Rome. Some went to provinces that had been assigned to them by Caesar, such as Decimus Brutus to Cisalpine Gaul; others seized provinces and asked the Senate to confirm their hold, such as Marcus Brutus in Macedonia and Gaius Cassius in Syria. Antony and Lepidus kept order in Rome. Antony, acting realistically, made compromises with the oligarchy. The assassins, on the one hand, were given amnesty; on the other, Caesar's acts were confirmed. But beneath the surface forces that would bring on another civil war were at work.

H. Resumption of Civil War to the End of the Republic

Second Triumvirate (43 B.C.)

A power struggle inevitably developed after Caesar was dead. The oligarchy, of course, attempted to regain control of the state; its leader was Cicero, who came out of semiretirement for the struggle. He saw the imperfections of the Republic but favored it over any possible alternative.

The grand-nephew of Caesar, Gaius Octavius—rather unexpectedly, for he was only nineteen years old—added a new dimension to the struggle. He was adopted by Caesar's will and became known as Gaius Julius Caesar Octavianus. Modern historians call him Octavius before his adoption, and Octavian from that point to 27 B.C., when the Senate conferred on him the name Augustus. Octavian disliked Antony's compromise with the assassins, who he felt should be punished. Moreover, he and Antony had a dispute over money; Octavian was Caesar's heir, but it was rather difficult to distinguish Caesar's funds from those of the state. Antony had just taken over all of it. Cicero and the Senate made an effort to use Octavian against Antony, for the young man was popular with Caesar's troops and veterans.

A struggle developed over Cisalpine Gaul. Decimus Brutus had taken it over, as we have noted. Antony, remembering its political importance, decided he wanted it and got a law passed giving it to him. Brutus, encouraged by the Senate, decided to fight. Cicero thundered against Antony in a series of abusive orations.

Octavian was made propraetor, and his army of Caesarian veterans was legitimized. Together with the consuls for 43 B.C., Hirtius and Pansa, he defeated Antony, but the consuls were killed in the battle. Acutely aware that the Senate meant only to use him and then get rid of him, Octavian now seized the opportunity for independent action.

He marched on Rome with the army and forced the Senate to name him consul. Then he moved north, theoretically against Antony, who had taken refuge with Lepidus, serving then as governor of Transalpine Gaul.

Instead of fighting against them, Octavian joined with Antony and Lepidus to form another triumvirate. One feature of their agreement was a proscription list, and among those proscribed was Cicero, who was assassinated at the end of that year. The orator's head was taken to Rome and hung in the Forum, where Antony's wife Fulvia stuck pins in Cicero's tongue as vengeance for his eloquent attacks on her husband.

The following year the last opposition to the triumvirs was put down in two battles in Macedonia, the battles of Philippi. There Octavian and Antony defeated Marcus Brutus and Cassius. The "republican" opposition was not yet ended, however, for Sextus Pompey, a son of Pompey the Great, held Sicily and Sardinia with a strong naval force. From there he was able to menace the grain supply for Rome, and so could not be ignored. It was not until 36 B.C. that Octavian defeated Sextus and drove him from Sicily. At the same time Octavian also got rid of Lepidus, the third member of the triumvirate, who had been relegated to an inferior position almost from the beginning. During the campaign against Sextus Pompey, Lepidus attempted to strengthen his position by using some of Pompey's troops who had surrendered to him. However, wearing a disguise, Octavian won over the troops in a dramatic night adventure. Lepidus gave up and was forced into retirement. Probably he escaped death only because he was also *pontifex maximus.*

Octavian, Octavia, Antony, and Cleopatra

Immediately after Philippi, Octavian and Antony in effect divided the Roman world between them. Octavian took charge of Italy and the West, where he had to worry about Lepidus, Sextus Pompey, demobilization of veterans, and numerous other problems. His efforts to find solutions led him to confiscate private property and to carry through other unpopular measures, but he was generally successful. In the East, Antony had to concern himself with the Parthians, numerous former supporters of Brutus and Cassius, uncertain client kings such as Herod the Great, and an ally of Rome, Egypt, which under Cleopatra had supported the wrong side. Antony enjoyed his greatest success with Cleopatra and took his worst defeat at the hands of the Parthians. In general, however, he too was able to control his half of the Mediterranean world.

Octavian and Antony tended to clash with each other from the beginning. At one point, Fulvia and Antony's brother Lucius actually fought a war against Octavian in Italy over a question of the relative authority of the triumvir and the consul (Antony's brother). As it happened, Antony was in Egypt renewing his acquaintance with Cleopatra at the time, unaware of events in Italy. When he found out, he was naturally incensed—but not only at Octavian. Fulvia soon died and the leaders patched up their relationship.

To seal the renewed agreement, Antony married Octavia, the sister of Octavian. She must have seemed a bit tame after the Egyptian queen, and after a couple of years he went back to Cleopatra. At length he sent Octavia a letter of divorce and formally married Cleopatra, who by then was the mother of twins, named Helios and Selene—the Sun and the Moon! Since Octavia was a most admirable woman, like many others in Roman history, Antony's behavior cost him much of his popularity. Octavian was quick to press his advantage and circulated stories of Antony's giving away Roman territory to Cleopatra (he did give her some territory in lower Syria) and of Antony's will. He wanted to be buried in Alexandria. Imagine, a Roman!

Antony and Cleopatra prepared well for the inevitable struggle. They were strong in seapower and about equal to Octavian in the number of legions. Perhaps Octavian's greatest advantage lay in his choice of his closest lieutenant, his childhood friend Marcus Agrippa. It was Agrippa who had really defeated Sextus Pompey, and he now organized the campaign against Antony. The latter had mobilized his sea and land forces at Actium, just across the Ionian Sea and southeast of the heel of the Italian mainland. But then, curiously, Antony became almost inactive, as if he expected an uprising in Italy that would make a battle with Octavian unnecessary.

Finally, in 31 B.C., surrounded on land and blockaded by sea, Antony and Cleopatra decided to risk all on a sea battle. Again their behavior seems curious. The battle was scarcely under way when Cleopatra's squadron veered off and left for Egypt. Perhaps she panicked; perhaps she saw defeat coming. Antony quickly joined her; they abandoned their navy and twenty or so legions of troops. Back in Egypt they made little effective preparation for the inevitable coming of Octavian's army. In 30 B.C., with no great difficulty, Octavian defeated Antony's skimpy forces and occupied Egypt. Antony soon committed suicide; Cleopatra, determined not to be led in a triumph at Rome and finding Octavian inflexible, took her own life also. (The story about the asp may be true.)

Octavian now ruled the whole Empire. He would not be seriously disputed again. The old leaders, for the most part, were dead; those who remained, along with all the Roman people, were sick of war. The famous Pax Romana thus was born of despair, exhaustion, and repeated disaster that had affected almost every person in the Mediterranean world.

Books for Further Reading

ADCOCK, F. E., *Marcus Crassus,* Cambridge, 1966.

BADIAN, E., *Publicans and Sinners,* Ithaca, 1972.

BADIAN, E., *Roman Imperialism in the Late Republic,* 2nd ed., Ithaca, 1968.

BAKER, G. P., *Sulla The Fortunate: The Great Dictator,* New York, 1927 (reissued 1967).

BUCHAN, J., *Caesar,* London, 1932.

COWELL, F. R., *Cicero and the Roman Republic,* London, 1948.

EARL, D. A., *The Moral and Political Tradition of Rome,* Ithaca, 1967.

GRUEN, E. S., *The Last Generation of the Roman Republic,* Berkeley, 1974.

KILDAHL, P. A., *Caius Marius,* New York, 1967.

SMITH, R. E., *Cicero the Statesman,* Cambridge, 1966.

TAYLOR, L. R., *Party Politics in the Age of Caesar,* Berkeley, 1949.

VOLKMANN, H., *Cleopatra,* New York, 1958.

CHART 6 The Roman Empire

PERIOD	ROME	OTHER
27 B.C.	Octavian named Augustus; announces restoration of the Republic; over a long period takes actions called the Augustan settlement; beginning of the Pax Romana.	Parthians negotiate with Augustus, return standards captured from Crassus.
	Golden Age of Latin literature: Vergil, Livy, Horace, Ovid.	
	Expansion in Illyria and north to the Danube; Illyria, Achaea, Raetia, Noricum, and Pannonia made provinces; conquest of the rest of Spain.	German resistance to Roman penetration; Arminius destroys three legions.
Julio-Claudians	Tiberius is successor to Augustus; nonexpansionist.	
	Sejanus' machinations; treason trials.	
	Gaius (Caligula) becomes emperor.	Continuing friction with Parthia. Beginnings of Christianity.
	Claudius; conquest of Mauretania and Britain (provinces); extensive building program, organization of the central bureaucracy.	Conquest of Mauretania.
	Nero on imperial throne; Seneca, Burrus contest the regency with Agrippina; Nero assumes control, kills his mother; Silver Age authors: Seneca, Lucan; Rome burns in great fire; the Golden House built; conspiracy and executions; revolt.	Parthian War, over Armenia. Revolt of the Jews.
68 A.D.		
69 A.D.	Civil Wars; succession of emperors: Galba, Otho, Vitellius.	
	Vespasian; economic retrenchment and recovery; opposition and exile of several philosophers; period of Pliny the Elder.	Destruction of Jerusalem.
Flavians	Titus; another fire at Rome; eruption of Vesuvius buries Pompeii and Herculaneum.	
	Domitian; continued opposition of philosophers; conspiracy and executions; assassination of Emperor.	Troubles along the Danube, especially with Dacians.
96 A.D.	Nerva; first official alimentary institutions.	
Five "Good Emperors"	Trajan; building projects; Dacian and Parthian wars; period of Tacitus, Martial, Plutarch.	Dacia made two provinces. Revolt of Jews, Cyrene and Egypt.
	Hadrian; military retrenchment; building projects all over the Empire; period of Suetonius and Juvenal.	Another Jewish revolt, led by Bar Kochba.
	Antoninus Pius	
180 A.D.	Marcus Aurelius (with Lucius Verus); wars in Parthia and along the Danube; plague.	Danubian tribesmen invade Empire.
193 A.D. Severi	Commodus; assassination of Emperor; civil war; Pertinax, Didius Julianus, Septimius Severus, and new dynasty; role of wife, Julia Domna.	Parthian wars with Rome.
	Caracalla; citizenship to most free persons throughout Empire.	
	Elagabalus replaces Macrinus after assassination of Caracalla.	
235 A.D.	Severus Alexander in turn replaces Elagabalus; primary role in two reigns of Julia Maesa and Julia Mamaea; assassination of Emperor.	Sassanid Persia replaces Parthia as primary foe in the East.
	Beginning of half-century of civil wars, complicated by foreign invasions and economic breakdown; military emperors, at least 30 major claimants to throne plus others; Aurelian builds new wall for Rome.	Persians, Goths, Franks, Alamanni, and others invade Empire from east and north; some get to Italy; Empire split in three parts.
284 A.D.	Diocletian restores order, reorganizes politically, militarily, and economically.	
312–337 A.D.	Constantine; first "Christian" emperor; Christianity now tolerated; building of Constantinople foreshadows division of Empire.	Persian War.

Pax Romana

18

The personal ascendancy of Octavian—soon to be revered as Augustus—over the Mediterranean world marks the beginning of a new era. This is true no matter what one thinks of Augustus: whether he was an adventurer who by accident inherited a great name and by systematic elimination of his opponents managed to survive and initiate the Empire, or whether he was a wise, tolerant and generally beneficent overseer who rescued Rome from chaos. Those who "put down" Augustus emphasize the less commendable actions of his earlier years and refuse to believe he could really mature and change as he grew more experienced. Those who praise him excessively refuse to give reasonable weight to the more unsavory things he did, mostly before 27 B.C.

That date, 27 B.C., the year when Octavian received from the Senate the title Augustus, was also the year when he announced that he was restoring the Republic. Ironically, this is the date most often taken as the beginning of Empire. Yet Augustus' announcement of a restoration of the Republic was not all sham. He had learned much, and one thing he knew well was this: the ruling class must be not merely tolerated but also fostered. This meant giving some consideration to their sensibilities. He therefore made the decision to permit the Senate and the government to function in many ways as they had in the past. One must note, moreover, that the term *res publica,* while usually translated "republic," really means "the state"—with an added connotation, for a Roman would have taken it to mean "like the traditional state." The point here is that Augustus should not be judged a hypocrite because of the announcement. He never promised to restore everything as it was before.

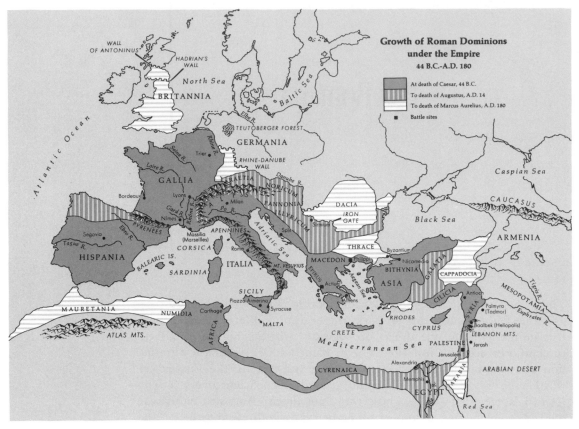

Growth of Roman Dominions
under the Empire
44 B.C.–A.D. 180

At death of Caesar, 44 B.C.
To death of Augustus, A.D. 14
To death of Marcus Aurelius, A.D. 180
■ Battle sites

Adapted from Brinton, Christopher, and Wolff, Civilization in the West, *third edition, volume one.*

The willingness of Augustus to learn, and to act on the basis of what he learned, was his greatest strength. From Caesar he learned not to exercise too much power too nakedly; from Pompey he learned that prestige alone was not enough, that a solid basis of authority was also required. Perhaps he learned most of all from Cicero. In the last two decades of his life the great orator had come to believe that coalitions dominated by powerful men—or by one man—now formed a permanent feature of the Roman political scene. It was only important that these men (or this man) be committed to the ideals of the Republic; such politicians should dominate but not destroy the ancestral state.

Augustus chose for himself an additional title, *princeps* ("chief citizen"). Historians therefore call the early Empire the Principate, to emphasize the role of the emperor as a sort of constitutional monarch, or partner with the Senate, as ruler of the state. Nevertheless, one must admit that Augustus' position had become so strong that no truly free institutions could exist alongside it; the old Republic could not actually

Augustus. Denarius of about 2 B.C. The inscription reads: CAESAR AUGUSTUS DIVI F (= Son of the Divine one—Caesar); PATER PATRIAE (= Father of his Country).

be restored. Ambitious men now could advance only with the approval of the Princeps. In retrospect, it is easy to discern the growing shoots of absolutism in the Augustan state—and the seeds of decline and ultimate decay as well.

A. The Early Empire

Structure of the State
under Augustus (27 B.C.–14 A.D.)

Augustus with clear vision saw that, though he must avoid the appearance of absolute power, he must nevertheless effectively control most of the offices, the army, and the money of the state. The legal basis for his control in the early years was provided by the consulate, which he held each year. The office of proconsul would hardly do, for the consul's power was technically superior. In 23 B.C., however, he was voted the *maius imperium,* which, with the additional powers he was given later, made his rank superior even to that of the consuls. Thus it was no longer necessary for him to retain the post of consul itself. He also had the power of a tribune, by which he could summon the Assembly, propose laws, and even veto them (though we know of no instance when he did so). He exercised the power of a censor to purge the Senate of Antony's men and of some of Caesar's as well. After the death of Lepidus in 12 B.C. Augustus also became *pontifex maximus.*

The elections continued somewhat as in the past. Augustus himself appeared in the Forum as candidates had of old; and he paid the gratuities that were by then expected of all candidates and were not considered bribes in any pejorative sense. He did not always indicate his preferences among the other candidates; but the favor of the Princeps meant more than any widespread canvass of voters. Before the end of his reign the prerogative centuries (those which voted first) were made up of men whose common sense Augustus could depend upon. In consequence, interest in the elections declined, and the number of Romans who exercised the suffrage declined also. When Augustus' successor Tiberius transferred the elections from the popular assembly to the Senate, it was only a formality.

The form, however, was mostly still there: elected consuls (usually four per year—two selected at the usual time and two more in midyear) served first in Rome, then later as provincial governors. Praetors and quaestors also were elected as before and served in routine ways. The Senate continued to make its disbursements from the traditional treasury. There were changes, too, however. The decrees of the Senate—a body more and more subservient to the will of the Princeps—had the force of law even more than before. Fewer and fewer laws were passed by assemblies of all the people. This latter process had become almost farcical in the late Republic, when small numbers of citizens living in Rome sometimes styled themselves "assemblies of all citizens." The Senate also acquired an increasingly important role as a judicial body, policing its members.

There were other important differences. Augustus governed about half of the provinces himself, by sending out personal legates who did the actual governing. As it happened, the territories so governed included the newest provinces (and consequently, the ones where Roman troops were needed). In this way, most of the army remained under his direct control. Egypt, richest of all the provinces, was tacitly considered Augustus' special preserve. Senators were not even permitted to travel there without special permission.

Control of Finance

Augustus did not tamper with the traditional public treasury, the Aerarium Saturni; yet the most important sources of revenue gradually came under his control. The taxes collected from each province were always, in part at least, used to meet the expenses of provincial government. Since Augustus controlled most provinces, he had access to these funds. The *fiscus* (treasury) in each province was in theory expected to send back to the state treasury in Rome all surpluses; in fact, Augustus probably assumed complete control over their operations. By the 2nd century A.D. these were connected with a single *fiscus* at Rome, which by then was the main treasury. It should be noted that those provinces which required sizable army units seldom produced a surplus of income over expenditures.

Augustus also established a special military treasury (Aerarium

Militare), with new sources of revenue, to distribute pensions to soldiers. As commander-in-chief, he naturally controlled its expenditures. The Emperor also had an important source of income from Egypt, with its special status and abundant crops. Finally, the Princeps had great private resources, for he had inherited rich properties from Julius Caesar and from his own family; and over the years his personal property (*patrimonium*) was vastly increased through inheritance. All important men at Rome listèd the Emperor in their wills, partly because it was the conventional thing to do—including important men in one's will was an old custom, going back at least a century or two—and partly because it was wise to do so. There would be no problem in validating such a will! This custom must have had a result similar to the inheritance taxes of our own day. The total disbursements personally controlled by Augustus at the end of his reign must have dwarfed the Senate's public expenditures from the Aerarium Saturni.

Control of the Army

During the Republic, the most important armies were those drafted to meet emergencies. The Senate authorized a set number of men and the money to pay them; then each commander did his own recruiting, and the troops took an oath to him. In the late Republic, however, a parallel practice grew up in the provinces that required standing armies. Troops there, over a period of time, might serve under two or more commanders. Augustus came to depend entirely on an adaptation of the latter system; he eliminated the traditional emergency army in favor of a larger standing army. In some senatorial provinces—Macedonia, for instance—proconsuls appointed by the Senate still had small armies under their command. Most troops, however, were under Augustus' legates, and recruiting was all managed under the authority of the Princeps. Through the Aerarium Militare the troops, on discharge, were pensioned by him in the form of discharge bonuses or land. Small wonder that the army always opposed any effort at a genuine return to the Republic.

Augustus also established nine new cohorts, the Praetorian Guard. Stationed in Italy (by later rulers, in Rome itself), these troops served both as imperial guards and as a strategic military reserve. During the early Empire, the praetorians were recruited among Roman citizens in Italy and served for sixteen years. The legionnaires, who were citizens from all over the Empire, served for twenty years. Auxiliary troops, recruited among the noncitizen population, served for twenty-four years and for the least pay but were rewarded with citizenship upon retirement. Colonies of veterans were established all over the Empire and became valuable sources of call-up reserves and new recruits. Such colonies helped to Romanize the provinces—a development that was ultimately of great significance.

Augustus brought order to the city of Rome, just as he did to the entire Mediterranean world. He formed the *vigiles,* police and fire-fighting units organized by district. Subject to strict discipline, they could also perform in paramilitary roles. The Urban Prefect, who controlled these forces, the Praetorian Prefect, who commanded the Praetorian Guard, and the Prefect of Egypt came to be quite powerful and influential men, although drawn from the Equestrian Class.

Manners and Morals

Like many another strong man in the world's history, Augustus was basically a conservative. This remains true even though he introduced great changes at Rome, and he was careful to cloak his actions with an appearance of legality. The Senate approved all major changes. A considerable number of Senators acting within an advisory council (the *consilium principis*) helped to set state policy.

This essential conservatism is seen also in Augustus' attachment to the ancestral state (*mos maiorum*). The Princeps reconstituted priesthoods which had all but dissolved; he conscientiously observed festivals, sacrifices, and the auguries; and he rebuilt scores of temples and completed several new ones. One of the latter was a temple which had been vowed to Mars by Caesar. Augustus added the name Ultor ("the Avenger"), to commemorate his vengeance of Caesar's murder. It was placed in the new Forum of Augustus, close by the old Forum and the later one of Caesar. He put up other public structures, including a theater dedicated to his nephew Marcellus, porticoes, and bridges. At the end of his life, he declared that he found Rome brick and left it marble.

A conservative must give attention to mores and morals; and in Rome of the early Empire it was easy to view the situation with alarm. Especially among the upper classes lax morals prevailed, along with frequent divorce. Over the previous two centuries women had emancipated themselves from the most binding restrictions, and at least some made the most of their new freedom. The birth rate of senatorial families declined, as senators desired to conserve their wealth and make possible a continuation of the extravagant life-style all too many Romans affected.

Augustus attempted to stem the tide. He lived a rather simple life and built no great palace for himself. Laws against extravagance and loose morals were passed. Adultery was severely punished when proved; even the Princeps' own daughter Julia was exiled when he learned of her illicit behavior. After a pattern going back to Cato the Censor, laws limiting the amounts that could be lavished on a single dinner were freshly enacted. Tax laws penalized bachelors, widowers, and married persons with fewer than three children. In his exercise of the powers of censor (three times during his reign), Augustus purged the Senate and the Equestrian Order of morally objectionable persons.

As in most other times and places, moralistic laws seem to have been ineffective. Yet, since the tone of society is usually set from above, Augustus' attitudes were somewhat influential. In the *Aeneid,* the poet Vergil's emphasis on the *pietas* of Aeneas toward the family and gods reflects the pervasive attitudes of the Princeps. On the other hand, the emphasis on sophisticated seduction seen in the *Ars Amatoria* of Ovid reflects the permissive mores of the younger set in Rome. This poem may have helped to draw the wrath of Augustus down upon the unfortunate Ovid, who was banished to the Black Sea region.

Augustus would probably have preferred to end the free distribution of grain to the urban plebs, but he found it impossible. Free distribution of grain came to be guaranteed to hundreds of thousands of persons not as a privilege but as a right. The great festivals, which were both religious spectacles and public entertainment, he did not wish to eliminate. "Bread and circuses" remained a part of the scene at Rome as long as the city was an imperial capital. Some emperors reveled in the cheers

The aqueduct of Claudius in the Campagna. *(Alinari-Scala)*

and applause of the city's poor; a satisfied proletariat, moreover, afforded a degree of public protection to a popular ruler.

Frontiers and Provinces under Augustus

For most of the 50 to 100 million residents of the Roman Empire under Augustus, the new order represented solid gain. First, of course, there was the blessing of peace. The Pax Romana established after 30 B.C. lasted, with only brief interruptions, for nearly three centuries. What fighting did occur was on distant frontiers, and the general populace could ignore such wars. The admirable road system, though developed chiefly for military reasons, brought benefits to all. Trade restrictions within the Empire were minimal; the coinage, though not completely unified, was well integrated.

Roman governors, now under better control from Rome and given excellent salaries, were on the average more competent and less avaricious than during the late Republic. Many imperial administrators, especially those of second rank, were career professionals whose future depended upon efficient performance. The Empire was built upon cities —city-states, really—everywhere except in the West, where tribes were the organized local units. A considerable degree of self-government was usual. Of course, official abuses were still to be found. Every reader of the New Testament knows, for example, that Jews equated publicans (tax collectors) with sinners. But as long as the central government in Rome was reasonably competent, the lot of the average provincial was better than ever before—in some areas, immeasurably better.

A modern state the size of the Empire under Augustus can support an immense military establishment; but an ancient state with little industry, resting on a rural economy, could not. The army with which Augustus manned Rome's sprawling frontiers was surprisingly small, averaging between twenty-two and twenty-five legions, with auxiliaries— or in all, about 250,000 to 300,000 men. In most areas he therefore adopted a somewhat conservative diplomacy. It was rather typical of him to attempt to get back through negotiation rather than military action the three legionary standards lost by Crassus to the Parthians in 53 B.C. —and to succeed. It was also typical that he publicize his success: he put *Signis receptis* on one issue of coins. The coinage became a constant vehicle of official propaganda, though mostly in good taste.

Along the Rhine-Danube frontier, for a time Augustus pressed vigorously to expand Rome's dominion. From the area of modern Switzerland to Thrace, Rome's armies "pacified" all the lands south of the Danube. Roman expeditions moved eastward across the Rhine and even beyond the Elbe. A disaster in the Teutoburger Forest in 9 A.D., however, brought the destruction of three entire legions. There the Roman commander Varus lost to the German tribal leader Arminius, who had previously served in the Roman army and been given equestrian status. After this serious defeat Augustus set the Rhine as the Roman frontier.

The whole of the Iberian Peninsula came under Roman control by 19 B.C. In one way or another, most of coastal North Africa was also Roman, held for the empire with but a single legion, backed up by two more in Egypt. Toward the end of Augustus' reign Germanicus, the Princeps' grandson by adoption, again ventured east of the Rhine—perhaps to the old Emperor's disapproval. A year after Augustus died, Germanicus nearly met disaster on the same battlefield where Varus had fallen. In general, however, at the death of Augustus peace reigned along all the imperial frontiers.

B. Julio-Claudian Line after Augustus

Tiberius (14–37 A.D.)

Tiberius was not Augustus' first choice as a successor—nor his second or third. Apparently Augustus found his adopted stepson somehow personally unacceptable as a future Princeps. Augustus' first choice was his nephew, Octavia's son Marcellus. His second was Agrippa, his childhood friend, most trusted lieutenant, and son-in-law. The third was Drusus, Tiberius' younger brother. And fourth and fifth came Augustus' grandsons Gaius and Lucius, the sons of Agrippa and the Emperor's daughter Julia, who were also called Caesar because Augustus adopted them (as he did Drusus and Tiberius as well). But Augustus outlived them all, and his choice eventually had to fall upon Tiberius. He forced Tiberius to divorce Vipsania (the daughter of Agrippa by a first marriage), whom he loved, and to marry his daughter Julia, Agrippa's widow, whom he disliked. This feeling was apparently mutual and perhaps helps to explain Julia's well-known adultery.

Tiberius, nevertheless, had proved himself a competent general and administrator. If he resented the treatment he got at the hands of his stepfather Augustus, it should not be surprising. Yet in some respects Augustus was right: Tiberius was a dour personality; reserved and cold, he was never popular. Even when trying to do something laudable, he tended to be obscure and ungracious. When he attempted to get the Senate to act more independently than it had in recent years, Tiberius only aroused the suspicion of the servile senators about his motives. He sat in on their judicial deliberations only when it was clear that the senators were not doing their job. As the historian Tacitus said, this was good for justice but bad for freedom. The results were always the same, and the fault lay in the system, not the men. The Emperor's powers were too great to share effectively, and in such a situation true freedom was not possible. Tiberius is a classical example of a man who, quite unwilling, was forced into the mold of a despot.

Tiberius had been required by Augustus to adopt his nephew Germanicus, who it was evidently intended should succeed Tiberius. Germanicus, his uncle felt, had been too rash in the German campaign mentioned earlier. Tiberius considered that the Rhine was the best frontier. In this, as elsewhere, a major tendency of Tiberius is seen: to continue all the major policies of Augustus. He recalled Germanicus from the Rhine frontier and sent him on a task in the Near East. Eventually Germanicus died—his devoted wife Agrippina believed from poison— and there were those who suspected the Emperor of complicity in his sudden death.

Tiberius also had difficulties with his officials at home. Lucius Aelius Sejanus, his Praetorian Prefect, seems to have set out to succeed Tiberius. (There is, among scholars, vast disagreement about the extent to which Sejanus schemed, was schemed against, or was used by Tiberius.) Germanicus' widow Agrippina was the daughter of Agrippa and Julia. Convinced her husband had been murdered, she was accused of instigating a conspiracy against Tiberius. She was imprisoned along with some of her sons, two of whom soon died or were murdered. It is possible that Sejanus fabricated the conspiracy as a means of getting rid of some obstacles to his own ambition. Sejanus may also have murdered Tiberius' son Drusus, as Tiberius was later told by Sejanus' estranged wife. The Prefect wanted to marry Livilla, the widow of Drusus, and a sister of Germanicus, but Tiberius withheld his permission.

Sejanus had wide scope for his intrigues when Tiberius virtually retired, to the island of Capri, for the last eleven years of his reign. From Antonia, the influential and rich daughter of Mark Antony and Octavia, Tiberius eventually heard of Sejanus' machinations, in spite of his isolation from affairs at Rome. The Emperor then entrapped and replaced the Prefect, who was soon executed. Tiberius had always been of a suspicious nature; now in old age he became embittered as well. In this period scores of persons were tried on charges of treason—as others had been in the days of Sejanus' ascendancy. The Emperor himself stopped some trials when he thought the charges unfounded, but he permitted far too many to go on. The whole proceedings were infamous: such charges were brought by private individuals, informers (*delatores*) who were rewarded from the property of the convicted men. The system itself was bad.

Most of the Empire enjoyed good government under Tiberius, nevertheless. In spite of Sejanus—and Pontius Pilate—Tiberius generally chose competent officials and governors of provinces. A revolt in North

Africa by the elusive Tacfarinas required attention for years, but mostly the frontiers were quiet.

The Empire seems also to have been generally prosperous; yet it was impossible for Tiberius through thrifty fiscal policy to amass the tremendous treasury surplus he did (almost 3,000,000,000 sesterces) without adversely affecting the economy, particularly in Rome itself. We know of a financial crisis in 33 A.D., during which Tiberius did lend money without interest to those most affected. He did not put on grand festivals and games at home or build lavishly. The financially depressing effects of this policy contributed to his unpopularity there. When at last the Emperor died in 37 A.D. at age seventy-seven, there was rejoicing in the streets.

Gaius (Caligula; 37–41 A.D.)

The young man not yet twenty-five who next succeeded to the throne of the Roman Empire had little training for his post, and little to commend him for his task except that he was the son of Germanicus, the most popular member of the dynasty. Gaius' earliest memories would have included the years in Gaul when his father was campaigning across the Rhine. The boy wore little soldiers' boots (*caligae*), and so was given the nickname Caligula. The following years brought turmoil to his life, and he lost his father and saw his mother and brothers imprisoned. He lived with his severe great-grandmother, then with his grandmother, and finally with Tiberius on Capri.

Gaius' reign began auspiciously, with cheers, honors, and sacrifices. He paid generous donatives to the praetorian guards and the city plebs, lowered taxes, released men from prison, and put on expensive extravaganzas. Incredible extravagance and personal vagaries, however, soon ended the new ruler's honeymoon, at least in so far as the governing class was concerned. Germanicus, Gaius' father, had implied he might restore the Republic. Gaius had no intention at all of following through on this, though it may have been expected of him.

It is possible to sift through ancient sources and conclude that many of the acts of Gaius which are presented as capricious idiocy really had some rational explanation: he was reacting to a conspiracy, rather than killing men without reason; he was training and disciplining his troops, rather than making an elaborate farce of an invasion of Britain which he mobilized for but never carried out; he was aiming at Hellenistic kingship, not merely making sport of the Senate. But to rationalize all the available evidence in this way is to reject much of it. Through it all, Gaius appears as distinctly unbalanced mentally, even if he did have intermittent periods of rational behavior.

Gaius spent huge sums to bridge the Bay of Naples with a causeway of ships, across which he paraded for a couple of days. No matter what the reason, this was a piece of enormously expensive idiocy. Though one may dismiss the stories of his sexual misbehavior even with wives of men invited to imperial parties or of incest with his sisters, there is no doubt that in this respect too he was eccentric. He was said to have appointed his favorite horse to a priesthood and declared that he would have it elected consul. He once gave 2,000,000 sesterces (the average Roman could not make so much in a thousand years) to his favorite charioteer.

Gaius deified one of his sisters, Drusilla; the other two he imprisoned. He himself did not follow the example of Tiberius, who declined when divine honors were offered him. Gaius seems to have wanted to be identified with Jupiter. He somehow extended his palace so that the Temple of Castor and Pollux in the Forum became a kind of entrance foyer, and he built a bridge from his home on the Palatine over to the Capitol to facilitate his communion with Jupiter there. He very nearly had a rebellion of the Jews on his hands in 40 A.D. through his insistence that his statue be placed in the temple precincts at Jerusalem, presumably to be accorded divine honors. (Yet most of the provinces do not seem to have suffered under Gaius.) These are only a few of his idiosyncracies reported in the sources.

One great difficulty for those around Gaius was his capriciousness, even in reaction to flattery. The sycophants of the court could never be sure what would please him or what might irritate him. A conspiracy headed by Guards officers finally did away with him before he had ruled four years.

Actually, Gaius well illustrates two lessons emphasized and reemphasized in history. First, as has been said above, free institutions cannot exist alongside absolutism. (Individual senators did try to end Gaius' reign but could do nothing without troops.) Second, any such system has as its greatest defect the succession problem: if successors are not chosen by a selection process that in some way relates to the abilities of the various candidates, it is inevitable that at some point a psychopath will end up in control of the government. Of course, one must admit that no governmental structure guarantees that this will not happen.

Claudius (41–54 A.D.)

It is surprising to find that hopes of a restoration of the traditional Republic still persisted in Rome among the upper classes, even after the reigns of Tiberius and Gaius had shown how hopeless an aspiration that was. This was perhaps more desperation than hope, born of years of suppression of the position of these classes. The sudden assassination of Gaius brought the Senate into session to consider what sort of government should follow. Such a body was inherently unable to act swiftly, however, and the decision would not go to the tardy.

Imperial guardsmen, roving about and probably looting, apprehensive because Caligula had been murdered by their own officers, by chance encountered Claudius hiding behind a curtain. This fifty-year-old brother of the famed Germanicus, uncle of the dead Gaius, was a logical candidate for the post of emperor. Perhaps, also, they could persuade him to grant amnesty to the Guards as a whole. They took Claudius, virtually a prisoner, to the Camp. Along the way Claudius encountered a friend, the Jewish prince Herodes Agrippa, who advised him to accept the proffered post.

The question immediately arises, why was Claudius not considered for succession at the death of Augustus or of Tiberius? The answer is that Claudius suffered from a physical disability, some sort of partial paralysis perhaps, which made his head and hands shake at times; he occasionally drooled, and his gait was clumsy. Augustus had not known quite what to do with him. He seemed intelligent enough and could even manage to stand well and make a decent speech in public. But at other times he seemed an embarrassment as a member of the imperial family. He was therefore allowed to hold only minor office and was generally kept out of the public eye. Gaius, though he sometimes made fun of Claudius (he once had him thrown into the Rhine), allowed him to be consul.

Claudius was, nonetheless, given a good education. He studied with the historian Livy and wrote history himself; none of his historical writing remains, but it was not belittled by later writers. He also was much interested in languages: he attempted to add three letters to the Latin alphabet to symbolize sounds not provided for. He wrote of both the history and the language of the Etruscans. Modern scholars would give much to possess these works.

In Claudius' study of history, we may, in fact, find the key to several of his most important policies. He seems to have been much impressed with two theses of Livy. That celebrated historian saw reasons for Rome's greatness in the enlightened treatment of the conquered peoples, Latins and Italians, and in Roman willingness to adopt proven ideas and practices of others. Similarly, Claudius accepted the traditional state but, at the same time, emphasized that change itself was an essential ingredient of it. Claudius seems to have been particularly impressed with the role of Julius Caesar—as well as Augustus—and with Caesar's specific plans.

Following the principles stated by Livy and Caesar's example, Claudius treated the provincials well and interested himself in their problems. He was broadly tolerant in religious matters. Reversing the practice of Augustus, he extended citizenship liberally and even, like Caesar, put some Gauls into the Senate. Caesar had invaded Britain twice and perhaps intended to conquer it; Claudius did conquer it, even joined the expeditionary force himself, and was acclaimed *imperator* a number of times. Caesar intended to build an artificial harbor for Rome at Ostia; Claudius did it, though his engineers attempted to dissuade him because of the enormous expense. Caesar planned to drain Lake Fucinus, around which was valuable farmland that was all but unusable because of the erratic water levels; Claudius did it, again at enormous expense and with only partial success.

Claudius' detractors in antiquity charged that he was dominated by his freedmen and his women. There is some truth in both charges, yet exaggeration also. Claudius attempted to rationalize the central government he found under his charge. Gifted freedmen were put in control of bureaucratic departments. Most important among these freed Greek slaves were Pallas, his financial officer, and Narcissus, his secretary. Perhaps Claudius chose freedmen to run these important departments because he felt he could trust them. Even if senators could have been persuaded to take such posts, the Emperor could hardly have trusted their loyalty to him. After all, the Senate generally had not approved his elevation to the imperial power, and many senators seem to have opposed him as best they could after he was installed. Not surprisingly, numerous senators and other officials were accused of such crimes as treason and executed during his reign.

This apparently well-grounded mistrust of the existing aristocracy may also have bolstered Claudius' view that a healthy state (of the ancestral type, as championed by both Livy and Cicero) required the constant infusion of "new men." Claudius' purging of the Senate lists and introduction of new senators, including Gauls, served not only to bring in new blood but also to remove the threat of dissidents. Claudius in several ways reduced the Senate's power in the provinces, especially in monetary and judicial matters. Yet it is certain that he did not feel he was deliberately destroying the power of the Senate, but rather that he was acting in a traditional and perfectly logical manner.

As for the women in Claudius' life, the charge that they dominated him must have referred primarily to the last two of his four wives, Messalina and Agrippina. Messalina was executed when, it was claimed, she went through with a public "marriage" ceremony with a young patrician named Gaius Silius. Perhaps she did conspire with the latter to get rid of Claudius and take over; but it is just as likely that she lost out to one of Claudius' wily freedmen in a game of power politics. Claudius next married Agrippina the Younger, who was actually his niece, the daughter of Germanicus and the elder Agrippina. There is little doubt that she had a great influence upon the aging Emperor; the succession at his death proves this well enough. Claudius had a son of his own, named Britannicus. But, instead, Agrippina's son by an earlier marriage (to Gnaeus Domitius Ahenobarbus)—Nero— succeeded to the throne, four years after she had persuaded Claudius to adopt him legally.

Nero (54–68 A.D.)

A complex person, Nero has been much maligned—with some justification—by Christians and historians. It is important to remember that he was a sixteen-year-old when he came to power and that he was not yet thirty-one when he died. During much of his life he struggled to assert himself over a dominant mother and strong governmental officials. His was the soul of an artist: he sang, not badly, though his voice was some-

Nero, who at 16 came to power only to have to struggle to assert himself over a dominant mother and strong governmental officials during most of his reign. He was a complex person who has been much maligned—with some justifications —by Christians and historians. (*Alinari-Scala*)

what muffled; he wrote passable poetry; he supported (perhaps initiated) important advances in architecture; he wished for Romans, of both upper and lower classes, to choose concerts over gladiatorial contests. It may be legitimately questioned, however, whether the Emperor ought to have given free rein to the arts at the expense of politics. He was, after all, the chief of state.

Nero's mother Agrippina had got the principate for her son, and expected to serve as a kind of regent, it seems. Here she ran afoul of basic Roman conservatism: women might indeed be emancipated in a sense, but they were not to hold political office or exercise direct political power. Two of Nero's chief ministers, the Stoic philosopher Seneca and the Praetorian Prefect Burrus, contested with Agrippina and gained ascendancy over her son. When Agrippina threatened in veiled fashion to support Claudius' own son Britannicus to replace Nero, the latter had Britannicus poisoned before his mother's face. A few years later, in 59 A.D., Nero had his mother killed also.

The plot to kill Agrippina was an elaborate charade. Both Nero and his mother were at residences on the Bay of Naples. Nero invited her to dinner and, so the sources say, pretended to be reconciled with her. He offered a boat to take her home, across the bay. It had been especially designed to open up suddenly and sink. Unfortunately for the plan, Agrippina escaped, but was killed by the sword when Nero learned of her escape. In justification, he put out a story that she had been conspiring against him. In 62 A.D. Nero divorced his wife Octavia, the daughter of Claudius, and married Poppaea Sabina, previously the wife of his youthful companion Otho, of whom we shall hear more later. A short time after, Octavia was executed on trumped-up charges.

Burrus, who had been a benign influence, died in 62 A.D. After a conspiracy headed by the senator Gaius Calpurnius Piso in 65, Seneca was implicated and forced to commit suicide, along with the poet Lucan and Piso himself. Nero had been playing a freer hand since the death of Agrippina, and now he was free of all earlier restraint. Much of his time was now given over to his art and architecture; increasingly, he performed in public, singing and playing the lyre. Finally he decided on a trip to Greece, where he participated in numerous events at the great games, some of which were held out of the usual cycle to honor his visit. He won all the gold medals, of course, hundreds of them. In gratitude he granted Greece an exemption from all taxation.

Rome was devastated by a great fire in 64 A.D, in which approximately half the city burned. About 160 acres of choice property in the burned-out area near the Forum was selected for Nero's greatest architectural project, the construction of his Domus Aurea ("Golden Palace"). It was to be a lavish country villa in the city, complete with a small lake about where the Colosseum now stands. An elaborate dining room somehow was turned by machinery to show, like the dome of a planetarium, the changes of the constellations; perfume and rose petals could, it was said, be sprinkled down on the guests.

Nero came up with plans for his new palace very quickly after the fire, along with general building regulations designed to make the reconstructed areas less like firetraps. There was nothing wrong with the latter: such safety regulations were much needed. And no one should have objected to Nero's building himself a palace; his old one *had* burned. But the speed of the planning and the grand scale of the new palace—which occupied lands formerly used for private residences—led to a report that Nero himself had set the fire. There seems no good reason to believe that he did. But the Emperor felt it critically important to find the culprits and, after investigation, decided that a new religious sect, the followers of one Christ ("Chrestus," as the historian Tacitus wrote it), was to blame. There was a brief, agonizing persecution, during which many innocent victims paid the penalty for arson, which was death by burning.

This necessarily brief sketch of Nero's reign might give the impression that the years of Nero's ascendancy were chaotic and that Nero himself was a monster. Yet the first claim is mostly wrong, and Nero was much less a monster than some (the Christians, for example) have judged. The provinces were very well governed in Nero's reign; some of those named to important posts were of exceptional caliber. Deprecators of Nero suggest that it was Seneca who made the best selections, but Nero at least approved them. An exception to this generally good picture was Judea, where misrule contributed to the outbreak of violent rebellion in 66 A.D. But the Jews were extraordinarily difficult to govern; the Romans thought their religion mostly atheistic, and the intensity of their devotion to it was beyond the Roman ken.

In Rome, Nero did try to raise the level of popular taste in entertainment. His energetic measures to help private persons rebuild the burned-out areas after the great fire were commendable, as was his new building code. One cannot doubt Nero's sincere devotion to the world of art; but he was chief of state, and such a man must be first of all a politician. Moreover, Nero's psyche troubled him from beginning to end. After Piso's conspiracy, he was frightened and permitted the execution of men who surely were guilty of no more than incurring the disapproval of the Emperor. Such a man was the Stoic Thrasea Paetus, whose silent protests (he walked out of the Senate when Nero's story of his mother's "conspiracy" was being told) at length brought on his condemnation. Thrasea's forced suicide in 66 A.D. wrung from Tacitus the protest that tyrannical emperors were a threat not merely to life but even to simple morality—since anyone whose life was wholly moral seemed to reproach the Emperor by his very example.

Perhaps Nero's greatest mistake was his neglect of the army. He did not inspect his units on the frontiers, and in the crisis that ultimately came, the soldiers showed no particular loyalty to him. Moreover, the officer class was alarmed when Nero forced his greatest general, Gnaeus Domitius Corbulo, to commit suicide in 67 A.D. presumably for implication in a conspiracy.

Another of Nero's mistakes was his extravagance. The wars conducted by Corbulo in the East in connection with Armenia (Rome vied with Parthia for control of this important kingdom), the cost of prolonged rebellions in Britain under Queen Boudicca and in Judea, and the expense of rebuilding Rome were quite costly enough without Nero's grand tour in Greece, an enormously expensive spectacle put on for the son of the Parthian monarch (who consented to be crowned King of Armenia at Rome), and the lavish expenditure on the Domus Aurea. Nero was forced to depreciate the silver coinage and reduce the weight of the gold; this was the first cheapening of the coinage in nearly three centuries. In many of the executions he ordered, Nero had as a secondary motive the confiscation of the property of those condemned.

The conspiracy that was to cost Nero his throne began while he was still away in Greece. A freedman made a dramatic dash to the East to inform Nero; yet the Emperor moved sluggishly, as if not quite sure what to do. Perhaps he did not really believe the threat was great. The first fighting took place in Gaul, where the provincial administrator Julius Vindex attempted to head a rebellion that would replace Nero with Servius Sulpicius Galba, governor of one of the Spanish provinces. However, Verginius Rufus, governor of Upper Germany, defeated Vindex's army. Perhaps Nero now thought the threat to his rule was over. But the revolt spread to Africa. Moreover, Galba could not back down, though he had taken little overt action. In Rome Nero found little support where it counted, among the Praetorian Guards. Promised huge gifts of money by a supporter of Galba, they abandoned Nero, who fled to the countryside near Rome and committed suicide, with the help of a slave. It was June of 68 A.D.

Galba proceeded slowly to Rome, where the Senate accepted him as successor to Nero. The crisis appeared to be over, and with a minimum of fighting.

The Year of the Four Emperors (69 A.D.)

Galba had no ties with the Julio-Claudian family but came of the old nobility. He had to act quickly and wisely if he was to retain the throne. From the beginning, several of the army commanders accepted him only with reluctance. Unfortunately for the new emperor, existing conditions made it difficult to please everyone; moreover, the seventy-three-year-old man did not always act with foresight.

Galba found the imperial finances in terrible condition. He therefore did not pay the Praetorian Guards all that had been promised them. And in attempting to recover money Nero had spent on court favorites, Galba alienated some powerful men who might otherwise have supported him. Attempts to discipline the praetorians and other troops pleased them not at all. Finally, his choice of a second-in-command was extremely important, since he was seventy-three years old—and Galba chose Lucius Calpurnius Piso, an old-line aristocrat, but a man who was not widely acceptable.

The legions in Upper and Lower Germany refused to take the regular New Year's oath to Galba in January of 69 A.D. He had been supported by Verginius Rufus after some hesitation; but then Galba had quickly replaced Rufus, to the disgruntlement of his troops. On January 2, the commander of Lower Germany, Aulus Vitellius, was acclaimed emperor by his troops at their encampment near present-day Cologne. (No doubt he engineered the affair, but the attitude of the troops was crucial.) Quickly the legions of Upper Germany fell in line, and soon other troops in the area joined the crowd.

In Rome, meanwhile, Marcus Salvius Otho, who had at first supported Galba, also led a revolt. Otho, husband of Poppaea until Nero decided he wanted her, had hoped to succeed the elderly Galba. The choice of Piso, coupled with the knowledge that Galba's regime was faltering, decided Otho to act decisively in his own interest. He got the support of the Praetorian Guard and killed Galba in the Forum on January 15.

Otho was curiously inactive in the early weeks of his reign. He apparently assumed the German legions wanted only to get rid of Galba and would support him. Eventually he began, too late, to concentrate troops in northern Italy. In a decisive battle at Bedriacum in April, the forces of Vitellius triumphed. Otho fled and then committed suicide, after having "reigned" just one day more than three months.

Vitellius' reign was to be equally short. He seems to have been remembered chiefly for his gluttony. The sources also tell of enormous extravagance and profligacy. Certainly he failed to maintain discipline in his army.

Once the idea took hold that the legions could be kingmakers, the process was not easily halted. Vitellius had not yet reached Rome (he was still in Germany when his supporters beat Otho's troops) before legions in the East and along the Danube decided to get into the act— prodded, of course, by certain ambitious commanders. Their choice was Titus Flavius Vespasianus, the sixty-year-old commander of the Roman legions besieging Jerusalem against the rebellious Jews.

A legate named Marcus Antonius Primus took the lead in promoting the interests of Vespasian with contingents from the Danubian armies. They marched into northern Italy and, in battles near Cremona, destroyed Vitellius' cause near the same place where it had been won. As Primus moved cautiously on Rome, the Urban Prefect Flavius Sabinus, Vespasian's brother, sought to negotiate with Vitellius for his abdication. But the Guardsmen surrounded Sabinus on the Capitol, defeated his forces, killed him, and burned the Temple of Jupiter Optimus Maximus. Primus arrived, however, and quickly took over the city, put down the praetorians and ended Vitellius' reign. This was on December 21. Mucianus, the governor of Syria who had first encouraged Vespasian to attempt to gain the purple, came to Rome and held it in trust until the new emperor belatedly arrived after some months.

These civil wars had dealt heavy blows to all Italy, especially to the area around Cremona, where several major battles were fought. In such circumstances, the troops were not well disciplined and looting was general; moreover, serious situations cropped up along the frontiers. Mucianus had the luck to pass by with his army as a semibarbarous force attempted to invade from across the Danube, and he put down this threat. In Gaul and Germany a Batavian leader named Julius Civilis, at first pretending to support Vespasian, gathered troops and waged a war of Gallic liberation. The Romans heaved a collective sigh of relief when at last Petillius Cerialis, a relative of Vespasian, succeeded in putting down the revolt of Civilis, and all was peaceful again in the interior of the Empire. After facing the chaos which had accompanied this free-for-all race for power, men of all stripes were ready to support Vespasian as the imperial successor, middle-class plebeian though he was. As usual, security was valued above elusive hopes of greater freedom—except by the Jews and the Gauls.

C. The Flavians

Vespasian (69–79 A.D.)

Before the civil wars Vespasian would have seemed an unlikely candidate for the principate. He was born in Sabine country to an obscure and undistinguished family. He had risen through the ranks in the usual sequence for one of the equestrian order who entered the Senate and was politically successful. He was military tribune, quaestor, aedile, praetor under Gaius, legionary commander in Britain under Claudius, and finally consul. Nero was irritated by Vespasian's habit of going to sleep during the Emperor's public performances, but still chose to make use of his proven abilities as a general when rebellion broke out in Judea in 66 A.D.

In Judea Vespasian commanded three legions plus other units, an aggregation of about 60,000 men. When at length he went on to Rome after his accession was assured, he left the army that was besieging Jerusalem under the command of his son Titus. Titus completed the conquest of Jerusalem and the subjugation of the Jews in 70 A.D. The last pocket of resistance was at Masada, near the Dead Sea, where a few hundred Zealots held out until 73. Titus returned to Rome to a triumph. Jewish prisoners were put to work building the Flavian Amphitheater, later known as the Colosseum.

Vespasian carefully paraded his intention to rule in the manner of Augustus, and his powers paralleled those of the earlier sovereign. But he held the consulship almost every year and exercised the censorial powers much more sweepingly than Augustus had. The latter action was perhaps necessary. Civil war and assassination had depleted the senatorial and equestrian orders, and Vespasian had to fill up their ranks. He seems to have chosen well, for many of the leading men in the next several decades were first given important positions by Vespasian, and even the emperors of the 2nd century were descended from men who first reached high position under his rule.

Vespasian needed political control, in order to prevent a continuing chaotic struggle for power; but he also needed money. He announced that he needed 40,000,000,000 sesterces (the equivalent perhaps of five billion dollars, but such a sum meant much more to the Roman government than it would to ours) to retrieve the economic fortunes of the Empire. He therefore had to invent new taxes and to obtain money in every way possible.

Vespasian thus gained a reputation for stinginess. It was claimed that he sometimes squeezed money out of the populace in disreputable ways. The story is told that he put a tax on buckets of urine from the toilets, collected for use in whitening fabrics. When his son Titus protested, Vespasian stuck a denarius under his nose and said, "This doesn't stink, does it?" In any case, Vespasian did stabilize the economy and was able to reduce taxes before the end of his reign. All the sources agree that he made wise use of the state's income. Some of the money was spent in the construction of probably the best-known structure ever erected, the vast Colosseum, which Romans called the Flavian Amphitheater. It was rather pointedly placed on the site of Nero's artificial lake. Vespasian carefully avoided the odium attached to Nero's Domus Aurea, which he left unfinished. Some scholars think he deliberately blackened Nero's memory before the populace to strengthen his own position.

The provinces were perhaps burdened heavily early in Vespasian's reign because of the great need for money; but provincials had mostly escaped the damage inflicted on Italy during the civil wars. Governors were well chosen, and when wise government brought a return to prosperity, taxes presumably were lowered. In Britain, conquest of new areas was begun at this time. Along the frontiers of the upper Rhine and the Danube, new boundaries made for a more defensible line.

The Flavians—especially Vespasian and Domitian—had their troubles with philosophers, just as Nero had. Both Stoics and Cynics criticized Vespasian. They did not feel that the civil strife had turned up the ideal "best man." The imperial biographer Suetonius relates that the Emperor took their criticisms in good humor; however, Vespasian finally did exile most of the philosophers. One of the chief Stoics, Helvidius Priscus, was banished and later executed; but Suetonius says Vespasian regretted his decision and sent a messenger to countermand the earlier order—unfortunately, he arrived too late. One wonders about the truth of this affair. It would not be at all astonishing if a *novus homo* like Vespasian was more vulnerable to criticism than Suetonius thought. Suetonius tells, also, of a time when Vespasian passed a Cynic who railed bitterly at him; the Emperor reached down, patted his head, and said, "Good dog." (The Greek word for Cynic derives from the word for dog.) Vespasian, though not an intellectual himself, was not anti-intellectual. He was the first to put professors of Latin and Greek on the state payroll.

Among other stories told of Vespasian's redeeming sense of humor was the one that when he was about to die he said, "Ah, me, I think I'm about to become a god!" Hereditary succession was Vespasian's definite plan, and his eldest son succeeded him with no difficulty.

Titus (79–81 A.D.)

Titus, handsome and congenial, was less like a plebeian masquerading as a king than his father was, from the aristocratic point of view. He was popular, so his accession was an occasion for joy. But his short reign was bedeviled by three great disasters: a plague worse than any in recent memory carried off many; there was another great fire in Rome; and Vesuvius, which had emitted preliminary warning shocks for years, erupted with devastating effect. Everyone knows of the resulting burial of the cities Pompeii and Herculaneum. Several villas and farmhouses also disappeared, and at Naples (Neapolis) volcanic ash lay knee-deep in the streets. It is ironic that this event, for so many a great misfortune, has been a boon for modern students of the ancient world. Archaeological excavations at these sites have turned up rich and graphic remains, some of which will be discussed in another chapter.

Titus was not so thrifty as his father, and perhaps his judgment was not so sound. Perhaps, also, the sources would have praised him less if he had lived longer. His untimely death brought to power his younger brother Domitian, who probably was no less competent but who was much less attractive personally.

Domitian (81–96 A.D.)

Ancient historians and Christian apologists cast Domitian in the same mold as Gaius and Nero—no doubt, with some justification. Domitian, apparently, did intend to rule as an absolute monarch and did, therefore, have relationships with the Senate that fell below the ideal. Perhaps the Emperor was marked psychologically as the consequence of a long-standing unfavorable comparison with his more handsome and popular older brother. This may perhaps explain the suspicion, cunning, and cruelty the sources emphasize among his traits.

Yet the sources also make it quite clear that Domitian was intelligent and that he gave meticulous attention to affairs of state, especially in choosing provincial governors and other officials. The researches of modern scholars have generally borne out the truth of this information. Domitian vigorously countered threats to the Empire's frontiers and even led his armies personally in campaigns in southern Germany and along the Danube. He permanently strengthened the military units in those areas. In general, the Empire enjoyed good government during his reign.

Domitian exalted his own position and liked to be addressed as Dominus et Deus ("Lord and God"). Like his father, he had trouble with the philosophers and exiled them. He put numerous senators to death for various reasons. Christians seem to have been persecuted because they did not consider themselves Jews—as Domitian regarded them—and therefore did not pay the double-drachma tax Vespasian had imposed on all Jews. At least that is what must have initiated the investigation that led to the Christian persecutions, which were spotty and not on an empire-wide scale.

In the executions of senators Domitian was not altogether at fault. There is no evidence of such purges in the early years of his rule. In later years he was frightened and angered by conspiracies against his life—fears that were real enough. Thus it is reasonable to conclude that Domitian was less the cruel egomaniac than a very human individual thrust unexpectedly into power and forced into cunning cruelty by urgent motives: his life depended on it.

The world will doubtless go on remembering Suetonius' story of Domitian sitting alone and engaging in one of his favorite pastimes: catching flies and stabbing them with his stylus, or plotting the death of someone who dared to utter even mild criticism of the Dominus. The final conspiracy that did away with the last of the Flavians, murdered in his bedroom, included even Domitian's wife. It was done with little planning for the future, and the result might have been another chaotic clash of arms like that of 68–69, except for the wiser and quicker action of the Senate and then of its candidate, Nerva, one of their own.

D. The "Good Emperors"

Nerva (96–98 A.D.)

Though he ruled but sixteen months, Nerva deserves his classification as one of the "Good Emperors," as he and the four who succeeded him were called. His attitude was one of tolerance in peripheral matters and firmness in important ones. He put no senator to death and, indeed, took an oath not to do so except upon trial by peers. He treated the ruling classes with respect and consulted the Senate often.

Nerva also started the practice of setting up institutions called *alimenta* for rearing and educating poor children, especially orphan boys. Following a procedure already developed by private benefactors, he used public money to establish trust funds in various towns in Italy. The money, controlled locally, was loaned to area landowners at a low rate of interest, and the income derived from it supported the children. Girls were sometimes supported in this way, too. The purpose was partly simple benevolence and partly a desire to keep Italy populated with young men available to the military. A secondary benefit may have resulted in some instances, when landowners got capital needed for improvements on their land. But since these loans were not repayable and became a permanent obligation on the land, this does not appear to have been a major purpose of the *alimenta*. Indeed, it is probable that the landowners may sometimes have been required to accept such loans.

In another most important way, Nerva also set the pattern for the "Good Emperors": he was childless and chose his successor wisely and well. It was important to conciliate the army in the choice and, of course, to choose a capable man. Nerva's choice was Trajan.

Trajan (98–117 A.D.)

Trajan came of an old Roman family that had long since migrated to Spain, where the future emperor was born in 53 A.D., in a colony called Italica. His father, Marcus Ulpius, was the first of the family to reach the consulship, under Vespasian, who also gave the family patrician status (a practice begun by Julius Caesar). Trajan had long years of army service, in positions ranging from military tribune to commander, and had much administrative experience also. He came well recommended to the imperial office.

It is interesting to compare the power exercised by Trajan with that of Nero or Domitian. Trajan was no less the absolute monarch; in fact, since Nero was so engrossed with his art, it is likely that Trajan supervised the whole structure of the Empire more closely than Nero. The differences lay in manner and method: Trajan was considerate, diplomatic, tolerant to a point. A number of his letters, preserved for us in the published collection of letters belonging to the younger Pliny, show that he made careful judgments, phrased economically but not bluntly. He put no senators to death—but then, he did not need to. He was called *optimus princeps,* possibly with the agreement even of the philosophers.

Trajan is particularly remembered for his military conquests and for his building achievements. His greatest projects were concentrated in Rome and elsewhere in Italy. His new forum, which completed the row of imperial fora begun by Augustus, was the largest, most magnificent, and most useful of all—except perhaps the oldest, which is always referred to simply as "the Forum." Colonnades, a basilica (for court use), a temple, and two libraries, Latin and Greek, made up his forum proper. Trajan's famous column stood between the libraries. On the side, fronting on outer streets, was a shopping area with stalls on three to four levels. Trajan also built an aqueduct into the city and a magnificent new harbor area at Ostia. Other harbor facilities, roads, and bridges improved the communications network of the peninsula. A less ambitious program of construction (aqueducts, public buildings, and the like) was undertaken in the provinces.

Trajan's wars of conquest were conducted primarily north of the Danube in Dacia (approximately, modern Rumania) and in the Near East. King Decebalus of the Dacians had presented problems on the Danube frontier for some years. In 90 A.D., Domitian had come to an agreement that involved regular subsidy payments to the Dacian ruler by Rome. Perhaps, in return, Decebalus actually performed some service beneficial to Rome. This mutual accord might have continued without war, but Decebalus made attacks on a Roman ally, and Trajan seems to have ended the arrangement. In two wars, in 100–101 and 105–106 A.D., he defeated Decebalus and made an imperial province of Dacia. At the beginning of the second campaign, Trajan built a bridge across the Danube, designed by a Syrian architect named Apollodorus, who also designed his forum. Some of its stone pylons remain, though the wooden superstructure was not left in place for long. The spiraling relief sculpture of the Column of Trajan, with its astonishing detail, helps to make up for a deficiency of literary sources not merely for the Dacian campaigns but also for the whole of Trajan's reign.

A major war in the East against the Parthians (114–117 A.D.) occupied most of Trajan's final years. Here he was again successful and conquered all of Mesopotamia. The Sinai Peninsula had also been occupied and became a province, Arabia Petraea. But Trajan had over-extended the Empire, and his successor found it necessary to retrench.

Near the end of the Emperor's life, a revolt of the Jews of the Diaspora (Dispersion; i.e., outside Palestine) brought new and unexpected problems. Antisemitism and Jew-baiting, unfortunately, are not only problems of the modern world. To polytheists, Jews seemed not only peculiar but, at times, a dissident sect who were a positive danger to established religious institutions and beliefs. At this point (116 A.D.) the goaded Jews lashed out fanatically and killed indiscriminant in Cyprus, Egypt, Cyrene, and Mesopotamia. It was claimed a million persons were slaughtered. Trajan put a general named Lusius Quietus in command of pacifying forces, and the inevitable operations that would in turn slaughter Jews began.

Trajan died rather unexpectedly in 117, as he was planning to return to Rome. Oddly, he had not yet named a successor; he was sixty-four and perhaps expected to live longer. It was announced that on his deathbed he had named his kinsman Hadrian his successor. Hadrian was a second cousin, had married Trajan's grand-niece, and had been given preferment. Yet Trajan must in some way have mistrusted him, not to have taken formal action. It was rumored that Trajan's wife Plotina, loved Hadrian, who was about her age, and that she with accomplices fabricated the "adoption." We cannot learn the truth, but in fact there seems to have been no other likely choice.

Hadrian (117–138 A.D.)

Though the new emperor had no real rival and the army supported him, the circumstances surrounding his accession were embarrassing. He had to make tough decisions quickly; there was no time to write courteously to the Senate and wait for a reply before assuming the imperial purple. The Jewish war still blazed, and the Parthian unrest was far from ended. Hadrian therefore took the supreme command and sent an apology to the Senate afterward. There were disturbances in Britain and North Africa and the threat of invasion along the Danube frontier.

Because of the manner of his "adoption" and because of the execution of four senators, Hadrian got off to a bad start in his relationship with the Senate. The praetorian prefect Attianus claimed to have sniffed out a conspiracy against Hadrian on the part of four consulars, including Lusius Quietus. The four accused were executed before Hadrian's arrival back in Rome. According to the Emperor, this was done without his knowledge and consent, but apparently not all senators believed his story. Hadrian did take an oath not to put senators to death.

Quick action by his subordinates ended the difficulties in the various parts of the Empire, and Hadrian made what must have been an unpopular decision: to withdraw from much of the Mesopotamian territories so recently conquered by Trajan. He retained some of these lands, however, enough to control several important trade routes, as well as Arabia Petraea and Dacia. One might say that Trajan had prevented serious trouble in the outposts of the Empire by his aggressive campaigning; but probably Hadrian was right in withdrawing from the most exposed, poorly defensible conquests. Trajan had overextended the imperial forces and resources. Elsewhere on the frontiers Hadrian adopted a similarly defensive stance. He built up the fortifications (*limes*) along the line connecting the Rhine and the Danube. In Britain, he built the celebrated wall across the island at a narrow stretch and abandoned the expansionary policies of his predecessor.

Still, it must not be thought that Hadrian was uninterested in military matters. Though he used the army little in actual war, he visited and inspected his legions even on the frontiers, put them through difficult maneuvers, and devised field exercises so effective that they were still standard a century later. His ancient biographer declares that this high state of military preparedness helped Hadrian to preserve peace.

In matters relating to the law and the judiciary, Hadrian brought about several innovations. He added salaried jurisconsults (*jurispru-*

Hadrian's mausoleum; in modern times known as the Castel Sant 'Angelo. Intended not just for Hadrian, but for use as an imperial tomb for many years. (*Italian Government Travel Office*)

dentes) to his council (the *consilium principis* initiated under Augustus), which under him became a more precisely organized and useful body. The opinions of the imperial jurisconsults naturally carried more authority than those of even the great lawyers who headed the unofficial schools of law. The Praetorian Prefect, who for a long time had been more than mere commander of the Praetorian Guard, was empowered to function more specifically as Hadrian's agent in judicial matters, especially in appeals. Hadrian also devised a more rational organization for the courts system in Italy: the peninsula was divided into four judicial districts, each administered by a new official chosen from among the consulars.

This latter change seemed to the senators to reduce their own power, even though the new magistrates were consulars (and hence senators, too), since the Emperor's role was thereby enlarged. Importuned by the Senate, Hadrian's successor Antoninus Pius rescinded this system, but Marcus Aurelius later restored it. The greater power of the praetorian prefects also meant a reduced role for the Senate. While this change was doubtless more efficient, because of the careful selection for the prefecture of men who were thoroughly competent in the law, this innovation irritated the Senate as well.

Hadrian's relations with the Senate, thus, were generally less serene than Trajan's had been. There were the dubious executions early in his reign, but other reasons for the abrasiveness of the relationship are more difficult to establish. Hadrian was a very complex personality, handsome, witty, and urbane; yet one should keep in mind that he, like Trajan, came from Italica in southern Spain. When as quaestor he gave his first speech before the Senate in 101 A.D., he was laughed at for his provincial accent. Perhaps, despite his sophistication, he felt that the capital's aristocrats looked down on him. Certainly he was never very fond of the city of Rome.

It is possible, also, to find some unattractive traits to remark about Hadrian. He was perhaps the first emperor to use the *frumentarii*—army commissaries—as a kind of secret police. He could hold a grudge. He rather overdid the glorification, and indeed deification, of his favorite young man Antinöus, after the latter drowned in the Nile. Yet the more attractive aspects of his personality seem to outbalance the rest by far.

Perhaps the most traveled of all the emperors to his time, Hadrian spent over half his reign away from the capital. He traveled in most of the provinces, and everywhere he went he inspected troops and military installations and also left practical tokens of his benevolence. Aqueducts, temples, and other public buildings arose quickly in the wake of his visits. Athens especially was the object of his largesse. There he built an entire new city, called Hadrianopolis (the gateway bearing this name still stands) in which he completed the huge Temple of

Zeus Olympius, which had been under construction intermittently since the time of Peisistratus (6th century B.C.). Some of the best-preserved monuments in Rome date from Hadrian's reign. These include his imposing mausoleum (called Castel Sant' Angelo since the Middle Ages), which he constructed because the Mausoleum of Augustus, across the Tiber, was by then full; the Pantheon, originally built by Agrippa (and attributed to him even after its complete reconstruction in this period); and the Temple of Venus and Roma, the remains of which are best seen from high atop the Colosseum. (A Christian church of considerable size now occupies less than half the original temple.)

One of Hadrian's building projects was ill-advised. He attempted to erect a pagan city, called Aelia Capitolina, on the site of ancient Jerusalem, which had suffered much destruction at the hands of the Romans, 70 A.D. The result was yet another rebellion of the Jews (132–135 A.D.), led by Bar Kochba ("Son of the Star"). Believing to the last that God would deliver them from the overwhelming power of Rome, the Jews suffered another, more enduring disaster; Palestine became almost depopulated of Jews. The Christian tradition, on the other hand, holds that under Hadrian all persecution ceased, by order of the enlightened Emperor.

Hadrian built almost a complete city as his residence at Tivoli, a few miles east of Rome at the foot of the Alban Hills. Modern tourists never cease to be amazed at the extensive ruins, which include two theaters, baths, and temples. This was somehow conceived as a showplace symbolizing the sprawling Empire. In one area symbolizing Egypt, for example, were a pool, a temple to Egyptian deities, and statuary representing the Nile. Other areas perhaps symbolized other provinces, and there was a large-scale mosaic map of the entire Empire. Perhaps Hadrian's Villa, as this summer residence is called, best epitomizes Hadrian the Emperor: he was not, narrowly speaking, a Roman but rather a cosmopolitan; he intended to be not merely a Roman dominating the known world but the unifier of that world. Hence his ambitious travels, his lavish benefices—and also, his bad relations with the less-broad-minded senators.

Hadrian, too, had no son to name as his heir. He not only adopted his immediate successor but attempted to make arrangements determining the man who would follow his adopted heir in the next generation as well.

Antoninus Pius (138–161 A.D.)

Hadrian chose his successors well—though Antoninus was his second, not his first choice. Antoninus Pius seems to have been a paragon of a ruler. The ancient evidence contains no hint of weakness or incapacity, nothing at all unfavorable. Part of the reason for Antoninus' popularity in Rome was his reversal of Hadrian's pan-imperial policies. This emperor stayed in Rome and showed his love of the city and of Italy in many ways (though his family had for some years lived at Nîmes, in what is today southern France). Moreover, Antoninus often consulted with and deferred to the Senate. Hadrian had, in some significant ways, reduced the functions of that body, such as in the judicial administration of Italy. Antoninus changed back to the older system. Hadrian's continual absences often meant taking important decisions without consulting large numbers of senators. Antoninus still had his consilium of advisers, only part of them senators, but he used the whole body much more frequently than his predecessor had.

Despite this emphasis on the Senate and on Rome itself, there is no indication that under Antoninus the provinces suffered in any way. He chose excellent governors, who served long terms. Existing evidence, partly archaeological and partly literary, indicates general satisfaction with his regime, and implies general prosperity as well, in the provinces. A rhetorician of Greek descent from Asia Minor, Aelius Aristides, delivered an oration in Rome during Antoninus' reign that told flatteringly of how, under the "Good Emperors," the world was well governed. Educated men like him could feel they were part of the governing class, even though they were not of Roman stock.

An outstanding feature of Antoninus' rule was his careful economy in ordinary expenses of government and his quick liberality in crises. He responded as swiftly with funds for earthquake-stricken Rhodes as for Rome when another fire burned down a portion of the city. Following earlier practice, Antoninus assiduously established *alimenta* for the rearing and education of orphans. To the modern mind, it must seem that no man could be so perfect as Antoninus is reputed to have been; somehow, there must have been feet of clay. Well, perhaps so; but the ancient authors were usually quick to report scandal and weakness. In this instance they did not.

Marcus Aurelius (161–180 A.D.)

It was Hadrian who had made Marcus Aurelius successor to Antoninus, when he insisted that the latter adopt Marcus, along with his cousin Lucius Verus, who ruled jointly with Marcus until his death in 169 A.D. Marcus, who had been preferred by Antoninus and who had married the Emperor's daughter Faustina, was clearly the dominant partner from the beginning.

Marcus Aurelius has been acclaimed as the sort of philosopher-king Plato dreamed of. This extraordinary man, born into a consular

Marcus Aurelius as a rather young ruler; denarius.

family long-resident in southern Spain, received the best education that 2nd-century Rome afforded. The finest teachers of law, rhetoric, and philosophy were found to instruct him. Best known among these was the rhetorician Marcus Cornelius Fronto, who remained the young man's close friend and correspondent for many years—even after the emperor-to-be had abandoned rhetoric in favor of Stoicism, which became the dominant intellectual influence of his adult life.

The Stoic who influenced young Marcus most strongly seems to have been the Greek Epictetus, who had begun study as a slave before he was freed by his Roman master, a freedman of Nero. Later he was exiled by Domitian, who like his father Vespasian had troubles with an opposition group led by certain philosophers (though probably not including Epictetus). The slave-become-philosopher finished out his life teaching in Epirus. Marcus Aurelius was only twelve or so at the philosopher's death and apparently never met him; but Epictetus' lectures, taken down by disciples and widely disseminated, were available to him. Epictetus emphasized that the individual's happiness lies within his own control; he must not permit anything outside himself, even though it may appear bad, to make him unhappy.

As his *Meditations* clearly show, Marcus Aurelius was a Stoic of the highest level, a high-minded man who wanted only to meet his obligations as an emperor should. His personal ethics were above reproach. Duty, for him, was in Stoic manner almost a religious concept. He was competent both in administration, especially in choosing subordinates, and also in military matters and the law. It has often been said he had only two faults: namely, he arranged for his son to succeed him, and he permitted—even endorsed—a persecution of Christians. To these might be added a third shortcoming: upon his succession, and occasionally afterward, he distributed too much money to the army, which gradually was becoming the kind of dominant and elitist force that in the not-too-distant future would take over the Empire as its right.

It is ironic that Marcus Aurelius, the man of peace, had to fight almost continuous wars. Perhaps Antoninus had given too little attention to diplomacy and the frontiers in the later years of his reign. Trouble with the Parthians began, as usual, over Armenia. In 162 A.D. the situation developed into a major war, and Lucius Verus was sent off to wage it. Victory was eventually achieved, but at considerable cost. Lucius seems to have been much given to luxury and ease, and the victories in the East were chiefly the work of Avidius Cassius, consular governor of Syria. It is generally agreed that when Lucius died in 169, leaving Marcus in sole charge of the Empire, the whole Roman world benefited.

Major wars had to be fought in the north along the Danube in the early 170's and again at the end of Marcus's reign. Marcomanni, Sarmatians, Jazyges, and others invaded across the Danube; some reached Aquileia, at the head of the Adriatic, and others penetrated far into Greece. Marcus himself, accompanied by his family, commanded this war, which was also waged successfully by the Romans. Marcus campaigned far north of the Danube and apparently intended to create new provinces as far north as the Baltic. This would have shortened Rome's northern frontiers, and might have affected the later history of the barbarian invasions. There were, besides, Moorish incursions into southern Spain and trouble in Britain. Moreover, in 175 A.D. the Syrian governor Avidius Cassius, whom Marcus had thought his friend, rebelled—perhaps because of a rumor that Marcus had been killed. Though Avidius controlled much of the Eastern Empire for a time, his revolt eventually collapsed without any major counter measures by Marcus, and the would-be emperor was killed, probably by his own subordinates.

Beyond the travail of war and the sadness of Cassius' abortive attempt to claim the throne, Marcus and the Empire reeled under a series of natural disasters. In the very first year of his reign terrible floods on the Tiber destroyed property on an unprecedented scale and brought on famine. The army that came back in triumph from the eastern wars brought with it the plague. Epidemic at certain times and places, the disease remained endemic and sporadically destructive of life for several years after. Estimates of the losses in human life run as high as a third of the entire population of the Empire. Even though this figure seems too high, there is no doubt that Rome never quite recovered from this grave blow.

Manpower shortages, especially in the military and in the important field of agriculture, were facts of life for every Roman emperor from this time on. As a result, more and more barbarous or semibarbarous units were used in the Roman army. Such groups were often encouraged to settle on vacant land inside the boundaries of the Empire; but they did not always settle down peacefully in their assigned spots. When an earthquake destroyed Smyrna, Marcus helped to rebuild it, at great cost.

Continual war and disaster bore down hard on the treasury. Despite the personal thriftiness of the Emperor, he was often hard-put to keep cash in the state coffers. He even resorted to an auction of some of the prized possessions of the imperial household. The symbolism of this act may have been even more important than the money involved. The coinage seems to show a progressive economic decline—and not just in Marcus's reign. The silver denarius had been gradually cheapened since the time of Nero, until by the end of Marcus's rule the silver content of this coin was only about 60 percent of what it had been under Augustus. It is likely, however, that this depreciation in part reflects a rise in the relative price of silver itself.

The persecution of Christians came in two periods, chiefly in the mid-160's and again about ten years later. The first persecution, in which Justin was martyred, reflects the troubled period of the plague; Christians, with their "atheism" (i.e., from the prevailing viewpoint), may have been held responsible for the anger of the gods. The second persecution, centered about Lugdunum (Lyons) in Gaul, was the result of local zeal against men marked as criminals merely by their professed religion and was a side effect—no doubt unexpected—of an imperial decree. Marcus, in attempting to take a heavy financial burden off the upper classes in the Empire, decreed that criminals might be used in place of trained slaves in the wild-animal baiting in public games. Marcus also seems to have believed the lurid stories of incest and child cannibalism that were widely told of Christians. Again, the great irony: here was an emperor whose concern for justice made him sit long hours in court and who made some landmark decisions, noted for their humanity. Yet he persecuted Christians without investigating the century-old false charges laid against them.

Marcus died in Vindobona (Vienna), while still on campaign. He had already made the arrangements that put the empire into the hands of his son Commodus. This was perhaps Marcus' worst decision, but he could have made a different one only if he were willing to kill his own son—too great a sacrifice to expect of any fond father.

E. The Empire at Its Height: A Look Back

Administration

Despite the idiosyncracies of some emperors, occasional injustice, and a series of disasters, the Roman Empire in the first two centuries must be accounted a resounding success. One does not expect perfection in the imperfect worlds that human beings fashion for themselves. Most inhabitants of the Empire lived out their lives in relative peace, with a fair degree of prosperity and little interference from the central government. True, the general emphasis was on security rather than freedom, but there was at least a modicum of each.

Local levels of government—city-state forms to the east and tribal forms to the west (but with gradual urbanization in the west also)—flourished vigorously. Yet there was an inevitable centralizing tendency in the interest of uniformity, and sometimes in the interest of the local residents. Provincial governors found it necessary to intervene in local affairs, often for financial reasons. In Trajan's reign, the younger Pliny found communities in his province of Bithynia that had vastly overextended their financial commitments for public works, sometimes illplanned. The tendency, which was to be more marked in future years, could already be observed for the local ruling classes to be forced more and more into service of the central state—as in collecting taxes and providing for the army's manpower needs—at the expense of local matters.

Provincial governors, whether legates of the Emperor, senatorial proconsuls, or Egyptian prefects, were now better chosen than in the last century of the Republic. They served longer terms, were salaried, and were much less likely to attempt to squeeze a fortune out of the provincials in a quick two-year tour of duty. They were much more closely supervised from Rome. They also referred many more local questions to the Emperor than provincial governors in the Republic had referred to the Senate. The consequence of these trends, again, was centralization: policy decisions were made at Rome, and important matters of detail were also decided by the Princeps or by his staff.

Augustus' household officials had functioned well enough as a staff, and he had extensively used a kind of cabinet of senators and others (*consilium principis*). Claudius put great power into the hands of a few freedmen and organized what in retrospect is considered the beginnings of a bureaucracy, a civil service. Hadrian made equestrians heads of the departments Claudius founded, and by his time the volume of work handled by the expanded bureaucracy was tremendous. Again the result was better administration, but also more centralization. As always, a civil service provided continuity in administration and organization along rational lines; yet, again as always, an extensive civil service meant that even an active and good emperor could influence the direction of the government less completely than before, could less satisfactorily implement any changes in policy.

Society

Already in the time of Augustus, Rome was a world empire and not the conquered property of a single city-state in western Italy. By the end of the period discussed here, this was even more markedly true.

The gradual extension of the citizenship and integration of the upper classes everywhere into the governmental structure helped make it so. The Christian apostle Paul, who was a Roman citizen, felt the universality of the Empire; his writings reflect his admiration for the universal state. In the 2nd century, Aelius Aristides of Smyrna in Asia Minor, as remarked above, could feel that Rome was in a sense his as well. Some few members of these upper classes, especially from Hellenized areas, even made their way into the highest imperial offices.

The lot of the lower classes in the Empire was surely less happy. The demands of the state for manpower, the natural heavy labor of agriculture, and wages that never rose much above subsistence level, in part because of slavery, all tended to depress the conditions of lower-class life. The plague during Marcus Aurelius' reign, of course, much accentuated the manpower shortages. Only a dramatic rise in general productivity through improved agricultural practices and through changes in other forms of production could have saved the situation for the lower classes—and, ultimately, for the Empire. These increases and improvements, generally speaking, never came.

An upper class with too much of privilege and money, a lower class kept at subsistence level, and lack of innovation in agricultural and other production meant, inevitably, that the Empire never developed a middle class of any size. Although there were the merchants and traders to produce and ship the pottery and other goods the society required, not enough of the small business owners and entrepreneurs prospered to make any real impact on the social and economic fiber of the state. Rome remained more a *two*-class than a *three*-class society. This division shows up in a tendency in law during the 2nd century and after: litigants in court were increasingly classified as *honestiores* and *humiliores* (actually, though not literally, upper-class and lower-class), with differing legal principles and penalties applying to each group.

Economy

The implications of the preceding paragraph for the economy are obvious—as are those of the demands of the central government for men and money, to fight the recurring wars in the east and north and to keep the upper classes in the style to which they had become accustomed. Then, too, there were the unfortunate consequences of the plague and the other natural disasters mentioned. Add to this an unfavorable balance of trade, the result of the shipment of large quantities of silver and gold to the East, especially to India, in exchange for silks and other luxuries. A gradually deteriorating economy was the inexorable consequence of all these factors.

Quite significant, also, was the economic deterioration at the central core of the Empire, in considerable part owing to commercial competition from the newer and richer provincial territories. Italy, which during the early Empire had shipped pottery (especially the famed red Arretine ware) all over the West, along with fine glassware and various metal items, gradually lost out to the increased provincial competition, particularly from Spain and Gaul. Imitations of Italian products soon began to be imported even into Italy itself. Commodities imported on a massive scale included not only grain, which had been imported in sizeable quantity for centuries, but also oil, wine, pungent fish sauce, and other foodstuffs. Italy held up financially, to some degree, because it was the center of government, and taxes and other moneys tended to flow toward the center. It has been said that imperial Rome exported government and imported everything else. While this exaggerates the case, it was decidedly not a healthy situation economically.

This gradual economic decline was masked during the 2nd century by the careful, thrifty policies of the "Good Emperors." Ideally, a long period of peace coupled with rule by a continued succession of wise emperors might have retrieved this worsening situation; but neither peace nor wise leadership lay in Rome's future.

Books for Further Reading

BALSDON, J., *The Emperor Gaius (Caligula)*, Oxford, 1934.

BALSDON, J., *Roman Women*, London, 1962.

BIRLEY, A., *Marcus Aurelius*, London, 1966.

BUCHAN, J., *Augustus*, London, 1937.

EARL, D. C., *The Age of Augustus*, New York, 1968.

GRANT, M., *Nero*, New York, 1970.

HAMMOND, M., *The Antonine Monarchy*, Rome, 1959.

HENDERSON, B. W., *The Life and Principate of the Emperor Hadrian*, London, 1923.

HENDERSON, B. W., *Five Roman Emperors*, Cambridge, 1927.

JONES, A. H. M., *Studies in Roman Government and Law*, New York, 1960.

MacMULLEN, R., *Enemies of the Roman Order*, Cambridge, Mass., 1966.

MARSH, F. B., *The Reign of Tiberius*, Oxford, 1931.

OGILVIE, R. M., *The Romans and their Gods in the Age of Augustus*, New York, 1970.

ROWELL, H., *Rome in the Augustan Age*, Norman, Okla., 1962.

SALMON, E. T., *A History of the Roman World, Thirty B.C. to A.D. 138*, 6th ed., London, 1968.

STEVENSON, G H., *Roman Provincial Administration*, Oxford, 1939.

SYME, R., *The Roman Revolution*, Oxford, 1939.

WARMINGTON, B. H., *Nero: Reality and Legend*, New York, 1970.

WATSON, G. R., *The Roman Soldier*, Ithaca, 1969.

Literature, Life, and Culture of Ancient Rome

19

The true greatness of Latin literature lies in its wide and enduring influence. Centuries after the fall of Rome, even into modern times, Latin remained the language of culture and scholarship in the Western world. Ecclesiastical documents and many doctoral theses were written in Latin as recently as the present century. Works in Latin were widely available and widely read for centuries, especially in the Renaissance period, and were correspondingly influential—often more influential than works of Greek literature that in scope were of greater value—because the Latin texts were more easily read. Plautus and Terence, though themselves imitators of the Greek "New Comedy," became lasting models for comedy, as Seneca was the model for tragedy, especially in Elizabethan England. Many generations of men learned the periodic, rhythmic style of Cicero or, perhaps when tastes changed, strove to imitate Caesar's lucid prose or affected the clipped, concise style of Tacitus. Countless aspiring poets have studied the stately meter of Vergil, the kindly satire of Horace, the lyrics of Catullus, the epigrams of Martial, and the biting sarcasm of Juvenal. As in so many past eras, literate persons today are at least aware of the most important works of Latin literature; literary people know them well, historians and other scholars pore over them carefully, and a surprisingly large number of people still read them for pleasure and intellectual profit.

The development of Latin literature was fairly steady—except for occasional lapses that marked periods of actual armed conflict—from the "Age of Cicero" to its full flowering in the early Augustan period, often termed the "Golden Age" of Latin literature. Then followed another period, extending well into the 2nd century A.D., called the "Silver Age." Thereafter, the quality of Latin literature waned rapidly.

A. The Age of Cicero

Marcus Tullius Cicero (106–43 B.C.) obviously was the greatest writer of the period named for him. In the two millennia since his death, his reputation has varied widely. Long praised extravagantly for political acumen that does not now seem so penetrating, and admired for a philosophical depth that was merely a restatement of Greek predecessors, Cicero later was condemned bitterly as a political opportunist and a borrower of ideas. In recent years, however, an interpretation both more sympathetic and realistic has presented him as a humane person who was out of place among the "direct action" politicians and generals of his day. His enduring greatness rests chiefly on his work of molding the Latin language and in his influence upon Western intellectuals through the centuries.

Cicero's writings fall into three categories: orations, philosophical treatises, and letters. Carefully composed with measured periods and deliberate cadences, the orations are still studied as examples of speechmaking but are now valued chiefly as historical source material. The texts were edited, and sometimes published well after the speeches themselves were actually delivered; in view of this, they sometimes represent what the orator wished he had said or intended to say, rather than what he did say.

His philosophical writings, such as the *Tusculan Disputations* (a stoical dialogue on virtue and happiness), the *Academica* (a treatise on theories of knowledge), and several others, were not represented as works of original scholarship. What Cicero did was to create a Latin vocabulary that could express Greek ideas, and he presented those ideas in ways understandable to the practical Roman. Several of Cicero's essays, however, were contributions of originality: among these, *De Legibus* ("On the Laws"); *De Re Publica* ("On the State"), a dialogue on ideal forms of government and statesmanly qualities recalling Plato's *Republic;* and several works on oratory. These are, of course, also of great value to the historian.

It is Cicero's numerous letters, however, which are most important to history. They are like brilliant windows through which one sees the real Cicero and also gets an intimate view of Rome and of many important Romans, including the great Caesar. Their scenes are sometimes indistinct, and tantalizing allusions are left unexplained, but without this collection of more than seven hundred letters our knowledge of the Rome of the eventful period from about 65 B.C. to his death in 43 B.C. would be much more obscure.

Another work notable for its historical as well as literary value is Caesar's chief contribution to Latin letters, *Commentaries on the Gallic War,* written in a concise, straightforward, effective prose. The work, which recounts Caesar's conquests north to the Rhine between 58 and 50 B.C., was admired by Cicero, who also praised the dictator's speeches, only fragments of which are extant. Like the *Commentaries on the Civil War* which followed (only part of which was written by Caesar), this personal memoir was at once a history, a literary work, and an astute piece of propaganda, as a defense of the Roman leader's own actions.

A notable historian of the Ciceronian age was Sallust (Gaius Sallustius Crispus c. 86–35 B.C.). A not-very-successful politician who became a partisan of Caesar, he somehow grew rather rich (some say by extortion while a provincial governor in North Africa) and in semiretirement turned to writing history. He produced an account of the Jugurthan War, another of the conspiracy of Catiline, and a *History* (only fragments remain), dealing with the second quarter of the 1st century B.C. Sallust disliked the oligarchs, his political opponents who dominated the nobility. Perhaps he overemphasized the venality of upper-class Romans and their unbridled ambition, but his moralizing was thoroughly Roman—it set something of a vogue—and his prejudices were fairly well hidden. In style he archaized, perhaps imitating the elder Cato; in structure he followed the great Greek historian Thucydides. Sallust is a most important source for a period made difficult for modern historians because of the loss of other works produced at that time, noteworthy among these the memoirs of Sulla.

The Ciceronian age produced two poets of consequence whose works have survived. Titus Lucretius Carus (c. 94–55 B.C.), a convinced Epicurean, wrote his lengthy poem *De Rerum Natura* ("On the Nature of Things") to teach that philosophy. Readers are often amazed at the apparently modern ideas set forth in this outstanding didactic poem. For example, it describes an atomic theory of the world and its creation and a sort of evolutionary theory of nature that includes the notion of the survival of the fittest. As pure science, the work of Lucretius, like that of his master of two centuries earlier, was not abreast of the most advanced work of Hellenistic scientists. The chief value of the poem today lies in its wealth of information about Epicureanism. This philosophy is otherwise not well known to us, for most of Epicurus' own writings have been lost.

Lucretius wanted to release the human mind from superstitious fear—fear of the wrath of the gods and of the dismal shades where the souls of the dead were said to dwell. With determination and almost evangelical enthusiasm, he attacked the established religious forms of his day and insisted that the soul does not live after death. A man, he taught, ought to die without fear and regret, like a banqueter who, filled with sustenance, lies down to sleep.

Catullus

The other great poet of Cicero's time, Catullus (Gaius Valerius Catullus; c. 84–54 B.C.), came from the Po Valley region and wrote on lighter subjects. Catullus belonged to a group of young aristocrats in Rome who, lightheartedly rejecting stern older values, led a gay and sometimes giddy existence. Catullus fell in love with Clodia, a sister of Publius Clodius, Cicero's archenemy, and who in the interest of late Republican politics, often terrorized the capital with gangsterish methods. To Clodia, whom he called Lesbia, Catullus wrote his finest lyrics, in which he ran the gamut from passionate love to equally passionate hate (after Clodia cast him off). Intense feeling is revealed with a simplicity and directness that gave Catullus his reputation as one of the world's foremost lyric poets. Yet somehow, in comparison with other and greater poets who overshadow him, Catullus' themes seem petty and his passions shallow.

B. The Golden Age

The great age of Latin literature came with the prolonged peace of the Augustan era (after 27 B.C.). One of Augustus' ministers, Gaius Maecenas, by his generous patronage made possible the sustained effort necessary to the creation of several important literary works. His interest in the arts and his support of such gifted poets as Vergil and Horace benefited the new regime as well as Latin culture in general. His work did something to win over intellectuals and creative artists to support of the new order. The Augustan poets produced great works of literature; they also sang the praises of their emperor and the Empire. The ensuing propaganda value was great for Augustus; yet one must not think these celebrated writers prostituted themselves to the regime. Calculated insincerity has never produced great works of art.

Vergil (Publius Vergilius Maro; 70–19 B.C.), born near Mantua in northern Italy, was educated there, at Cremona and Mediolanum (Milan), and in Rome. The family suffered a blow when its farm was confiscated by Octavian about 41 B.C., along with many other estates belonging to men of republican sympathies, to provide colonies for veterans of the victorious armies. Through the interest of Maecenas, it seems, Vergil was later given another farm in rich Campania and was received almost as court poet by the Emperor Augustus.

Vergil's first major works, the *Eclogues,* are pastoral poems written in imitation of the Greek idylls of Theocritus. These are generally inferior to his later works, though the Fourth Eclogue was popular even until early modern times because of its similarity to Messianic passages in Isaiah. In it Vergil predicted a golden age of peace and prosperity under the beneficent rule of an infant yet to be born. Rather than Christ (as interpreted by Early Christian writers), however, it appears that Vergil referred to the unborn child of Octavian, who unfortunately turned out to be the notorious Julia.

The *Georgics,* didactic poems on farming, appeared next. Modeled after the Greek poet Hesiod's *Works and Days,* Vergil's poetic cycle has little of the gloom and stern practicality of the earlier work. Instead, he presents farming as a glorious activity in a happy, well-ordered world of nature. The technique is flawless, and many have considered these poems the most perfect works in all Latin literature.

Vergil's fame rests chiefly on the *Aeneid,* the great Roman epic that gained for the poet the preeminent position in Latin letters he has ever held. Like Homer's *Iliad* and *Odyssey,* the *Aeneid* may be read for its gripping story, for its poetic excellence, or for the light it throws on the civilization that produced it. The poem linked Roman civilization —quite properly, if somewhat fancifully—with the Greek, through the person of Aeneas, who fled burning Troy and ultimately settled in Latium. Vergil made it clear that the Roman branch was from this very early time (soon after the fall of Troy, traditionally set about 1184 B.C.) fated to be far greater than its Greek predecessor. Praising the glories and eminence of the Romans, the poet managed to exalt Augustus also—going so far as to have him named in an underworld prophecy by the dead Anchises, father of Aeneas, as one who would bring a golden age and finally live in heaven as a god. Yet, despite these propagandistic overtones, we need not doubt Vergil's sincerity or his deep loyalty to Rome and his faith in its destiny to rule men well. The *Aeneid* seems to reflect accurately the thoughtful Roman's view of imperial Rome's mission in the world.

Horace

Another of Maecenas' circle, the poet Horace (Quintus Horatius Flaccus; 65–8 B.C.) similarly became a strong supporter of the new order of things, although he had served with the republican forces of Brutus at Philippi in 42 B.C. He too found his family farm in southern Italy confiscated, but through Maecenas was given another in the Sabine Hills, which he much loved. His poetry, much of it satire, lacks the biting sarcasm of Gaius Lucilius or of Juvenal. His *Epodes,* based on the early Greek poet Archilochus, contain political and personal mockery and invective, but it is mostly sham. His urbane *Satires* deal mostly with harmless topics and are filled with laughter, more than contempt, for the faults and foibles of mankind. In his chief work, the *Odes,* Horace sometimes informs the reader in polished rhythm that politics should be left to others; that one should enjoy his blessings, be thankful, and let it go at that. Horace's sensible advice and pious sentiments are often attacked as commonplaces—as they nearly always are. His great gift was that he said everything superlatively well. It is easy to underestimate the depth of Horace's feelings or to overestimate his inner qualities because of his felicitous phrasing.

Ovid

A third important poet of the Augustan period was Ovid (Publius Ovidius Naso; 43 B.C.–17 A.D.). Like Catullus a half century before, Ovid belonged to the younger social set at Rome. The long period of peace and growing wealth and luxury led this group increasingly to despise the old virtues; for them Ovid was spokesman. Augustus' own daughter, the dissolute Julia, was one of this group. As we have seen, she was eventually banished by the Emperor for adultery. Ovid's poem *Ars Amatoria* ("The Art of Love"), basically a handbook on seduction, may have been what brought down Augustus' wrath on the hapless poet. There was also some scandalous affair. The harsh sentence came nine years after publication of the poem; poor Ovid was banished to Tomi, a frontier community on the Black Sea, his personal Siberia. Ovid's most useful work is his *Metamorphoses,* a kind of encyclopedia of mythology, though the artful storyteller often added to the great myths his own details that on occasion conflict with other narratives. Also quite valuable for the student of Rome is his *Fasti,* a poetic calendar of events at Rome, such as the great festivals. Unfortunately, only the books for the first six months of the year remain.

Another writer who extolled Rome's glorious destiny was Livy (Titus Livius; 59 B.C.–17 A.D.), greatest of the Latin historians. Though Livy admired Augustus, he nevertheless felt great nostalgia for the Republic. Augustus is said to have called him, good-naturedly, "the Pompeian." Not connected with the court in the same fashion of patronage that Vergil and Horace were, Livy was nevertheless close to the family of Augustus and was a sort of tutor to his grandson by adoption, the future emperor Claudius.

Livy's huge chronicle—which if printed in full today would run to sixteen average-sized volumes—was, like the *Aeneid,* the story of the rise of Rome from humble beginnings to worldwide greatness. Only about one-fourth of its original 142 books are extant, but summaries of the whole still exist. The extant books deal with early Rome and with the period from the outbreak of the Second Punic War to 167 B.C.

The work has its weaknesses: Livy was not sufficiently discriminating in using his sources, did not go to the most basic source materials, and on occasion contradicts himself. Yet his became the standard history of Rome and was never completely redone. While it is true he ignored non-Romans, he did state explicitly that his purpose in writing was to perpetuate the achievements of the Romans. His task was great enough without broadening the base of his work. Livy was somehow able to feel himself a part of the past he re-created, and the picture he evoked carries the stamp of authenticity. As a work of art—and history is, in some part, just that—Livy's narrative was never surpassed in antiquity.

Livy's history has been likened to a funeral eulogy delivered over the grave of the Republic. The historian typifies for us the attitude of the average upper-class Roman; he mourned the old order but accepted the new. In his heart he knew the Republic was dead beyond recovery.

C. The Silver Age

As the name implies, the so-called Silver Age of Latin literature produced authors whose work fails to measure up to that of the greatest writers of the Augustan period. In style, these writers of the 1st and 2nd centuries A.D. evidence, first, a revulsion against the ample, flowing Latin of Cicero, Vergil, and Livy, and then an imitation of it. Next came a determined effort to be different, which all too often only emphasized the mediocrity of the writer.

Seneca

In literary content, morality and ethical conduct were much emphasized. Stoicism was the motivating philosophy of several writers, including Seneca (Lucius Annaeus Seneca; c. 4 B.C.–65 A.D.), tutor and for several years a sort of prime minister to Nero. Seneca was born in Spain, where his family was then resident. He was brought to Rome as a child and educated there. His dignified tragedies are written in a peculiar one-dimensional style, evidently intended not to be acted out onstage but to be declaimed. These plays seem dull and draggy today, but they contain occasional brilliant lines, and Seneca's tragedy was long a significant literary influence, especially during the Renaissance. Seneca's *Moral Essays* and *Letters* display moral teaching of the highest caliber, though their author does not seem always to have conformed to his own lofty idealism. During his time at the imperial court he became enormously rich. The last three years of his life, devoted to literary activity, were spent in retirement from public life. Then, accused of complicity in a plot on Nero's life, Seneca was forced to commit suicide.

Lucan

The idealistic morality of Stoicism is summed up in a passage from *Pharsalia*, a long, sometimes tiresome epic by Seneca's nephew Lucan (Marcus Annaeus Lucanus; 39–65 A.D.), written in praise of Pompey's cause. When asked to consult the oracle of Jupiter Hammon, Cato the Younger, a leader of the hard-pressed opponents of Caesar and a professed Stoic, replied: [1]

> *What, Labienus, would'st thou have me ask?*
> *Whether 'tis better to die free in arms*
> *Than live to see a tyranny? If life*
> *Is nothing worth, however long? If age*
> *Doth profit? Whether any force can harm*
> *The good? If Fortune threatens virtue vainly?*
> *If 'tis enough to will what merits praise,*
> *And right ne'er needs the crown of good success?*

Lucan's poem, filled with republican sentiment, naturally aroused Nero's anger, and Lucan was forbidden to give public readings of his works in the salons of the day. The resentful poet joined Piso's conspiracy

---

[1] A. N. Bryan-Brown, trans., in *The Mind of Rome*, ed. by C. Bailey (Oxford, 1926), p. 57.

against the Emperor and was forced to commit suicide at a tragically early age—less than half that of his philosopher uncle, implicated in the same conspiracy.

Columella

The 1st century A.D. saw several writers who combined literature and scholarship in the manner that Cicero had so well exemplified. Their works range widely, from Columella's *De Re Rustica* ("On Agriculture"; c. 65 A.D.) to Quintilian's work on rhetorical training. Columella, like Seneca, came from Spain; their ages, too, were similar. Columella was concerned rather more with practical than with literary matters. Despite certain advice that to us may seem ridiculous or even fantastic, it is apparent from his writings that the educated Roman farmer had a good knowledge of such important farm practices as fertilization and crop rotation. Absentee landlordism and slavery, it is equally apparent, were still the bane of agricultural well-being.

Quintilian

Quintilian (Marcus Fabius Quintilianus; c. 30–95 A.D.), also from Roman Spain, was an outstanding educator and had his own rather exclusive academy. His *Principles of Oratory* commend a broad educational program designed to produce a polished orator and cultured gentleman. More important to the modern scholar are his judgments of literature and sketches of authors he considered important: for example, he greatly admired Cicero. Interestingly, he advised that parents first teach their children Greek; Latin they could easily pick up later.

Pliny The Elder

Another 1st-century work of scholarship is the encyclopedic *Natural History* of Pliny the Elder (23–79 A.D.), which covers a broad field, from zoology and botany to mining and metallurgy, anthropology, and medicine. Not valued highly today either as literature or as science, it nevertheless does have valuable elements of each. Pliny, who knew a good story and could tell it well, included much trivial information of interest: Augustus' favorite wine, the color of Tiberius' eyes. The scholar, who did not have the modern zeal for experimentation and careful method, also included much information that now seems patently incredible. During his lifetime Pliny held both military and provincial administrative posts. He was asphyxiated near Mount Vesuvius during the celebrated eruption that caused the obliteration of

Pompeii, where he had gone while others were fleeing. As commander of the imperial fleet as Misenum, he probably wished to give aid as well as to make careful empiric observation. The typical bookish scholar, Pliny read constantly, slept little, and kept several secretaries busy.

Petronius

One of the most interesting works of antiquity is the bawdy, picaresque *Satyricon* of Gaius Petronius (d. 65 A.D.), which approaches the modern novel in form, although there does not appear to be a connected plot. Of the extant fragments, one of the most vivid and amusing deals with a lavish banquet given by one Trimalchio, a new-rich "climber." Anxious to flaunt his culture, he makes many ludicrous errors: for example, saying that Corinthian bronze is the metal that resulted when, at the fall of Troy, *Hannibal* put all the metal loot in a huge pile and burned it!

Tacitus wrote of Petronius (probably, but not certainly, the same man) that he was a kind of professional debauchee. Closely associated with Nero, Petronius became his official judge of elegance and taste and even bore the surname "Arbiter." Charged with treason by a jealous rival, he ended his life by opening his veins. Written in the pithy, vulgar, and sometimes indecent language of the common man, perhaps the *Satyricon* was created purely for the hilarity and pleasure of the imperial court. Some modern scholars, however, detect an undertone of criticism of the corrupt Roman world of which its author was a part. Whatever his real attitude, the originality of the work seems unquestionable.

Apuleius

The next century—actually beyond the limits of the Silver Age proper— saw the production of still another work somewhat resembling a novel. The *Metamorphoses* (best known as *The Golden Ass*) of Lucius Apuleius (c. 123–185 A.D.) combines a series of tales, often hilarious and sometimes risqué, into a loosely connected narrative. The story relates the adventures of a man temporarily turned, through magic that backfired, into an ass. In the 14th century Boccaccio made use of these stories, many of which probably were not original with Apuleius. This work is interesting because of its anti-Christian bias. Its author was an initiate in the mysteries of Isis, and later a priest of Isis, Osiris, and Aesculapius. Some other, rather florid rhetorical works by him also survive. Apuleius' distinctive language perhaps relates to his background; he was a North African educated in Carthage and Athens.

Good-humored satire of the type found also in Horace may be seen in the work of Petronius. But quite a different form, biting and sarcastic, is found in other Silver Age authors. Seneca lampooned the emperor Claudius in a short work (*Apocolocyntosis*) relating the events in heaven immediately after Claudius' death. When it is proposed that Claudius be made a god, as Caesar and Augustus were supposed to have been, there is much objection to the idea, and finally Gaius, who had often tyrannized over his uncle in life, asserts his authority and has Claudius made clerk to a freedman!

Satire is cutting and merciless in the *Epigrams* of Martial (Marcus Valerius Martialis; c. 40–104 A.D.), another notable Latin writer born in Spain. Martial's work is an unconscionable mixture of good and bad, mingling condemnation of hypocrisy with condonation of every moral indecency. Since Martial named names in these lampoons, it is astonishing he was not strangled by some victim of his cruel wit in a dark alley, instead of dying a peaceful death after having retired to the Spanish countryside.

Somewhat similar are the poetic works of the last of the great Roman satirists, Juvenal (Decimus Junius Juvenalis; c. 55–133 A.D.). Writing in the first third of the 2nd century, Juvenal was driven by indignation, relieved with occasional flashes of a serious-minded humor. He ridiculed the faults and affectations of Romans, especially women, whom he hated with an unrelieved pessimism. He detested the "sewage" of foreign influence and condemned vice, which he nevertheless described in vivid detail. Stoic influence is evident in the Tenth Satire, where the poet advises that peace of mind can be attained through virtue and counsels that one should pray for "a sound mind in a sound body" (*mens sana in corpore sano*). Despite his obvious exaggeration, Juvenal's somber and sordid picture of a gross, decadent Rome has too often been totally accepted and written indiscriminantly into our histories of this era.

Historians: Tacitus, Suetonius, and Others

This same picture of deteriorating moral fiber is the chief impression derived from study of the two important historians of the Silver Age: Cornelius Tacitus (c. 5–115 A.D.) and Gaius Suetonius (about 69–130 A.D.).

Tacitus' chief works are his books of history, the *Annals* and the *Histories,* which together cover the period between the death of Augustus (14 A.D.) and the assassination of Domitian (96 A.D.). The surviving books recount nothing later than the civil wars of 69 A.D., and there are earlier gaps as well, notably for Nero's last years. Tacitus writes of almost unrelieved tyranny, rife with vice and depravity at the top. Many critics call him the greatest of Roman historians, but he falls short of this rank. Though he claimed he wrote without prejudice, prejudice warps his whole work. To the emperor Tiberius, for example, against whom Tacitus had a special animus, the historian confidently, on very flimsy evidence, ascribes the basest motives—motives the author could not possibly have known. That is, Tacitus claimed to know what Tiberius *thought*. Similarly, his *Germania* is less an attempt to present a factual account of Germanic life and tribal institutions than an expression of an ideal of discipline and simplicity to which Tacitus felt Rome must return. His biography of his father-in-law, *Agricola,* also has the obvious purpose of recommending a return to austere older standards of military discipline and imperial aggressiveness.

Nevertheless, Tacitus used his sources more carefully than any other Roman historian and did not deliberately falsify facts. This keen discrimination, his terse, forceful prose style, and the acute perception evident in numerous startlingly lucid generalizations have justly earned for him a high reputation. For Tacitus, history was much more than an accurate presentation of past events of significance; it was a powerful tool with which he might influence the direction of events.

As a historian Suetonius does not rank with Tacitus, for his *Lives of the Caesars* (covering twelve emperors, from Julius Caesar to Domitian) is a motley collection of fact and scandalous fiction. Nevertheless, it is fascinating and even convincing to read. Some of his stories are of that type which, if not true, ought to be, because they seem to illustrate the character of the subject so well. Moreover, Suetonius did use some excellent sources and thereby has preserved for us some of this worthwhile basic material; for example, he quotes from Augustus' letters. If the reader discounts the colorful scandal Suetonius could not bring himself to leave out, the ancedotal *Lives* becomes a valuable work for today's historians.

A different segment of Roman society from that so bleakly described by Juvenal and Tacitus is revealed in the letters of Pliny the Younger (61/62–c. 113 A.D.), nephew of Pliny the Elder. In his voluminous letters—cultured, civilized, and sensible—may be discerned something of that more responsible class of Romans upon whom fell the tasks of empire. One of the best-known of his letters, written to Trajan about 111 A.D. from Bithynia, where Pliny was serving as governor, asks for advice on methods of dealing with Christians, whose "depraved, excessive superstition" had spread extensively in that area. His own procedure, he said, was to execute only those accused who refused to curse Christ and sacrifice to the Emperor. Trajan's answer was that he was doing quite right: no general rule could be laid down; Pliny was not to engage in active persecution nor to accept anonymous accusations, but if a Christian was denounced before him and persisted in refusing to adore the gods, he must of course be punished.

Not a Roman but very important to Roman history is the famous Plutarch (c. 46–120 A.D.), whose *Parallel Lives* of celebrated Greeks and Romans has inspired leaders of many generations. Eminently readable and studded with illustrative anecdotes, Plutarch's *Lives* gave Shakespeare most of the information used in his plays set in antiquity and provided, in quite another way, serious reading for the young Napoleon Bonaparte. In his distinctive biographical scheme Plutarch paired Alexander the Great with Caesar, Demosthenes with Cicero. The Roman *Lives* are mostly those of great figures from the last two centuries of the Republic.

During the 2nd century and after, Latin literature skidded rapidly from good to mediocre, and from mediocre to worse. A current-day scholar has written about this period and termed it the "Silver-Plated Age." [2] Some writings of this era were important, notably in law; but the best of Roman literature was produced during the two middle centuries of Roman history, which encompassed both the Golden and Silver Ages.

D. Life in the Roman Empire

A generally excellent administration, a fine roads system, well-constructed aqueducts and public buildings, provision for sanitation facilities and the like: all these amenities produced an age in which a greater percentage of men could live comfortable, relatively secure lives than was possible at any time before in human history, or at any later time until perhaps the nineteenth century.

Rome

Rome itself, of course, was the queen of cities—with the most cosmopolitan population, the most surging crowds, the most exciting events, and the most marvelous buildings and public squares. By the time of Trajan, there were five forums, boasting numerous temples, basilicas, libraries, and other public buildings, as well as colonnades and open space for socializing. Adjoining the forums were innumerable shops, arranged on as many as five levels.

The population of Rome, by the best estimates, reached nearly a million by the reign of Augustus and was somewhat larger still in the 2nd century A.D. The major streets were paved—though others remained dirt (or mud)—and along the best streets were sidewalks. The city aque-

2 T. B. Jones, *The Silver-Plated Age* (Sandoval, N.M., 1962).

Panoramic view of the Roman Forum. *(Alinari-Scala)*

ducts, which brought in water from as far away as fifty or sixty miles, had a capacity of more than 300,000,000 gallons per day—though the actual delivery must have been considerably less. The water was distributed all over the city, even to the hilltops, and poured continuously into the many public fountains. The privileged had water brought to their residences by lead pipe and with some pressure. There were valves and other plumbing amenities such as flush toilets.

The concentration of forums and shops produced almost overwhelming crowds and traffic. "Noise pollution" is no modern phenomenon. When shopkeepers and peddlers shouted out their wares or metalworkers and carpenters hammered, all in narrow echoing streets, the noise level was irritatingly high. Nor did this din subside in the evening. Rome's narrow, often steep and twisting streets simply could not accommodate both pedestrian and cart and wagon traffic. From the time of Julius Caesar on, therefore, most carts and wagons were barred from the downtown area during the day. Juvenal relates graphically how

338

impossible it was to sleep at night when the iron tires of heavy wagons ground on the cobbled streets below, the drivers swearing at the tops of their voices at unwilling beasts. Seneca tells what it was like to live above a bathhouse, where one could hear, for weary hours, the slap of the masseur, the grunts of the exercisers, and the shouting of participants in the various games. Many of Rome's thousands lived in insulae, or great apartment houses, which sometimes were cheaply constructed and occasionally collapsed. Often they must have lived on streets so narrow that balconies on the floors above shut out much of the natural light.

Despite the *vigiles,* a police force organized by Augustus, travel in the streets at night could be risky business. If muggers didn't assault the lone wayfarer, he might suffer the indignity of being drenched with filth thrown from upper-story windows. Streets were supposed to be swept by the property owners every day (again, by decree of Julius Caesar), but this regulation must often have been violated. City codes incorporating rules of this sort were gradually extended throughout the cities of Italy and, eventually, the whole Empire. Despite problems in enforcing these rules, there is no doubt that Rome was a more sanitary and healthful place to live in the early Empire than many a European city was in early modern times.

Rome was above all the place to be. The center of the Mediterranean world, this was where things happened, and all things naturally gravitated to that center. Most exciting were the great spectacles, officially supported in lavish style. Juvenal said, contemptuously, that the Roman mob cared only for bread and circuses. Food was provided for two or three hundred thousand inhabitants through free grain distribution (the *annona*). The circuses too were free, or almost so. In the mid-1st century A.D., about forty percent of the calendar days were designated as holidays (though it should not be assumed that all Romans were permitted to cease work on all those days). On about a hundred days each year, public games of one sort or another were provided; these were most often associated with the great festivals, some of which had been celebrated for centuries. Most of these occasions had some religious or semireligious connection. The greatest festivals, which included games and theatrical performances, were those in honor of Jupiter, Apollo, Ceres, Cybele, and Flora.

Perhaps the most exciting events were the horse and chariot races, held in the huge Circus Maximus, seating about 150,000 persons. Including standing room, perhaps a quarter of a million persons could see the races here. Even in its present rather bare, excavated form it remains impressive. There were two or three other outdoor circuses of this type in the city. Anyone who has seen the movie *Ben Hur* can have some impression of the excitement of the race itself, but only the imagination can conjure up the overwhelming effect of the betting, the hawking, the roar of the crowd, and the tremendous competition between the various factions supporting the Blues, the Greens, the Whites, or the Reds. The owners and drivers of the best horses commanded large fees, just as premier athletes and horses do today. There is one story of an official who, feeling the demands of the chariot crews were unreasonably high, put on dog races instead! Though we have no information on crowd reaction, it is known that the usual races were quickly restored.

Just as exciting, and in a more feral way, were the games presented in the various amphitheaters. Largest of these was the Flavian Amphitheater, later known as the Colosseum. It derived its familiar name from the Colossus, a statue of Nero about 125 feet tall, wearing the radiate crown of the sun god and built nearby as part of his reconstruction of the city after the great fire. The Colosseum was built in large part with the labor of thousands of Jewish slaves brought to Rome after the de-

The Flavian amphitheater, commonly called the Colosseum, built by Vespasian and Titus. (Italian Government Travel Office)

struction of Jerusalem in 70 A.D. It is perhaps the most impressive of all the monuments from the ancient Roman past; the remaining portion gives the modern viewer a feeling for the days of imperial Rome as nothing else can. Built of travertine that, over the centuries, has mellowed to a yellowish white that almost glows at sunset or by the lights illuminating its arches at night, it was constructed in four tiers of arches in three classic styles (Doric, Ionic, and Corinthian). The capacity of the immense oval structure has been estimated at from about 50,000 to 90,000. From accounts of how the crowds pressed into other similar structures (50,000 persons were once said to have been killed or injured in a much smaller amphitheater in an Italian town), the higher figure is most likely, though spectators would then have been packed into every conceivable space.

In these amphitheaters were held the infamous gladiatorial combats, the contests between men and wild animals, combats of animals (lion versus elephant, etc.), animal hunts, and all the various other chilling spectacles that could be devised by the most ingenious minds in show business. There were, indeed, some more civilized treats, such as acrobatics, juggling, and the antics of trained beasts performing much as they might in a modern circus. But the Roman mob demanded blood, and Romans were happiest when shouting "Jugula" to a gladiator, mercilessly urging him to slay his fallen adversary.

Both members of a pair of gladiators often survived combat in the arena, but there were deaths in great numbers: there are existing accounts of the events that mention the total numbers who fought and the number who died. Some of those who fought—hardly professional gladiators—were condemned criminals. The demand for healthy male slaves to make into gladiators must have been tremendous, for it was not Rome alone that thirsted for spilled blood in the arena. The slave system itself was dehumanizing enough; the gory public spectacles can only have contributed to the cheapening of human (and animal) life.

The Italian towns all had arenas, as did towns in the provinces, especially in Gaul and Spain. The remains of the amphitheater at Arles in southern France are of impressive scale. There were fewer public slaughters in the Hellenized East, but even there some were held. Information turned up at Pompeii shows intense public interest in the spectacles there. At some games in the local arena, riots broke out in which several persons were killed; in consequence, the Emperor forbade further games there for several years.

Ostia, Pompeii, and Herculaneum

Time and circumstance, unkind to the ancient inhabitants but generous to modern scholarship, have preserved more or less intact large sections of Ostia, the port for Rome, and two small cities on the Bay of Naples,

Pompeii, and Herculaneum. No visitor to Italy should miss spending some time at each of these sites.

Ostia was abandoned in the early Middle Ages and gradually crumbled into ruin. The durable Roman brick resisted the elements, however; temples, a theater, a public building or two, and many apartment structures have remained well preserved enough to show their form. A local museum houses important objects of art found on the site. Especially impressive to the casual tourist are the apartment houses, which with the addition of electricity and somewhat improved modern plumbing would, if still intact, make attractive and modern-looking quarters acceptable to tenants of discriminating taste even today.

Pompeii was covered with fifteen to twenty feet or more of volcanic ash in the eruption of Vesuvius in 79 A.D., and is still only about two-thirds excavated. Here, perhaps more than at any other existing site, one can feel himself transported back into the 1st century. The huge paving stones of the streets show the grooves carved out by the groaning iron wheels of ancient wagons. The shops lining the major streets seem

Painting found in a Pompeian house. The snake probably symbolizes the household deities.

Pompeii. Street Scene with shops. Note the stepping-stones, spaced to permit cart wheels to pass between them.

ready to be filled again with goods and customers. Graffiti, perhaps supporting a political candidate or making a sardonic comment on life, can still be read on walls. The comfortable, livable houses, attractive inside (though not so much on the exterior), are typical of Roman life in the seaside resorts of the Naples area.

In this leisurely setting, disaster came suddenly, and because of this sudden catastrophe much remained in situ for modern rediscovery. We may see the remains of a loaf of bread, carbonized but still in its original form. Jewelry, cooking utensils, surgical instruments—so many items of beauty or practical use that they cannot be listed in full—may be seen in the National Archaeological Museum in Naples. There are marvelous detached mosaics and frescoes as well as statuary. There are also the obscenities and pornography that marked the houses of prostitution. Expert excavators learned to pour plaster into the cavities where once something living had lain. The resulting casts reproduce faithfully such poignant traces as the chained dog who died in agony and the mother

343

and daughter who died while fleeing, the mother's arm thrown protectively around her child.

Herculaneum, buried much more deeply under lava and mud, is thus more intact even than Pompeii. It has been excavated more slowly and with greater difficulty, particularly because much of it lay beneath a modern urban site. Some valuable objects were retrieved in antiquity from the ashes of Pompeii, but most everything remained for the modern archaeologist at Herculaneum. Moreover, archaeologists there are, laudably, attempting to leave more of the frescoes and other objects in their original site for greater realism and appreciation. Unfortunately, the amount of money available for such projects from the Italian government is insufficient—so much so that some of these valuable sites are actually imperiled.

The total impression gained from these graphic remains is of pleasant living in well-planned, clean, and prosperous towns. Ostia prospered because of trade; Pompeii and Herculaneum were favored by location in a resort area. Thus they cannot be entirely typical, and one should remember that most Italians—like most residents of the Empire elsewhere—must have lived in far less satisfactory conditions. But it is equally certain that most inhabitants of the Empire at its height were better housed and lived in better circumstances than people in the same areas were to enjoy again for many centuries after.

E. Philosophy and Religion

Prosperous and pragmatic, the Romans obviously did not provide the most fertile soil for widespread growth of any philosophical system; yet the major philosophical schools were in evidence at Rome—Epicureans, Cynics, Skeptics, and Pythagoreans. Recently uncovered evidence indicates that in the first two centuries of the Empire the last-named group was more numerous and influential than previously was thought. The philosophy that took deep root and acquired distinctively Roman characteristics, however, was Stoicism.

Stoicism

As we have seen, it was Panaetius, a Greek Stoic teacher who lived at the home of Scipio Aemilianus in the 2nd century B.C., who first popularized Stoicism in Italy. This philosophy, mostly stripped of its cosmogony and stressing self-sufficiency, virtue, and public service, strongly appealed to important Romans during the next three centuries of Roman history. Mucius Scaevola, the great jurist of the 1st century B.C., analyzed and organized the law in accordance with Stoic principles. Cicero, though he proclaimed himself a skeptical Academic, often reflected Stoic influence. Cato the Younger was a professed Stoic. Authors of the 1st century B.C. as was pointed out earlier in this chapter, often were infused with Stoic idealism. Seneca, Nero's great tutor and minister, wrote essays and letters explicitly elaborating his Stoic convictions. Such men strove for moral reform and moral integrity, rather than for a commitment to abstruse logic or subtle philosophical principle.

Some Stoics and other philosophers felt compelled to oppose certain of the Roman emperors and formed a core of opposition the rulers found it difficult to deal with. One such adversary was Thrasea Paetus. He was far from being an activist, however; he once expressed his disapproval of Nero's actions merely by walking out of the Senate. Yet, after Piso's conspiracy, Thrasea was condemned and forced to commit suicide. His son-in-law Helvidius Priscus attacked the Flavian regime; Vespasian exiled and finally executed him. Later Domitian put to death his son. These philosophers apparently felt that only the "best man" somehow was fit to rule—and the prevailing system was not turning up such men.

One of the most notable Stoic teachers of the age was Epictetus, an ex-slave, mentioned above in connection with Marcus Aurelius. He did not involve himself in political criticism, though his teacher Musonius Rufus, a contemporary of Seneca, had been banished by both Nero and Vespasian. Epictetus nonetheless was caught up in a general expulsion of philosophers by Domitian and lived out most of his life in Epirus. His best efforts were directed to the common man rather than to the educated elite. A commonly reproduced prayer of our own times—"Oh, Lord, help me to accept what I cannot change, to change for the better what can be changed, and to have the wisdom to distinguish between the two"—could have been the prayer of Epictetus, for these words convey the central impact of his teaching.

With the advent of the "Good Emperors," philosophical opposition to the government tended to subside. Hadrian was especially interested in philosophy; and of course, Marcus Aurelius made a personal profession of Stoicism in his *Meditations.*

Oriental Influences in Roman Religion

From earliest times, the most important influences for religious change came to Rome from Greece and the East. During the late Republic, Rome was infiltrated by devotees of several new exotic religions. Most of these were mystery religions: that is, each jealously preserved some secret lore promising special benefit to the initiate, usually involving a hope of life after death. The new religions were brought in mostly by immigrants—

slaves, traders, and others. The worship of Cybele (Magna Mater) had been brought in under the sponsorship of the ruling classes during the Second Punic War; but most of these new religions arrived unofficially.

The new cults were the products of Hellenistic religious syncretism. This process, operative especially in the centuries after Alexander, had transformed both deity and religion, giving a universal aspect to all important gods. From Egypt, for example, came the worship of Isis and Osiris, once Nile gods but now deities whose power and influence were felt to be all-pervasive. A prayer to Isis found in Apuleius' *Golden Ass* indicates a concept of a beneficent, omnipresent, omnipotent deity— or almost that. Shrines to Isis were torn down in Rome during the anti-Egyptian reaction that accompanied the last phase of the civil war. Only in the reign of the Emperor Gaius was a temple dedicated to the Egyptian goddess permitted within Rome's sacred boundaries.

One of the more important of the newer Oriental religions was Mithraism, which gained numerous adherents and became one of the most powerful competitors of Christianity. Roman troops who served in Asia in the 1st century B.C. brought back this form of worship. Mithra was a chief lieutenant of Ahura-Mazda in the Zoroastrian religion, and therefore of Persian origin, and was closely identified with the sun. Many characteristics of Zoroastrianism carried over into this later sect: an emphasis on light vs. darkness, purity of life, strong connections with the sun, and a Persian mythology.

Mithra was conceived as a creator-benefactor of mankind. In the Mithraic creation myth he was said to have pursued and killed the sacred bull, from the blood and parts of which all things were made. The cult statue that was the focal feature of the Mithraeum, the half-buried structure where the initiates met, shows Mithra astride the bull, in the act of pulling its head back by the nostrils and stabbing it with his dagger. Pictured below are several creatures—zodiacal figures, for the most part— whose role is not always clear. Fine examples of these cult statues may be seen in the world's great museums, the best of them being in the Louvre and the British Museum.

Mithraism was a man's religion (women were not admitted into its mysteries) and so had a special appeal to soldiers. The religion first spread among the camps marking the Danube and Rhine frontiers. Numerous Mithraea have been found in Roman cities—Rome and Ostia, for example. There were several degrees of progression for the initiates. As with some other Oriental cults, the ceremony of the taurobolium was practiced: a bull was sacrificed above a grate, while below the initiates allowed themselves to be bathed in its dripping blood. Christian writers ridiculed this ceremony, though its symbolism certainly would not have been alien to them.

Mithraists worshiped the sun on the first day of the week ("Sunday"), observed the birthday of the sun about December 25, made use of ceremonial washings for purification, and held ceremonial meals. The several parallels with Christianity are obvious, but it is not always certain who borrowed from whom, or indeed whether either borrowed directly from the other. Christians probably set December 25 as the birthdate of Christ to offset the Mithraic and other pagan celebrations such as the Roman Saturnalia. But Christian baptism derived from an old Jewish practice, and the tradition of the Lord's Supper seems to bear little relation to Mithraic practice.

Christianity

Though Christianity is often presented as just another of the Oriental mystery religions that arrived in Rome from the East, it was much more than that, of course. This religion, like its parent Judaism, had its roots in history. Moses, the prophets, Jesus—all are real figures set in real history, even if they have acquired an admixture of myth. The influence of Jesus rests less, perhaps, on the claims that his followers made for his divinity than upon the record of his teaching. This was in many ways similar to the ethical pronouncements of the Jewish scriptures or of the greatest of the Greek philosophers. Probably the Greek Orphics and the Mithraists also taught a code of lofty ethics. But in its simplicity and depth of feeling, its probing and enlightening impact, Jesus' teaching was unique.

The similarities between Christianity and certain pagan cults sometimes appall modern Christians, who, ignorant of the world of the past, imagine that Christianity burst upon history totally unique, completely different from other contemporary cults. Actually these very correspondences made it easier for Christianity to spread. For example, a man who was attracted by the high ethical pronouncements of the Stoics but repelled by their stern, almost inhuman *apatheia* (determination to be unmoved by emotions, even the gentler ones) would quite likely have been ripe for Christian conversion.

As everyone knows, Christianity began as a sect of Judaism in Palestine. After a period of success in Jerusalem, adherents of the new group were scattered by persecution. Thereafter the movement flourished among the more Hellenized Jews outside Palestine. One of these, Paul, became the most influential of the "apostles" (personal messengers) of Christ in propagating the new religion and soon was converting gentiles as well as Jews, so that after a time gentiles predominated. By the time of Trajan, as we learn from Pliny's letters, Christianity seemed about to overwhelm paganism in Asia Minor.

We have already noted the deadly flareup of persecution under Nero. This wave of persecution was brief and not widespread. However, at this time or soon after, it became firm policy that Christians, by their profession of the religion, upon admission that they wore the name, were automatically branded enemies of the state, subject to the death penalty. It was this policy which Tertullian, in the late 2nd century, so strongly protested. Arguing that Christians were basically good citizens, he said, it was unreasonable to condemn them except for a specific crime. Sporadic persecution did not halt the growth of the new movement, and may indeed have helped. One did not profess this new religion lightly, and those who did so were dedicated. The problems that were later to beset the church—heresies, questions of church-state relations, of the internal government of the church itself, or of the nature of Christ—all these concerns were of secondary importance in an era when persecution and martyrdom seemed always near.

The reasons for the phenomenal growth of these new religions are not easy to discern. The world was mostly at peace and mostly prosperous, yet men by the thousands felt the need for something more, a deeper dimension to their lives. They were asking important questions, seeking spiritual sustenance. The new cults appealed mostly, it is true, to the lower classes. Their ethical and spiritual emphasis contrasted strongly with the world portrayed by Suetonius, Juvenal, and Martial. They thought the world was going to pieces, morally; obviously, it was not. The decline the next chapter must deal with cannot have resulted principally from a deteriorating moral fiber in society—as men have so often mistakenly claimed.

F. Roman Law

Growth of the Law

The mid-2nd century A.D., which saw the decline of Latin literature, witnessed great strides in the study of law and its codification. From the Twelve Tables of the 5th century B.C.—the first written Roman code —the law had developed as Rome evolved into empire. Applied to many peoples, backward and advanced, it developed equitably and effectively but also became complex, sometimes jumbled and confused. Now began a great period of juridical compilation, classification, and clarification. Through legal opinions and publications, a series of great jurists of the 2nd and the early 3rd century, the period termed the classical age of Roman law, drew from centuries of accumulated experience the great legal principles still taught in law schools everywhere in the Western world. Perhaps the greatest of these jurists were Gaius, Paul, Papinian, and Ulpian.

Romans had been forced at an early date to distinguish between civil or domestic law and the more or less international law they encountered when away from their home city. The edicts of the urban praetors, formulas developed by them to instruct judges in specific cases, decisions actually rendered, and the opinions of jurists (jurisconsults) all contributed much to the formulation of the Civil Law, which applied to Roman citizens.

As Rome acquired provinces, the praetors, proconsuls or propraetors who administered them were given wide lattitude in establishing fundamental law in their territories. Each governor published his edict, setting forth the law for the area under his jurisdiction. These edicts were not, of course, newly formulated each time a new governor arrived. Some, such as that of Mucius Scaevola, a distinguished jurisconsult who was governor of the province of Asia in 94 B.C., became models that were used again and again, with necessary modification.

Centralization and Elaboration under the Empire

The imperial system brought gradual centralization of the sources of law and a more unified administration of it. The popular assemblies gradually lost their legislative power, and even the decrees of the Senate mostly reflected the will of the Princeps. Decisions of the emperors had virtually the force of law, and indeed this became an explicit principle toward the end of the 2nd century. The spectacular jury trials that had made the reputations of such men as Cicero under the Republic were finally eliminated, and pleading took place before judges only, except for cases in the Senate or personally heard by the emperor. At least in the early Empire, the Roman citizen enjoyed an appeals system that could go straight to the Emperor himself. The Christian Apostle Paul could gain a hearing before the highest officer of the Empire by saying simply, "I appeal to Caesar."

During the early years of the Empire, the concept of *jus gentium*—law of nations—evolved, both philosophically and legally. From the idea of common custom, it had come to mean a kind of universal law. Combined with this was the concept of *jus naturalis,* or natural law, often connected with Stoicism. Its basic provisions or, rather, ideals were conceived of as embodying natural rights. It seems ironic that the late 2nd and early 3rd centuries, an age which saw growing autocracy in Roman government, should also have been the age known as the classical period of Roman law, during which the great jurists were elaborating important principles of human rights. The concept of equality before the law was based, ultimately, on the idea that all men are born equal—a principle specifically stated by Ulpian, praetorian prefect under Alexander Severus in the 220's. Yet during the same period, as we have seen, citizens were divided into *honestiores* and *humiliores* (roughly, the rich and the poor), and to each group were applied differing procedures and penalties.

The great jurists strove to bring order out of chaos, to classify, simplify, and point up clearly the philosophical concepts inherent in the law. The first effective condensations were unofficial works designed for use as textbooks in the private schools of law. After the work of generations of jurisconsults showed that their interpretations of the law were in many instances as important as the law itself, the emperors decreed that the opinions of certain of them were to be followed by the courts. Eventually, official classified condensations, or codifications, were produced for judicial guidance. Historically the most important of these is the famous Justinian Code, the chief edition of which appeared in 534 A.D.

Corpus Juris Civilis of Justinian

The Justinian corpus consisted of four parts: the Code itself, a condensed and orderly arrangement of law; the Digest, important opinions of the most distinguished jurists (also called the Pandects); the Institutes, a treatise on the elements of law; and the Novels, additional constitutions the emperor Justinian saw fit to add from time to time. Other codes were important; the Theodosian Code of 438 A.D., for example, served as the basis of law for several of the great Germanic tribes that by then dominated most of Western Europe. The Justinian Code, however, became the model of Roman law in its later diffusion about the world. The influence of Roman law is more indirect in the English-speaking nations than in other nations of Western Europe (exceptions to this generality are the Union of South Africa and the state of Louisiana). These first-named nations use the British Common Law, with its dependence on prior judicial opinion and precedent, rather than on a definitive code, and its use of the jury system instead of trial before judges. But the most important of the common-law jurists were conversant with Roman law and were influenced by it.

It is thus quite accurate to say that the whole Western world still feels the impact of Roman legal experience and thought, in a continuing development now extending back through two and a half millennia.

ALTHEIM, R., *A History of Roman Religion,* tr. H. Mattingly, New York, 1938.

ARNOLD, E. V., *Roman Stoicism,* London, 1911.

BALSDON, J., *Roman Women,* New York, 1963.

BRION, M., *Pompeii and Herculaneum; the Glory and the Grief,* tr. J. Rosenberg, New York, 1961.

BURFORD, A., *Craftsmen in Greek and Roman Society,* London, 1972.

CARCOPINO, J., *Daily Life in Ancient Rome,* New Haven, 1940.

CLARKE, M. L., *The Roman Mind,* New York, 1968.

DILL, S., *Roman Society from Nero to Marcus Aurelius,* New York, 1956.

DUFF, J. W., *Golden Age of Latin Literature,* New York, 1953.

DUFF, J. W., *Silver Age of Latin Literature,* London, 1927.

GLOVER, T. R., *The Conflict of Religion in the Early Roman Empire,* London, 1920.

GWYNN, A., *Roman Education from Cicero to Quintilian,* Oxford, 1926.

JONES, T., *The Silver Plated Age,* Sandoval, 1962.

MATTINGLY, H., *The Man on the Roman Street,* New York, 1966.

MOORE, R., *The Roman Commonwealth,* London, 1942.

STARR, C. G., *Civilization and the Caesars,* Ithaca, 1954.

WHITE, K. D., *Roman Farming,* New York, 1970.

20

Collapse and Recovery:
Military Monarchy
and Oriental Despotism

The general harmony and appearance of partnership between the emperor and the Senate—important even if it was in part only an elaborate facade—disintegrated with the death of Marcus Aurelius. Within a few years the Empire was beset within and without by all but insurmountable problems. By the mid-3rd century, the only security remaining lay with the soldiers; effective military commanders therefore became the most important administrators. Generals, one after another, seized and briefly held power. Meanwhile trade collapsed, the tax structure suffered, and the monetary system almost dissolved in unchecked inflation. At length one general, Diocletian, clung to power long enough to achieve a period of unified peace and, to a degree, retrieved the situation. By then, however, it was impossible to restore fully what had been lost; too much of the foundation had been destroyed. The structure of the state that Constantine and his successors ruled over little resembled the Empire of Augustus. By that time—the early 4th century A.D.—Rome had entered an age of Orientalized absolutism.

Lucius Commodus (180–192 A.D.), only nineteen when his father Marcus Aurelius died, quickly made peace in the north. He soon dismissed the advisers bequeathed him along with the Empire and, with bad judgment that was truly exceptional, appointed new ones. General misgovernment brought on a conspiracy, which was detected in time; but thereafter Commodus was frightened. As a result, he executed large numbers of persons and listened willingly to new tales of treason. He began not to trust even his own ministers, who tended to be deposed and executed with marked regularity. At one point his praetorian prefect (by now the most important person in Rome after the emperor) was a freedman whose venality set new records.

Commodus was a simpleminded man who gave himself over to personal pleasure and the games. Tall and strong, he himself wrestled, hunted wild beasts, and played the role of gladiator—sometimes in public, it seems. He commissioned statues of himself carrying the club and wearing the lionskin that were the accouterments of Hercules, with whom he identified.

In the last years of Commodus's reign, some of the more prominent persons who were condemned, it was said, were guilty only of owning property to be confiscated for replenishing the depleted imperial coffers. Inevitably a new conspiracy was hatched that at length did away with Commodus. He was first poisoned, then strangled by his wrestling partner.

Relying on the precedent set at the assassination of Domitian, the Senate attempted to seize the initiative and named a distinguished older man, Pertinax, to replace Commodus. This action did not please the Praetorian Guard, however, which, as the historian Dio Cassius says, had gotten used to "delicate" living. There was not enough money in the treasury to buy the praetorians' acquiescence, although the attempt was made. Less than three months after his reluctant acceptance of power, a group of praetorians murdered Pertinax. Then they conducted a kind of auction for his successor at their camp between the father-in-law of Pertinax and Didius Julianus, who finally made the highest bid (that is, agreed to pay them the most for their support) and was acclaimed emperor. This spectacle was too much for even the city populace, and more repugnant still to the legions, who were not about to allow the praetorians to name emperors in such fashion.

Such a turbulent situation roused the ambitions of every charismatic general, and soon there were three serious candidates for the imperial post: Clodius Albinus, governor of Britain; Pescennius Niger (who surely had a dark-skinned man among his ancestors), governor of Syria; and Lucius Septimius Severus, governor of Pannonia. Didius Julianus was executed only a little more than two months after assuming power. Severus made an ally of Albinus while he struggled to defeat Niger, and then he turned on Albinus. Victory against him in 197 A.D. made Septimius Severus the sole ruler of the Empire he had largely commanded since being acclaimed by the provincial legions in 193.

A. The Severi

Lucius Septimius Severus (193–211 A.D.)

Although Septimius Severus in several ways ruled well and managed to stabilize and unify the Empire, in some ways he also symbolizes all that was wrong with the imperial system. He was first a general, only secondarily an administrator of empire. This is seen in the advice he is reported to have given his sons at his death—that they should live in concord, enrich the army, and despise everyone else. The army was now the sole basis of power, and Septimius never forgot this. He was rather vindictive, even against persons who had been forced to support one of the other early candidates for the throne. Born in North Africa, he spoke Latin with an accent. He was by no means uneducated but had little feeling for long-established tradition.

Septimius was superstitious and, even more than some of his predecessors, depended on the horoscopes cast by his astrologers. It was said than when he married for the second time (he was already an important administrator who had reached the consulship and governed two or three provinces) he looked for a woman whose horoscope predicted great things for her husband. This search led him to Julia Domna, who came of a Syrian noble family that included several remarkable women—about whom more later.

Septimius successfully fought wars in Britain and Parthia; in the latter, he even captured the enemy capital, Ctesiphon, in 198 A.D. It is ironic that Roman campaigns against their perennial foe Parthia only weakened that kingdom, so that it eventually became prey to a successor state, that of the Sassanid Persians, who fought the Romans as fiercely as the Parthians had.

As emperor, Septimius found it necessary to enlarge the army, which now comprised several legions more than in the days of Augustus. The praetorian guard, which had deteriorated especially under Commodus, was simply disbanded by Septimius, who then reconstituted it immediately, in effect, but with troops drawn from the loyal legions. For a time, at least, their position as elite, privileged guards was reduced.

Septimius also militarized the government, by making extensive use of generals in positions of power. In a sense, of course, important officials had always been generals also. But now the situation was reversed: the officials in question came from a lower rank—the equestrian order rather than the senatorial—and they proved themselves in the army rather than through the usual sequence of promotion in civilian positions. It was not merely the fact of the emperor as effective commanding general that induces historians to designate the Roman state of the century following Septimius Severus' accession a "military monarchy."

Septimius conducted internal affairs with great efficiency—especially the collection of taxes and tribute. He was able to raise the pay of soldiers, give them special donatives, and still leave his successor a treasury far from empty. The city of Rome itself he also nurtured with care; at his death he left, it was said, enough grain and oil to feed the city for several years. He spent huge sums on building programs, particularly in adding massively to the complex of imperial palaces on the Palatine in Rome. In his native North Africa he practically re-

Caracalla, son of Septimius, remembered for making citizens of almost all free persons in Europe and for the public bath in Rome. *(The Metropolitan Museum of Art, Samuel D. Lee, Fund, 1940)*

built whole cities, as the remains of his birthplace Leptis Magna demonstrate to present-day tourists there.

Caracalla (211–217 A.D.)

Septimius left his power jointly to his two sons: Caracalla, the elder, and Geta. Julia Domna, their dynamic mother, was doubtless expected to play an important role in preserving harmony between them. She failed in this, however, and Geta was soon killed, in an attack in Julia's own presence; she herself was wounded. Before the end of Caracalla's reign, nevertheless, she reasserted herself; she received official petitions, answered official correspondence, and was named jointly with Caracalla on imperial dispatches.

Caracalla is remembered chiefly for two things. In 212 A.D. he made citizens of almost all free persons in the Empire. The citizenship had gradually been extended, so that perhaps a majority of free persons were already citizens; yet this was a notable move. Some of his contemporaries were unkind enough to suggest that, since citizens paid an accession tax, Caracalla's main intention was to make a bigger tax haul. In any case, the move did not mean equality for all, since other distinctions were as marked as ever: for example, that between those termed *humiliores* and those called *honestiores* in law and the courts. *Humiliores* could be beaten or subjected to other corporal punishment; *honestiores* could not. The other notable accomplishment for which Caracalla is remembered is his huge public baths in Rome. Even in ruins, their brick-and-concrete core (which now houses one of the largest outdoor opera theaters in the world) is still impressive and of staggering scale to the modern viewer.

Caracalla liked to see himself in the image of Alexander the Great. He even had an army unit called the Macedonians. Perhaps it was chiefly this personal fantasy which led him to prepare an expedition to intervene in the affairs of the divided and decadent Parthian kingdom in the East. Caracalla, however, had few of Alexander's finer qualities. He made many enemies and was killed in the sixth year of his reign, during the Eastern campaign, at Edessa. Julia perhaps considered seizing power in her own name, but was prevented by the praetorian prefect Macrinus, who himself laid hold on the Empire for a little more than a year. Julia was already sick with the cancer that would soon carry her off.

Other equally competent women of her family, however, continued to fashion positions of power for themselves. Her sister Julia Maesa had two daughters, Soaemias and Mamaea. All were important in the intrigues of state. Julia Maesa persuaded the soldiers to rise against Macrinus; she and Soaemias actually joined the ensuing battle and rallied the troops at a critical point. Macrinus was killed, and Maesa was able to arrange the accession first of one, then of the other of her grandsons, Elagabalus and Alexander Severus.

Elagabalus (218–222 A.D.)

The eldest of Julia Maesa's grandsons was Varius Avitus, better known as Elagabalus. At the time when the army gave him its support he was almost fifteen years old. His chief interests were exotic religion and sex. Fortunately for the Empire, his mother and grandmother actually administered public affairs. He introduced the Eastern solar deity after whom he was named to Rome (symbolized in a black stone) and celebrated a marriage to another sun-god in some sort of syncretic emphasis on worship of the sun as the chief god of the Empire. He himself, perhaps in the guise of a deity, married a vestal virgin.

Probably under his grandmother's guidance, Elagabalus set up a Senate of Women—who concerned themselves primarily with making rules on the behavior and dress of women. When in his extraordinary perversion the Emperor made himself look more a woman than a man, he numbered his days, for the army would not long support such a monarch. Julia Maesa persuaded him to adopt his cousin Alexander in 221 A.D., so that when the praetorian guards predictably murdered Elagabalus (and his mother as well) this boy succeeded to the throne.

Since Alexander was not yet fourteen years old when he was acclaimed emperor, some sort of regency was inevitable. His mother and his grandmother, Mamaea and Maesa, acting somewhat more circumspectly than the dead Soaemias had, saw to affairs. Historical sources indicate that, as Alexander grew up, he acquired the finer virtues of dedication and equity. It is interesting that he displayed a surprising religious eclecticism; in his private shrine, besides deified former emperors, he kept busts of Orpheus, the Pythagorean mystic Apollonius of Tyana, Abraham, and Christ. There is a Christian tradition that his mother, Mamaea, became a Christian.

Alexander did not have a forceful character, despite his virtues. Unhappily he chose as praetorian prefect the great jurist Ulpian, highly competent in the law but unpopular with the soldiers of the Guard. When emergency demonstrated Alexander's incompetence as general, the legions also became disaffected.

The crises that exposed the military incapacity of Alexander, and of course of his mother as well, occurred on the Empire's eastern and northern frontiers. In the East, the dynast of the rising Sassanid Persian kingdom invaded Roman territory. The Persians at length were fended off, but the Roman troops did not behave well in battle; nor did their commanders, including Alexander. A similar threat arose in the North with an invasion of Germans across the Rhine. Alexander and Mamaea arrived in the area to do their best, only to be murdered by mutinous Roman troops there. Perhaps the disgruntled troops blamed petticoat government for the Empire's military problems—which seem to have included some attempt by the slain emperor to curtail the political sway of the army.

B. Barrack-Room Emperors; Administrative Chaos

In the half century after the death of Alexander Severus, Rome was racked by civil war, barbarian and Persian invasions, and the plague. There were scores of claimants to the throne, at least twenty-five or thirty of whom must be classified as serious contenders. For instance, in a single ten-year-period, one emperor (Gallienus) fought off eighteen challengers. All civilian concerns had to be subordinated to the overriding problems of defense, against both invaders and would-be emperors. The foreign invasions probably should be regarded as the most serious problem: from the north, Franks, Alamanni, Goths, and other Germanic peoples poured by the hundred thousand into the Empire. Repeatedly they penetrated Asia Minor, Greece, the Danubian and Gallic provinces, Spain, and even Italy itself. Only by the greatest efforts, the fortunate competence of several of the emperors, and sheer luck did the Empire survive. In the following paragraphs we shall mention only a few of the more important rulers during this troubled age.

Maximinus to Decius (235–251 A.D.)

It seems somehow symbolic that Gaius Julius Maximinus was a Thracian of Germanic parentage who was noted more for his great physical stature than for anything else. Proclaimed emperor by his soldiers in 235 A.D., he ignored the Roman Senate (which still functioned, but with much-reduced power and status), fought numerous opponents unsuccessfully, and was killed by his own men within three years. Succeeding emperors were named by the Senate or, more often, seized power from positions of strength. One of these latter was known as "Philip the Arab" (Marcus Julius Philippus), who celebrated the one-thousandth anniversary of the city of Rome (753 B.C.–248 A.D.; note that in our reckoning there is no year zero)—but it looked as if there would never be a future jubilee for any emperor to celebrate. Philip was killed by Gaius Decius, an Illyrian who gained power with the help of his troops.

Decius reigned less than three years (249–251), and during this time the plague struck, along with the fierce Goths. He died in battle against the invaders—something a bit unique, for most emperors of this era were killed by their own men or fell in battle against challengers to their power.

Decius is remembered by Christians as a great persecutor. Philip was said to have favored the Christians, and perhaps Decius was in part reacting to the policy of his slain enemy. This was the first empire-wide persecution. Decius required all citizens to appear before local officials to take an oath to the Emperor—such an oath as Christians could not swear. Every man then had to carry on his person notarized proof of having sworn the oath. Some Christians yielded, and others yielded through the ruse of sending paid surrogates to appear and take the oath in their names. They argued bitterly among themselves about the ethics of this latter practice. Certainly they rejoiced at the death of Decius, as the first systematic persecutor on a broad scale.

Valerian, Gallienus, and Aurelian (253–275 A.D.)

Valerian and Gallienus, a father-and-son team, were not at all incompetent, and in fact—unusual in these years—were not uncultivated men. As emperor, Valerian (Publius Valerianus; 253–260) occupied himself

An Antoninianus (= two denarii?) of Trajan Decius (249-251 A.D.). Note the radiate crown. Decius first mounted an empire-wide persecution of Christians.

chiefly with a Persian invasion which achieved even the capture of Antioch. This war was accompanied by plague. Valerian won an initial battle and then penetrated into Mesopotamia, where he was defeated. When he attempted to negotiate with the Persian monarch Sapor I, Valerian was treacherously taken prisoner and ultimately died in captivity. The world was treated to the spectacle (memorialized on a Persian coin of the time) of a captive Roman emperor on his knees in humiliation before King Sapor.

Publius Gallienus (260–268), meanwhile, with little better success attempted to stem the migration of hordes of Franks, Alamanni, and Goths, who were near to overwhelming the Rhine and Danube defenses. The Goths overran Dacia, and one small group penetrated as far as the walls of Athens. Only by vigorous action did Gallienus salvage the central segment of the Empire. To make matters worse, a Roman general named Postumus seized Britain, Gaul, and Spain and carved out an independent state. Gallienus, hampered by a continuous succession of Roman challengers to his power, could not regain the lost provinces. His successor Claudius II (268–270) was eventually able to roll back the invading Gothic hordes, and thus earned the surname "Gothicus."

In the East, a bit of luck saved the situation: Odenathus, king of the rich trading city of Palmyra in Syria, chose to make an alliance with the Romans and inflicted a serious defeat on the Persians. But soon Odenathus himself, and after his assassination in 267 A.D. his beautiful widow Zenobia, seized a large chunk of Roman territory and ruled as independent monarchs. The Empire had effectively broken up into three parts.

Aurelian (Lucius Domitius Aurelianus; 270–275 A.D.), son of a small farmer in the Danube Valley, performed heroically in restoring the unity of the Empire—though he was forced to abandon Dacia, held by Rome since Trajan's time. He twice defeated Palmyra; the second time he destroyed it. Its ruins are among the most imposing in the ancient Roman world. Queen Zenobia was led in Aurelian's triumph at Rome but was afterward permitted to live out her life in a villa near Tivoli.

A threat to Italy caused Aurelian to begin building a great wall about the city of Rome, the first such fortification since Hannibal's menace. It is this wall, with medieval additions, which is admired by tourists at various places within the present city.

Aurelian restored order along the Danube and at last reconquered the Gallic kingdom, which was ruled by Gaius Tetricus from his capital at Treverorum (Trèves). He was justly hailed as *restitutor orbis* ("restorer of the world"), a title Hadrian had once enjoyed for quite different accomplishments. Ironically, Aurelian was killed by some of his own officers who believed the false story, circulated by a clerk who knew he was being investigated for irregularities, that they were about to be executed.

When the truth of this affair came out, Aurelian's generals were so chagrined that they did not name a successor; instead, they actually asked the Senate at Rome to do so. After some understandable hesitation—did the generals really mean it?—the Senate, so long accustomed to being ignored, named an elderly senator called Marcus Tacitus. No return to civilian direction of affairs was to be hoped for, however, and in a few months some soldiers killed Tacitus. The fatal pattern of barrack-room intrigue continued. Rome had to suffer nearly another decade until at last Diocletian was able to restore a measure of stability.

C. Economic and Social Collapse

No state could withstand such buffeting as Rome endured in the 3rd century without serious damage. Indeed, most other states could not have survived. The most serious damage, ultimately, came not to the army nor to the top-level administration but to the economy and to society at the lower levels.

Economic Chaos

The economic decline, catastrophic and complete, hardly needs to be documented. The cost of maintaining huge standing armies for continual civil wars and foreign invasion would alone have bankrupted the Empire. But in addition, trade of all sorts shrank; plague contributed to the chronic manpower shortage; and the production of farms and the typical small industry declined ruinously. Except for those whose farms adjoined the frontiers, those who owned farms along the great military roads suffered most. When troops have no money, they still must eat; if the legionaries did not simply seize what they needed, they requisitioned it, and for the produce taken they gave paper which, though legal, often was worthless.

The coinage portrays graphically to modern eyes the deterioration of the monetary system along with the economy. Rampant inflation brought cheapening of the coins: gold disappeared; the silver was adulterated with base metals so that, finally, "silver" coins had only the thinnest coating of precious metal. Remaining specimens sometimes show only flecks of silver over the bronze core. The standard silver coin at the beginning of this period was the *denarius*. Even then, under the Severi, this was worth only about half the value of the *denarius* prior to Nero. Soon it was all but abandoned in favor of another coin, larger but with a smaller percentage of silver—the *antoninianus,* apparently valued at double the *denarius*. Within a few decades this coin too was debased, until it became almost worthless. Those who possessed valuable coins hoarded them. In some places, barter replaced a money economy.

Damage to Social Classes

The aristocracy naturally suffered; in Rome the senators lost power as well as wealth and influence. Perhaps it would be more accurate to say the generals were now the aristocrats, for success could make an equestrian commander an instant noble—if not an instant emperor. The middle class of traders, bankers, and moneylenders suffered most of all. This class, which had always been too small for the good of the Empire, now all but disappeared.

As for the lower classes, especially the rural small farmers, they too suffered. Chaotic politics, wars, and uncertain markets hurt their living standard, but perhaps the manpower drain of the draft hurt them most of all. As soldiers the peasants might be well cared for; the soldiers were probably the best-treated of any social group. But the overall health of the state demanded that they be in the business of production, not of destruction.

Restoration of society and the economy would require herculean labor. Perhaps it is not too pessimistic to say that a complete restoration was impossible; but human affairs must always proceed, no matter what the tasks.

D. Return to Order: Diocletian and Constantine

What had happened during a half century of civil war, foreign invasion, and economic and social dislocation was something akin to revolution. Power now resided in new hands; the class structures had been altered, and talented men of all ranks could rise to the top. Traditions of all sorts had been swept away. The results were chaotic; but at least if a strong figure rose, he would find less organized resistance to his efforts at reconstruction. The man who was to begin such a process was Diocletian.

Diocletian and the Tetrarchy (285–305 A.D.)

Like several of his predecessors, Gaius Aurelius Diocletianus came of Illyrian peasant stock. He rose through a combination of military and administrative skill, the latter quality being the more notable. The man had a certain charisma; he chose strong men as subordinates and retained their loyalty. More than anything else, it was his ability to control the generals that made possible a break in the long series of civil wars in which most emperors had been overthrown by their own lieutenants. Thus Diocletian could devote himself primarily to the tasks of administration. His subordinates, especially Maximian, did most of the work of restoring peace on the frontiers. It should be remembered, too, that in the tasks of unifying and protecting the Empire Diocletian was much aided by the work of his immediate predecessors, among them Aurelian.

What Diocletian created is often referred to as an Oriental despotism. Those who use such terms refer in part to the manner in which, from this time on, the emperors made themselves inaccessible and surrounded themselves with the trappings, even the dress, of Oriental monarchs. But the powers of the Emperor also had become more nakedly absolute.

Diocletian, as a general himself, could hardly be expected to attempt to reestablish the sort of partnership between emperor and Senate that had characterized the first two centuries of empire. Moreover, such a course would have been impossible. The problems he faced were great and required drastic solutions. The army had to be maintained at a high level, and the Emperor must command it directly, at least at times. He could not share his power with the Senate; nor could he stay in Rome for constant consultation with that body. The Senate, though retaining some of its ancient prestige, was by now little more than a city council for the capital. Even this claim is not quite accurate, for Rome, though it retained its mystique as the Eternal City, was no longer a real capital: Diocletian usually resided at Nicomedia, in Asia Minor near the Bosporus, and his chief lieutenant Maximian usually governed from Milan.

Diocletian's greatest achievement was to bring an end to the internal competition for office. This was absolutely necessary before he could improve the chaotic economic situation. Doubtless the most important ingredient in this achievement was the quality of the Emperor himself; but there was new administrative machinery, too. Almost at once, Diocletian made Maximian a Caesar, subordinate to himself as Augustus. Then, when Maximian's troops hailed him as Augustus after he crushed some invading Germanic tribesmen, Diocletian accepted that. The two commanders thus became theoretically equal, though Diocletian, in true military style, maintained his seniority in rank. Each of the Augusti soon took a Caesar as his chief lieutenant: for Diocletian, it was Galerius; for Maximian, Constantius Chlorus.

The Empire as restructured was basically divided in half (shades of the future!), with Diocletian ruling the Eastern part and Maximian the West. The halves were further subdivided into quarters, with the Caesars each controlling one segment. Any of the four rulers could, in time of crisis, lend help to his nearest comrade in the chain of command. Thus, when Constantius campaigned against a Gallic usurper, Carausius, in northwest Gaul and Britain, Maximian moved up from his head-quarters in Milan to look out for the Rhine frontier. The death of any of the four rulers would not have precipitated a crisis, since one of the others would have stepped in to keep order and a successor would have been quickly named.

Diocletian reorganized the army into smaller and more mobile units, stationed along the frontiers. Reserve detachments were positioned some distance back from the frontiers, for defense in depth and greater flexibility. Adding to its mobility was an emphasis on cavalry.

The civilian government also was reorganized. While the four rulers gave their chief attention to military matters, four praetorian prefects governed civilian affairs. The number of administrative provinces was increased to more than a hundred; perhaps the intent was to prevent rebellion on the part of a powerful provincial governor. The provinces were grouped into twelve *dioceses,* headed by officials called *vicars.* The provincial governors now were often termed *duces.*

Constantine the Great (306–337 A.D.)

Diocletian decided to abdicate, effective in 305 A.D. This was a rather astonishing and unprecedented move. He persuaded—perhaps coerced—Maximian to retire at the same time. As expected, the younger Caesars became Augusti, and two new Caesars were appointed. Though Constantius technically outranked Galerius, Diocletian permitted Galerius to make the new designations.

Notably left out of the new tetrarchy by Galerius were Constantine, the son of Constantius, and Maxentius, the son of Maximian. At the death of Constantius the next year, Constantine was hailed Augustus in his place. At this, Maxentius seized Rome and declared himself Augustus as well. Maximian came out of retirement to help his son and resumed his title of Augustus. After a series of events that included some actual fighting, six persons all now claimed the title of Augustus! At one point Diocletian came out of retirement and made new arrangements in an effort to perpetuate his system, but soon the struggle resumed.

Galerius died of a wasting disease in 311. By then, Maximian had been killed. This left four rulers: Constantine in the extreme west, Maxentius in Italy and Africa, Licinius on the Danube, and Maximin Daia in Asia. Constantine and Maxentius prepared for a confrontation. Constantine seemingly claimed right to the whole Empire by saying he was descended from an earlier emperor, Claudius Gothicus; he emphasized this relationship by adopting as his chief god Sol Invictus, the "Unconquered Sun," in the manner of Claudius and several other emperors from Aurelian on. In this, perhaps, Constantine was wooing the large number of Roman soldiers who also worshiped the sun in the Mithraic religion.

In 312 Constantine mounted an expedition and marched on Maxentius in Italy. He could manage only 40,000 men; Maxentius had two or three times as many available. The adventure seemed foolhardy and has been explained in religious terms; perhaps Constantine was already influenced by the Christian views he later accepted. At any rate, it was later written by his biographers that one evening on the march he saw a cross in the sky with the writing, in Greek, "In this sign, conquer." This, it was said, was confirmed by a vision that night which told him to put the monogram for Christ in Greek, the Chi-Rho, on the armor of his troops.

Whatever the truth, Constantine dared a great deal. He gained some preliminary victories in northern Italy, but his great triumph came at the Milvian Bridge, just north of Rome. Constantine won that battle, and with it control of all the West. Superior tactics had forced Maxentius to fight at a disadvantage; but, of course, Christians attributed the victory to the intervention of God. The Roman Senate named Constantine senior Augustus, and almost immediately the Emperor attempted to use his power to stop all persecution of Christians in the East. Licinius, who had become Augustus of the East, joined with Constantine in this act and, together with him, signed the Edict of Milan, in 313, proclaiming toleration of Chrstianity throughout the Empire.

The strife among and attrition of the Augusti continued until only two remained: Constantine in the West and Licinius in the East. This arrangement lasted until 324, when the two came to war. Ambition was the most likely reason for their clash, but there was also a difference in religious policy: Licinius had begun to attack the Christians, in an attempt to destroy the higher levels of organization in the Church, whereas Constantine was attempting to take over the Church hierarchy. Whatever the cause, the result was victory for Constantine, and the whole Empire was again ruled by one man.

There was a kind of inevitability about the struggle between Christianity and the pagan state of Rome. Jesus' own position was not intransigent ("Render unto Caesar the things that are Caesar's and unto God the things that are God's"), and the apostle Paul was essentially loyal to the Roman state ("The powers that exist are appointed by God"). Yet Rome's pagan religiosity was so completely intertwined with the state itself that any attack on its religion must ultimately be an attack on the state as well.

The Jews' and Christians' exclusiveness not only precluded them from practicing anything pagan in nature but led them to deny the existence of gods other than the One. They were thus labeled atheists. Judaism had at least the advantage of being a legally recognized religion, but Christianity was long denied that status. Moreover, after the elimination of the Jewish state during the wars of Vespasian and Hadrian, the Jews no longer seemed a real threat to the secular state. Christianity, however, seemed the more dangerous as it grew apace; its hierarchical organization grew also, and to emperors such as Decius and Aurelian it seemed a state within a state, essentially unpatriotic and sapping the foundations of Roman society and government. They therefore tried to stamp it out.

Diocletian had severely persecuted Christians. Perhaps this was a result of the influence of his Caesar, Galerius; most Christian writers thought so. The worst persecution came toward the end of Diocletian's reign. Galerius continued the harsh attacks until he was afflicted with a terrible disease and had second thoughts. Then, in 311 he reversed himself and issued an edict of toleration; but the change did not stay the progress of his disease. After him, Maximin Daia again began persecuting the Church, and eventually, as we have seen, so did Licinius. In the West, even in Diocletian's time, the persecutions were always less severe and less extensive than elsewhere, and after Constantine gained power they of course ceased.

Constantine therefore is accounted the first Christian Emperor. Exactly when and in what way he was converted, it is difficult to say. He may have been much influenced by the painful fate of the arch-persecutor Galerius. One cannot reject out of hand the reports that he saw a vision and had a dream before the Battle of the Milvian Bridge. Some sort of personal conviction must have been there, since Christians were hardly strong enough to have made it politically advantageous to favor them. The Emperor continued to be *pontifex maximus;* to use pagan themes— even the radiate crown of the sun-god—on his coinage; and was not baptized until the very end of his life. Yet he embraced the Church and dominated it, and even coerced bishops when he felt it necessary.

Above all, under him Christianity was recognized as an officially acceptable religion, a status dating from the Edict of Milan. It remained for Constantine's successors, in particular Theodosius the Great (379–395), to ban paganism and to permit those once persecuted to become in their turn persecutors—and, increasingly, to denounce and persecute each other as heretics or schismatics.

Economic Policy under
Diocletian and Constantine

The disastrous economic collapse in the 3rd century had been caused largely by invasions and civil wars, with all their attendant evils: ravaging of cities and fields (not always by non-Roman armies), heavy tax burdens, the military draft, and the decline of trade and small industry. Inflation and debasement of the coinage were results rather than causes, but were painful nonetheless. Obviously the most important single blessing for the stricken economy was the restoration of order, both along the frontiers and internally. Equally important was a restored discipline in the army, for the undisciplined individual soldier could manage a good deal of depredation on his own. These positive changes Diocletian and Constantine in large part accomplished, with beneficial economic effect.

Improvement was not always immediate. We hear of productive lands that lay idle for lack of tenants. Inflation also, which so often becomes a psychological phenomenon as well as one based on economic necessity, was not easily stemmed. Diocletian thus found it necessary to issue his famous price edict in 301, setting maximum prices for commodities and labor all over the Empire. The prices established seem a bit high for antiquity; yet they are surely much below those which were then being extorted. One tends to doubt how successfully this measure—extreme and characteristic of absolutist thinking—curbed prices in the marketplace.

Diocletian and Constantine reformed the coinage and issued a new gold coin, the *solidus,* somewhat lighter than the old *aureus,* which had disappeared during the preceding half century. New and finer silver coins were also introduced. In the time of Constantine the *solidus* appears to have been minted in sufficient quantity to form the basis of the monetary system; in Diocletian's reign these coins were probably not available in sufficient numbers. It is notable that Diocletian, in reforming the tax system, arranged for the collection of taxes in kind, that is, in produce. Much of the government's disbursements were also made in produce—which hardly implies total success on the monetary front.

Many of the changes of the catastrophic 3rd century proved irreversible. The ruined middle class could not be re-created. On the level of local government, a large segment of the governing classes—those which furnished the members of the city councils, the *decuriones*—had been ruined. These classes did reestablish themselves to a degree in the more secure times, but never to their old levels in numbers and prosperity. The decuriones were saddled by law with compulsory and heavy financial burdens. Eventually laws were added to force well-to-do persons to serve as decurions. The effect of all this was stifling.

One notable and permanent change of this era saw many tenant farmers changed virtually into serfs; no longer free to leave their tenant contracts, they were thus bound to the soil. Whether these *coloni* derived from slaves made into tenants, barbarian prisoners converted into tenants, or free men who under pressure of an age of disorder had slipped into this half-free status is not known. Their condition, which developed gradually over many decades, was firmly established by the time of Constantine. This tendency to bind men to their occupations was not limited to agrarian activities. Before the end of this period, edicts of the central government attempted to tie men of all sorts to their occupations. Their work became a hereditary obligation to the state.

The degree to which the Roman state now attempted to control the lives of all its citizens was unprecedented; compelled by the turmoil of the times, its effects were ultimately deadly.

A Look Ahead

Rome had survived, but at the cost of great damage to her institutions, her economy, the social order, and even the spirit of her people. The Empire would somehow continue for a century and a half after Constantine; then the West would break up. The Eastern Empire would survive, however, for another thousand years.

This division of the Empire, which had been foreshadowed in the arrangements of Diocletian, was further symbolized in the establishment (330 A.D.) of the new capital city, Constantinople, on the site of the old Greek colony Byzantium, at a strategic location on the Bosporus. Constantine made it in many ways a duplicate of Rome, complete with Senate and other similar official bodies. Though Rome's walls would be breached several times in the next century and a half, the massive fortifications of Constantinople would not fail their defenders until 1453.

Alaric the Goth sacked Rome in 410—almost exactly 800 years after the city was last sacked. Not so bad a record. Gaiseric and his Vandals, operating from their recently established base in North Africa, did a more thorough job in 455. Finally, in 476, a date often given as the end of the Empire, the last emperor who could be called Roman ended his reign. Appropriately enough, he was called Romulus Augustulus (Little Augustus). The ensuing change was not really notable for residents of Rome and Italy, since Odoacer and the Ostrogothic rulers who followed him were neither incompetent nor uncivilized. Still, in some sense it was an end—and a beginning.

Books for Further Reading

BIRLEY, A., *Septimius Severus: The African Emperor,* New York, 1972.

DÖRRIES, H., *Constantine The Great,* New York, 1972.

GRANT, M., *The Climax of Rome,* New York, 1970.

GUTERMAN, S. L., *Religious Toleration and Persecution in Ancient Rome,* London, 1951.

HYDE, W., *Paganism to Christianity in the Roman Empire,* Philadelphia, 1946.

JONES, A. H. M., *Constantine and the Conversion of Europe,* London, 1948.

MACMULLEN, R., *Constantine,* New York, 1969.

PARKER, H., *The Roman Legions,* Oxford, 1928.

PAUL, LOUIS, *Ancient Rome at Work: An Economic History of Rome,* New York, 1927.

ROSTOVTZEFF, M., *Social and Economic History of the Roman Empire,* Oxford, 1957.

WHEELER, M., *Rome Beyond the Imperial Frontiers,* London, 1954.

Our Heritage from Antiquity :
The Essential Substructures of Modern Civilization

21

The Most Basic Foundations

The first tender plants of civilization were nourished in the Near East—and nurtured to maturity. Among those tender plants was the capacity to produce food, and the development of that capacity led to population growth. The greater density of population in turn created problems, each of which, when solved produced new social institutions and, ultimately, political institutions as well. Problem-solving in one area thus led to the earliest law codes, as we have seen.

A systematic agriculture with an increasing variety of tools was absolutely essential to the genesis of this early civilization. The economy of all the ancient world rested on agriculture. Indeed, even the economy of the modern world rests on agriculture to a degree that is often unsuspected. The ability of 20th century, industrial nations to import needed foodstuffs sometimes leads statesmen to overemphasize the industry and neglect agriculture. But the readers of this book may see the day when a highly industrialized state may no longer count confidently on the easy availability of foodstuffs from other regions of the world.

The intellectual basis for civilization, too, was laid in the Near East, where the accumulation of information was made possible by systems of writing. The alphabet is the gift of the Near East. The first seeds of literature, philosophy, medicine, surgery, pharmacology—all the fruits of the mind of man that may be recorded in writing and preserved for the future—were sown in the ancient Near East.

369

A Religious Outlook on Life

It may sometimes seem that modern man's god is Materialism and that Scientists are his prophets. Yet it is nonetheless true that religion remains a vital ingredient in the lives of many—perhaps most—peoples of our world, Americans among them. The threads of our beliefs go back to the ancient Near East. The unique contributions of the Hebrews and Persians are well known, but religion was a fundamental element in all civilizations of the Near East from the very beginning.

At its worst, religion has served as a tool—all the more effective when those who use it also believe in it—used by the upper classes to help them control those beneath them. At its best, religion has called forth the most spiritual thought and the most altruistic actions of which humans are capable. Some of both the best and the worst can be found in the heritage of the Near East.

As is usual with historians of Western civilization, we have passed in this book from the ancient Near East to Greece and Rome with only an occasional look back to the cradle of civilization. It would be a mistake to assume, however, that in these later phases of history the Near East—and at intervals the Far East—had no impact on the direction of events or the development of occidental culture. The great philosophical systems of the West were drawn up by men who felt the influence of the older and more mature Near East. The Roman Empire, in both structure and ideal, gradually acquired an orientalized form. And at last an oriental religion—Christianity—suffused all of Western civilization and inexorable changed all it touched.

B. The Heritage of Greece

The Rational Approach to Life

Since the days of the Renaissance, modern man in the Western World has attempted, none too successfully, to combine the religious approach to life characteristic of the Orient (especially the Judeo-Christian view of God and man) with the rational approach first worked out by Greek thinkers. Reason made possible the separation of superstition from real religion, and tended to relegate religion to its proper sphere. Reason brought the beginnings of science and with it the first systematic approach to an understanding of the nature of the physical world. Reason caused men to take fresh looks at all their institutions, with some various and interesting results. Reason developed philosophical systems that brought a free-ranging revaluation of man's position in the universe, his ethical values. In all these things Greeks were pioneers of the mind.

370

Several categories of literature were either created by the Greeks or given form and style by them. Homer may have had the advantage of an epic tradition that went back to the Sumerian's saga of Gilgamesh. Yet he created the world's greatest epic. Herodotus knew of works of a basic historical nature that were ancient when he was born, yet to a considerable degree he created history as a discipline; and Thucydides has been the most-imitated historian who ever lived. The myriad forms and styles of Greek poetry have served as models for every generation of poets since the days of Sappho—which is not to say, of course, that nothing new developed after the Greeks.

The Theater and Art

The theater was purely a Greek invention. Of the world's greatest playwrights, whether tragic or comic, several must be accounted Greek. No more influential way than the theater has yet been devised for transmitting and disseminating thought and feeling, though, to be sure, modern television and movie screens make possible a wider viewing of dramatic productions.

In architecture and sculpture the Greek influence has been as tremendous as it has been enduring. Though today's architects no longer place Greek-style columns and porticoes on their buildings, their ideas of line and function show that they still drink from Greek springs. It is, in short, impossible to imagine a world in which the ancient Greeks will not continue to have an enormous intellectual impact.

C. The Heritage of Rome

In many ways Rome served as a transmitter of ideas, not a creator. Yet to many things Rome imparted her own peculiar stamp, and in some ways the Romans did make original contributions.

Government: Idea and Structure

A most important idea passed on by Rome was that of the unity of the civilized world. The idea was transmitted by Rome not so much on the basis of theory as on the basis of political achievement. The idea itself derived in part from the ephemeral achievement of Alexander the Great and from the great oriental empires that preceded him, in particular the Persian with its concept of One World. Kings of the European states in the centuries after the fall of Rome often aspired to a Roman—that is to say, a universal—state. Hence the medieval use of the name Holy Roman Empire, which, despite its name, never approached the ideal. Statesmen, not only of the Roman Empire's immediate successor states in the West, but also those of states existing into recent times, looked to Rome also for ideas about specific structures. In the French revolutionary period there were consuls, tribunes, tribunates, and other bodies named after Roman structures, though they were hardly Roman in reality. And in the New World, it was no accident that the upper house of the United States Congress was given the name "Senate."

Much of a society's governmental structure is expressed in law, and here, it must be reemphasized, is one of Rome's greatest achievements. Again the influence was perhaps stronger a century and a half ago—the Code Napoleon, for example, was specifically based on Roman law—but all the codes and procedures used in Western countries today still owe much to Rome.

Language and Literature

Several of the major languages of the Western World are termed Romance because they derive directly from Rome, from dialects of the Latin. Several other of the major tongues of the world have been affected by the Latin vocabulary and Latin grammar. The grammatical influence has not always been beneficial: attempts to impose the Latin forms upon German and English, for example, have not always yielded happy results.

Latin literature must rank second to Greek. It was not, however, merely imitative; on the contrary, Latin prose and poetry have real distinction. The influence of Latin literature was great in early modern times partly because Latin was more easily read by Western scholars than Greek. Yet men by the thousand who could read both have preferred, say, Cicero's congenial style to the heavier language of Thucydides or the more difficult dialectics of Plato. Satire, history, and biography are among the strengths often noted in Latin literature.

D. Ancient Influence Today: Disparate Views

That the minds of those knowledgeable about the heritage of the ancient world should be impressed with such disparate views regarding that heritage is rather amusing. On the one hand, some, remembering the wealth of ideas and practices that still persist, and feeling that the basic changes in modern times are fundamentally inconsequential and technological, think that everything of importance in the modern world owes much to the ancient. On the other hand, others, feeling perhaps overwhelmed in a world of change, a world that seems to have lost its awareness of its traditions, and with that its stability, feel that the ancient world's influence has shunk to nothingness. Doubtless the truth lies somewhere between. Wherever it lies, no educated person in today's Western World can doubt that the wellsprings of his civilization have their sources deep in ancient soil.

Books for Further Reading

BAILEY, C., *The Legacy of Rome,* Oxford, 1923.

BROWN, P., *The World of Late Antiquity,* London, 1971.

JONES, A. H. M., *The Decline of the Ancient World,* New York, 1966.

KATZ, S., *The Decline of Rome,* Ithaca, 1955.

LOT, F., *The End of the Ancient World,* London, 1931.

SCHULZ, F., *A History of Roman Legal Science,* Oxford, 1953.

STAHL, W. H., *Roman Science,* Madison, 1962.

VOGT, J., *The Decline of Rome,* London, 1967.

WATSON, A., *The Law of the Ancient Romans,* Dallas, 1970.

Index